A POLYVALENT MEDIA POLICY IN THE ENLARGED EUROPEAN UNION

Journalism, Media and Social Communication

Beata Klimkiewicz's, *A Polyvalent Media Policy in the Enlarged European Union* initiates English editions in this series

These books were published in the series on *Journalism, Media and Social Communication* in Polish:

Media a integracja europejska, red. Teresa Sasińska-Klas, Agnieszka Hess, Kraków 2004

Media. Władza. Prawo, red. Maria Magoska, Kraków 2005

Bogdan Fischer, Weronika Świerczyńska-Głownia, *Dostęp do informacji ustawowo chronionych, zarządzanie informacją. Zagadnienia podstawowe dla dziennikarzy*, Kraków 2006

Agnieszka Hess, *Promocja małej i średniej przedsiębiorczości w Unii Europejskiej*, Kraków 2007

Teresa Sasińska-Klas, Agnieszka Szymańska, *Małopolski przedsiębiorca na rynku Unii Europejskiej. Założenia, doświadczenia, rezultaty*, Kraków 2007

Wybory samorządowe w kontekście mediów i polityki, red. Maria Magoska, Kraków 2008

Andrzej Nowosad, *Władza i media w Bułgarii*, Kraków 2008

Agnieszka Hess, Agnieszka Szymańska, *Pomost medialny. Rola mediów w międzynarodowej komunikacji politycznej na przykładzie relacji polsko-niemieckich*, Kraków 2009

Magdalena Hodalska, *Śmierć Papieża, narodziny mitu*, Kraków 2010

Agnieszka Szymańska, *Medialne fiasko zjednoczenia? Rola prasy prestiżowej w sytuacji przełomu politycznego na przykładzie niemieckiego zjednoczenia*, Kraków 2010

Teresa Sławińska, *Prasa regionalna na nowe czasy? Historia sukcesu francuskiego przedsiębiorstwa prasowego Ouest-France*, Kraków 2011

Michał Bukowski, Jarosław Flis, Agnieszka Hess, Agnieszka Szymańska, *Opcja czy osoba? Upartyjnienie* versus *personalizacja w wyborach samorządowych*, Kraków 2011

Monika Wawer, *Dziennikarze o sztuce, czyli opowieści medialnie nielogiczne*, Kraków 2012

Przodownicy prasy, red. Rafał Wietoszko, Kraków 2013

BEATA
KLIMKIEWICZ

A POLYVALENT MEDIA POLICY IN THE ENLARGED EUROPEAN UNION

Jagiellonian University Press

Series: Journalism, Media and Social Communication

Reviewer
dr hab. Jacek H. Kołodziej

Cover design
Pracownia Register

ISBN 978-83-233-3715-7

The publication of this volume was financed by the Jean Monnet Programme awarded by the Education, Audiovisual and Culture Executive Agency of the European Commission and the Faculty of Management and Social Communication, Jagiellonian University

JAGIELLONIAN UNIVERSITY PRESS

www.wuj.pl

Jagiellonian University Press
Editorial Offices: Michałowskiego St. 9/2, 31-126 Cracow
Phone: +48 12 663 23 81, +48 12 663 23 82, Fax: +48 12 663 23 83
Distribution: Phone: +48 12 631 01 97, Fax: +48 12 631 01 98
Cell Phone: + 48 506 006 674, e-mail: sprzedaz@wuj.pl
Bank: PEKAO SA, IBAN PL80 1240 4722 1111 0000 4856 3325

Contents

ACKNOWLEDGEMENTS

Writing a book is a long process that one enters with a handful of inspirations, mellowing gradually into a more systematic structure. This book arose as a result of several research ideas and activities revolving around the complex and challenging field of media policy, both at the EU level and in the region of Central and Eastern Europe. The strands of views and concepts crystallised over the course of smaller empirical investigations, the outcomes of which were published in various journals and collective volumes.

The publication of this book would not be possible without a grant from the Jean Monnet Programme awarded by the Education, Audiovisual and Culture Executive Agency of the European Commission. I was fortunate enough to spend three months at Visiting Fellowship in the St Anthony's College in Oxford University within the framework of the research project Media and Democracy in Central and Eastern Europe sponsored by the European Research Council. This important experience contributed to the final outcome of my research on media policies. I would wish to acknowledge in particular the kind support of Jan Zielonka and Paolo Manicini during this fruitful stay. I am also grateful for the possibility of being able to contribute to policy-oriented studies and co-operation with the Centre for Media Pluralism and Media Freedom affiliated with the European University Institute, Hans-Bredow-Institut, UNESCO, Open Society Foundations, Peace Institute and other institutions. Certainly, many ideas of this book benefited from the shared awareness of the policy background and process. Additionally, an inspiring academic exchange under the COST Action 30 *East of West: Setting a New Central and Eastern European Media Research Agenda* should be mentioned.

I feel indebted for the opportunity to conduct part of the research for this book at the Center for Media and Communication Studies in the Central European University in Budapest. I am grateful for the help from various media regulatory authorities, in particular the Hungarian Media Council and the Polish National Broadcasting Council, and a number of policy practitioners and experts who kindly shared their experience and knowledge in this field. I highly appreciate important debates with a number of my friends and colleagues from the Institute of Journalism and Social Communication at the Jagiellonian University in Kraków, and other academic institutions around Europe.

I owe debts of gratitude to Karol Jakubowicz, who, before his premature death, kindly shared with me many brilliant ideas and his experience, all of which helped to shape a more multi-dimensional understanding of media and communication policies. I wish to thank tremendously Jacek Kołodziej for his insightful comments and advice that tested this work on fundamental and normative grounds of basic values and conceptions.

I owe most of all, to Sonja, Dawid and Klara, all for being so understanding and supportive. I wish to thank Konrad as well for new venues in thinking about well-known concepts. Last, but not least, I would like to thank Chris, for all the inspiration, tough but truly important questions and steady support.

1. CHANGING MEDIA, CHANGING PUBLIC SPHERES: THE CONCEPTUAL GROUNDS FOR STUDYING MEDIA POLICY

1.1. An Introduction

Media and communication policy can be studied following two parallel paths: one aiming at understanding the role, function and structural development of communication media in contemporary societies, the other tracing the development of a public policy, largely manifested in the intended actions of political institutions that respond to strategically defined problems. These two paths meet especially in one territory: it takes shape when the communication media become objects of public policy. This book aims at mapping a territory of this intersection in the context of the enlarged geopolitical space of the European Union and new media environments shaped by technological, economic and cultural transformations.

The first important question to start with is: *why are the media and communication in general objects of public policy?* For almost one hundred years, the mass media and the concept of mass communication have captured the attention of media and communication scholars in Europe and around the world. These concepts evolved as an intellectual reaction to the industrialisation of news and print press production, as well as the emergence of 'new' channels and modes of communication including film, radio and television. It does not seem to be a historical coincidence that the period of the rise of terrestrial linear television and broadcasting in general, induced a perception of this 'new' media environment at that time, as an interconnected system. Particularly Marshall McLuhan's (1967) theoretical attempt to aggregate disparate media of communication into a synthetic whole of a media system, proved to be highly influential. Denis McQuail (2002: 4) argues that such theorising about the mass media had its origins in a consciousness of the changed character of a society. In other words, the mass media and system of communication media were seen as the lifeblood of society, playing a principal role in the processes of social change. An everyday operation of the system, was perceived as fundamental in terms of consequences for the way in which social life is organised, how societies function and how they construct their sense of collective identity.

Although both mediatisation and media-centric approaches have met a wave of criticism, especially from audience studies, they seem to justify the high interest of political institutions in incorporating communication media systems into the more complex network of public policies and governance. Moreover, nowadays, with the rise of new forms of communication and media architecture, we face similar intellectual reactions underlying the pivotal role of the new media for social life. They are seen pervasive and ubiquitous, penetrating all aspects of contemporary life (Deuze, 2011), *intrinsic* to the functioning of modern societies (Craig, 2004). A new communication environment is recognised as 'post-mass mediated' and 'post-industrial'. The fundamental changes that societies and individuals undergo, are once again in history proclaimed to result from the spread of new communication technologies and the use of new media. At the same time, the concept of 'the media' is less obviously and frequently associated with a coherent and centrally institutionalised *mass* media. New media and communication environments crystallise, on the one hand, around the legacy media, that have existed for centuries and evolved before the advent of the Internet, on the other hand, they thrive through networks and contents generated by users, new platforms and forms of content and services. The provision of news and information is increasingly fragmented, elusive, delivered in many forms, formats and combinations of media and communication networks. Mining, collecting and aggregating of information almost instantly from a vast array of sources, reached a scale never experienced in media past. A predominant perception of the media as 'external agents' providing the technological infrastructure for transferring the content to *masses* of users, is being replaced by the concept of 'networks' through which users compose their own individualised and singularised information spaces. These 'individualised media systems' are invisible, and at the same time, indivisible from all aspects of everyday life (Deuze, 2011).

The new media architecture of communicative abundance is not only increasingly *invisible* but also plural. This move towards a plurality of mutually-opaque networks (each of which presents different problems of inclusion and exclusion) demands new skills and capacities from media users and different forms of literacy (Nieminen and Sparks, 2012). Do these changes and new evolving structures transform rationales and justification for public policy in the area of media and communication? In order to answer this question, it would be instructive to consider and reconsider the specific roles and functions of the communication media in contemporary societies. This will subsequently lead us to the question: Why do we have policies? And how are objects of policies defined and constantly adapted to changing social and technological conditions? An important perspective to study policies in this respect is a process. In other words, how the field of policies developed, changed and how did research on media policies react to these changes? And finally, all these reflections will be linked to the geographical and geopolitical context of this book. The methodological approach and scope of the book will be briefly explained in the later sections of this chapter.

1.2. Media are so specific: five functions and five arguments

One of the leading justifications across changing paradigms of media and communication policies has been the assertion of the *specificity* of the media. In other words, the communication media have played multiple functions in societies, each of which grew from a particular field of social life and action such as economy, politics, culture and education. At the same time, the media are so *specific* that they seem to be conducive and indispensable for the operation of these particular fields. For example in the field of politics, the system of a well-functioning democracy and full exercise of citizenship rights presupposes an informed and participant body of citizens that can access, validate and negotiate their preferences and understanding of social reality through the communication media. In the economic field, effective models of production and distribution universally depend upon a media function to advertise commercial products. Evidently, the media are businesses, but they are also ascribed a special function in the democratic health of a society (Craig, 2004: 3), education and yet they are technologies and cultural institutions disseminating and reproducing cultural expressions.

Communication scholars have distinguished various sets of functions (McQuail, 1992; Schulz, 2004) some of which are seen as fundamental, others (e.g. integrative and unifying) as supportive. These resonate with certain expectations and responsibilities that ultimately, restrict the operations and performance of the media (Voltmer, 2013: 25). Hence, the media are not seen in isolation from their social environment, but as a means to various societal ends, and consequently, justifications for media freedom, independence and autonomy – as leading policy rationales – are derived from a shared sense of importance of the media and agreement on the functions they play in other fields of social life. The arrangement and hierarchical ordering of the functions might depend on the preferences and leading paradigms of institutions developing and enacting communication policies. The section below summarises the five main functions and arguments for a media and communication policy.

Technological argument – one of the specific functions of the media is to transfer, disseminate and channel various forms of communication over spatial and/or temporal distances according to their channel and storage capacities (Schulz, 2004: 90). In this sense, technological solutions and infrastructures broaden human communication capacities, act as technological 'extensions of a man' and improve the natural limits of human communication (McLuhan, 1967; Schulz, 2004).

One has to recognise, however, that the forms of mediation, relay, transfer, dissemination, delivery, bridging and storage have evolved and changed fundamentally over time. Also, it became apparent from communication studies that media technologies are not neutral, but their structural features shape the meaning of the messages they convey as well as patterns of interactions of those who are using them (Voltmer, 2013: 60). The scale of mediation has reached unprecedented ubiquity, while the change is also qualitative. Opposite forms of communication (interpersonal, mass and mass-self communication) coexist, interact and complement each other (Castells, 2009: 55). These also rearrange the very nature of mediation among individuals and between individuals and a larger society, encompassing mass communication and self communication at the same time: mass communication because it can potentially reach a global audience and self-communication because the production of the message is self-generated and the retrieval of specific messages or content self-selected (Livingstone, 2009; Castells, 2009: 55). The technological implications are that media connect and isolate users at the same time, make the world concurrently larger and smaller (Deuze, 2011: 142).

The 'technological argument' for a media and communication policy seems to be operational and assisting in the fulfilment of other functions. In other words, technological infrastructures and solutions have to be established, put in place, and have to be made openly accessible before other functions are exercised. In this respect, the basic values justifying policies in terms of access to enabling technologies, are those of *freedom, universality* and *equality*. Free and universal access to new communication and media technologies, and the Internet in particular, is considered to be a basic condition and communication right in the world. It can be illustrated by the new UNESCO concept of *Internet Universality* proclaimed at the WSIS 10+ summit in Paris in 2013. Likewise in Europe and the US, the policy initiatives aiming at eliminating the digital divide and the broad resonance of such concepts as 'knowledge-based societies', 'an information society for all' and 'e-inclusion' demonstrate that importance of access to the physical infrastructure necessary for the use of new technologies is perceived as an instrument of societal progress and development.

Yet, the question of technological access is directly linked with technological use: how does it vary among those who are better skilled and more competent to use advanced technologies and those who are not? Christian Katzenbach (2012: 125) stresses that technology in use does not blindly follow any inherent logic but is always appropriated, reinterpreted and domesticated by its users. Media technologies seem to appear 'naturally', but they reflect the social relations and needs of the society in which they are used (Voltmer, 2013: 58). Moreover, technological prerequisites may impact different forms of use and control by users. These, as is the case of AVMS Directive (European Parliament and the Council, 2010a) may justify differentiated regulation. Thus, for example, non-linear or on demand audiovisual media services are regulated differently than linear services on the grounds of the fact that it is the user who decides what services are chosen and when are they being used.[1]

Freedom, universality and *equality* as guiding principles for the access and use of communication technologies may be understood differently in various societies. Jan van Dijk argues that in the developed countries, universality of access usually means household access for all:

> For those not connected at home, public access and public service in community and government buildings, libraries, telecenters and Internet cafés are the second option. In developing countries household access is a luxury that is far beyond reach. Here public access is the first option; access in public buildings, community centres and commercial telecenters or cafés is the only achievable aim of access in a short or medium term (van Dijk, 2008: 289–290).

As it comes to the value of equality, equal access is usually addressed in terms of settlement, geographical location and costs of connecting to new media technologies such as digital TV or broadband Internet. Equal access to technologies by users regardless of place of residence (whether it might be a big urban agglomeration or remote countryside) or material

[1] For more on this issue, see in the Chapters 2 and 4.

status, can be seen instrumental in terms of structuring and framing of social communication, and thus also the exercise of communication rights.

Cultural argument – a cultural function of the communication media allows for the reproduction of cultural expressions and representations, content processing and validation of knowledge in a particular cultural environment. Specifically, it is linked to the process of encoding, decoding and formatting of communication forms in a way suitable for human perception, thus also entailing acts of interpretation, recognition and evaluation (Schulz, 2004: 92). It goes without saying that the media do not operate in a cultural vacuum, likewise culture does not evolve in a communication void. To paraphrase a well-known sentence of Edward T. Hall: the communication media determine culture, culture determines the communication media.[2] Culture is mostly embedded in the processes of communication, and reciprocally, the media enable social perception and information processing through cultural encoding, decoding and formatting. The communication media reproduce fundamental categories, values and norms, according to which communities of culture conduct their lives and construct their identities and sense of being (Cottle, 2000). Thus, cultural identities do not seem to be completed in the private sphere and then simply applied to the public sphere of the communication media. Communication contents, flows and practices incorporate and recognise a myriad of identity layers that individuals and communities bring to them from their manifold roles and activities in society.

In a similar vein, cultural diversity is not only manifested in the mediating cultural differences through media contents, services, activities, etc., but it is also embodied in media institutions and *their* practices. In that sense the communication media are *cultural* institutions shaping a symbolic environment in which cultures thrive. Culture and the communication media are linked through a networked infrastructure, and operations of *common* institutions and practices providing their users with meaningful ways of life. These need to be socially and spatially transmitted to guarantee cultural self-sustainability over generations. Yet despite self-sustainability, societies transform culturally.

No contemporary society is characterised by a single culture, and spatial boundaries of societies and cultures now rarely coincide (McQuail, 1992: 276). Joseph Straubhaar argues that the movement from traditional press and national broadcasting mass media to the use of Internet and

[2] Edward T. Hall, a 'founding father' of intercultural communication, formulated the key maxim: "Culture is communication and communication is culture" (Hall, 1959: 186).

multi- and cross-media services has produced identities that are multi-layered with cultural, geographic elements that are local, regional, national, transnational and global. As in geology, the layers often interact, they sometimes break and form new layers out of the pre-existing ones (2008: 12). Manuel Castells (2009) distinguishes four cultural patterns shaped by communication flows that illustrate the currents of cultural evolution and change. These patterns are characterised by the opposition between globalisation and identification, and by the tension between individualism and communalism (2009: 136). The patterns and layers of cultural identity are present in media and communication environments across different markets, geographical spaces and media structures. At the same time, alongside this restless dynamics of cultural change with an ongoing hybridisation and possibilities of cultural bypassing and transverse, the view that mediated communication should maintain symbolic cultures characteristic for particular societies, still marks cultural policies related to the media and communication processes.

Policy implications in the field of culture are often guided by the values of *diversity*, *uniqueness* and *authenticity*. On the one hand, they may cover such structural aspects as balancing asymmetries in cultural flows through protecting transnational media spaces against external players (e.g. against external ownership, capital flows), supporting domestic players (e.g. with subsidies for media production), co-production treaties, must-carry obligations that favour the distribution of domestic channels (e.g. in cable networks or on digital platforms). Relevant policy initiatives often resonate with political debates and originate within the frameworks of supra-national governmental organisations such as the European Union. At the same time, national states, although significantly weaker, still play a leading role in designing policies that seek to protect national cultures within the globalised communication sphere. Hallin and Mancini (2004: 43) see a crucial form of such an intervention in the institutionalisation of the public service media (PSM) that have been "present in every country in Western Europe and North America except the smallest", and in most countries public service media have until recently served as the primary source of broadcasting. Examples of the BBC, France Télévisions and others prove likewise that the PSM are viewed in many countries as an integral part of national cultural heritage and national cultural brands attracting worldwide respect.

The PSM have certainly not been the only media institutions, through which national states as well as supranational institutions sought and seek to defend cultural identity, cultural expressions and language. In addition to structural and institutional arrangements, communication policies in this regard often focus on the matters of content and performance: promotion of cultural works (especially works produced by domestic, indigenous producers or produced in a given country), language requirements (e.g. quota or proportions of works originally produced in a national/regional/minority language), support for locally-oriented or locally-produced content or media services for ethnic and national minorities. In addition to structural and content-related solutions, culturally motivated policies may also involve tax policies supporting minority ownership and employment policies designed to stimulate an active recruitment, retention and advancement of minorities (Gandy, 1998).

Educational and knowledge-generating argument – An educational function of the communication media has been frequently associated in past policy initiatives with the role and performance of the PSM. This partly resulted from a paternalistic model of the PSM, developed particularly in the UK and successfully exported to some other parts of the world (e.g. Japan). Yet, also in countries with a predominantly commercial model of media landscapes (USA), the educational and knowledge-generating media function has been used as an argument supporting, e.g. broadcasting licence policies requiring from broadcasters in the early years of radio and TV broadcasting to comply with 'public responsibility' or a 'fairness doctrine.' This has gradually been replaced with a pro-competition, non-interventionist policy imposing a minimum information requirement for licence renewals (Noam, 1994). The trend of deregulatory policies in the media environment, that has gained influence in the course of the last 30 years in most European countries and the US (but also other parts of the world), washed away most of the pro-educational commitments placed upon the commercial media by relevant policy-makers.

At the same time, increasingly commercial media systems tended to disappoint those seeking more ambitious performance satisfying knowledge-generating expectations. The mechanisms in the commercially-dominated systems are generally based on maximising audiences valuable to advertisers not on the grounds of the users' ability to mindfully acquire media contents but on the grounds of attracting their attention. As a result, the media use and reuse well-proven schemes serving popular culture, omit social and cultural controversies, and minority interests, bypass imbalances in the programmes and avoid antagonising any segment of the population that may be potentially appealing to advertisers.

A renewed interest in the educational and knowledge-generating function of the media has spread with new modes of media delivery and use. In media and communication policy, it found its manifestation in such concepts as media literacy, the protection of minors and a safe Internet. An important turning point in this respect has been the shift from a passive media user, to the person who is not only able to actively interact with the media, but more significantly, who is fully aware, *autonomous*, and has a strong personal locus in his/her media use and choices. The concept of 'personal locus' reflects the personal motivation of media users, and is composed of personal, autonomous and intentional goals of the users (Potter, 2011). These personal cognitive goals and reasons are usually very different from the political, economic, cultural and technological goals of the media institutions being composed of the goals of owners, producers, journalists and other actors contributing to, or influencing media performance.

Naturally, the communication media cannot be seen as substitutes for universities or educational institutions in general. At the same time, the way how we acquire and use the information in the media and through the media influences our organisation of knowledge. This information resides in messages and is composed of facts. Knowledge is formed in a person's mind and requires structure to provide context and thereby exhibit meaning (Potter, 2011: 17). Thus, media literacy starts with mindfulness. The point is to be rather reasonable than reactive. With a conscious attention to media use and constant linking it with personal purpose, information can be more thoroughly transformed into subtle knowledge structures. Mindful and fully conscious media use prevents an automatic processing of the information that lacks clear intentions and purposes. Why then, all these mental efforts of selection and meaning construction seem to be so important in new and dynamic media environments?

James Potter puts forward this explanation: "The information problem has shifted from one of gaining access to one of protecting ourselves from too much" (Potter, 2011: 3). Moreover, current media users face at least three false impressions. First, a high saturation with information and communication is often wrongly identified with huge variety and diversity. Second, there is a false sense of being well-informed and third, a false sense of control (Potter, 2011: 8). Paradoxically, having a greater control on the time and form of media use, users spend increasingly more time on searching and using the content that does not necessarily meet their personal purpose.

This becomes even more evident with younger segments of the population. Undoubtedly, as content consumption opportunities have multiplied and increased in thematic specialisation, minors have emerged as one of the most financially viable target groups for increasingly differentiated media products (Füg, 2008: 165). At the same time, exposure to various forms of media content acquired through manifold platforms became significantly higher. This also implies a different risk profile of children's media consumption. As the risk profile evolves mainly due to new technological possibilities, the issue of protection of minors and safe internet became more frequently addressed as salient areas in the media and communication policy.

At the same time, media literacy has been conceived more frequently by the public service media in some countries as a quite blanket concept combining informal learning with formal education concerning various age groups in societies. Interestingly, the BBC understands this part of the remit as covering a wide range of factual subjects that ultimately help audiences to form their knowledge (including natural history, science and medicine, leading to scientific literacy; history, art, music and religion leading to cultural literacy; the democratic process, business, law and consumer affairs leading to civic literacy; parenting, health, nutrition and gardening leading to life literacy; and an understanding of how and why the media are made and presented in the way that they are, leading to media literacy). On the other hand, the mere provision of facts, is to be completed by selecting, organising and interpreting them to spark debate and deepen understanding.[3] Thus, the educational and knowledge-generating function seems to be much broader than a quite limited understanding of media literacy itself. Additionally, the function wouldn't work as 'one size fits all'. The services with particular educational purposes and knowledge-building are to be adjusted to specific target audiences in ways and in subjects which are most relevant to them. For example, services for teenagers or young adults are to tackle relevant topics such as health, body image, careers and personal finance. Children are to be encouraged to find out more about the world around them through drama, comedy and entertainment, as well as factual programming on the CBBC, and pre-school children are to be provided with the opportunity to learn through play on CBeebies.[4]

Immersing oneself in the contemporary media environment sometimes resembles an overindulgence. It leaves us with the feeling of consuming too much, and of satiation with unwanted products. There is no doubt that 'media nutrition' affects our mental health and overall emotional and cognitive balance. One of the great strengths of the educational/knowledge-generating function of the media is that it makes

---

[3] BBC (2013) *Public purposes: Promoting education and learning* (available at: http://www.bbc.co.uk/aboutthebbc/insidethebbc/whoweare/publicpurposes/education.html; retrieved 25.08.2013).

[4] Ibidem.

the users *aware* and *conscious* of their personal goals, and eventually of what might be 'healthy' as regards their communication needs on the one hand, and communication habits, on the other hand. A healthy media diet is a choice. As taste in food can be changed, so can be taste in certain media contents, services and products. Thus, being curious and brave enough to go outside given and ready-to-use media frameworks, to look for a solution that meet personal locus, ultimately leads to better-informed political choices, more engaged citizenship, cultural creativity and personal experience of knowledge. This however requires abandoning certain expectations and prejudgments. The appropriate media 'diet' should be proportionally composed of a great variety of content types, yet this diversity needs to be reasonable. As with quality food, sometimes a quite small proportion of ingredients of high quality can better replace the empty calories of a large quantity of junk food.

Economic argument – an economic function of the communication media is closely linked with the development of media industries that have been customarily defined in terms of mass production by large scale organisations of a distinct product – such as a TV programme or news content – distributed in particular ways (Hoskins et al., 2004). The communication media are predominantly seen as businesses and in the words of Manuel Castells they operate mostly according to a business logic, regardless of their legal status (Castells, 2009: 71). In other words, they depend on economic mechanisms of supply and demand that include financing from sales, subscription, advertising, corporate sponsors and are expected to generate a profit. At the same time, the communication media are not the *same businesses* as other economic activities. This happens because the media perform other important societal functions (including the political/democratic function), but also because their economic operations are specific and incomparable with other businesses. First, the economies of scale shape comparatively low costs of mass media production, especially the costs of multiplying and distributing messages. Second, the communication media have two types of clients: advertisers and media users. In fact, the costs of media products are hidden in the prices of goods and services for which the media carry advertising (Kleinsteuber, 1997, quoted in: Schulz, 2004: 93). Thus in some respects, the media market is *not* responsive to audiences (Croteau and Hoynes, 2006: 27). Some authors even argue that the media, selling in fact the attention of their audiences, are primarily answerable to their 'advertising clients' and there is no effective process that makes the media accountable to consumers of their contents (Voltmer, 2013: 166).

Ideally, market mechanisms should provide a continuous mechanism of trial and error, of innovation, product improvement and flexible response to changing needs of media users (McQuail, 1992). Yet in practice, the communication wants and needs of users are not always congruent as they do not coincide with the interests of the users and advertisers. In other words, media products are 'merit goods'; they have significant social value, but individual consumers, if let to themselves, are likely to under-invest in these products, thus underestimating their long-term interests (Graham et al., 1999: 5; Freedman, 2008: 9). Many authors have frequently addressed the failures of communication media markets, that cannot be corrected from inside the system of economic operations and may lead to an under-serving of media users as well as may have an impact on other media functions (e.g. democratic, cultural) (Graham et al., 1999; Baker, 2002; Croteau and Hoynes, 2006; Freedman, 2008).

First, media content is a public good. In the case of these types of products, one person's use does not affect its use by another person. (Baker, 2002: 8). Second, media performance often produces significant externalities, including e.g. the advance or destruction of someone's reputation, strengthening or weakening of a democratic debate, promoting or discouraging a healthy lifestyles, etc. Third, media markets display a strong tendency towards concentration because of the economies of scale and scope; and the Internet is not excluded from this norm. Fourth, unlike in other industries, a certain number of media companies tend to target the same middle ground of consumers with relatively homogenous services, rather than distance themselves from the mainstream. Fifth, media systems are most productive when seen as distribution networks rather than the producers of discrete products (Freedman, 2008: 8).

Moreover, the definition of media markets, as well as industries is becoming more elusive. In economic terms (justifying e.g. competition policy), markets usually refer to structures and entities supplying substitute goods or services to a common group of users. In addition, to a product dimension, the market has a geographic dimension (Hoskins et al., 2004: 142). Yet, in a changing communication environment the notion of 'substitute goods' becomes less clear. Can e.g. news content based on investigative journalism be seen as a substitute for user-generated news? As regards the geographic dimension, the current trends of globalisation, digitisation, networking and deregulation – have removed most of the limits to corporate media expansion allowing for the consolidation of control by a relatively small number of companies benefiting mainly from their ability to build and use global media networks (Castells, 2009: 72).

In the current circumstances of communicative abundance and growing availability of content from alternative sources, traditional business models, especially of news production by the legacy media, are facing many challenges. In the last five years, print press circulation has declined by 17% in Western Europe and the US (Kilman, 2012). At the same time, newspaper advertising revenues have been declining as revenues lost in print have not been replaced by digital advertising. Audiovisual markets have been affected by audience fragmentation, while technological convergence has accelerated ownership consolidation across platforms, and has been widely used to justify further de-regulation of ownership (OSF, 2012a). These new economic conditions and trends will determine greater differentiation among media users willing (and able) to pay more or less for new technological devices and content, more frequently tailored for individual needs. Some analytical findings already suggest that high-quality (and often specially targeted) news is becoming more expensive, and to a certain extent, restricted to elitist users that are able to pay for it (OECD, 2010: 61). These new emerging communication divides reveal a twofold challenge of a market operation in the new media environment: on the one hand, the business models will lead to cheaper solutions in production of news for mainstream users (implying greater standardisation and routinisation in news production, less original content, thematic recycling of news). On the other hand, more sophisticated packages and portfolios of news and analyses will be prepared for the elite users paying the extra costs for quality and match of these packages with their individual needs.

So far, economic rationales that justify media and communication policy are mainly built on the values of economic *freedom*, *equality* and *diversity*, and more specifically they involve such notions as pluralism of media ownership, fair and effective competition, and fair or reasonable pricing for media and communication services. It is worth mentioning in this context that an economic logic has been a main driving force in media and communication policy in recent years. This has been mainly caused by the fact that both governments and supranational institutions (the EU in particular) have perceived – as their prior interest – well-developing communication media markets with a stable, eventually increasing employment. Denis McQuail and Jan van Cuilenburg observe that there has been a tendency to resign from "regulation where it interferes with market development and giving relatively more priority to economic over social-cultural and political welfare when priorities have to be set" (van Cuilenburg and McQuail, 2003: 198). At the same time, even in communication media policies framed by economic criteria (e.g. media specific ownership policies, merger controls, state aid rules, subsidies), economic justifications are often combined with or weighed against cultural and political arguments.

Political, democratic argument – a political or democratic function of the communication media has long been viewed as overriding in importance all other functions. In traditional liberal theory, the pivotal role of the media is to act as a check on the state and to monitor systematically all aspects of state activities, including failures, wrongdoings and abuses of power (Curran, 2002). Yet, a sole 'watchdog' or critical function does not certainly cover all the complexities of communication media involvement in a political and democratic process.

A minimalist approach to democracy in national politics is traditionally built around the arrangement of competitive and free elections. So is the role of the media that are largely expected to offer a source for well-informed choices that reflect citizens' preferences and provide guidance for political participation. Yet, democracy can also be seen as a structure of power rather than a procedure of method (Ringen, 2007). Such a structure of power is based on collective exercise and trust of citizens, that decisions are made and will continue to be made on the basis of respect for their interests (2007: 25). The method by which democracy works is not only elections, but more generally, it is maintained by structures of power, including a structure for public communication.

In normative terms, such a structure should ensure the formation of a plurality of "considered public opinions" (Habermas, 2006: 416), "enlightened understanding" (Dahl, 1979) and the "simultaneous presence of innumerable perspectives and aspects in which the common world presents itself" (Arendt, 1958: 57). Plurality and variety is thus conditionally linked to the public sphere. It is this diversity of perspectives and constant bargaining, in which shared social and political meaning is constructed and social reality defined. Moreover, the exchange of information and views of common concern are conducive to the formation of public opinion that can act as a political will. Reconsidering the classical concept of the public sphere, Jürgen Habermas argues that it can be best described as *a network* for communicating information and points of view, which enables the streams of communication to be filtered and synthesised in such a way that "they coalesce into bundles of topically specified public opinions" (Habermas, 1996: 360). Public opinion, however, does not seem to be representative in the statistical sense, nor does it seem to be an aggregate of individually gathered, privately expressed opinions (1996: 362). The process of its formation involves a shared practice of communication, collective experience, and process of imagination and representation. In Hannah Arendt's words it is an 'enlarged mentality' that validates the opinion: the very quality of an opinion as of a judgment depends upon careful consideration of other people's standpoints, on imagination of their preferences, and thus, ultimately, upon its degree of representativeness and impartiality (Arendt, 1969). Though collectively forged, the formation of public opinion has an important individual dimension: Robert Dahl emphasises that a concept of enlightened understanding implies adequate and equal opportunities of citizens for discovering and validating what their preferences are on the matter to be decided (Dahl, 1979: 104–105). In other words, to take autonomous and well-informed decisions, citizens need access to alternative, essentially diverse, but also trustworthy sources of information.

As the public sphere has become more and more separated from the public's physical presence and extended to the virtual presence of dispersed media users and communities, the communication media have evolved into central channels carrying, locating and constructing shared public meaning. Ideally, these communication structures ensure that a structure of power is democratic, and create the conditions for the legitimate exercising of power: power that crystallises in and through the process of deliberation and that is centred around the values, interests and choices citizens articulate by means of their debate. In democratic and media practice however, the exercise of the process of deliberation through the communication media has various limits, as supporters of critical theories observe.

First, the users of media content and services cannot be easily identified with *the public* or *citizens*. Publics emerge through a more complex processes of information collecting, discursive interaction and performance of citizens (Meyer, 2002: viii).

Second, the blurring the boundaries between discursive media practices, e.g. between news journalism and entertainment, public relations and advertising, news and advertising, leads to the erosion of a rational explanation and exchange of views, and thus ultimately to citizens' inability of political judgement and validation of their preferences (Postman, 1985; Bourdieu, 1998). Jaap de Wilde argues that in today's television democracy, in which arguments are defeated by sound bites and slogans, "the concept of democracy has been hollowed out" (de Wilde, 2011: 8). Numerous studies on news contents have demonstrated directions that seem to confirm these critical observations: they depict a growing trend of depoliticisation and commercialisation (McQuail and Siune, 1998; Lucht and Udris, 2010); a weakening of the divide between editorial and advertising content, particularly in local newspapers (OSF, 2012a) and redirecting funding from the production of content to technology and marketing (Baldi and Hassebrink, 2007: 10).

Third, communication media do not just reflect political life or the democratic process, but generate a political 'reality' that is tailored to their own requirements (Meyer, 2002: viii). This leads to a profound functional transformation of democracy in media societies that touches not merely the level at which politics is portrayed or represented, but alters the political process itself in every one of its aspects. Thus, media democracy is a new political regime with its own rules, options, resources, channels of influence, and limitations (Meyer, 2002). These critical views exposing the limitations of media performance in a democratic process are few examples of many similar observations. Even though they detect discrepancies between normative expectations, and actual practices, they do not undermine the validity of normative approaches.

Some authors argue that the age of communicative abundance changes the logic of democratic involvement. Compared with the era of representative democracy, when print culture and broadcasting media were much more closely aligned with political parties and governments, the age of monitory democracy witnesses constant public scrutiny and spats about power where it seems that "no organisation or leader from a political system is immune from affects of public surveillance" (Keane, 2009: 15). In this view, the process of deliberation seems to be less systematic, less organised, more spontaneous, and focused on constant scrutiny. Michael Schudson emphasises that in monitory democracy "citizens scan (rather than read) the informational environment in a way so that they may be altered on a very wide variety of issues for a very wide variety of ends and may be mobilised around those issues in a large variety of ways" (Schudson, 1998: 310). Thus, monitory democracy modifies citizens' engagement in a democratic process and it does modify communicative practices shared through the use of the communication media. At the same time, the civic mobilisation and call for forging public attention into some form of action or changed decision becomes more difficult due to a particularistic fragmentation of media user communities.

There is no doubt that the communication media play a decisive role in functioning democracies. Individuals are tremendously affected by collectively made decisions. The quality of these decisions depends, to a certain extent, on the politically-relevant qualities of the communication media: how they contribute to the formation of the public sphere, construction of the public opinion, the quality of political participation, general welfare, the adherence to ideas of community, togetherness and interdependence, the exercise of human rights (and communication rights in particular), maintenance of conditions that allow the sustainability of collective life and social order, and importantly, how they contribute to preserving the integrity between political rhetoric, media expression of political goals on the one hand, and the political action and decision – and realisation of these goals – on the other hand.

Because the communication media influence the qualities of democratic societies, they also enjoy a high status in terms of legal protection incomparable to other institutions of business or culture. Freedom of the press, broadcasting media, as well as the right to engage in these areas, safeguards the media infrastructure of public communication (Habermas, 1996: 368). Thus, basic implications in media and communication policies involve those rights and liberties that aim to preserve an openness and diversity of media systems and ultimately, facilitate deliberative legitimation processes. Most scholars agree that such operations are possible only if a self-regulating media system gains independence from its social environment (Habermas, 2006: 411–412). At the same time, the independence of the communication media is to be particularly protected against state power and political pressure as for their immediate political importance. The sheer function of providing information should be fulfilled only outside the political realm strictly speaking, and no political action and no decision should be involved in this process (Arendt, 1969: 131). Following this argument, there are reasons for public policies protecting the democratic/political functions of the communication media: these, mainly derived from values of *freedom* and *diversity*, are needed to guarantee the independence of the media and journalistic autonomy in order to facilitate the potential of democratic deliberation.

The five main functions and arguments for media and communication policy have painted the main paths delineating a specific territory of media policy for decades regardless of changing technological, societal, geopolitical and economic conditions in which the communication media have operated so far and continue to operate. This is not to say however, that these are the *only* functions and *only* policy rationales. Moreover, the changing conditions make policy recognition of a particular normative conceptual framing enormously difficult. This happens because normative policy considerations have to be translated into concrete actions, and as such, they often attempt to catch up to a 'moving target' of actual communication, cultural, political and economic environments. An elusive character of contemporary societies linked by communication networks puzzles policymakers: how to define the risks, problems and threats in such fluid environments? How to conceptualise, operationalise, measure? What 'framing' perspective to choose in order to crystallise a right understanding of a problem? How to achieve pragmatic coherence about a definition of the problem as well as about the claims made by relevant groups?

In this connection, it is important to start from the description of the key elements of a media and communication policy and ask: *what specifically* is/are the object/objects of these policies? The answers might not be as easy as they seem to be at first sight. With rapid technological changes, mediated communication more frequently migrates to the channels and performances that are not controlled by traditional legacy media institutions, but often by the media users themselves. Karol Jakubowicz observed that in these circumstances, it is increasingly difficult to distinguish between 'media' and 'non-media' or to know the scope of policy and regulation and what regulatory regime to apply to which service (Jakubowicz, 2012a: 240). The section below reflects on these important questions.

1.3. Media systems, media environments and other objects of media and communication policy

The term *mass media* has been used for decades to name and define the technologies, modalities, institutions, contents and services as well as forms of performance with a primary aim to mediate communication. Thus, broadly understood, the media are intermediate agencies that enable communication to take place (O'Sullivan et al., 1994: 176; Craig, 2004: 3). Niklas Luhmann pointed out, that the term mass media includes all those institutions of society which make use of copying technologies to disseminate communication (Luhmann, 2000: 2). It is the technology of dissemination that plays a fundamental role in differentiating the media from other spheres of social activities – the technology constitutes a medium which deals with information, or more precisely distinguishes between information and non-information (Luhmann, 2000). The growth and evolution of the communication media is significantly marked by the emergence of new technologies. Newer segments of media landscapes grew at an extraordinary pace with new technologies and social forms of media use, thus resulting in the omnipresence of the *new* media in social life.

Disregarding for a while the whole dispute about the changing nature of contemporary communication media, and the questions whether they still (or not) constitute coherent institutions and technologies, we can observe that the media compose various structures – from macro to micro societal levels. These include multiple hierarchical layers that embrace environments, systems, networks, practices, forms of performance, contents and services with a global, transnational, national, regional and local relevance. Thus, both media and communication policies are multilevel as all the media structures addressed by policies are interdependent. Yet, there are media systems and communication environments at a macro level that attract the ultimate policy focus manifested in organising principles, prevailing order or paradigms of communication. It is the overall quality of such a system as a whole that should be examined by what it offers to users and citizens, and how it addresses their communication needs. In other words, media systems have various potentials (e.g. potential of diversity) but taking full advantage of these potentials depends on actual media use and on the way this use affects the lives of individuals in general.

Some scholars argue that *media systems* do not emerge spontaneously from the logic of communication technologies, or from the business strategies and actions, but are instead purposefully created by competing political interests (Freedman, 2008: 1). Others point out that media systems are as much the outcome of chance (or self-organisation) as of policy design and there are always gaps and inconsistencies (McQuail, 1992: 152). Certainly, both assertions hold a grain of truth. The formation of particular media systems results from various factors – endogenous (historical, political, legal, cultural), exogenous (globalisation, technological convergence, transnational economy and governance), empirical (population size, demographic structure, density of population) and normative (cultural and political values, distinctive social imaginaries, historical traditions, legal principles and norms). In other words, media systems grow from a common historical-cultural ground, and are formed by a concrete constitutional and legal framework, they reflect manifold views and orientations and economic relations in an ever-changing social context (Golka, 2004: 6).

Even though media systems posses certain distinctive organisational and regulatory features (Humphreys, 1996), they do not constitute single uniform systems with single purposes or philosophies, but are usually composed of many separate elements including diverse normative expectations (McQuail, 1994: 240). At the same time, we may quite clearly see intrinsic differences between the French and British media systems, or French and German model of media regulation. Thus, media systems are distinct, unique and nonreplicable, but not uniform or internally homogenous. They resemble living organisms in their dynamics and originality, while they also share certain characteristics with other systems or media environments. To state that the media systems constantly change, transform, develop and evolve, is self-evident. This development is usually seen by scholars as a progressive evolution or the process of increasing capacity of the media system to fulfil perceived communication needs at progressively higher levels of material and cultural well-being (Tehranian, 1994: 276). Yet, the realities of media system transformations show that change may be progressive as well as regressive: sometimes periods of media proliferation, increasing quality and diversity of offerings are followed by media decline. Media policies then may be seen, in normative terms, as potential corrections of such a volatile development.

Media systems are macrostructures, in which media entities, operations and performances are arranged together in a particular way, also (but not only) due to the fact that media systems have been, historically, objects, and thus also the results of communication policies. At the same time, media systems exhibit a reasonable autonomy: they differentiate themselves from other spheres of social actions, are constituted and reproduced through their own operations, or more precisely 'observing operations' (Luhmann, 2000). Thus, media systems are characterised by a certain degree of coherence (and thus also internal selectivity) and at the same time by sufficient redundancy and variety. Both forces – autonomy and dependency of media systems on political, cultural, historical and geographical circumstances – are integrated into media and communication policies, sometimes as ends (e.g. autonomy from political interferences), sometimes as conditions to be preserved (e.g. dependency on distinct cultural and linguistic characteristics).

The most frequently studied media systems are national systems. Though the forces of economy and technology tend to produce quite convergent patterns in the development of media systems, nationally specific political, social, and cultural factors explain much of the divergence (Lowenstein and Merrill, 1990; Kleinsteuber, 1993; Humphreys, 1996; Hallin and Mancini, 2004; Humphreys, 2012). The phenomenon of convergence refers to both technological and geographical boundaries. On the one hand, convergence of media systems leads to the fading of the once clear boundaries between print, broadcast and telecommunication-based media (McQuail, 1994: 240). On the other hand, the boundaries of national media systems become more permeable due to globalisation, a widespread use of new technological applications and economic forces.

The converging forces caused by technological development create certain characteristics of new media types such as online media that tend to unite media systems in terms contents and performances across national boundaries (Deuze, 2003; Benson et al., 2012). Such characteristics include e.g. a dominance of promotion and advertising as well as a more prominent presence of deliberation, opinion and excessive commenting in the online media (Barnhurst and Nerone, 2002; OECD, 2010; Benson et al., 2012). Hallin and Mancini (2004: 261) point out that the homogenisation produced by technological innovation involves the spread of a global culture of technical expertise that gradually replaces professional journalism once rooted in national cultures. The economic forces of media system homogenisation include not only trends in media commercialisation and development of global media markets (with transnational ownership structures, modes of financing, organisation, production and distribution activities and use), but also the deregulation and harmonisation of media policies. This trend reduces the distinctiveness of the media experience in any country and extends perceived policy problems and solutions over an area wider than the nation state (McQuail, 1994: 241).

Table 1: Factors of convergence of media systems

Technological	Economic
interconnectedness of media production and distribution across various media platforms and sectors	commercialisation of media systems
formation of media and communication networks without boundaries between print, broadcast, online and telecommunication	harmonisation and deregulation of media policies
new media forms (both in terms of content and performance)	globalising media markets (with transnational ownership structures, modes of financing, organisation production and distribution networks)
globalising pattern of professional journalism and technical expertise resulting from the spread of new technologies	

Sources: Elaborated on the basis of: Klimkiewicz (2010b), Castells (2009), Hallin and Mancini (2004).

Still, the distinctiveness plays an essential role in the variation of media systems. Among the relevant factors geographical and demographic variables should be mentioned in the first place – these embrace e.g. size of media markets (correlated usually with the size of a population), density of settlement, proportion of urban population, and proportion of a population settled in a capital city. Larger systems are likely to generate more varied media structures, while in smaller systems, internal differentiation might be stalled by consolidation processes or other market determinants (Klimkiewicz, 2010b). Hallin, however, warns of oversimplifications and points out that a state's size interacts with other variables (such as linguistic boundaries, the level of GDP, etc.), and therefore, its effects are not consistent (2009: 101). Variations in media distribution may be caused by the density of settlement (e.g. an early entry and dominance of cable) or the proportion of an urban population, while centralisation of the media system might also be a result of a significant proportion of population settled in a capital. These factors do influence and are influenced by policymaking process – it can matter greatly whether such a process is centralised or decentralised as is the case of Germany or Spain (Humphreys, 2012: 165).

Socio-cultural factors are equally important for an explanation of media system variations. Media systems are not only organised according to certain visions and cultural cleavages, but they do play a crucial role in sustaining, reproducing and transforming the forms of socio-cultural inclusion and exclusion (Downey and Mihelj, 2012: 7). The forms of media segmentation in this respect differ from country to country and they reflect various ways of acknowledgement of ethnic and cultural diversity. This great variety stems not only from the fact that countries are composed of different proportions of minority groups (some are relatively homogenous, some have significant proportions of historical autochtonous minorities while others are multicultural due to the presence of allochtonous immigrant groups), but also from the fact that there is lack of agreement on what are the *ethnic, national minorities, cultural* and *regional* communities and moreover, what are the *communication rights* of these groups. Thus, media services and adequate media provision for various ethnic minority groups are debated not only in demographic terms (how big are these minority groups) but also in terms of historic settlements, political arrangements, migration flows developing over time. The question of political recognition or nonrecognition draws a main defining line as the appropriate media provision is rarely satisfied by pure market forces.

Political factors determining the variation of media systems were comparatively analysed by Daniel Hallin and Paolo Mancini (2004) in their groundbreaking work on comparing media systems. In addition to political systems factors (majoritarian versus consensual democracies, the role of rational-legal authority) the dimensions of scrutiny included the extent to which the media reflected political orientations in a society (political parallelism), the degree of professionalism and the scope of state intervention. Peter Humphreys (2012) argues that other relevant factors in terms of the political and legal tradition should also reflect historical disjunctures. They refer to different legacies that disconnect the historical paths of political development. In Europe, for example, countries having their experiences with dictatorial or authoritarian regimes adapt different ways of media system democratisation (Humphreys, 2012: 166–167). This can be illustrated by the example of Germany, Spain, as well as the post-communist countries in Central and Eastern Europe (CEE). Other important political/legal factors include legal system traditions. Common law and civil law traditions suggest quite different approaches to the media, especially in legal terms, the former being conducive to 'judge-made law', the latter being conducive to a codified body of a special press law (Humphreys, 1996). Moreover, the role of judicial review also impacts functioning of the media system and policy-making process (Humphreys, 2012). In addition, a specific 'logic' or 'climate' of media policy affects a dynamic process of media system architecture. For example, applying market logic to media regulation results in prioritising economic qualities, such as economic efficiencies or healthy competition, over other normative goals, including the qualities of democracy, cultural values, social inclusion, etc. Peter Humphreys (2012) also mentions the relevance of national regulatory approaches and 'styles' in their implications.

Finally, economic factors do not only generate forces of convergence but also contribute to national variations. Some media systems may be economically quite self-sustainable in their particular environments, others might highly depend on external resources in terms of financing, know-how, human capital, but also policy schemes (imposed directly or indirectly) and the rules of action. Manuel Puppis rightly observes that a high penetration of foreign media has implications for the media landscapes (2009: 11). Greater dependence on external forces might negatively influence the system's own ability to generate the necessary diversity, but one has to be sensitive to historical nuances in this process. In cases of important turning points, some media systems have a capacity to reorganise their structure according to available resources, while others absorb solutions from outside (Klimkiewicz, 2010b). Also, patterns of media ownership and strategies of concentration vary from a system to system. Numerous and highly complex symbiotic relationships between media owners and politicians might lead to fundamental structural changes, cementing, for instance, the positions of principal media players in the media system. Besides, in some media systems advertising by state or public institutions crucially shapes the conditions under which the media operate. There seems to be a great affinity between the modes of financing and functions performed by media outlets within a system. Structural diversity generated by different funding sources may be more proportionate, e.g. when it does involve the coexistence of the public service media (PSM) financed predominantly from licence fees, privately owned entities financed by advertising or subscription, as well as community or alternative media supported by public grants and donations.

Factors of convergence and distinctiveness of media systems are involved simultaneously in developments of media systems. Yet, it is also apparent that some factors of distinctiveness make factors of convergence more influential. An interesting example to illustrate this is media transformation in the CEE.[5] Both types of factors as well as their balancing play a decisive role in the formation of media policies.

Table 2: Factors of distinctiveness of media systems

Geographic/ demographic	**Cultural/ linguistic**	**Political/legal tradition**	**Economic**
population size (large, medium, small)	linguistic structure of society (language/languages spoken)	the level of political decentralisation and regional autonomies: multinational democracies, federalist structures versus centralised national states	the level of media concentration (high, medium, small)
density of settlement (high, medium, small)	cultural, ethnic and religious structure of a society (proportion of minorities)	consensual power-sharing systems versus majoritarian executive system	dependence on external forces versus self-sustainability of media systems
proportion of urban population	inclusion/exclusion of particular cultural/linguistic groups (political representation and legal recognition of the groups)	intervention of the state (strong, medium, weak)	modes of media financing (various proportions across national media systems)

[5] More on this issue see in the Chapter 3.

proportion of a population in the capital		ideological polarisation (high, moderate, low)	forms of employment (institutionalised, outsourced)
demographic structure (age, income, education)		legal tradition (common law versus civil law)	forms and types of media ownership (private, public, NGO, staff-owned)
		influence of judicial law making versus constitutional legal rulings	

Sources: Elaborated on the basis of: Klimkiewicz (2010b), Humphreys (2012).

Although media systems are ultimate policy objects, they are rarely referred to and defined as such in policy and regulatory instruments. These often tend to minimise and precisely delineate the object of regulation. The manner and form in which the objects are recognised and defined are important determinants of how they will ultimately be addressed by policymakers (Howlett and Ramesh, 1995: 104). Clarification of a language, the narrowing of a concern in question as well as an exclusion of specific categories stem usually from a gradual reconciliation of various interests. On the other hand, an acceptance of a broad definition of the objects leaves policymakers with a greater freedom of deliberate actions. The two examples below illustrate how policy and regulatory definition of the media – the object of public policies – can serve as a battleground for clarifying various interests of involved actors.

The first, demonstrates a gradual narrowing of the 'media' definition for regulatory purposes. An adoption of the concept of (audiovisual) media service in the Audiovisual Media Services Directive (AVMSD) (European Parliament and the Council, 2010a) leaves no doubt that 'the media' component is confined to a *particular* kind of media services. The Recitals 5, 21, 22 and 28 of the Preamble and Article 1(a) bring up the following criteria:

- audiovisual media services are as much cultural services as they are economic services,
- the definition covers mass media in their function to inform, entertain and educate the general public,

- the definition includes audiovisual commercial communication but excludes any form of private correspondence, such as e-mails sent to a limited number of recipients as well as electronic versions of newspapers and magazines,
- the definition refers to a service, thus requiring an economic activity that is under the editorial responsibility of a media service provider (hence excluding e.g. private websites),
- the definition covers services, which are mass media, that is which are intended for reception by, and which could have a clear impact on, a significant proportion of the general public.[6]

Taking into consideration also the 'audiovisual' component of definition, *the media* as the object of eventual regulation would be even more severely confined to a relatively limited number of services. Yet, as it comes to policy goals and rationales justifying the adoption of AVMSD, these certainly aim to reach a more general level of media operations in European societies.[7]

The second example sketches a critical discussion concerning the adoption of a broad definition of the media by the US Federal Communication Commission (FCC) in the case of measuring media diversity in local markets. In its critical analysis of FCC policies Mark Cooper quotes the discussion of the Supreme Court regarding the *Prometheus Radio Project* versus FCC (2004) that aimed to correct the definition of the media for regulatory purposes:

> Media outlets have an entirely different character from individual or organisations' websites and thus contribute to diversity in an entirely different way. They provide an aggregator function (bringing news/information to one place) as well as a distillation function (making a judgement as to what is interesting, important, entertaining, etc.) (quoted in Cooper, 2007: 203).

Thus, the concept of the media is not only technologically determined, but has also functional relevance in a given society. Both cases prove that the conceptual approach to the object of the media policy is quite complicated and largely depends on weighing various interests involved. The next section will examine the field of media and communication policies.

---

[6] See Jakubowicz (2012a) for a similar discussion on defining the object of media/communications policies.

[7] See more on this issue in the Chapter 4.

1.4. Media and communication policy: a conceptual framework and evolving paradigms

Media and communication policy as other thematically distinguished public policy fields stands for conscious (public) projects that aim to achieve chosen goals with the proposed forms and means of action, available resources and in a foreseen time horizon. Pioneering public policy research, Harold Lasswell conceptualised the complexity of policymaking by breaking its process down into a number of distinct stages: intelligence, promotion, prescription, invocation, application, termination and appraisal (Lasswell, 1956). The cyclic model integrating various consecutive stages and phases of action inspired a vast number of scholars. Michael Howlett and M. Ramesh (1995:11) summarised these variations of scholarly scrutiny into five phases of applied problem-solving and corresponding stages in a policy cycle:

- Problem recognition – agenda-setting,
- Proposal of a solution – policy formulation,
- Choice of a solution – decision-making,
- Putting the solution into effect – policy implementation,
- Monitoring results – policy evaluation.

Although the concept of 'cyclic' policies has been one of the most popular in theoretical terms, a vast number of other approaches has offered a helpful catalogue of systematising the relatively opaque and often impenetrable field of public policies. Peter Levin (1997: 24) argues that two aspects have to be borne to mind when conceptualising policies. First, an equating a 'policy' with 'action' may be sometimes misleading as it results in the inability to explore the relationship *between* policy and action. Second, the policymakers use the term 'policy' as a label to denote the belongingness, commitment and status of a proposal. Thus, the appropriate question should be: what do policymakers mean by 'policy' (1997: 24)? Scholarly approaches to studying policies have revolved around various dichotomies:

- 'thematic' versus 'analytical',
- 'administrative' versus 'critical',
- 'processual' versus 'problem-oriented',
- 'comparative' (usually cross-national) versus 'one case' (national),
- 'paradigm-oriented' versus 'action-oriented'.

For the purpose of this book, the first two dichotomies deserve a brief explanation, as they overlap to some extent. The distinction between a 'thematic' versus an 'analytical' approach is derived mostly from their goals: the 'thematic' approach seeks generalisations that reveal certain regularities, while the 'analytical' approach follows elaboration and description. Hence, the 'thematic' approach employs theories to explain policies, while the 'analytical' approach focuses on mechanisms and circumstances (Levin, 1997: 30). The methods used in the 'thematic' approach operate with norms, values, and offer rather normative significance. The methods of the 'analytical' approach often seek to provide hard evidence for a case and are rather descriptive.

The distinction between an 'administrative' and 'critical' approach was originally introduced by Paul Lazarsfield (1941) (quoted in Puppis and Just, 2012:17). The 'administrative' approach denotes research carried through in the service of some kind of administrative agency and is often associated with positivist, analytical methods (2012: 17). Thus, 'administrative' research seems to be less autonomous, mainly descriptive, analytical, evidence-driven, to a large extent based on quantitative data. The critical approach on the other hand, "develops a theory of prevailing social trends of our times" (Lazarsfield, 1941: 9; quoted in Puppis and Just, 2012: 17) and aims to explain the logic behind the policy process and values involved. Thus, the critical research seems to be more autonomous, mainly evaluative, often discourse-oriented, value-driven, to the large extent exploring historical narratives and using qualitative data.

Media policy as a specific type of public policies is usually seen as a set of goals, modes and measures by which public authorities shape, or try to shape, the structures and practices of the media (Freedman, 2008: 10; Psychogiopoulou, 2012: 5). Thus, media and communication policy embraces a totality of enforced laws, settled norms and principles that govern activities of the communication media on various levels (Goban-Klas, 1999: 173). A complex media policy process can be divided into various stages, but two are substantive: setting down the policy goals (agenda-setting, formulating and framing of policy issues) and realisation. The policy process is always determined by leading values, the societal needs and actual resources that can be invested into the policy enactment (Goban-Klas, 1999: 173). Much of the media policy research has followed these elements tracing how media policy goals are chosen, how policy outcomes come about, what factors shape different policies in different countries, why certain interests and priorities rather than others prevail, what actors are involved in policymaking and decision making process and how power is distributed amongst them (Humphreys, 1996; Fischer, 2003; Freedman, 2008; van den Bulck, 2012).

As a complex field of social and political action, a media and communication policy is often studied through media regulation. Yet, there is an important difference between a 'policy' and 'regulation'. While a 'policy' denotes a broader field, where various ideas and assumptions about the expected structure and performance of a media system circulate (Freedman, 2008: 13) and are shaped into a more consistent way of action, regulation refers to the specific actions and mechanisms, in which policy makers require or proscribe certain desired activities and behavior on the part of individuals and institutions (Howlett and Ramesh, 1995: 87). In this sense, a policy precedes regulation (Psychogiopoulou, 2012: 8). Media regulation takes various forms including rules, standards, forms of protection, prohibition, legal measures, executive orders and other forms of intervention (e.g. distribution and redistribution of resources in the form of subsidies) that are composed in a regulatory regime or regulatory pattern. Such a regime or pattern counts for one of the principal four building factors in the framework for communication policy: the underlying goal, the medium, the technology and the policy/regulatory regime (Bar and Sandvig, 2008; quoted in Jakubowicz, 2012a: 239). Referring back to the two distinctive stages in a media policy process, media regulation would come to the shape in the second stage focusing on policy realisation. In other words, media regulation implies the application of rules developed through the policymaking process, it also deals with the operation of specific, often legally binding tools that are deployed on the media structures and performance (Freedman, 2008: 14).

The concept of media governance has a broader relevance than the terms 'regulation' and 'policy'. Media governance incorporates various influences, claims, demands, forms of control and encouragement used by different actors in society (also beyond national authorities), including guiding principles and values that aim to shape media structures and performance (Karppinen and Moe, 2012: 188). In this sense, the concept of media governance reflects the increasing importance of informal networks, non-governmental actors, supranational bodies, as well as mechanisms affecting media structures and performance that combine divergent objectives and logics of action. Media governance covers the totality of mechanisms both formal and informal, national and supranational, centralised and dispersed, that aim to organise media systems along with media policy strategies (Freedman, 2008: 14).

Another interesting current that spurs conceptual debates concerns the terminological choice between a 'media policy' and 'media policies'. A media policy serves as an overarching term to embrace a totality of various public projects, visions and collective forms of action, guided by manifold principles and values, often with different objectives that aim to shape media structures and performance at multiple levels. Media policies on the other hand refer to specific projects, visions and forms of actions. They may depend on the distinct medium under consideration (the press, broadcasting, online) or sector (public, private, community) or function (economic, educational, cultural, democratic) or collective actor (media owners, content producers, content providers, journalists, media users). Thus, both designations are seen relevant in their own terms and are used in this work.

Finally, terminological concerns have to be completed with some reflection on a 'media' policy and a 'communication' policy. Van Cuilenburg and McQuail (2003) associate media policy with a traditional understanding of policies focusing mainly on newspapers, broadcasting and cable, and other similar means of general public distribution, directed towards political welfare goals while by contrast, a 'communications' or 'telecommunications' policy involves more attention to infrastructure and architecture, market conditions, regulation of monopoly, etc. (2003: 186). Other authors (Puppis and Just, 2012) replace the term 'media' with a mere 'communication' policy marking a new policy trend that responds to technological and economic convergence in the media and communication sector. This volume focuses on media policy as it is examining forces that shape or aim to shape media system architecture rather than telecommunication architecture, but both terms 'media' and 'media and communication' policy are used to denote either a policy field dealing with the communication media or a more broader policy area tackling the media operations that interact with electronic communication networks.

Media policy discourse is shaped to the great extent by various rationalities and theoretical understandings of the communication media and their roles in a society. The way how these understandings and perceptions are formed, activated, used and institutionalised affects the evolution of media policy paradigms. Two paradoxes or ambiguities characterise the field of media and communication policies: the state as a principal actor in media and communication policy has been historically perceived as the main agent of press freedom restriction. In other words, there is a genuine ambivalence in the historical and expected role of the state in shaping a socially desired media architecture. The state, that has been responsible (and is still responsible in many autocratic and non-democratic regimes throughout the world) for constraining freedom of expression and the free operations of the media, is also expected to actively guarantee this freedom through constitutional, legal arrangements and other complementing policy measures in conditions of functioning democracies. Second, although media and communication policies are viewed by many authors as essential for sustaining functioning democracies (Habermas,

1996; Napoli, 1999), the related policy issues are often low profile, and do not receive the same attention as budgetary decisions or tax policies (Puppis and Just, 2012). These two paradoxes are obviously interrelated and prove again that the communication media are *special* objects of, and media policy a *special* type of, public policies.

Media policy paradigms, are to certain extent, formed within these limits. In their groundbreaking work on media policy paradigm shifts, van Cuilenburg and McQuail (2003) explain the change of paradigms by the transformation of underlying goals. The three distinguished paradigms (communication industry policy until World War II, public service media policy 1945–1980/90 and a new communication policy paradigm – since 1990) were guided by a different – and unique for each phase – set of goals. These were conceptualised by van Cuilenburg and McQuail as political welfare, social welfare and economic welfare. Though a media policy has been directed towards political welfare goals traditionally, a current search for a new communication policy paradigm is mainly driven by an economic and technological logic, even when enriched with certain normative elements. These are in fact more 'communicative' and less 'political' and 'cultural' in character. They can be summarised by the following principles:

- freedom of communication;
- access – understood as the possibility for individuals, groups, organisations and institutions to share society's communication resources, both as senders and receivers;
- control/accountability – accountability meaning the possibility of securing from those who control and make use of access; control in a sense of deciding who gets access to what communication resources, when, where, how, and on what conditions (van Cuilenburg and McQuail, 2003: 203–205).

It should be also added in this respect that the paradigm shift reflects the changing weights of actors involved in the media and communication policy process, the state in particular.

The next section of this chapter attempts to develop a model for studying the media policy in this book.

1.5. Polyvalent media, polyvalent policy: A methodological note

Media policy research deals interchangeably with a dual subject of examination: on the one hand it aims to scrutinise the policies, on the other hand it studies media structures and performance – either as part of these policies, or independently. Thus, methodological choices should resonate with this duality and provide a framework that logically connects both elements. The model below attempts to incorporate both policies and media, together with normative and empirical perspectives. A media policy is perceived both as a collective conceptualisation and collective action: it does involve various groups of actors with various positions, roles and levels of control over the action and conceptualisation, which interact in order to shape communication media structures and media performance.

In normative terms, any policy should be justified by rationales. In the case of the communication media, these rationales are derived from five specific functions the media play in societies. In other words, media policies do support (or should improve) certain *qualities* of the media that facilitate these functions. Qualities can be seen in comparison of one level with the other or through the interplay of potential and realisation (Ringen, 2007: 31). It is this second understanding that seems more relevant for studying a media policy. In other words, a media system may contain various potentials: for example of media freedom, media pluralism, access for all, inclusive representation of various social groups, etc. But only when the system allows for freedom, performs diversity, guarantees access and inclusive representation of media users, the qualities take shape and come to terms with plural expectations of the public vis-à-vis the media, and as such, they respond to communication needs.

Communication needs reflect both the collective and individual aspects of mediated communication. They do not only strengthen political and civil rights, but manifest manifold purposes for which individuals and communities interact with the media. Thus, communication needs can be divided into three broad categories. The first embraces the need for knowledge, information and orientation that affect society as a whole. These needs are associated with the processes of collecting, receiving information, learning about social realities, interpreting politics and distilling views that resonate with various orientations. The second category of needs involves the processes of representation, exchange and sharing. These are the needs for an understanding, representation, deliberation and expression of social and cultural communality. Finally, the third category of needs demonstrates the need to understand and express oneself, and is linked with the process of self-expression (Stevenson, 1995). To accept that communication needs have to be met in societies is to recognise communication rights that imply obligations and responsibilities, and that can be demanded. Although these rights have been internationally agreed upon and confirmed in different arenas, they have not been collected into a unified framework and thus, also not adopted as a part of international law (Nieminen, 2010).[8]

In normative terms, media and communication environments should proportionally balance the five functions media play in societies, respond to communication needs and guarantee the fulfillment of communication rights. Media policy rationales are usually distilled from this *polyvalent* normative view. In other words, the media and communication policy is a *polyvalent* phenomenon as are the very objects of the policy – the communication media themselves. Stein Ringen (2007: 272) observes that if the job of the media was only to inform, we could judge the media on a single standard. But if the purpose is a mixed one, we need to consider several criteria at the same time, criteria which may well be in conflict with each other (2007: 272). Thus ideally, the polyvalent media policy aims to shape desired media functions and prioritise qualities that help to meet the communication needs and exercise communication rights of individuals and communities proportionally. In practice though, the policy is a product of rationales that may be contradictory or complementary. In other words, policy rationales exhibit a certain degree of elasticity as they have to be adaptable to very specific projects. Hence, the polyvalent media policy is always a selective, and at the same time a complex and sophisticated process. It may be seen as an outcome in itself, but also as the process balancing various goals and leading to multiple ends.

The process itself involves a set of actors with various positions and roles played as well as different levels of control over the selection of allowable actions. Policy actors hold different positions to decide how are media functions balanced or whether they are balanced at all, what are the proportions among them, and what issues are prioritised. In such a dynamics of balancing, an imagined media architecture plays an important role as the policy ends are marked by a will to correct perceived asymmetries. Thus, it is important how factors of distinctiveness and convergence of media systems are incorporated in this imaginary, eventually whether they are seen important at all. Ulrike Klinger (2012: 142)

[8] Hannu Nieminen (2010: 15) summarises the concept of communications rights in four dimensions:

- the right to information concerns the claim for factuality and accuracy of public representations,
- the right to orientation concerns plurality and diversity of opinions that are publicly offered or available,
- the right to social and cultural communality refers to the availability of a rich variety of cultural representations, including those of both art and entertainment, and
- the right to self-expression includes an access to channels and platforms where citizens can make themselves heard and seen, and also listened to.

notices that usually, a media policy evokes little mass public mobilisation and is negotiated among political elites, media owners, journalists and media activists. An important aspect, that distinguishes policy from other collective actions is the commitment (Levin 1997: 31) and willingness to translate norms and beliefs held by the actors into the policy process (Sabatier, 1988).

The actors in the polyvalent media process use a vast array of strategies for the selection of particular courses of action. Naturally, the core decision-makers occupy a central position in this process: their consent is indispensable to change the status quo of a previous policy pattern. Some scholars describe these decisive actors as veto players (Tsebelis, 2002; Klinger, 2012). The core decision-makers as collective actors represent public institutions and their position often results from specific political configurations that reflect a given political system. Yet, the decision-making process involves another strong collective actor representing the media industry. Klinger (2012: 149) argues that media owners in particular have strong incentives to influence media policy but also "convincing means of doing so: as they can control access to the mediated public sphere and the qualitative appearance of political actors in this arena, they are crucial partners and gate-keepers of political parties". Paradoxically, though one of the functions of the media is to hold accountable those who exercise political power, the strong dependency relationship between the core political decision-makers and the core media actors determines collective consideration of selected policy actions, the desired outcomes and outcomes to be avoided, the costs, benefits, means and resources associated with each possible action and outcome.

Thus, the key component of the polyvalent media policy is collective conceptualisation of a policy problem, and the greatest challenge coherence between policy actors and congruence of their policy choices. When the decisions in the polyvalent media policy are set, potential outcomes defined, means linked with expected ends, the collective action completes conceptualisation. In principle, the action should be consistent with the objectives adopted. In empirical terms, it often faces numerous constraints marked by available resources, co-operation in implementation, and formal versus factual exercise of standards. Moreover, in a supra-national policy framework, as is the case of EU media policy, possible policy constraints are evoked by a discord between the supranational and national level of policymaking and harmonisation.

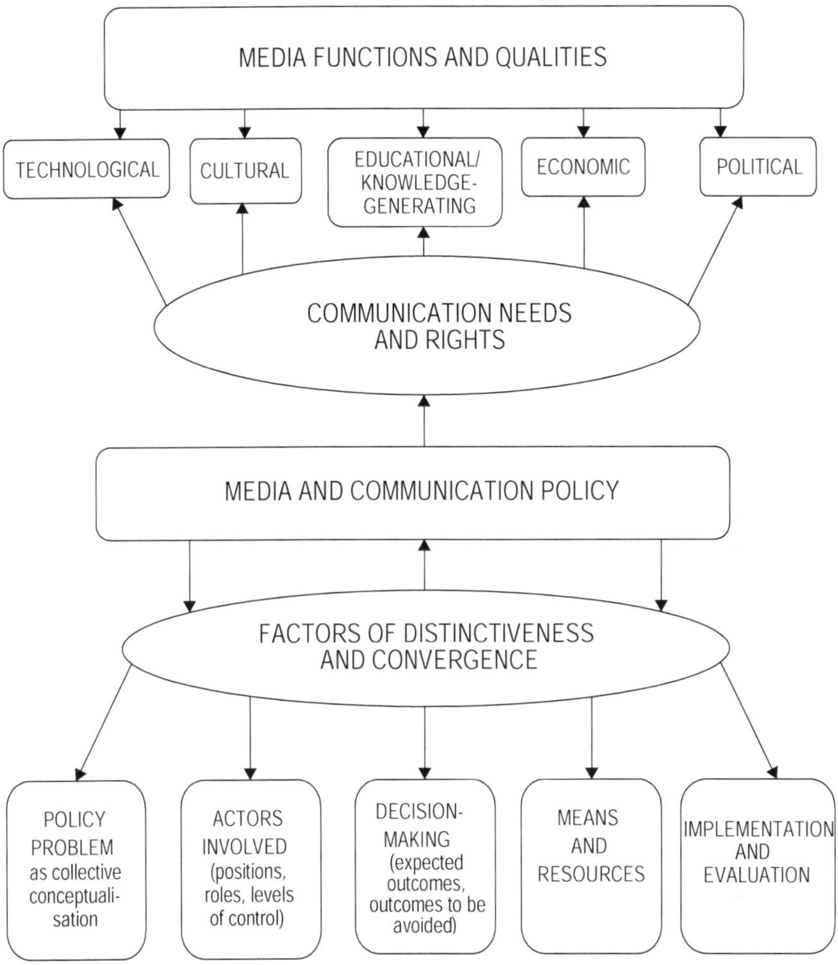

Figure 1: The model for studying communication media policy

The figure above outlines the conceptual framework used for the analysis of policies in this book. In this model, polyvalent media policy rationales are derived from the normative categories of media functions, media qualities, communication needs and communication rights. The polyvalent media policy process encompasses collective conceptualisation (policy problem) and collective action (decision-making, allocation of means and resources, implementation and evaluation) controlled to various extents by the actors involved, among which the core actors make decisions on allowable actions.

Using this conceptual framework, the present volume seeks to systematise major media policy developments related with the European Union, through the perspective of younger EU member states. The role of other international institutions (Council of Europe and UNESCO in particular) will be considered as well. The historical fifth, sixth and seventh EU-eastward enlargement waves generated institutional change both at the EU macro-level and the level of Central and East European media regulatory institutions and regimes (especially in terms of opening media markets for EU ownership, promotion of EU audiovisual contents and services, control of state aid provided to the public service media and telecom industry, and privatisation of the communication sector). A constant adoption of EU media policy and Council of Europe's standards affected various facets of media systems that shared some specific features from the past (Klimkiewicz, 2010a). Yet to assess how deep, substantial and ultimately successful these changes were, and to what extent previous legacies of media transformation and path dependency overshadowed these processes, various thematic, diachronic and sectoral strands in the policymaking will be studied in this volume.

To understand the conditions in making, an analytical approach has been chosen to study media policy as a polyvalent phenomenon consisting of collective conceptualisation and collective action regarding main problem areas (as perceived by policy actors). In terms of techniques, the research combines various methods. Most importantly, it builds on document analysis using various types of documents including legal, policy, strategic documents, background and evaluation reports, annual reports, position papers, statements, press releases. The documents are treated mainly as sources expressing political commitment, interests and the goals of actors involved, yet they are also seen as symbolic fields where the vocabulary used, a way of reasoning and operationalisation of policy problems denote policy conditions. These may be understood as particular circumstances (for instance a supportive political climate), but also reflect the positions and levels of control of the actors involved. In analysing selected media and communication policy problem areas, various case studies are adopted to illustrate the situation in one or more new CEE member states. Also, in studies, data collection and analysis combines several techniques, such as a secondary analysis of the quantitative data, the document research and semi-structured interviews with various actors involved in relevant media policy processes.

1.6. Outline of the Book

This introductory chapter focused on conceptual and methodological concerns that provide some ground for studying media policies in the context of profoundly changing media environments and in an enlarged geopolitical space of the European Union. The second chapter, following on these theoretical introductory thoughts, explores nine main problem areas that emerge from current policy and regulatory developments in the European Union, including among others: audiovisual media services regulation, support for the European media and audiovisual works, media pluralism and digital agenda. The aim of the chapter is to provide a map, both in terms of timeframe and institutional involvement that helps to navigate through a highly complex field of policies targeting media structures and performance. The third chapter addresses an issue of EU enlargement as a specific condition for the development and implementation of a polyvalent media policy. The process of conditionality during the fifth EU accession and especially the Commission's monitoring exercise in the area of media policy was marked by a certain tension between formal monitoring and enforcement of coherent criteria.

The next section of the book examines selected media policy areas. The fourth chapter elaborates on efforts to form the EU audiovisual landscape, especially through content and service-related regulation. The chapter follows policy conceptualisation leading to the introduction of Television Without Frontiers (TWF) Directive and analyses rationales justifying far-reaching modernisation through the Audiovisual Media Services (AVMS) Directive. It also gives an overview on the implementation of the Directive in the new CEE EU member states, especially with reference to the European quota. The fifth chapter explores the issue of media pluralism – one that has been perceived as a big failure of EU institutions (both the Commission and Parliament). Despite raising the need for harmonised European rules on media pluralism and various new initiatives brought by new policy actors at the EU, media pluralism still remains to be dealt with in the national context. This might, indeed, result in fundamentally diverging practices, mechanisms and even anomalies. In this respect, the chapter studies empirical examples of the structural developments of ownership patterns, functional and geographical diversity in the CEE countries. The sixth chapter focuses on the independence of media regulatory agencies and public service media. First, it seeks to explore the field of harmonising regulatory regimes and the role of national media and communication regulators that are largely responsible for the implementation and monitoring of EU regulation. These institutions are expected to carry out their work in full autonomy, impartially and transparently, in accordance with their professional remit (defined by the administrative, supervisory, rule-making and monitoring functions), eliminating a potential risk of political or economic interference. Second, the chapter considers policies affecting the position of the PSM in the EU especially in the context of substantial challenges these institutions currently undergo. These are related on the one hand to an increasing regulatory pressure from the European Commission in terms of clarifying the PSM's remit and financial relationship with the respective states, but also to the new political choices inspired by commercial incentives or populist reasons. The situation in CEE countries seems to be instructive in many respects, as PSM have been created through a far-reaching media system reform only 25 years ago (formerly, the same institutions served as state-controlled media) and since then, in conditions of 'compressed time' they went through similar challenges and regulatory changes as their older European counterparts. The seventh chapter summarises the conclusions of the volume.

To sum up this chapter, three points should be mentioned: first, studying media and communication policy as a polyvalent phenomenon enables a reconsideration of the normative grounds for policymaking in a broader context of the interplay of various social fields where the media play specific roles rather than seeing policy as a battlefield between economic or cultural/political values. Second, examining the policies through policy conceptualisation and action as well as media structures, reopens the possibility to compare the changing object of policies with the policies themselves. Finally, the combination of supra-national (EU) and national level of the media governance helps to see the policy as a constant flow between the potential and its realisation.

2. EUROPEAN MEDIA POLICIES: STAGES OF HARMONISATION AND DISCORD

2.1. Three introductory observations

As has been observed in the previous chapter, one of the paradoxes of media policy is that although the communication media are attributed high importance in the cultural, political, economic and technological development of contemporary societies, the related policy issues are often ranked lower than is the case of other sectors. Due to their specific role and polyvalent character, the communication media are also seen as one of the most challenging object of regulation. This seems to be one of the reasons why this policy field still remains predominantly the domain of member states. Yet, with the evolution of the European Union (EU) and its competencies, the mandate of EU institutions – and in particular the European Commission (EC) – grew considerably into the area of electronic media. Some authors even argue that over the last 20 years, EU policy initiatives have steadily increased in number and expanded to cover a wide range of issues, effectively limiting the capacity of member states to frame their national cultural and media policies (Ariño, 2011: 328).

Many scholars argue that there has been a fundamental divide or asymmetry between a reliance on economic arguments and a technocratic approach to media policy, and on the other hand, consideration of communication needs based on cultural, political (democratic) and social values (Ward, 2002; Harcourt, 2005; Humphreys, 2008; Psychogiopoulou, 2012). Thus, mainly due to the legal confines in the Treaties and prevailing concept of the single market, communication media, as a policy object, have been predominantly defined in economic terms – as markets or services delivered to consumers. In a similar vein, rationales justifying regulation have sought to correct failures in the effectiveness of the media's economic functions. Although certainly well-grounded in empirical terms, a critique of asymmetry tends to create an opposition of economic to all the other media functions putting them in one overarching category of non-economic goals. And even though other accounts seek to contrast industrial/economic and cultural approaches in EU policy concerning the media, one grand line of distinction still points to the asymmetry of economic goals. Schlesinger and Doyle (1995: 26) observe that:

> We are being offered two quite distinct images: one of a society of consumers founded in notions of economic choice, the other – increasingly marginalised in respect of media and communication policy – of a society of complexity rooted in persistent cultural difference.

Michalis (quoted in Humphreys, 2008: 152) connects industrial/cultural distinctions with sectoral divides and with diverging national interests:

> On the one side, a cultural policy coalition of interests embracing public service broadcasters, the European production industry and countries like France, which have been very concerned about the impact of the market – and globalisation – on cultural identity. On the other side, pro-liberalisation coalition of interests aligning the advertising industry, the private broadcasting lobby, the telecommunications industry, new media operators and aggressively deregulatory pro-market countries like Luxembourg and the UK.

Various national courses of action in media policy, and thus also national preferences at the EU level, evidently reflect the distinct compositions of functions attributed to the media and qualities expected to be achieved. Some of these may be thought to resonate better with what Fritz Scharpf (1999) defines as 'negative' or 'positive' integration. In his well-known and extensively quoted work, Scharpf (1999: 45) addresses the unbalance between pro-market deregulatory 'negative integration' and market-correcting regulatory and 'positive integration' in EU policies. Scharpf argues that 'negative integration' refers to the removal of barriers to free and undistorted competition. 'Positive integration' on the other hand concerns the reconstitution of an economic system of regulation through market-correcting measures. Scharpf emphasises the structural asymmetry of EU governance, gravitating toward 'negative integration', while 'positive integration' has little contributed to the increase of institutional capacity and problem solving and remains tied to the national level (Sharpf, 1999: 157). In this manner, Scharpf observes that 'negative integration' has been transposed to the European level, while 'positive integration' encompassing the need to fulfil communication rights resides at the national level.

The assumption of asymmetry of economic functions in EU media and communication policy is not disproved by an empirical assessment, and after all also by the recognition of the EU institutions themselves. Still, conceiving media functions in a more multidimensional way may open a plausible course to reflect not only on policy outcomes but also policy conceptualisation; not only intended engineered actions but also more spontaneous strands in policymaking evoked by unexpected problems and risks. It also allows us to observe how EU institutions exercise their powers in informal ways (e.g. through the promotion of certain concepts such as digital agenda), or offer soft law instruments (e.g. guidelines, recommendations, green papers, communications). Along this vein, the second chapter will test policy responses of the EU institutions to the core five media functions described in the previous chapter.

It should be also mentioned in this context, that views vary whether the EU has a media, audiovisual or communication policy at all. To quote Karol Jakubowicz (2004a: 277): "The EU does claim to have an audiovisual policy (...), but it is doubtful whether it has a media policy properly so called". Many scholars, indeed prefer to analyse the audiovisual policy leaning towards a safe territory mainly framed by the Audiovisual Media Services (AVMS) Directive and other corresponding regulations and policy programmes. The fact that certain policy issues are omitted is also part of a policy; the actions taken are as important as solutions ignored and after all, an unequal and non-proportionate distribution of a policy attention among various media sectors, or even discouragement regarding certain services, epitomises the policy as a dynamic process. Moreover, referring back to the policy model described in the previous chapter, this largely complex field does not only include 'hard' policy actions such as legal measures and their implementation, but also policy conceptualisation, standard-making, soft means that might ultimately lead to the change or shift in previous policies. In this sense, the use of media policy or media and communication policy is justified in the EU context. Besides, media and communication-related issues are officially recognised within the range of key policy areas administered by the European Commission. Among the 15 principal policies of the Commission, media-related activities are exposed under the two policy categories: *Culture, education and youth* and *Science and technology*. Both policy areas cover media-related issues in four aspects:

- Audiovisual and media policies,
- Media coordination MTF (Media Task Force),
- Media Literacy,
- MEDIA Programme.[1]

[1] European Commission: The policies, available at: http://ec.europa.eu/policies/; retrieved 4.05.2013.

Although not distinctively addressed as one of the EU core policy areas, media and communication policies are recognised as a legitimate field to be dealt with by several Directorates General of the Commission.

Finally, acknowledging the complexity and interpretational richness of media policy issues as well as possible policy impasses at the EU level, an important question is that about harmonisation. How far-reaching are the implications for media systems and performance, of continuous integration of media regulatory functions of the nation state into the European Union, as well as adaptation and incorporation of European decisions and strategies into domestic policy discourse and practice? Alison Harcourt (2005: 3) argues that there has been a rather high occurrence of convergence rather than divergence in media policy, not only between the larger member state countries, but also across the European Union. Yet, convergence in media policies does not automatically presupposes the harmonisation of media systems and performance. To what extent did the enlarged EU structures generate observable change in media policy both at the EU macro-level and the level of Eastern and Central European media regulatory institutions, regimes and systems will be studied in the next chapters. The sections below will attempt to bring together various stages and thematic angles of the EU media policy and tie these to the model for studying media and communication policy elaborated in the first chapter. Challenges and constraints will be examined in this context as well.

2.2. A difficult terrain for ambitious projects

Providing a short, condensed overview of EU media and communication policies is a demanding task. The highly complex character of the overall picture manifests itself in a diversity of actors, rationales, policy issues, information and outcomes that compose a fragmented field. Individual media policy issues and solutions are linked in a rather unsystematic, although not necessarily inconsistent way. As will be demonstrated in the next sections of this chapter, media-related problems and policy responses have emerged from a series of negotiations and compromises among the range of options limited by many factors: the EU mandate in the area of media and communication, conflicting national interests and approaches, politically sensitive media questions, cultural proximities, historical specificities and others. Thus, as a map depicting a mountainous terrain shows that routes and connecting lines are largely allowed to be built on the safe ground of valleys, so also EU media policy has been exercised quite carefully through the least contentious terrain. Certainly, technical sophistication allows for more ambitious projects: tunnels and viaducts that bridge steep hillsides of opposing mountains. This would certainly be the case of the EU media policy if supported as a priority field with the necessary intellectual and political investment. At the same time, the constraints are serious.

David Ward (2008: 4) observes that the EU's complex architecture, together with a restricted mandate based on the EC Treaty, are perhaps not most suitable foundations for the regulation of media and communication environments. Yet, the institutional layer of the EU media and communication policy does not only rest on competences derived from legally defined scope of possible policy actions. It is structurally shaped and consolidated by intended and accidental interactions along political cleavages (especially visible in the EP), national interests, cultural and historical proximities and most importantly, the constant scrutiny of the media. In an environment where the political success of EU institutions depends very much on effective media strategies, the need for news management provides a durable context of media regulation where in turn, the media do not act as partners in public relations but are approached as objects of communication policies.

Drawing on the multiple, but also selective roles of the EU institutions (including among others the initiation of law and policy, control of implementation, mediating between national and sectoral interests, negotiating) many scholars argue that the EU's complex structure stimulates a 'democratic deficit'. This may be augmented, as some scholars argue (Fossum and Schlesinger, 2007: 9) by a further element of technocracy. Some analysts observe that the EU is becoming a closed and self-contained bureaucratic system (Siedentop, 2001) unable to develop a demos that would make the institutions accountable directly to the public (Ward, 2002: 9). Thus, the EU's own legitimacy becomes based on its performance, and is conditional with regards to public support that may be withdrawn whenever public expectations are not met (Fossum and Schlesinger, 2007: 13). In the field of policymaking in particular, EU decision-making system is perceived by citizens, in view of some scholars, as being too remote and too complex, not to mention the fact that core executive EU institutions are generally unelected (Sükösd and Jakubowicz, 2011:11).

In addition to the democratic deficit, Sükösd and Jakubowicz (2011) distinguish other deficits in EU policy-making:

- legitimation deficit,
- identity deficit,
- media deficit,

- communication deficit,
- media policy deficit.

The *legitimation deficit* manifests in a relatively weak cohesive forces of the EU to act as a 'community' or 'union' enjoying full legitimacy in the eyes of its citizens. On the other hand, the EU reached the point of intrusiveness into the operation of nation-states and "the lives of their people where there can be little expectation of popular support for further steps without genuine emotional identification with, and commitment to, the whole process" (2011: 15). The *identity deficit* can be attributed to the fact that for most of EU citizens national or regional identity remains a basic framework of a social, cultural and political identification, formation of worldview and references. Not only do the EU citizens not share a common language but also collective cultural identity has not been constituted and shared at the supra-national level. The *media deficit* can be conceived at various levels of media structures and operation: at the level of performance of individual media organisations the deficit manifests in insufficient coverage of transnational European politics, culture, and common issues of public importance. A media system level demonstrates that media structures in the EU still rely on national rather than transnational dimensions, not to mention the fact that pan-European media institutions have rather an elite character and occupy a fairly marginal position in European media landscapes. The *communication deficit* refers to an inability of the EU institutions to convincingly justify political actions at the EU level and communicate this successfully to its citizens. The *media policy deficit* manifests itself mainly in a dominance of an industrial approach in regulating media landscapes. All these deficits are closely related with each other and present barriers to further European integration in the area of media and communication (Sükösd and Jakubowicz, 2011: 6).

Reflecting on constraints and conditions of media policymaking, it would be worth to contextualise them with current challenges the Union is facing at the important moment of its historical juncture. A number of analysts observe a manifold crisis of the EU. In political terms, an attempt to anchor the EU to a constitutional framework failed due to the lack of popular support. Moreover, participation rates in European parliamentary elections have diminished gradually over the past 30 years. Future EU accession waves have been postponed for some years yet with the exception of a couple of single country cases like Croatia and Serbia. Another force that has been gaining influence recently is the financial and fiscal crisis: it urges the EU to rebuild the Economic and Monetary Union on stronger foundations, and introduce a centralised banking supervision with improved budgetary and economic policies. In a competitive global environment, the EU struggles with dynamising and innovating its mature economies. Aging populations, growing debts and high social costs, pose demographic and political challenges that require a more consistent political response. Political leaders acknowledge that the work to be done is considerable and cannot be finalised without strengthening democratic legitimacy and accountability in the European Union (Monti, 2013), yet designing a concrete scenario for this difficult journey into a shaking and highly fragmented territory seems to be for now a mission-impossible task.

Understandably, media and communication policy could not remain immune to such momentum conditions. Important shifts and modifications in the previous course of policy action were signalled by the change in the departmental structure of the Commission. In July 2012, the former DG Information Society and the Media (DG INFSO), was replaced by the DG for the Communications Networks, Content and Technology (DG CONNECT). The previous DG INFSO (2005–2012) was dealing with a variety of issues such as research, policy and regulation in the areas of information and communication, but the media were quite highly exposed as a policy object approached by technological, economic, cultural and societal considerations. The DG Connect has been equipped with the responsibility to manage the 2012 Digital Agenda of the EU. Thus, its activities are and will be focused on the development and use of information and communication technologies in order to create jobs and generate economic growth in the EU. This overall goal resonates well with the urgent EU effort of revitalising economies and stabilising financial structures. Concomitant aims of the DG Connect are centred on provision of better goods and services for all, and greater empowerment digital technologies can bring in the EU. Policy objects covered by the DG Connect are grouped in nine categories most of which refer to computing systems, electronic communication networks and the internet. The media are clearly not a priority in this departmental design, moreover the media issues dealt with in the unit *Media and data* are mainly seen in terms of creative and innovative media use and media convergence. It should be noted however that the DG Connect is not the only rightful place for an EU media policy. An important role in this respect is played by the DG Education and Culture (DG EAC), DG Competition (DG COMP), DG Justice (DG JUST) and to the lesser extent, by some other directorates.

2.3. Four symptoms of complexity

As stated above, the EU media and communication policy is a highly complex and composite phenomena. Four` symptoms of complexity include in particular:

- policy actors' interdependence,
- polyvalent rationality,
- complementarity and functional convergence,
- knowledge and data asymmetries.

Policy actors' interdependence

The institutional architecture of the EU is rich and tied together through a set of reciprocal relations. The European Commission representing the supranational interests of the EU, initiates legislation, often at the request of the Council representing the member states, or the Parliament representing the EU's citizens (Humphreys, 2008: 153). The legislation encompassing directives, regulations, recommendations and decisions is ratified by the Council of Ministers and the European Parliament. Intra-institutional priorities vary according to thematic units and their specific agendas (Directorates General in the EC or thematic committees in EP), political affiliations (EP political groups representing more than 150 political parties) or national interests (represented in the Council). As described above, the European Commission has been a key actor in the EU media policy. Although it has initiated media policies mainly by DG INFSO until 2012 and since 2012 by DG Connect, involvement of other DGs became crucial. Especially, the role of DG COMP (Competition) has been decisive as regards state-aid policies concerning the public service media. Also, the DG EAC (Education and Culture) has occupied an important position especially with respect to the Media 2007 Programme, Media Mundus Programme, Media Literacy initiative and involvement in the UNESCO Convention on the Protection and Promotion of the Diversity of Cultural Expressions. Other DGs too have been frequently invited and consulted by the DG INFSO/DG Connect to represent their agendas during the development of new policy initiatives. These include in particular the DG JUST (Justice), DG MARKT (Internal Market and Services) and DG ELARG (Enlargement).

Despite its weaker legislative powers, the European Parliament has been intensely involved in media policymaking. Verhulst and Goldberg argue that the EP has more frequently initiated many aspects of EU media policy than have the Commission or the Council (Verhulst and Goldberg, 1998). These included, in particular aspects neglected by the EC due to its limited competencies: the policy on safeguarding media pluralism, public service media, community media and others. In addition to EU institutions, the EU media policy has been shaped to the certain extent by a relatively large number of formally independent but functionally interdependent actors and institutions. These include member states, international organisations – such as the Council of Europe, UNESCO; media industry consortia – such as the Association of Commercial Television (ACT), European Newspaper Publishers' Association (ENPA), European Publishers Council (EPC); pan-European groups – such as the European Broadcasting Union (EBU), European Platform of Regulatory Authorities (EPRA), European Federation of Journalists (EFJ) and the International Federation of Journalists (IFJ), various interest groups and NGOs – such as the Open Society Foundations (OSF), Article XIX; expert, think tank and consulting institutions such as the European Audiovisual Observatory (EAO), European University Institute (EUI) and others.

The environment of these institutional actors seems fairly diffuse and shaped by quite contradictory interests, at the same time they are linked together through the network of co-operative exchange acting simultaneously to other networks in different functional arenas (Ansell, 2000: 322). Although slightly different configurations of actors are brought together for individual media policy projects, the core group of principal actors is often the same. The institutional network of policy actors generates interactions with various outcomes. Institutional interdependence manifests, on the one hand, in attunement and harmonisation of policy goals and objectives over various institutional levels (between DGs, between EP and EC, etc.) and over various functional arenas (e.g. competition, audiovisual policy, human rights). Other 'positive' ends include policy diffusion, policy learning, and parametric adjustment (Grande, 2001: 10). On the other hand, policy projects have to be always compromised and thus designed in an enormously complex manner that may impede rather than facilitate implementation at the national level. Sometimes it may even lead to the policy deadlock. Moreover, the institutional actors not only follow diverging interests, they also compete: for resources, media attention, a broader support of smaller actors and the primary role in setting and determining the policy agenda.

Polyvalent rationality

The polyvalent character of the media policy implies an involvement of multiple values in policy reasoning and justification. These values are rooted in various fields of social life where the media perform important and decisive functions. The values, provided they might be facilitated by the media operation and policy support, are expected to foster qualities that contribute to desired functional outcomes in the fields of technology, culture, economy and politics. A classical concept of rationality in policy studies refers to logical behavior based on rational choice. Determining whether a policy is rational is a matter of determining whether it efficiently and effectively accomplishes its given goals (Thacher, 2004: 1). More generally, rationality refers to the way of reasoning which is logical and consistent with given rationales, firm convictions or beliefs and problematisation of, a given fragment of the social reality. In this sense, the concept of rationality in a media and communication policy is a polyvalent phenomenon. Convictions based on various values (e.g. economic, cultural, political, technological) may indicate divergent, even conflicting choices preceding a policy action. These choices may be perfectly rationale given the different logic and way of reality conceptualisation. Thus, for example, media qualities that guarantee economically efficient markets, may not necessarily be viewed as sufficient for guaranteeing a healthy democracy and a well-functioning public sphere. Along a similar vein, market-oriented deregulatory and culturally-oriented pro-regulatory rationales may be addressed by diverse (even contradictory) measures, but at the same time, both may be viewed as rational choices in their own rights.

David Thacher (2004: 1) drawing on a work of John Rawls argues that good conceptions of policy goals are "those that satisfy a test of reflective equilibrium, in that they are consistent with a wide range of firm convictions". We may question, elaborate and improve normative views by reflecting on their relationship to a variety of abstract and concrete commitments that we hold. Thus for example, the conviction that the media should freely develop in undistorted markets to offer a wide range of quality services to their users, may be re-examined in the light of the conviction about the legitimacy of public service media financed mainly from public sources (and thus, also having a huge impact on media markets). The PSM, to follow their audiences and comprehensively fulfill their remit generating public value, are currently extending their activities to the online world and mobile platforms. This however is perceived by many as a form of competition distorting media markets. In 2009, the Commission adopted a Communication on the state aid rules to public service broadcasters in the light of new technological developments (European Commission, 2009a). The Communication suggests to enforce a public consultation regarding significant new services launched by the PSM, thus allowing a broad examination of the relationship of these services to the market, other media players, and most importantly, value for society. This process will require balancing the convictions about the social need of public value generated through the PSM's new services, with the expectations concerning a well-functioning market.

The search for reflective equilibrium starts with identifying a set of considered judgments that serve as fixed normative points (Rawls, 1971: 47 quoted in Thacher, 2004: 5). These are to be revised in light of other convictions and continuously accommodated or harmonised in a process of reflection to achieve consistent, even though polyvalent reasoning behind the policy goals set. Polyvalent rationality poses one of the most demanding aspect of a media policy process, and certainly so with the respect to clarifying whether the communication media (in terms of their progressive development and accessibility by users) are seen as the main and primary goal of policy or whether they are perceived as instrumental to other policy goals – e.g. economic welfare, the growth of jobs, innovation, etc.

Complementarity and functional convergence

Another important symptom of complexity in the EU media policy is its complementarity. It refers to such a policymaking process, in which policy means (mainly embodied in media and communication laws, regulatory mechanisms, self-regulation, monitoring, distribution of resources or dissemination of knowledge) are increasingly designed in a complementary manner. This process involves, although not at an equal stance, interdependent policy actors, such as EU institutions, national media regulatory authorities, government ministries, professional and media industry organisations, NGOs, etc. (Klimkiewicz, 2010a). The complementary approach requires from policymakers to adjust the respective policy means (not necessarily the goals) to other functional fields. This may inevitably lead to the exclusion of some areas of implementation (or reduction of an interest in monitoring these), while others may be more easily promoted as they could be smoothly converged with a surrounding thematic spectrum. Accordingly, some scholars have observed that the European Commission has been more preoccupied with the implementation of the provision on cross-border broadcasting than other provisions in the TWF/AVMS Directives (Harcourt, 2005: 208). Yet, complementarity does not only present limits in a policymaking process, it can be seen as an opportunity especially in terms of facilitating knowledge dissemination and transfer as well as integration of policies.

Functional convergence is closely linked with complementarity. On the one hand, it is largely driven by a new technological environment, in which traditional media services and structures merge with new services and structures such as the Internet. On the other hand, functional convergence implies the process of policy attunement: the objects of policy analysis and regulation become accepted as common in various public spheres (Sarikakis, 2008). Multiple media and communication services regulated by different sectoral policy in the past (e.g. broadcasting, telecommunications), are more increasingly dealt with in a common 'media and communication' umbrella framework. Policy attunement therefore reaches different levels of governance: regional, national, supra-national.

Knowledge and data asymmetries

The policymaking process increasingly relies on research evidence, relevant data and knowledge integration in order to support policymaking decisions and choices. P. Napoli and J. Karaganis point to the paradox between this growing demand of empirical knowledge (often encompassing rigorous and large-scale empirical analysis) on the one hand, and limited public accessibility to of high quality data (Napoli and Karaganis, 2010). Ideally, equal participation in a process of knowledge integration and sharing ensures a proportionate reflection of various perspectives on a policy problem. Such a proportionate participation however depends on access to relevant data and available knowledge or resources that sufficiently support the particular perspective with necessary empirical evidence. In current media policymaking, there are whole sets of large-scale or longitudinal data (in addition to publicly accessible statistical and other data) that are controlled, aggregated, tailored for specific purposes and often protected by private consulting or research institutions. These include such crucial data areas as audience and advertising shares, readership, use of online services, media ownership and others.

Another paradox that illustrates data and knowledge asymmetries stems from the fact that specialised knowledge supporting policy choices becomes increasingly available through digital databases or various net-based institutions. Many of these are publicly available, whilst they are often reformatted and correlated with other data for specific purposes by private agencies. At the same time, the abundance of low quality information renders it difficult or eventually excessively time-consuming and expensive to filter and search for highly specialised and focused information. Thus, existing knowledge and data asymmetries and resource imbalances allow certain participants (more often industry than other types of organisations) to have a disproportionate influence over policy outcomes (Napoli and Karaganis, 2010; Harcourt, 2008b). An important catalyst for redressing this imbalance are EU rules on data transparency and the EU policy on open data.

Within the area of media policymaking, valuable information on media landscapes and markets is being collated by various international and national organisations, including especially the European Audiovisual Observatory, MAVISE and IRIS databases covering mainly audiovisual media services. However, more focused, targeted and comparable data are often difficult to be extracted without the necessary background of specialised knowledge. One of the policy areas with relatively difficult public access to relevant data is media ownership. Media ownership and control play a crucial role in the internal differentiation of media structures. Usually, there are the ministries or regulatory authorities at the national level that are responsible for systematic monitoring of structural developments on media markets. Even though the information on ownership might be compulsory for overseeing the fulfillment of licensing conditions, in many cases it needs to be supported with additional relational background to find out not only 'who owns' but 'who effectively controls' particular media outlets. Research by Access Info Europe has found that the legal framework in many EU countries is insufficient to guarantee full transparency of media ownership. Key information about media ownership is not collected, either by media regulators or through disclosures required under company law (Open Society Foundations, Access Info Europe, 2012). Alison Harcourt pays attention to two main drawbacks in national monitoring practices (on which collection of information at the EU level depends): firstly, regulatory authorities and ministries are dependent upon provision of ownership information by the company. Secondly, accounts are not necessarily made available publicly which restricts public scrutiny and independent market analysis (e.g. by think tanks and academic research institutes) (Harcourt, 2008b).

The symptoms of complexity result from the fact that various strands in EU media and communication policy developed along distinct phases, thematic clusters (audiovisual field, media pluralism, electronic communication, EU support for media production, the public service media and community media, media literacy, digital agenda for Europe and digital divide and others) and media levels (structural, content and performance-related policies). The next sections of this chapter will seek to present an overview of the EU media and communication policy initiatives with regards to various stages, and topics. They also attempt to reflect on various media levels in the policy process, that has traditionally distinguished content-related and performance-related aspects (such as the ban on hate speech, promotion of national, local, European works, protection of minors) and structural aspects (such as rules on media ownership, the PSM, community media, and subsidies for local media). The table and figure below depict an institutional and policy-actor framework for the EU media policy and a policy scheme illustrating various thematic areas and stages attributed to distinct media functions.

Table 3: Relevant policy units and issues concerning the media and communication policy within the European Commission

DG CONNECT	DG COMP	DG EAC	DG MARKT	DG JUST
AVMS DIRECTIVE (2007), renewed 2010 European works TV advertising Jurisdiction Right of reply Media pluralism Media literacy Protection of minors STATE & CINEMA state aids to cinema MEDIA PLURALISM monitoring EU MEDIA FUTURE FORUM advice on new media and digital revolution	STATE AID RULES TO PSM financing and control of PSM PSM remit STATE AID TO CINEMA AND TELECOMS	MEDIA 2007 PROGRAMME support for EU audiovisual production MEDIA MUNDUS MEDIA LITERACY UNESCO CCD (2005) international tool for preservation and promotion of cultural diversity CREATIVE EUROPE	TEU AND TFEU DIRECTIVE ON SERVICES IN THE INTERNAL MARKET (2006) DIRECTIVE ON LEGAL PROTECTION OF DATABASES (1996) EUROPEAN OBSERVATORY ON COUNTERFEITING AND PIRACY – fight against illegal downloads and other infringements of intellectual property rights	EU CHARTER FOR FUNDAMENTAL RIGHTS freedom of expression freedom and pluralism of the media GENDER EQUALITY COUNCIL FRAMEWORK DECISION ON COMBATING RACISM AND XENOPHOBIA (2008)

ELECTRONIC COMMUNICATION PACKAGE MOBILE TV interoperability, licencing, spectrum DIGITAL SWITCHOVER SPECTRUM POLICY DIGITAL AGENDA EUROPE SAFER INTERNET PROGRAMME			A SINGLE MARKET FOR INTELLECTUAL PROPERTY RIGHTS TRANSPARENCY DIRECTIVE (2004)	

Sources: Elaborated on the basis of the European Commission, various DGs and policies (available at: http://europa.eu/index_en.htm; retrieved 25.08.2013).

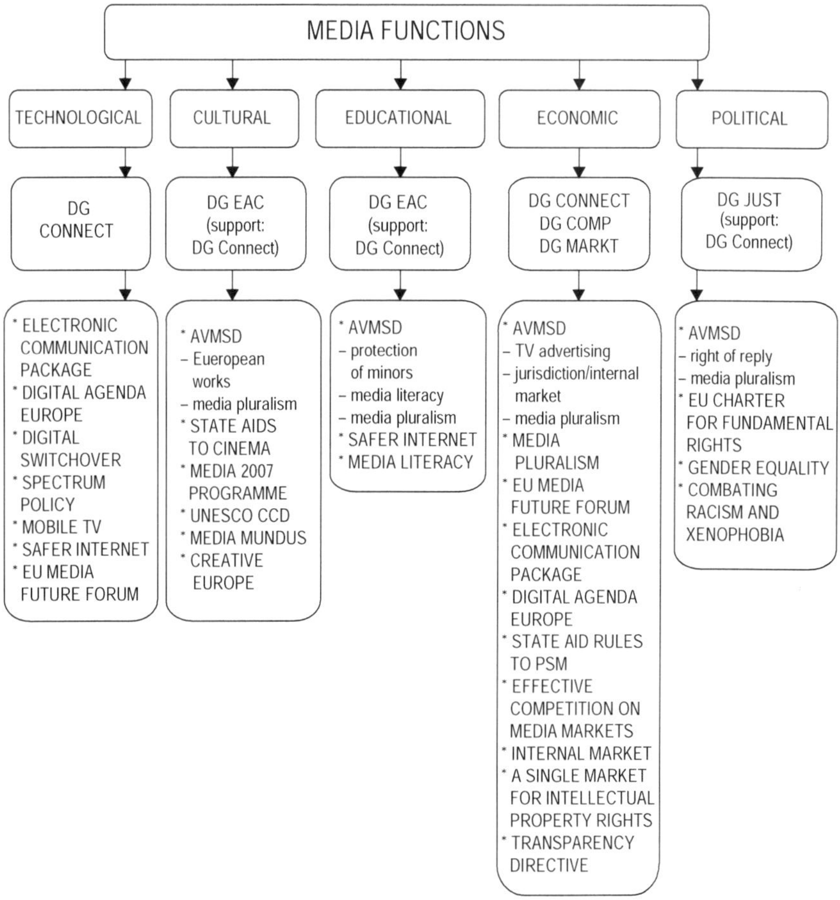

Figure 2: Five media functions attributed to relevant policy units and issues within the European Commission

Sources: Elaborated on the basis of the European Commission, various DGs and policies (available at: http://europa.eu/index_en.htm; retrieved 25.08.2013).

An overarching regulatory rationale for multiple areas of the EU media policy has been freedom of expression and the media protected under Article 10 of the ECHR. Freedom of expression and the media has been recognised as a basic communication need and right, and increasingly acknowledged as a positive right (the citizen's right to be fully and impartially informed). Media freedom and pluralism are also enshrined in Article 11 of the The Charter of Fundamental Rights of the European

Union (European Parliament and the Council, 2010b).[2] Moreover, with the Lisbon Treaty coming into force on 1 December 2009, the Charter was made legally binding. It is worth adding in this context that Article 11 of the EU Charter (unlike Article 10 of the ECHR) expressively emphasises that freedom and pluralism of the media shall be respected. At the same time, the Charter does not establish new rights or any new power or task for the Union (European Union, 2012).[3] It mainly assembles existing rights that were previously scattered over a handful of international sources. With regard to freedom of expression and the media, the Charter now can be used to assist in cases where EU law is in issue. In general, a vast array of problem areas of the EU media policy has grown in light of and compatibility with this principle. The section below identifies nine specific areas of media and communication policies that evolved over time across various topics and media levels.

2.4. United for competitiveness of European markets and cultures: TWF and AVMS Directives

The EU audiovisual policy centered around the enactment of the TWF and AVMS Directives epitomises a hard balancing between harmonisation and discord, between a search for unity on the one hand, and acceptance of diversity, where unification proves unachievable. It also brings together two dimensions: the pragmatic and symbolic. The pragmatic is associated with a free and more symmetrical operation of audiovisual markets and players, whilst the symbolic is attributed to a pertinent way of correcting proportions between media representations of cultures on a global scale. Finally, it presents also a sort of battleground of three rival conceptions over the meaning of transnational audiovisual space: economic (a support for unity in the transnational dimension), cultural and political (both reconciliation of unity and diversity in the transnational dimension).

One of the earliest phases of media and communication policies (1980–1989) was guided by a will to form a common, and thus also united European audiovisual space (mainly subsumed under TV broadcasting and the film industry) and to protect this area against US media

[2] The first version of the Charter was published in the Official Journal in 2000. European Parliament, the Council and the Commission (2000) *Charter of Fundamental Rights of the European Union* 2000/C 364/01. O.J. 18.12.2000 C 364/01–22.

[3] TEU, Article 51(2); European Union (2012).

imports. Karol Jakubowicz (2011: 275) observed that the original impetus behind the legal development was in fact the hope that EC-regulated transfrontier television could promote the emergence of a common European culture and identity. Philip Schlesinger (1995: 11) adds that the role of audiovisual media in constructing a European identity has been officially defined in opposition to a culturally invasive Other, namely the USA. The broadcasting media were perceived not only through their economic function, but also through their potential to contribute to European integration, democratic structure, creation of European identity and protection of common European cultural values, thus political concerns were involved in the early stages of policy conceptualisation.

The European Commission's Green Paper *Television without Frontiers* (1984: 15) stated that the purpose of the Green Paper is to "demonstrate the importance of broadcasting (...) for European integration and, in particular for **the democratic structure** of the European Communities" (emphasis added by BK). In one of the working papers, prepared for the Commission and also quoted in the Green Paper, the following reasoning was offered:

> European unification will only be achieved if Europeans want it. Europeans will only want it if there is such a thing as European identity. A European identity will only develop if Europeans are adequately informed. At present, information via the mass media is controlled at a national level.[4]

Although one can certainly point to a weakness in linking the process of identity formation with creation of the media that could provide such a basis, this reasoning shows that in an early stage, cultural and symbolic concerns occupied an important place in media policy objectives and rationales. This changed in the subsequent period (since the second half of 1980s). Paradoxically, many authors point out (Harcourt, 2005; Humphreys, 2008; Jakubowicz, 2011; Ariño, 2011), that it was only with the Maastricht Treaty (since 1992) that the EC gained a legal competence to deal with cultural matters. Even though, EU competencies in media policies (and cultural field in particular) have not been defined clearly in Article 128 of the Maastricht Treaty (Article 151 of the Amsterdam Treaty and now Article 167 of the Lisbon Treaty[5]), but instead attributed to numerous complementary objectives. Thus, in the later period of the TWF

---

[4] European Communities, European Parliament (1982) Working Documents 1981–1982, Doc. 1-1013/18 of 23.02.1982 (PE 73.271/fin.), p. 10.

[5] Consolidated Version of the Treaty on the Functioning of the European Union (TFEU) (European Union, 2010).

enactment, economic objectives became prioritised, although not isolated from cultural concerns.

The Television Without Frontiers (TWF) Directive was adopted in 1989 to create conditions for the free movement of television broadcasts. The Directive also implied basic common requirements concerning advertising, the protection of minors, and the promotion of European works. Alison Harcourt argues that the Directive was drafted in the spirit of the single market (2005: 199). Likewise, Peter Humphreys (2008: 155) supports this account with a suggestion that the TWF has to be seen for what it was: part of a single European market legislation. Though the Directive systematised and set priorities in regulatory regime for television content, it did not provide detailed harmonised European rules which remained primarily a member state competence. In other words, the member states, while required to ensure that broadcasters comply with the minimum program standards set out in the Directive, retained a significant degree of autonomy to apply stricter rules and regulations on those broadcasters licensed in their jurisdictions.

The Directive was modified in 1997. The revisions focused on relaxing the limits in teleshopping and regulating the free broadcasting of events of major social and cultural importance. This initiative is often perceived as the pursuit of public interest goals. It has largely grown from reactions of free-to-air broadcasters across Europe to the relatively successful attempts of large commercial groups to acquire exclusive rights to broadcast important sporting events (Ariño, 2011: 338). The European Parliament has targeted the Commission and Council with an initiative to make certain major events of social and cultural importance (including prominent sporting events in the first place) accessible to all citizens on free-to-air, rather than on pay television. The agreement with the Council was made on a condition that relevant lists of events with social and cultural importance are defined by the member states rather than at the EU level (Humphreys, 2008: 160).

In 2005–2007 the TWF Directive underwent far-reaching modernisation and was renamed as the Audiovisual Media Services (AVMS) Directive. The current version of the Directive contains a justification for the regulation that recognises important political, cultural and economic functions of the audiovisual media:

> Audiovisual media services are as much cultural services as they are economic services. Their growing importance for societies, democracy — in particular by ensuring freedom of information, diversity of opinion and media pluralism —

> education and culture justifies the application of specific rules to these services (European Parliament and the Council, 2010a, Recital 5: 1).

The AVMS Directive has extended regulation to new media services and offered 'a differentiated framework' for regulation: more flexible rules apply with regard to non-linear, on demand services; while stricter rules involve linear, 'traditional' broadcasting services. The new approach to regulation was prompted by a technological progress, changes in media use and transforming economic landscape (the number of channels increased 30 times since the first Directive was adopted and business models have changed fundamentally).

On the one hand, the Commission emphasised regulation of audiovisual content under the principle of 'technological neutrality', on the other hand, the distinction has been made between linear services encompassing traditional broadcasting and non-linear on demand services on the grounds of user's choice and control. The argument that it is the user who decides upon the moment in time when specific content is transmitted and chosen from an available catalogue, justified, in the view of the Commission, a differentiated regulation. As a result, some of the rules are common for both linear and non-linear services, some are applicable only for on-demand services, while stricter rules apply to television services. In general, on-demand services became subjected to light touch regulation covering such aspects as: identification of the responsible editor (Article 5), separation of advertising from editorial content (Article 9), prohibition of tobacco advertising, restrictions on advertising of alcohol to minors (Article 9), product placement (Article 11), recognition of sponsorship (Article 10), protection of minors (Article 12) and human dignity (protection against content inciting hatred on the basis of sex, religion, race and nationality) (Article 6), promotion of the production and distribution of European works (Article 13).

A higher tier of regulatory controls applicable to linear services covers most of the rules developed in the TWF Directive with some modifications. In general, linear services are subject to advertising rules (Articles 19, 20, 21, 22, 23, 24, 25, 26), product placement (permitted in certain genres and under specific conditions) (Article 11) recognition of sponsorship (Article 10) quota of European works and works produced by independent European producers (Articles 16, 17, 18), short news reporting rules (Articles 14 and 15), protection of minors (Article 27) and human dignity (Article 6), identification of the responsible editor (Article 5), right of reply (Article 28).

There has been a strong recognition by the Commission that 'no heavy regulation' is needed to implement the Directive. Co- and self-regulation are encouraged provided that the latter is state-entrusted. The Directive also recognises the importance of media literacy and encourages the member states to monitor media literacy levels in light of the skills, abilities and competences of media users. Media pluralism has been mentioned explicitly in the AVMS Directive as one of the particular rationales along with freedom of information and diversity of opinions (all linked to democracy) that justifies the application of specific rules to audiovisual media services.

The member states were given two years to transpose the new provisions into the national law. In reality, many countries stretched this deadline over several years and as will be shown in the Chapter 4, new EU member states were well represented among the delayers. It is important to remember that the Directive establishes only minimum requirements, leaving a larger scope for the stricter rules for member states. As Ariño observes, most of the states certainly applied stricter rules on broadcasting according to their national interests and culture (Ariño, 2011: 332).

2.5. Pan-European Media

Concomitantly with the legal efforts, the European policy has also dealt with the structural dimension of a pan-European media system. The selective means has mainly focused on support to pan-European audiovisual and website projects that would help to establish pan-European media outlets.

The pan-European press landscape seems rather poorly developed in comparison with the examples of transnational press in other regions of the world, not to speak of the much more robust and widely used national press structures. Olivier Baisnée (2007) points out that the socially and numerically limited audience of the pan-European press does not mean, however, that it has to be neglected when considering the existence and vitality of the European public sphere. The limited pan-European press' audience might well be the real public of the EU as can be drawn from the study on user profiles (Baisnée, 2007: 500). Some studies prove indeed, that not only trans-national and pan-European coverage of the news is much more intense in these outlets, but also that hit-rates of covered EU institutions are significantly higher in the pan-European than national outlets (Economisti Associati et al., 2011).

A brief glance at the pan-European press reveals that it is comprised of a tiny number of international quality dailies targeting mostly economic and political elites, and a smaller-scale, Europe-specific press outlets (most of them operating online). The first group of outlets grew out of regional markets to reach pan-European scope (Varga, 2011: 126). The publications in this group include dailies with a particular focus on finance, economics and international relations: the *Financial Times* (both in English and German), *Wall Street Journal Europe* (in English), the *International Herald Tribune* (in English), the weekly *Economist* (in English) and the monthly *Le Monde Diplomatique* (in French). Their European circulation varies from 400,000 (*The Economist*) to 85,000 (*Wall Street Journal Europe*). These papers obviously do not focus exclusively on European matters, but a European dimension is often exposed more significantly than other geographic angles. Established by large-scale media companies, these outlets have not been direct subjects of EU media policy through financial support, but it is noteworthy that they construct an important discursive space where EU policies resonate, are exposed as the currents of visible activities (selected out of a wide array of the invisible one), justified, questioned and refined. Moreover, the outlets as integral parts of larger media groups (e.g. News Corporation) present stakeholders and actors involved in media and communication policy process negotiated at the EU level.

In the Europe-specific group of outlets perhaps the most prominent place has been occupied by the largely known weekly *European Voice*, originated in 1995. Since its establishment, the *European Voice* positioned itself as more user-friendly and less specialised (in particular as it comes to use of language) than *Europolitique/Europolitics*, a daily newsletter, published since 1972 in Brussels. Despite aspiring to attract a more general audience beyond Brussels, the newspaper's paid circulation (around 5000–6000 copies) amounts to only 30%, with the rest distributed to various EU administrative units and officers, including policy-makers (Varga, 2011: 131). Since the end of 1990s, various web-based publications emerged with a potential to function as pan-European media, including news website *EU Observer* (2001), EU policy web portal *EurActiv* (1999) and online magazine *Café Babel* (2001). They have been supported with both public and private grants, sponsorship and advertising. The active policy role of the EU in respect to all these print and online activities has been rather limited and informal. After all, pan-European print and online media present a fairly selective set in terms of topics portrayed and audiences served, particularly in comparison to television that has long been seen as a primary platform for forging a pan-European community through pan-European TV media events and services as well as channels. But also in this field, the designed activities failed to reach the desired mainstream.

Until the early 1980s, television broadcasting in Europe has been structured almost exclusively through the national systems, and there has been a little space for pan-European projects with the exception of exchange of broadcasts and *Eurovision*. Since the 1980s, television in Europe has been going through a process of decentralisation and regionalisation on the one hand, and a process of transnationalisation on the other hand (Chalaby, 2002: 185). The process of transnationalisation can be viewed through the expansion of the international television trade, but also through the linking national television services at a supra-national level to offer pan-European broadcasting. It has been this broader context of change that encouraged European broadcasters to experiment with a pan-European offer.

Paradoxically, the creation and use of transnational pan-European media has met less vivid response among European audiences than in other parts of the world despite the strong support coming from pan-European media policy initiatives. Jérôme Bourdon (2007) paints a skeptical picture of numerous media projects, including simultaneous broadcasts and services, multinational and satellite channels that have all repeatedly failed to influence a European identity formation. The most active actor of these initiatives has been the EBU (European Broadcasting Union), established in 1950 in order to facilitate co-operation between member organisations – public service broadcasters (originally 23 broadcasters signed the agreement). Responding to early EU policy ideas on creating a common European media space, the EBU launched the Eurikon project in 1982 and TV Europa since 1985 to 1986. These projects aimed to test a possibility for creating a pan-European satellite channel. Both activities received the support of European institutions, including the Commission and the European Space Agency (Bourdon, 2007: 271).

Though these experiments failed, the EBU continued with efforts to establish a genuinely European news channel that dared to provide aggregated news formats from various broadcasters in multiple language versions. The Lyon-based *Euronews* channel was launched in 1993 by 11 members of the EBU, later joined by a further eight members (Chalaby, 2002: 190). Jérôme Bourdon argues that *Euronews* failed to meet the goal it was created for – to offer news with a European point of view, largely because the reference to Europe as a common space simply did not function (Bourdon, 2007). Another pan-European channel *Eurosport* has been more thematically focused and the European dimension has served mainly as a geographical and territorial reference. Also in this case, the EBU was a launching partner of the News International in the channel's onset in 1989. The partnership did not last long as NI withdrew shortly afterwards (Chalaby, 2002: 190).

One of possible and repeatedly used explanations for the failures of pan-European media structures would be the historical embeddedness of the European media systems in distinct linguistic, cultural and political environments. Continuing research conducted by Eurobarometer proves not only that Europeans prefer to learn about European matters from their national media systems rather than from pan-European media, but also that EU coverage attracts much less attention from audiences than other thematic clusters such as social issues, economics, sport, and national politics. Hannu Nieminen argues that one of the leading factor contributing to the lack of a common normative approach in the construction of a common EU public sphere and transnational EU media, is the regulatory and political weakness of the leading EU institutions (Nieminen, 2010). Richard Collins emphasises the lack of cultural proximity:

> What principles of cohesion remain to bind together complex, large scale, modern social structures – and few are more complex and on a larger scale than the European Union – characterised by polyglot populations, cultural hybridisation, fissuring and penetration by exogenous symbolic systems? (Collins, 2007: 28).

European cultural proximity serving as a potential glue to transnational media systems seems to be rather weak given the uncertain self-recognition by Europeans of the 'European identity' and stronger adherence to national and regional cultures and languages.

For these reasons, the issue of pan-European media has been discretely replaced in the EU's policy agenda with the 'European dimension of the media' or 'European media sphere'. These conceptual shifts demonstrate that where structures are impossible a substance may come into a policy focus. An interesting comeback of the concept of a common European public/media sphere has marked the 2006 activities of the Commission on European communication policy. The White Paper on a European Communication Policy not only mentions the European public sphere, but observes that it has not been adequately developed due to the limited coverage of European issues. The paper therefore calls for the necessary creation of such a sphere that should incorporate inclusiveness, diversity and participation (European Commission, 2006). Three years later, the European Parliament used the concept of the 'European media sphere' to suggest a preparatory action for a new EU programme provisionally called 'Erasmus for journalists'. The rationale behind this initiative assumed that if journalists will experience the situation in other European countries directly, the coverage of trans-national and European affairs in the media at various levels will be enhanced (Economisti Associati et al., 2011: 88). The 'European media sphere' is thus very much related to political and cultural dimension of journalism and should not be confused with the concept of the 'European media area' that has been widely used to denote the single European media market in purely economic terms (2011: 88). The manifold activities supporting transnational European journalism are, however, not seen without controversies inside and outside journalistic communities. Some authors argue that the reciprocity links between European institutions and journalists (not to speak about media managers and owners) go beyond pure professional relations and amalgamate into forms of instrumentalisation in order to promote an EU-friendly coverage. Voltmer (2013: 208) describes some of the practices where journalists are indirectly 'paid' or supported to boost coverage of EU institutions and issues. This includes for instance widely practiced free hotel stays and dinners (so called 'freebies') offered to Brussels correspondents by EU institutions. In this sense, the European media sphere seems to be rather shaped by discretion than openly promoted (and successfully enacted) policies. In consequence, it becomes a part of the process where policy horizons are lowered in the pursuit of what is perceived as 'realistic' and 'feasible'.

2.6. EU support for audiovisual production

In addition to their legal dimension, EU audiovisual policies have been carried out through distributive means where subsidies have been allocated to media production and dissemination activities in order to contribute to competitiveness and strengthening of European audiovisual production in a global context. The legal basis for this intervention is enshrined in the Treaties where Article 167 (2) (European Union, 2012) envisages to support and supplement the member states actions in the area of the audiovisual sector. The first of four series of the MEDIA programme were established in 1988 and adopted by the Council in 1990. The initial mission of the programme was to promote the production and dissemination of audiovisual works throughout the EU, with a specific focus on training, pre-productions, multilingualism of programmes, and easier access to venture capital (Venturelli, 1998; Boyer and Sükösd, 2011). The last MEDIA 2007 programme (2007–2013) emphasised the objectives of preserving European cultural diversity and the competitiveness of the European audiovisual sector in the framework of an open and competitive market. A new aspect of the latest MEDIA programme edition focused on the technological and market consequences of digital revolution and strengthening the production structures of small businesses (Humphreys, 2008: 158).

Noticeable in this respect would be to reflect briefly on the changing cultural objectives of the programme. Shalini Venturelli may sound provocative to observe that the MEDIA programme, in fact, has supported counter-unification as it has subsidised individual producers in member states who produce indigenous cultural forms (Venturelli, 1998: 208). Interestingly enough, the MEDIA II programme (1996–2000) proclaimed more explicitly a focus on 'non-national European' production and signalled that in addition to supporting national cultural production, a transnational pan-European dimension is needed. To this end, the evaluation of the MEDIA programmes demonstrated that the strategic objectives of reversing market trends and generating pan-European production and distribution mechanisms was not achieved (Boyer and Sükösd, 2011: 234). In the fourth edition of MEDIA 2007 however, the 'supranational dimension' evaporates, and instead, a 'European cultural diversity' is promoted as a quite enigmatic label for an audiovisual heritage to be supported in the spirit of 'intercultural dialogue'.

Undoubtedly, the allocated subsidies gradually increased:

- from the EUR 200 million (for the period 1991–1996),
- to EUR 310 million (for the period 1996–2000),
- to EUR 400 million (for the period 2000–2006),
- to EUR 755 million (for the period 2007–2013).

Still these budgets count for rather modest than generous support when compared with expenditures in the audiovisual industry (not to speak about the support for audiovisual productions in some other parts of the world) or EU support in other policy areas. Moreover, as the amount of subsidies has to be agreed upon and negotiated by the Council of Ministers, it is always contested by the member states. Humphreys (2008: 159) brings to the surface the national impulses of the three key EU national actors: the British and German governments have consistently succeeded in lowering the amounts of subsidies demanded by the French government and others. At the same time, public support for quality audiovisual content enjoys one of the most enduring legacies in the European media policy. The report *Fast-forward Europe: 8 solutions to thrive in the digital world* (EU Media Futures Forum, 2012) admits that global competition is fierce while Europe is still hampered by cultural and linguistic specificities. Arguably, the future public support policies should aim at better co-ordination between national financing schemes promoting the creation and distribution of audiovisual works that go beyond national/regional borders (2012: 19). This message calls for greater harmonisation between the EU support and national policies, while also the role of technologies overcoming linguistic barriers has been recognised.

The EU's new programme *Creative Europe* envisages the allocation of EUR 900 million in support for the cinema and audiovisual sector (areas covered by current MEDIA programme) and almost EUR 500 million for culture. More than EUR 210 million is also proposed for a new financial guarantee facility, which would enable small operators to access up to EUR 1 billion in bank loans, as well as around EUR 60 million in support of policy cooperation and fostering innovative approaches to audience building and new business models. Yet it has been quite clear from changing models of media operations that the most vulnerable element in current media industries is original and quality creative production that seems to depend more than ever on effective ways and channels of distribution.

2.7. The Public Service Media

The public service media have long occupied and still occupy (although to a lesser extent) a central position in audiovisual landscapes of many EU countries, especially as regards TV audience share (e.g. in Austria, Denmark, Finland, France, Germany, Italy, Netherlands, Sweden and the UK) (EAO, 2011). Understandably, PSM structures and performance have not only been shaped by national media and cultural policies, but also by EU decisions and regulations, particularly in the area of competition and state aid rules where the European Commission has direct competence. This has certainly been an ambiguous field of interference. It is interesting to observe that while in the initial phases of EU audiovisual policies, PSM were seen as close allies of the EU institutions in their attempt to create common pan-European channels and services (mainly through activities endorsed by the EBU at that time), in the later period this elusive symbiosis has been discretely replaced by policy neglect. This partly stemmed from a broader trend in the EU media policy where political and democratic media functions (and the PSM stood for institutions epitomising democratic expectations) were surpassed by cultural and economic objectives. Moreover, this period was marked by a profound transformation of broadcasting markets from public and national to private and transnational (Bardoel and Vochteloo, 2012: 303).

However, the end of the 1990s brought a slight shift in policy silence. The Protocol on the system of public broadcasting appended to the EC Treaty by the Treaty of Amsterdam, linked public service broadcasting (PSB) with the democratic, social and cultural needs of each society and with the requirement to protect media pluralism.[6] This allowed the member states to provide the funding of the PSM insofar as such funding has been used for the fulfillment of the public service remit, and has not severely affected trading conditions and competition in the Community. Complaints which have been brought in the 1990s and a subsequent period by private broadcasters of 'an unfair competitive regime giving privileges to the PSM', provide compelling evidence of ambiguity in the interpretation of the Protocol and a growing tension between the wish to permit the PSM to realise fully their mission and the general rules of European competition and state aid policy.

David Ward observes that the lack of a clear regulatory framework foreseeing the expansion of the range of services supplied by the PSM at the EU level, will continue to act as a source of contest between public and commercial operators as the debate about the funding and activities of PSMs is played out on the EU stage (Ward, 2008: 60). The media industry consortia have repeatedly emphasised a growing discrepancy between the mission statements and the actual activities of Europe's PSM (ACT, AER, EPC; 2004), and "distortion of markets (due to collecting advertising revenues in addition to state aid) in excess of what is acceptable to private operators" (European Publisher's Forum, 2005). The fact, that the PSM is the third most subsidised 'industry' in Europe, adversely affects, in the view of the private stakeholders, the whole media market in Europe including the press and internet publishing, not only private TV and radio broadcasters (European Publishers Council, 2005). Peter Humphreys argues that the vast majority of rulings that the EC competition authorities have made regarding the development of new media services by the PSM have been in their favour, thus supporting the principle of subsidiarity in the audiovisual sector (Humphreys, 2008: 170–171). Other authors observe however, that the Commission has gradually encouraged procedures that tend to narrow the public service remit in the new media to offerings not already available on the market (Bardoel and Vochteloo, 2012: 304).

---

[6] Protocol on the System of Public Broadcasting in the Member States, 2.10.1997, O.J. 1997, C 340, p. 109.

Whilst the Communication on public service broadcasting 2001 recognised the right of member states to support the PSM and the EC representatives repeatedly reaffirmed the PSM's right to make available socially valuable content on other platforms, the Commission clearly suggested that there are limits and areas where public funding should not be used to support certain new media services (European Commission, 2001). David Ward notes, that online services of the PSM and their move into new platforms is likely to increase the conflict between the public sector and commercial operators (Ward, 2008: 78). There has been also a growing assertion in the important policy documents that the PSM through their activities and operations affect conditions on audiovisual markets. The Commission's Green Paper *Preparing for a Fully Converged Audiovisual World: Growth, Creation and Values* observes that an extension of the PSMs' activities to the online world with applications or webpages is perceived by some actors as "a direct competition with their commercial offers, which do not benefit from public funding" (European Commission, 2013a: 7). In these circumstances, the PSM – as 'institutions distorting media markets' – not only have to justify their activities and their very existence, but member states too are called to carefully re-consider their funding policies. In the 2009 Communication on the application of State aid rules to public service broadcasting, the Commission describes how the impact on the market should be measured and under which circumstances such an impact can be accepted:

> In assessing the impact on the market, relevant aspects include, for example, the existence of similar or substitutable offers, editorial competition, market structure, market position of the public service broadcaster, level of competition and potential impact on private initiatives. This impact needs to be balanced with the value of the services in question for society. In the case of predominantly negative effects on the market, State funding for audiovisual services would appear proportionate only if it is justified by the added value in terms of serving the social, democratic and cultural needs of society, taking also into account the existing overall public service offer (European Commission, 2009a: 12–13).

Hence, the Communication proposes the member states to introduce an *ex ante* test. In such a test, the member states weigh the impact of a new media service launched by the PSM on the market against the public or social value of this service for society. As a result, various EU states, e.g. the UK, Germany, and the Netherlands have implemented public value tests or a prior evaluation procedures for their PSM. In this sense, the PSM are not only increasingly affected by the EU state aid rules (Bardoel and Vochteloo, 2012), but also a supra-national regulatory pressure has intensified in terms of clarifying and justifying PSM remit in a new media environment (Meier 2003; Bardoel and d'Haenens 2008; Ward, 2008). Prior evaluation and public value tests imply for the PSM, on the one hand, a greater investment in the measurement and parametrisation of new media services, on the other hand, closer liaisons with state administration responsible for funding and supervision. This can potentially lead to exerting political influence over editorial decisions within the PSM (Bardoel and Vochteloo, 2012: 312).

These trends champion a technocratic approach to PSM and pave the way to the quantification, parametrisation and weighing PSM output in terms of palpable social and public values. In other words, the policy shifts frame debates about PSM future with procedures, quantified values and translation of operations into 'market impact'. It comes as no surprise that a response from other policy actors seeks a balance in a greater emphasis on the specific role and function of the PSM in European media landscapes conditioned by their editorial independence and autonomy. The High Level Group on Media Freedom and Pluralism and the European Parliament in their recent policy documents highlight the necessity of maintaining the PSM and securing public funding for the fulfilment of their remit. European Parliament's Resolution *The EU Charter: standard setting for media freedom across the EU* underlies "the fundamental role of a genuinely balanced European dual system". The document observes that in a multimedia society with a growing number of commercially-driven market players the PSM, funded by citizens through the state, provide high quality, accurate and reliable information for a wide range of audiences, also offering spaces for niches that may not be profitable for the private media (European Parliament, 2013d: Recital 8) The Resolution warns before 'the current trend in some member states' manifesting in PSM budget cuts or scaling down their activities as it reduces their ability to fulfil their mission. In short, the Parliament calls for reversing this trend and ensuring "stable, sustainable, adequate and predictable funding" (2013d: Recital 12).

The High Level Group's Report *A free and pluralistic media to sustain European democracy* devotes one of its sections to 'public service broadcasting' recognising differences in PSM operation between the North and South of Europe, as well as between the West and East, providing some set of normative features: such as institutionalisation over decades, support for civil society, a tool for distance education, enlightenment and the strengthening of national cohesion (HLGMFP, 2013: 38). The Report recommends that "there should be a provision of state funding for media which are essential for media pluralism" (2013: 39). At the same time, the PSM should be subject to strict rules prohibiting governmental interference and placed under the supervision of an independent body representing all stakeholders (2013: 39).

These soft policy initiatives prove that there is no wide agreement on the conceptualisation of the PSM in terms of 'an impact on the digital market' and as an exception to the rule of media market operations. A legal obligation to render for internal pluralism within PSM services that has long shaped the European perspective on media policy does not seem to be less valid in a new communication environment.

2.8. Media pluralism and structural regulation

The European supra-national approach to structural regulation on the grounds of protecting media pluralism has been largely overshadowed by content and performance-related regulation in the area of audiovisual policy. This is not to assert that media pluralism has not been the subject of vivid policy debates at the EU level, but to admit that the policy outcomes were rather limited.

During the 1990s 'media pluralism' has been conceptualised by the European Commission merely through anti-concentration and media ownership policies. The fact that media pluralism served as a shorthand to economically diverse and competitive ownership structures was partly dictated by constraints in competences. These largely allowed the Commission to focus predominantly on safeguarding competition and economic plurality in the internal market, and thus influence the media sector through the internal-market and competition rules. In 1992, at the request of the European Parliament, the European Commission published a Green Paper: *Pluralism and Media Concentration in the Internal Market*. Its main purpose was to assess the need for Community action on the question of concentration in the media (television, radio, press) and to evaluate different approaches of the involved parties, with a possible outcome of media-specific pan-European regulation. Neither this document however, nor the follow-up paper (1994) helped to successfully design and implement a possible 1996 draft directive on media pluralism/ownership that would have regulated the media as a specific sector. Underscoring the difficulty to propose any kind of harmonised rules between the EU member states on media pluralism, the Commission has withdrawn from this policy area emphasising the importance of other European actions. In this case, the strong lobbying of some member states has not been insignificant in a discrete removal of the issue from the Commission's agenda. Evidently, (external, structural) media pluralism was not seen as a value to be generated through EU media policy instruments, but rather as an 'added value' to be addressed by other European (Council of Europe) or national institutions. In this respect, media ownership regulation and mergers in particular, fall only under the EC Merger Control Regulation (Council Regulation (EC) 139/2004[7]) at the EU level. It is important to remember that the regulation does not aim to reach goals and outcomes other than effective competition, which is why those media mergers subject to it are examined solely on the grounds of economic criteria and through the framework of competition policy (Just, 2009: 100). Moreover, the Merger Control Regulation identifies media plurality as a national task, and thus, entitles ultimately responsible national authorities rather than European authorities not to permit the merger on media plurality grounds (2009: 104).

The role of the media industry in distillation of policy approaches to media pluralism can be described as directing the issue towards a mute venue. Any policy, so is the case of media pluralism, is made in distinct institutional arenas or 'venues' (Baungartner and Jones, 1993; Princen, 2011). Such venues do not only incorporate administrative units where the problems are being dealt with but also the perspectives in which the issues are framed. In the case of media pluralism, media industry associations repeatedly attempted to prevent any new legislation at the European level (European Publishers Council, 2005). The publishing industry has also unitedly reminded the Commission that there has not been and there should continue not to be, a competence for the EU to intervene on matters of media pluralism other than its current rules on competition and merger regulation (ENPA, 2005). This position has been once again articulated in the ENPA's position paper on *Preserving Pluralism in a Rapidly Changing Media Market* (ENPA, 2011). The paper seems to distinguish between a 'negative' and 'positive' approach to media pluralism. While the former is clearly seen as a possible legislative measure on media ownership (e.g. limiting ownership concentration), the latter is associated with a range of fairly diverging activities. Evidently, the paper argues with a strong tone that the EU has no competence to regulate media diversity with an exception of competition rules and that national media markets are so diverse that only member states are appropriately equipped to offer sound solutions. Positive actions though can involve the EU role, especial-

[7] Council Regulation (EC) No. 139/2004 of 20.01.2004 on the control of concentration between undertakings (the EC Merger Regulation) 0.J. 29.01.2004 L 24/1.

ly in the area of indirect subsidies. Thus, the EU should ensure that a zero or super reduced rates of the VAT for printed newspapers are maintained, and even extended to the newspapers in their digital formats (ENPA, 2011: 3). At the same time, the ENPA questions public service remit in the digital environment and lists a limitation of PSM's activities in Internet and mobile platforms among 'positive actions' promoting media pluralism.

More generally, a relatively strong influence of the industry has not been the only factor redirecting media pluralism towards the mute policy venue. Global pressures and regulatory changes taking place in other parts of the world, led to prioritising, especially by some DGs, the logic of global competitiveness of European media players. An influence of the WTO, but also a decisive deregulatory and liberalising trend in the US, pushed for reconsideration of external and internal media policy goals in the EU. Most importantly, the 1996 Telecommunications Act eased media ownership rules in the US. Countries like Brazil and India liberalised significantly their media markets in the 1990s, and in China, the state has encouraged national media giant groups to merge, expand their corporate assets and sales revenues to achieve transnational competitiveness (Hong, 2011). Progressive relaxing of media ownership rules worldwide and the increased capacity of transnational media networks to use synergies resulting from the digitisation of information and distribution via online and mobile platforms, redefined understanding of competitiveness in media and communication markets.

At the same time, other EU policy actors, the European Parliament in particular, have gradually sharpened their stance on media pluralism viewed largely as an important policy outcome in democratic societies. The European Parliament itself adopted quite an impressive number of reports some of which were developed into resolutions addressing various facets of media pluralism. Katharine Sarikakis emphasises that despite internal and ideological differences, the European Parliament did not find it difficult to reach consensus on two major issues: the definition of the problem itself and the action needed in terms of policy (Sarikakis, 2004). The constant reframing of the issue cultivated a fairly complex understanding of media pluralism, although there was a shared conviction that media ownership occupies a central position as it is directly linked to the fundamental question of media control. One of the attempts to endorse complex media pluralism regulation at the EU level took shape in the *Resolution on Media Concentration and Diversity of Opinions* (European Parliament, 1992). Neither this initiative however, nor other renewed efforts of the Parliament did prove successful in the 90s. In the later periods, the Parliament addressed the issue of media pluralism in the context of some particular problems in member states – as was the case of Silvio Berlusconi in Italy.[8] One of the newest initiatives the *Resolution on the EU Charter: standard settings for media freedom across the EU* (European Parliament, 2013d) intends to reinforce the question of the competence and standard setting especially with the regard to Article 11 of the EU Charter. The Resolution does not explicitly mention media pluralism in its title, but focuses to a great extent on this issue. The European Parliament reminds the Commission that on several occasions in the past the EC has been asked to introduce media specific legal measures preventing concentration of ownership. The Parliament justifies these efforts by the specific role the media play in societies – media power may arise not only from monopoly pricing power but also from political influence. Thus, the Commission and the member states, should apply, in the view of the Parliament, media and competition rules setting lower thresholds in the media industry than in other markets to guarantee the access of new entrants (European Parliament, 2013d).

The profound difficulty to firmly place media pluralism in the EU policy agenda (not only as an object of soft policies) is linked to what Sebastian Princen (2011) calls the dual challenge at the EU level: the first revolves around gaining attention for an issue. The second challenge manifests itself in building sufficient credibility for the EU to deal with the issue. Especially this latter type of challenge has been problematic with media pluralism.

First, the question of competencies has to be considered in this respect. As described above, the formal aspect of the EU's legal competence has been questioned repeatedly by some actors, in particular the industry. On January 16, 2007 the Commission published a staff working document *Media Pluralism in the Member States of the European Union* (European Commission, 2007a). The Commission sustained a familiar argument against submitting a legal Community initiative regarding media pluralism on grounds of the absent competence. The document initiated the monitoring process of media pluralism alongside two actions: an independent study on media pluralism indicators (published in 2009) and Communication from the Commission concerning these indicators (never published). This already indicates that transferring of past commitments to present actions very much depends on discrete policy adjustments with veto players and changing external conditions resonating, in this case with prioritising a sustainable growth of digital economies.

---

[8] The *Resolution on the risks of violation, in the EU and especially in Italy, of freedom of expression and information* (European Parliament, 2004) did not refer to Italy only, but analysed problematic developments in other member states too.

The new relevance of the EU Charter on Fundamental Rights reopened once again discussions, especially when some recent cases in Europe (the hacking-phone scandal in the UK, the Hungarian media law) put media pluralism at stake. This new wave of interest on media pluralism includes a more prominent linkage of media pluralism with media freedom (as it is enshrined in the Charter) and marks a clear departure from encapsulating media pluralism as a sole problem of media ownership and concentration. Hence, despite a general agreement that EU competences to deal with media pluralism are patchy, many actors have affirmed that the European Union has not been, and cannot be, 'neutral' to this issue (CMFP, 2013: 10; European Parliament, 2013d; HLGMFP, 2013; PEFMPNM, 2013). These arguments defending EU competencies by institutional actors and expert groups can be summarised as follows:

- *Democratic/political argument:* The EU should be considered an appropriate venue to protect media freedom and pluralism, not only because this is the substance of Article 11 in the Charter, but also because there is a direct link between media freedom and pluralism and EU democracy. This link justifies connecting the issue of media pluralism with guaranteeing the rights granted by the Treaties to EU citizens, in particular the rights of free movement and representative democracy (HLGMFP, 2013; CMFP, 2013).
- *Cultural argument:* The EU should use more extensively Article 167 (4) of the TFEU that allows possibly to support media pluralism/diversity on the basis of non-economic and cultural arguments. Also the member states should contribute to these schemes with funding for media which are essential for pluralism (including geographical, linguistic, cultural and political pluralism) (HLGMFP, 2013; CMFP, 2013).
- *Economic argument:* The EU should adopt minimum harmonisation rules on media ownership to improve the functioning of the single market. The legal basis for EU intervention in Article 352 TFEU could possibly lead to a revision of Treaties by introducing specific principles on media freedom and pluralism (HLGMFP, 2013; CMFP, 2013; European Parliament, 2013d).
- *Technological argument:* The EU should take into account the increasing merging of different channels of communication in various EU policy fields, including the definition of the relevant markets and enforcing a principle of network and net neutrality. Moreover, the dominant position held by some network access providers or Internet information providers should not be allowed to restrict media freedom and pluralism (HLGMFP, 2013).

- *Monitoring/operational argument:* The EU should facilitate the creation of a network of national Media Regulatory Authorities (MRA) to share common good practices and quality standards in protection and monitoring of media pluralism (HLGMFP, 2013; CMFP, 2013).
- Finally, EU institutions can expressly ask the EU Agency for Fundamental Rights to monitor the media freedom and pluralism situation in the EU and report on this to the Commission and the Parliament (HLGMFP, 2013; CMFP, 2013).

Expressing views of the Commission, Neelie Kroes (Vice-President of the EC and Commissioner for DG Connect) has offered a more modest and cautious vision of the Commission's competencies during the Pan-European Forum on Media Pluralism and New Media *Wider? World? Web?* Her model is to build on existing measures relating to media ownership transparency, independence of media regulators from state and industry, the right of reply and media literacy (PEFMPM, 2013). At the same time, the repeated reference to the Charter and the fact that the Commission frames the issue in broader terms than ownership inevitably raises the question of whether the Commission, more frequently encouraged by other policy actors, is trying to establish grounds for extended competencies (Just, 2009: 100).

Second, in addition to the case of competencies, the question of capabilities should be briefly examined. In this regard, media pluralism can be seen partly a victim of its 'own' complexity and diversity: too often arguments have been made that a richness of perspectives in which media pluralism can be approached makes it impossible to elaborate a succinct distinct European legal instrument. An illustration from the EP's Resolution on the EU Charter can be instructive. The concept of media pluralism, derived from previous attempts to define the issue, resembles various layers that construct a quite heterogeneous structure, at the same time, the levels may function independently. In other words, media pluralism refers to the level of media ownership diversity, prohibition of censorship, protection of sources, issues related to pressures from political actors and market forces, transparency, working conditions of journalists, independence of media regulatory bodies, cultural diversity, the development of new technologies, unrestricted access to information and communication, uncensored access to the Internet, and the digital divide (European Parliament, 2013d).

Such a complexity translates into the question of an expertise and other organisational capabilities that allow policies to be designed and enacted. It can be seen as symptomatic that the Commission commissioned three important studies/reports regarding media pluralism to external groups of experts. The first *The Independent Study on Indicators for Me-*

dia Pluralism in the Member States – Towards a Risk-Based Approach has developed a monitoring mechanism to detect and assess risks for media pluralism in a particular country (K.U. Leuven, 2009). Proposing a highly robust scheme of empirical assessment of various dimensions of media pluralism (political, cultural, geographical, type and genres, ownership and control) the study aims, at the first place, to collect empirical data according to analytical risk-based framework – offering the Media Pluralism Monitor (MPM). The interpretation of these data and a subsequent choice of regulatory action thus depends on a member state's 'risk appetite' or 'risk tolerance', "that being the amount of risk that one is willing to take in pursuit of value" (2009: 6). If a member state prefers to accept a higher level of risk, it can favour minimal regulation. The study certainly provides a step forward to break down the policy deadlock, but its highly flexible and robust structure (including a comprehensive User Guide) may pose challenges in its applicability. In 2013/2014 the DG Connect decided to support the pilot monitoring study implementing the Media Pluralism Monitor in nine selected EU countries. The already mentioned CMPF's policy report on *European Union Competencies in Respect of Media Pluralism and Media Freedom* (2013) has been a product of two-years activities of the Centre for Media Pluralism and Media Freedom established at the European University Institute to analyse the issue of media pluralism and freedom at the EU. The report aims to offer a substantial review on previous policy activities related to media pluralism and propose new policy solutions. Finally, a High Level Group on Media Freedom and Pluralism was established in 2012, with a remit to provide a set of recommendations for the respect, the protection and the promotion of pluralism and freedom of the media in Europe. The results and findings of the group's work were published in the report *A free and pluralistic media to sustain European democracy* (HLGMFP, 2013). What all these reports and assessments share, is the assertion that common, minimal pluralism standards are needed and justified at the EU level. At the same time, an endemic variety of national media systems shaped by population size, linguistic diversity, historical traditions, political arrangements, makes a strong case for restating nationally/culturally/regionally differentiated policies.

As stated above, new configurations of media power, inclusion of the Charter into the Lisbon Treaty and some of the new developments in European media landscapes, mobilised a new policy interest in media pluralism among new coalitions of civic organisations and expert groups. Two initiatives, employing quite different strategies, deserve closer attention. The Pan-European Forum on Media Pluralism and New Media took place in June 2012. The event, organised in the European Parliament, was framed in three questions *Wider? World? Web?* This helped to reposition media pluralism as a fresh issue that needs to be reexamined in light of new technological developments. The summary report identifies various threats to media pluralism, in particular state intervention and undue influence (the case of the Hungarian media law), undue private media power (the case of News International and the political influences of Rupert Murdoch), changing business models (lack of sources for original and quality reporting) and paradoxically, an enhanced consumer choice (departure of users themselves from diverse content). The report argues that although the member states are best placed to develop policies that will support media pluralism in their own country, the EU could play a more central role in ensuring that a threshold level of pluralism is maintained in all states (PEFMPM, 2013). The second initiative – the European Initiative for Media Pluralism – is a classical example of a bottom-up policy action aiming at submitting a legal proposal for the EU Directive.[9] The project, inspired by two organisations – the European Alternatives and International Federation of Journalists, seeks to readdress media pluralism through the process of transnational participation of EU citizens. The idea is to collect the electronic signatures of one million citizens supporting the legal proposal. The initiative is using strong words: the slogans 'Media for all not the few' and 'Hands off the Media' manifest that there is a strong pro-democratic and political purpose of the action.

Summarising this section of the chapter, it is hard to find any other media policy area that would raise so many discussions and attempts to introduce hard and focused policy means at the EU level and that would, at the same time, bring only soft and highly dispersed means. This perhaps results partly from a high normativity and polyvalence of media pluralism. There is a broad agreement that the aim of media pluralism in public deliberation is to expand knowledge and overcome biases (Voltmer, 2013: 45) and that various forms of media financing and dispersion of control would contribute to authentic and deep diversity of performance. At the same time, media diversity is conceived in fundamentally different ways when approached from economic, political, cultural and technological perspectives. The question is, of course, whether policy bridges can be built between these understandings and whether some cohesion can be achieved at the EU level.

[9] The proposed legal document covers such areas as: anti-concentration media rules, the independence of media regulatory authorities, a definition of conflict of interests with media ownership to prevent abuse of media power in special interests and rules enforcing transparency to identify the ultimate beneficial owners of media outlets (European Initiative for Media Pluralism, 2013).

2.9. Convergence: from information society to the Digital Agenda for Europe

Unlike the cultural and political, the technological role of the media has been addressed until very recently by the EU institutions mainly as supportive, contextual to the leading economic goals of the Union. Notwithstanding, electronic communication and digital policies paradoxically gained a greater priority in policy actions than other thematic activities. Since the 1990s, the strand of emerging information society agenda played an increasing role in EU media and communication policy. The development of information or knowledge-based societies was seen as a key to economic development of the Union. A great enthusiasm and high expectations, linked with the visions of societies enriched by new knowledge capacities, were well-exposed in the Commission's white paper on *Growth, Competitiveness and Employment* and the Bangemann Report *Europe and the Global Information Society* (European Commission, 1994). The Bangemann Report described the information society as a structural change (and possible means to achieve so many of the Union's objectives), but the document critically assessed its fragmentation across the EU. Thereby, the report encouraged to master at the EU a risk of a potential creation of a two-tier society in which only part of the population would have access to new technologies (European Commission, 1994). The proposed option for the EU in this regard envisaged regulatory changes that would support a competitive, Europe-wide market for information services. It is important to add, that no public funding was foreseen for this goal, and the report emphasised largely a deregulatory action avoiding 'dirigisme' and 'protectionism'.

By the end of 1990, a high-reaching vision of the information society, offering widely spread and proportionally used digital communication technologies, had been replaced by the technical concept of convergence. This was dictated mainly by the observed changes in media and communication use: convergence across different media platforms brought multimedia and interactive services to European households. Also, the communication environment became more dynamic, unpredictable, elusive, diverse and highly dependent on the users' involvement. It became obvious that different regulatory models that have been applied to distinct media technologies and channels of delivery will have to change. The Commission's green paper on *Convergence of the Telecommunications, Media and Information Technology Sectors, and the Implications for Regulation* (European Commission, 1997) offered various options for revamping the regulatory model at the EU level. Concerned with promoting investment in the new media and IT industry, the DG Information Society tended to favour a new 'horizontal' regulatory model to cover existing and new services under one framework (Humphreys, 2008). This would have meant, that media content (e.g. audiovisual content regulated then by the Television Without Frontiers Directive) would come under a 'technology' neutral approach and be regulated together with new electronic communication networks and their services. Not surprisingly, this highly ambitious idea did not find many supporters at that time, and a majority of policy actors would rather opt for evolutionary than revolutionary changes. Finally, the Commission separated the regulation of infrastructure (delivery of electronic communication) and content (European Commission, 1999). In the 1999 Communication *Principles and Guidelines for the Community's Audiovisual Policy in the Digital Age* the Commission stated: "(...) audiovisual content should be regulated according to their nature and not according to their means of delivery" (1999: 2).

Yet the principles of technological neutrality and horizontal regulation have served a blueprint for a new regulatory framework for electronic communication that came into force in the member states in 2003. The principle of technological neutrality can be read in many different ways, sometimes in the context of international trade and country-specific standards, but for the purpose of a new regulatory package in the EU, neutrality has been most notoriously understood as the principle under which the regulation should not favour one technology over the other, should be flexible and open to technological change and should endorse universal service to users irrespective of the technology used. The horizontal approach to regulation has referred to the same regulatory principles that are to be applied to all transmission infrastructures, irrespective of the services carried over them, thus enabling the structuring of delivery systems along the activities line (Ariño and Llorens, 2008: 133–134).

The new regulatory framework for electronic communication introduced five directives: the Framework Directive (European Parliament and the Council, 2002a), the Access Directive (European Parliament and the Council, 2002b), the Authorisation Directive (European Parliament and the Council, 2002c), the Universal Service Directive (European Parliament and the Council, 2002d) and the Directive on Privacy and Electronic Communications (European Parliament and the Council, 2002e). In addition, the EC issued a Decision on Radio Spectrum (European Parliament and the Council, 2002f). In general, the electronic communication package reflects a policy wish to universally integrate the EU population with new communication services, at the same time, the regulatory rationale clearly demonstrates that the proposed technological arrangements aim to shore up economic goals. For instance, the Framework Directive emphasises a minimum approach to regulation: the regulation should only be imposed if competition policy proves insufficient or when market forces do not satisfy the public interest and needs of consumers (European Parliament and the Council, 2002a). Unrestricted access and universal service are obviously powerful regulatory motifs: the Access Directive stipulates a fair and non-discriminatory access of users to all electronic communication networks and services (European Parliament and the Council, 2002b). The Universal Service Directive addresses the provision of a defined minimum set of services to all end-users. These include for instance, a possibility to impose 'must-carry' rules for broadcasting services that are used as principal by a large number of end-users and meet 'general interest' objectives (e.g. public service media) (Article 31, European Parliament and the Council, 2002d).

In 2009, the electronic communication package underwent modernisation, largely referred as the 'Telecom Reform Package'. The reform included enactment of two amending directives (European Parliament and the Council, 2009a; European Parliament and the Council, 2009b) and the regulation establishing the Body of European Regulators for Electronic Communications (BEREC) (European Parliament and the Council, 2009c). The most important element of this reform was an attempt to overcome regulatory fragmentation and inconsistencies between national regulatory authorities. BEREC has been equipped with the competence to contribute to a better functioning of the internal market for electronic communications networks and services, to ensure consistent application of the EU regulatory framework and to develop and disseminate among national authorities the best regulatory practices. It is also worth to mention that the role of the Internet has been strongly reaffirmed as essential for "education and the practical exercise of freedom of expression and access to information", thus any possible regulatory restrictions in this environment are to be examined against the backdrop of the ECHR (European Parliament and the Council, 2009a). The reform also echoed the Lisbon Agenda in its focus on investment in new high-speed networks, innovation and strengthening the international competitiveness of the European Union.

The Digital Agenda for Europe (DAE) was adopted in 2010 as an integral part of the Europe 2020 strategy to stimulate the digital economy and address societal challenges through the ICT (European Commission, 2012a: 3). The use of the term 'agenda' is not accidental. It demonstrates a seriousness and principal place of digital development in the hierarchy of post-Lisbon EU policies. Needless to say, the EU experiencing a profound economic crisis, is forcefully searching for policies and visions that could restore a sense of collective purpose. The idea of a single digital market offers some kind of positive appeal as a possible integrative force. It provides a vision of Europe connected through fast-speed digital infrastructures, where the digital skills of users will swiftly improve and digital jobs grow. Yet, as the Communication from the Commission *Digital Agenda for Europe – Driving European Growth Digitally* observes critically "the EU is not positioning itself well enough to benefit from these digital developments" (European Commission, 2012a: 3). 20 years after the first strategic documents concerning information society have been published, the EC again warns of a risk of loosing global competitiveness and economic growth. The implications for the communication media have been examined by the EU Media Futures Forum installed by Neelie Kroes in 2012. The members of the group representing a whole value chain of the media business identified 8 bottlenecks hampering the digital development of the media. These included, among others, an uncompleted digital single market, barriers to developing new business models and fragmented support policies to the audiovisual sector (EU Media Futures Forum, 2012). The scenarios for policy underlined the need to create a digital single market by 2015 (through the harmonisation of rules, and tax policies), the promotion of new business models and a more efficient and well-endowed European support programme for the creation and distribution of audiovisual works (2012: 17–19).

The European Commission has been also vividly interested in the transition from analogue to digital broadcasting. In its ambitious plan designed in the Communication on accelerating the transition from analogue to digital broadcasting, the Commission set the deadline for a switch-off in all member states in 2012 (European Commission, 2005a). In 2013 however, only 22 of 27 member states have completed the digital switchover. Pay DTT services were available in 17 EU countries (Digital TV Europe, 2013). At the same time, Poland, Hungary, Bulgaria and Greece have scheduled to complete the switchover in 2013.

Since the Digital Agenda has been endorsed as one of the policy priorities, media convergence and its economic and social consequences have also generated a renewed policy interest in the Commission, especially the DG Connect. This was accentuated in particular in the Green Paper *Preparing for a Fully Converged Audiovisual World: Growth, Creation and Values* (European Commission, 2013a). The Green Paper is structured along three crucial lines: growth, creation and values. 'Growth' refers to the development of converged audiovisual markets. Still, the potential of connectable TV in Europe is not fully used and US players are seen as those who address the EU's fragmented market more successfully than some EU groups (2013a: 5). 'Creation' mainly addresses questions of content production, copyright, and financing models. Finally, 'values' manifest the Commission's commitment to rules that support freedom of expression and media pluralism, the promotion of cultural diversity, protection of personal data as well as the protection of consumers, including vulnerable groups such as minors and persons with disabilities. The Green Paper does not presuppose any action, but in following up, the Commission might explore regulatory and policy responses including self-regulation. In its invitation to the consultation process, the Commission emphasised its particular interest in views on the changing media landscape and borderless Internet, in particular on market conditions, interoperability and infrastructure, and implications for EU rules.[10]

The new media environment is certainly more complex and unpredictable than ever. It is also more elastic, chaotic and more easily adaptable to specific users needs, as the users are those who ultimately decide about how and what media infrastructures and services will be domesticated. There is no doubt that changes in communication structures and use induced by digitisation are without precedent and go beyond a mere quality and quantity improvement (Ariño and Llorens, 2008: 141). There are though, many paradoxes that affect simultaneously policy decisions and choices. On the one hand, convergence and digitisation deeply penetrate media structures, communication performance, various geographic and cultural levels. On the other hand, some expected trends have not reached the predicted scale and have not met social realities of media use. The audiovisual single market has been implemented for some years now, yet media systems in the EU member states still maintain the specific characteristics based on cultural, linguistic and political diversity. Analogically, the future and pace of the development of the single digital market will very much depend on the ability of EU users to get accustomed to, create and reproduce a borderless digital media space. After twenty years of reiterated interest in regulating what has been once called the information society, now converged digital environment, regulators face significant uncertainties. This stems on the hand from the pressure to keep the pace with developments, promoting innovation and competition, on the other hand from ensuring that users benefit proportionally and universally from digital services (Ariño and Llorens, 2008: 141).

---

[10] Digital Agenda for Europe (2013) Public consultations on media issues (available at: https://ec.europa.eu/digital-agenda/en/public-consultations-media-issues; retrieved 15.07.2013).

2.10. Media literacy and digital divide

Media literacy has been broadly used in the media and communication policies of the European Union at least for a decade, and as a broad concept completing information society policies even earlier. Peter Humphreys (2008: 166) describes media literacy policies in opposition to top-down EU legislation and in terms of their nature, as soft, facilitative and supportive. This is certainly a justified view. Many scholars (Humphreys, 2008; Harro-Loit, 2010) argue that media literacy actions have been inspired by the overall strategy for the EU development set by the 2000 Lisbon European Council. The strategy underlined importance of the transition to a knowledge-based economy and society with the help of supportive policies. The goal of achieving a more competitive knowledge economy induced also an encouragement to take better benefit from media digitalisation by societies, to invest in people and combat social exclusion.[11] Thus, economic goals have met, in the case of media literacy, a more profound accentuation of social goals (social inclusion), political goals (the exercise of a well-informed citizenship) and cultural goals (the right to self-expression and intercultural exchange). At the same time, it should be borne in mind that the enduring legacy of media literacy is much longer and resonates well with previous goals framed by the concepts of the information society and digitisation.

The cumulative initiatives on media literacy designed by the European Commission in a follow-up to the Lisbon strategy were gradually stimulated by the involvement of the European Parliament. The Parliament has always taken more prominent stance on issues that were promoted largely through a non-economic perspective, such as media pluralism, community and minority media, media transparency. A leading role in the Commission was played by the DG Education and Culture (EAC). Already in 2004, the Directorate differentiated eight competencies for lifelong learning among which 'digital competence' was listed (Harro-Loit, 2010). In 2006, A Media Literacy Expert Group was set up with the aim of analysing and defining media literacy objectives and trends, examining good practices at the European level and proposing actions in this field. Setting up and convening the expert group was a useful way for the Commission to unpack a new thematic area and build credibility vis-à-vis external actors. In addition, the DG EAC launched public consultation in

[11] European Parliament (2013) Lisbon European Council 23 and 24.04.2000: *Presidency Conclusions* (available at: http://www.europarl.europa.eu/summits/lis1_en.htm; retrieved 17.07.2013)

the last quarter of 2006 and commissioned a study *Current trends and approaches to media literacy in Europe* in May 2006. All these initiatives paved the way to the Communication from Commission *A European approach to media literacy in the digital environment* (European Commission, 2007b). In 2008, the Council and the European Parliament adopted respectively conclusions, and the Parliament endorsed its own report and resolution on media literacy in a digital world (European Parliament, 2008c).

The Communication (European Commission, 2007b) defines media literacy as the ability to access the media, to understand and to critically evaluate different aspects of the media and media contents and to create communications in a variety of contexts (2007b: 3). Three separate branches can be distinguished in this exercise, pointing to three groups of competencies developed by media users:

- *the ability to access the media* presupposes access to various media types, services, digital media forms, but also understanding differences between enabling infrastructures, platforms of delivery and the content they provide;
- *the ability to understand and to critically evaluate* different aspects of the media and media contents refers to skills that enable media users to analyse, organise and critically evaluate received information, also in the context of knowledge of media type (e.g. commercial, public service), media ownership structures and economic conditions of media operations (including a conscious exposure to advertising). The Commission's focus on understanding commercial communication does not only hint at the importance of advertising among content received (Koltay, 2011: 217), but also connects the concept of media literacy with a broader regulatory environment (in this case the rules on commercial communication forms in the AVMS Directive);
- *the ability to create communications in a variety of contexts* is directly linked to the active use of the media and participation in virtual communities. It is closely connected with the basic communication need of self-expression, and as Mark Deuze observes – generally with our life *in* media that primarily depends on mediated self-creation in the context of an always-available global connectivity (Deuze, 2011: 145).

Paradoxically, this relatively clear formulation of the concept does not easily translate into concrete policy actions. There are three reasons for this. First, a challenge of reduction can be mentioned. Recently, the concept of media literacy has undergone a quite intense scrutiny, yet there is still a struggle for a coherent understanding of the term (Tyner, 2010). Media literacy is encompassing an astonishingly large territory as it has been linked with such processes as digitisation, convergence and mediatisation on the one hand, and globalisation and commercialisation on the other hand. Thus, any attempt to demarcate and select categories and approaches for preferential treatment will necessarily imply reduction.

Second, there seems to be a challenge of motivation. Media literacy is essentially self-directing and self-governing quality: there are the media users themselves who decide what skills and competencies will they cater for and what is their *motivation* in developing quite unique exposure to the media. Thus, the question – what is needed in order to be a literate person in the digital communication environment? – is very much linked to the personal goals of users and these do not necessarily have to be congruent with the media goals, or political goals framed by approaches of relevant institutions. In this sense, any institutionally-inspired policies should find a broader resonance with actual media use.

Finally, in addition to abilities to access/receive information and create content, Koltay also distinguishes competencies that are built around creative re-use of existing materials and contents (Koltay, 2011). The superabundance of communication forms and contents increasingly involves various practices of selection, verification, search, scrutiny, reproduction and modification in new ways. This also becomes a part of media literacy with an indispensable recognition of intellectual property and copyright.

Such challenges and potential limits of media literacy as a policy concept direct actions of the EU institutional actors to the existing 'catalogue' of available set of rules and promoted standards. Hence, media literacy is echoed in manifold EU policy initiatives. In particular, the AVMS Directive refers to media literacy in its Recital 47 as a quality, that allows "consumers to use media effectively and safely". Effectiveness basically manifests in taking advantage of the full range of opportunities offered by the media and new communications technologies, while safety is embedded in an ability to protect oneself from harmful or offensive material (European Parliament and the Council, 2010a). The AVMS Directive also sets out a reporting obligation for the Commission to measure levels of media literacy in all the member states.[12] In 2009, the Commission endorsed the *Recommendation on media literacy in the digital environment for a more competitive audiovisual and content industry and an inclusive knowledge*

[12] Article 26: the Commission shall submit "a report on the application of this Directive and, if necessary, make further proposals to adapt it to developments in the field of audiovisual media services, in particular in the light of recent technological developments, the competitiveness of the sector and levels of media literacy in all Member States".

society (European Commission, 2009b). The Recommendation seeks to encourage member states and their media regulatory authorities together with media industry, to develop and implement co-regulatory initiatives facilitating practices that help media users to be more knowledgeable in their search and use of information, content production and creation. In addition to these standard-setting initiatives, the DG Education and Culture (EAC) financially supports projects that meet following criteria:

- analyse media representations and media values in a multimedia perspective;
- encourage the production and distribution of media literacy related content;
- stimulate the use of the media in order to improve participation in social and community life;
- intensify networking around media education related issues;
- concentrate on the implementation of media literacy initiatives bridging the media industry and the education world, in a 'hands-on' approach.[13]

Since November 2000–2011, in the framework of the Lisbon Agenda, the Commission has organised three workshops on media literacy and provided EUR 3.5 million of financial support to some thirty projects (through the eLearning initiative). These projects generally aimed at creating networks for an exchange of knowledge and experience concerning media literacy.

2.11. EU initiatives on community and minority media

One of the areas where media literacy can be forged through practical exercise is the sector of community media. Though specific definitions of community media vary, the concept generally refers to self-organised, participatory, non-profit media that address local communities and communities linked by interest or identity (Coyer and Hintz, 2010). Minority media may be run by professionals and can eventually generate profit, at the same time they contribute to the creation of identity, promote common interests and preserve cultural and linguistic diversity. Structurally, both types of media compose a third sector in the EU media landscapes, challenging traditional conceptions of a dual system consisting of public service and privately owned commercial media.

[13] Media Literacy (Available at: http://ec.europa.eu/culture/media/media-literacy/; retrieved 22.07.2013).

Genuinely alternative in terms of their function and performance, minority and community media play a vital role in fostering media pluralism. How this potential is used and exercised in practice, depends heavily on national policies of regulation, subsidies and control. Since the community and minority media have small audiences, they cannot benefit from economies of scale. Rather, they could rely on high volunteer activity stemming from a feeling of community of shared values and common interests (Gruffydd Jones 1998).

In the European Union, the strength and structure of community media vary from state to state. In some countries, community media have enjoyed a relatively strong position in terms of regulatory safeguards, available services and funding. These include the Netherlands, Germany, France, Denmark. Also in the UK and Ireland, regulation supporting the development of community media has been introduced (European Parliament, 2007). In other countries, community media have been legally recognised, but public funding has not been provided or community media activities have been rather limited (European Parliament, 2007). The same applies to minority media, while the variety of media outlets and services, as well as their sustainability, very much depends on the legal and political recognition of particular minority groups. And this significantly differs from country to country, where in some cases, national and ethnic minorities are not recognised at all, or only historical minorities are being acknowledged.

Community media have been more frequently recognised as a third sector of the media ecosystem inevitably strengthening pluralism and diversity by EU institutions. Still, a harmonised regulatory environment is largely missing at the EU level as media policies in this regard remain the responsibility of national authorities (Coyer and Hintz, 2010). In 2007, the European Parliament published the study *The State of Community Media in the European Union* (European Parliament, 2007). The report describes the regulatory context and examines examples of community media as well as public policies that support them. The document calls for legal recognition of community media in media laws, designing regulation that provides access to licences in both analogue and digital environments, and offering financial support for the sector. The study was followed by the *Report on Community Media in Europe* (European Parliament, 2008a) that put forward motion for the *Resolution on Community Media in Europe* (European Parliament, 2008b). The Report in its explanatory note, defines the community media, provides a historical context and describes a status quo of the sector. It also links community media with media literacy in the affirmation of their training and production potential: the community media may strengthen individual skills and competences in media-related professions (European Parliament, 2008a). Likewise, the Resolution points out that the community media improve citizens' media literacy, strengthen media pluralism and support a value of localism. Therefore, the European Commission and member states should legally recognise community media as a distinct group alongside commercial and public service media. The Resolution calls for a more pronounced support of community media and more active use of the EU funding schemes, through the implementation of a number of specific programmes, such as those of the European Regional Development Fund and the European Social Fund as well as the opportunities for educating and training journalists through the Lifelong Learning Programmes and others (European Parliament, 2008b).

Certainly, an involvement of the community media themselves as policy actors in a policy-making process presented an important incentive in this renewed interest in the sector contributing to the functional completeness of media systems. Also, a responsive and supportive policy climate of other international institutions such as the Council of Europe and UNESCO, played a facilitative role. A noticeable development has been the establishment of network organisations representing the interests of the 'Third Media Sector' in EU discussions and decision-making processes. Thus, the Community Media Forum Europe (CMFE) was created in 2004 to represent the concerns of the sector in various working groups at the pan-European level, alongside other associations representing the public and the commercial media sectors, as well as media and civil society stakeholders.[14] In addition, AMARC Europe – the European branch of the World Association of Community Broadcasters – was re-created in 2006 and has joined the CMFE as a representative of the community media. Both associations have collaborated closely since then and have overlapping membership (Coyer and Hintz, 2010). More often than not, community media were able through these structures to get involved more actively in the policy-making process at the EU level, at least when it comes to an affirmation and a greater recognition of the sector.

The minority media (the media of ethnic, cultural and linguistic minorities) have also been gradually recognised at the EU level, in part with a connection to the value of cultural/linguistic diversity, and more generally, as part of the new post-Lisbon rights' architecture. Consequently, the DG Justice has incorporated more prominently fundamental rights in its

---

[14] Community Media Forum Europe (available at: http://www.cmfe.eu/about-cmfe; retrieved 22.07.2013).

policy agenda. This agenda is relevant for the minority media especially in reference to Article 21 and 22 of the Charter. Article 21 prohibits any discrimination based on any ground such as "(...) race, colour, ethnic or social origin, (...) language, religion or belief, (...) membership of a national minority...". Article 22 promotes the cultural and linguistic diversity of the Union (European Parliament and the Council, 2010b). The DG Justice paying greater attention to strengthening the culture of fundamental rights and mainstreaming fundamental rights, has developed some distributive policies to fund studies, conferences and other initiatives that either seek to examine representations of minorities in the media or support structures of minority media. Paradoxically though, few initiatives that started successfully in the 80s did not find continuation. These include for instance, the EBLUL (The European Bureau for Lesser Used Languages) that was established in 1982 and ceased to function in 2010 because the funding mechanism has not been suitable.[15] Also Mercator, founded by the European Commission as a communication and media forum for the exchange of information and co-operation between communities speaking regional and minority languages has gradually limited its activities. Eurolang – the news portal for lesser used languages established in 2000 by the EBLUL moved to the facebook in 2010 to continue provision of the news from linguistic and national minorities in the EU. Some of these developments were discussed during the meetings of the Intergroup for Traditional and Minority Languages, set up in the European Parliament in 2010. The Intergroup also called for a more specific EU policy on linguistic minorities, including support for newspapers published in regional and minority languages. Some scholars argue though (Cormack and Hourigan, 2007) that indigenous linguistic minorities have enjoyed a relatively privileged position within the media and language policies of the EU. In creating a 'Europe of the Regions', EU institutions have explicitly sought to support indigenous regional and minority identities (2007: 249). On the other hand, immigrant groups have relied primarily on satellite broadcasts of television services from their country of origin, with some exceptional cases, such as the participation of immigrant communities in community radio broadcasting initiatives in the UK, France and Germany (Cormack and Hourigan, 2007).

[15] EBLUL (available at: http://eblul.eurolang.net/, retrieved 22.07.2013).

2.12. International trade and cultural diversity

Cultural diversity, although not directly pertaining to the media and communication, has been an important concept deployed by EU institutions to defend the internal market and also a more symbolic cultural landscape, against perceived threats from global trade and as justification to the state, and EU support for creative and audiovisual industries (contents and services in particular). At a more general level, cultural diversity has been acknowledged as a core value of the European Union (Charter of Fundamental Rights of the EU) and as a defining characteristic of humanity (UNESCO Convention on the Protection and Promotion of the Diversity of Cultural Expressions, 2005). More specifically, adequate representation of different cultural values, lifestyles, languages and heritages in the mainstream media, development of minority media and minorities access to media services have been repeatedly considered to contribute to a culture of tolerance, media pluralism and consequently, consolidation of democracy.

Cultural diversity as a principal imperative for media and communication policy has been supported by several rationales derived from the functions media play in societies. For example, political rationales reinforced cultural diversity as a quality closely connected with human rights and fundamental freedoms, including freedom of expression and the media. Growing concerns of loss of cultural specificities and local heritage justified a progressive affirmation of cultural diversity by the EU at the international level (Ariño, 2011: 324). Yet, in the context of EU media policies, in particular the economic argument has occupied a dominant role. It has been broadly believed that 'economic justification' more easily meets the convictions of policy makers and as such, is more smoothly translatable into governance, regulatory, institutional structures and practices.

One of the most important periods for an active involvement of the EU in this matter were negotiations with the World Trade Organisation (WTO) during the GATT and GATS Uruguay Round in the early 1990s and the Doha Round on the GATS in 2000/2001. By highlighting the importance of cultural diversity the EU attempted a countermanoeuvre to the free trade doctrine of the WTO (Puppis, 2008). The EU strived ambitiously to exempt cultural goods and services from these negotiations (Humphreys, 2008: 167). These moves implied differentiation among goods and services in the media and communication sector, and in consequence, delineating two mechanisms: the GATT applying to cross-border trade with cultural goods (including films, CDs, books, newspapers and magazines); and GATS concerning trade in services, in particular telecommunication and broadcasting. In comparison with GATT, the impact of GATS, especially in the area of audiovisual services has been minor as only fewer than 30 countries committed to free trade in this sector (Puppis, 2008: 411).

It should nevertheless be recognised that the position of WTO as an international governmental organisation principally dealing with eliminating barriers in free trade has been remarkably strong. The involvement of the EU in the negotiations with the WTO has been a reasonable option to amplify the stance of European national actors and demonstrate a supranational dimension in policy bargaining. The EU augmented its efforts by mobilising another international governmental organisation – UNESCO. The 'cultural exception' in the EU policies has received political support from the side of UNESCO (Humphreys, 2008: 168), especially as regards the development of standard-setting and legally-binding provisions.

The UNESCO Universal Declaration on Cultural Diversity (UNESCO, 2001) manifested the first step in this process, offering general standards to national states to protect cultural diversity. The European Commission continued to advance the legally-binding project and in 2003, the Communication *Towards an International Instrument on Cultural Diversity* was published (European Commission, 2003). Finally, in 2005, the Convention on the Protection and Promotion of the Diversity of Cultural Expressions (CCD) (UNESCO, 2005) was adopted. Significantly, there has been widespread support for the Convention from the EU member states with France, characteristically adopting a leadership role (Humphreys, 2008: 168), but it should be also added that the EU position was encouraged by a high number of stakeholders in the European cultural and media industries.

The Convention represents a semantic and conceptual shift from the Declaration (McGoonagle, 2008) as the Convention focuses on diversity of 'cultural expressions' rather than on 'cultural diversity', thus seeking an enabling environment in which and through which diverse cultures can thrive. Tarlach McGoonagle argues that the Convention is clearly of symbolic and political importance: it reaffirms the principle of state sovereignty in cultural matters and its universal approach to the diversity of cultural expressions counterbalances the predominantly commercial or trade-oriented approaches at the international level, e.g. under GATT and GATS (McGoonagle, 2008: 7). Some other authors though emphasise that a major shortcoming of the Convention is its normative and operational weakness. In contrast to the WTO agreements, the CCD does not impose binding and enforceable obligations on the contracting parties but merely proclaims the right of states to protect and promote cultural diversity (Puppis, 2008: 418)

The EU commitments to cultural diversity have not been confined to external policy initiatives, but have been strengthened also internally, in particular under the Lisbon Treaty. Among relevant legal provisions, especially Article 167 (TFEU), former Article 151 of TEC, plays the principal role. The Article states: "The EU shall contribute to the flowering of the cultures of the Member States, while respecting their national and regional diversity and at the same time bringing the common cultural heritage to the fore" (European Union, 2010). In addition, Article 22 of the Charter asserts: "The Union shall respect cultural, religious and linguistic diversity" (European Parliament and the Council, 2010b). The Preamble of AVMS Directive abounds with references to cultural diversity in the European audiovisual sector, in particular in Recitals 4, 5, 7, 12 and 48 (McGoonagle, 2008).

Supplementary to these legally-binding measures, the EU has continued to address cultural diversity as a salient issue in relatively recent policy documents. After series of consultations in 2006, the European Commission published a Communication concerning the *European agenda for culture in a globalizing world* (European Commission, 2007c). The Communication begins with a motto of Denis de Rougemont: "Culture requests a paradoxical pact: diversity must be the principle of unity, taking stock of differences is necessary not to divide, but to enrich culture even more. Europe is a culture or it is not". The Communication once again proclaims the well-known slogan 'unity in diversity' stating that the originality and success of the EU results from its respect of varied and intertwined history, languages and cultures, while forging common understanding and rules which have guaranteed peace, stability, prosperity and solidarity (European Commission, 2007c: 3). These principles need to be even more prominently recognised in a globalising world where the exposure to more diverse cultures from throughout the world increased and against which, the EU's identities need to gain greater intercultural cohesiveness. Thus, the EU must aspire to become an example of soft power founded on respect for diversity and intercultural dialogue. The Communication affirms the role of internal EU policies and programmes, but also external actions, such as the EU's involvement in the UNESCO CCD. Thus, cultural diversity is seen as a vital element in international relations.

Finally, the Communication from the Commission *Promoting cultural and creative sectors for growth and jobs in the EU* (European Commission,

2012b) exposes even more prominently the potential of European cultural industries to generate soft power in the globalising world. The Communication is a product of the post-Lisbon agenda, which is particularly visible in its language and logic. Cultural and creative sectors are seen as catalysts for innovation. Moreover, they play important role not only in a desired internal development of the EU, but are seen as key elements in global competition and as means of soft power. The Communication argues that countries such as China, South Korea and India make massive public investments to boost their economic potential and 'soft power.' The cultural and creative sectors in the EU are faced with a rapidly changing environment driven by a digital shift and globalisation, leading to the emergence of new players, the coexistence of very big structures with micro-entities (European Commission, 2012b: 4). These developments urge, in the view of the Commission, a number of initiatives and modes of funding to support EU cultural and creative industries with a potential global appeal.

2.13. Harmonisation or discord?

The short review of the EU media and communication policies demonstrates that there has been a fatal attraction between the two contradictory pursuits. On the one hand, the will to harmonise and unite certain aspects and functions of media environments proved to push forward visions of European media space integrated through the internal market, common rules on audiovisual media services, support (although quite unsuccessful) for pan-European media projects. On the other hand, a strong leaning toward nationally different and specific approaches cemented a discord on the protection of media pluralism, state aid to the PSM and support to other media sectors such as print press or community and minority media.

European media and communication policy resembles a process of gradual creation of quite varied thematic 'layers' of action, regulation and proposed standards. These layers or strata are deposed on one another in the course of policy crystallisation and use. It is a multidimensional, polyvalent and complex process that involves a wide array of actors, values and goals, at the same time, there are forces that make these layers more coherent and united, while also distant from each other and divided by a clear demarcation line.

Quite frequently, the confined attempts of harmonisation have been explained by the limited EU mandate in the area of media and communication and conflicting national interests and approaches. Yet it seems that also other factors are at play. Most notably, these are uncertainties arising from tensions along following axes:

- public versus private,
- catch-all versus specialised problems and themes,
- EU versus the rest of the world,
- value orientations and logics of action.

One of the key uncertainties revolves around the question of involvement of the public sector in media and communication environment dominated largely by private actors. The EU's recent role as the premier promoter of digital agenda owes much to supporting the private sector to do the job, or in other words, to boost the possibilities of digital technologies and communication networks in various fields of social life. Yet, there is also a clear understanding that in the more competitive and finance-driven economy, the private sector tends to be less willing to bear risks that involve investment in innovation. In the challenging reconfiguration of media landscapes with new modes of media use, the private media and communication companies tend to invest more in conventional rather than innovate technological solutions, and more in legal services securing business performance than in content production and journalism. At the same time, the role of the public sector is increasingly criticised by the private companies, especially in reference to the PSM. This results in many cases in a more cautious allocation of public funds to the broadcasting sector and questioning both financing from advertising as well as licence fees. The point then, is of course, how to overcome this hesitative approach and open up truly innovative possibilities of media and communication networks that constitute the European symbolic environments. Policy solutions need to be complex and at the same time simple, easily manageable and favouring users rather than network providers to overpass control of access, use and programming of content and services. Ultimately, the success of the digital agenda depends on users and their willingness to embark on a digital potential the communication networks offer.

Secondly, there are uncertainties how to practically deal with 'catch-all' policy problems and more specific issues. The catch-all themes, often accommodating numerous meanings, such as media pluralism, cultural diversity, media literacy, might be tempting at the conceptual level as they usually attract broad consensus of involved policy actors. However, there is a risk of translating these concepts into concrete policy actions. Issue boundaries fluctuate, when participants guided by different values and rationalities are activated, and the marginal elements of competing coalitions increase (Zahariadis, 2013: 811). Incorporated in various policy streams and resonating in manifold policy documents, the catch-all issues proved to be more rhetorically ambitious than effectively implemented in policy practice. On the other hand, more specific concepts such as the internal market resulted in the selective treatment of media environments with one dominating function linked, in this case, to economic qualities and expectations.

Thirdly, when prioritising issues and composing an agenda for the media and communication policies, the EU more frequently refers to the rest of the world, in particular the US, and recently also to China and India. Uncertainty that arises from this comparison manifests in a will to protect European media markets, cultural industries and heritage on the one hand, and to increase external competitiveness and export of European 'excellence' on the other hand. Although policy on promotion and protection of cultural diversity proved quite successful to maintain the European 'cultural exception', it is unclear how this course can be sustained in the future. Finally, one of the most challenging aspects of policy harmonisation has been a polyvalent approach to the media and communication environment. Uncertainty as how to balance, sometimes contradictory, values has paved the way for prioritising economic values in the EU media and communication policies. This also proved to be the least contentious option and a most comfortable policy choice that has not required a more sophisticated reconciliation of societal needs and interests.

The EU has clearly shown the tendency to act rather as a landscape architect than a gardener in media environments. In terms of a policy rhetoric ambitions seem to be ponderous while succinct visions are often confined by the complexities of negotiations and actors. In fluid, unstable and transforming media and communication landscapes, the quiet gardening turned into a series of modest actions – yet guided by a clear and bold vision of the ultimate harmonious result – might more importantly contribute to creating communication environments meeting its users' needs.

3. EU ENLARGEMENT AND MEDIA POLICY: A SUPERFICIAL SYNCHRONICITY

3.1. An Introduction: elusive boundaries and normative expectations

Interestingly, the EU enlargement has been one of the areas where the EU media and communication policy could be tested perhaps most comprehensively in a period of time clearly marked by following deadlines. It offered also a condensed framework of conditions that could potentially verify a normative integrity and balance of values, media policy choices rooted in various media functions as well as responsiveness to communication needs and rights. The EU has undergone several waves of enlargement since its creation. However, particularly the fifth enlargement – which the EU underwent in 2004 – has been considered as the *historic one* not only because the highest number of countries ever, joined the Union (including the Czech Republic, Estonia, Cyprus, Latvia, Lithuania, Hungary, Malta, Poland, Slovakia and Slovenia), but also because it was seen as an important act of a political will signifying the reunification of Europe after decades of geopolitical disjuncture. Although the accession policy towards the CEE has been generally described as a policy of conditionality, involving a bargaining strategy of reinforcement by reward (Schimmelfennig and Sedelmeier, 2004: 662), this process has not only been defined by sharply applied technocratic procedures, but had a very strong symbolic relevance. Certainly, it cannot be seen in isolation from the preceding political change in the region, and subsequent absorption of the CEE countries by other international governance organisations – such as the Council of Europe (CoE), Organisation for the Economic Co-operation and Development OECD (OECD), not to speak about World Trade Organisation (WTO).

Media systems and environments have always been defined by some boundaries, regardless of the fact whether these boundaries have become more permeable or contestable (e.g. by new forms of media use). On this point, an 'elusive geometry of boundaries' has shaped a largely varied response of the CEE countries to the media system change and EU ac-

Table 4: Membership of the CEE countries in international governmental organisations

	Organisation for Security and Co-operation in Europe (OSCE)[1]	Council of Europe (CoE)	World Trade Organisation (WTO)	Organisation for Economic Co-operation and Development (OECD)	Accession to the European Union (EU)
CZECH REPUBLIC	1.01.1993*	30.06.1993*	1.01.1995	21.12.1995	1.05.2004
HUNGARY	25.06.1973	6.11.1990	1.01.1995	7.05.1996	1.05.2004
POLAND	25.06.1973	26.11.1991	1.01.1995	22.11.1996	1.05.2004
SLOVAKIA	1.01.1993*	30.06.1993*	1.07.1995	14.12.2000	1.05.2004

Note: An apparently later membership of the Czech Republic and Slovakia in the OSCE and Coe in comparison with their neighbours results from establishment of the two independent states from the previously single federal state of Czechoslovakia on 1.01.1993. Czechoslovakia has been a member of the OSCE since 1973 and the CoE since 1991.

cession policy in the media and communication field. Firstly, boundaries have migrated in CEE more frequently than in other parts of Europe. This might be an explanation why it seems so difficult to rely on geographical coherence and contiguity, as well as shared historical, cultural, linguistic, ethnic, dynastic, political or religious roots, when it comes to the delimitation of regional proximity. Secondly, the boundaries that have been dissolved in 1989, still continue to serve as a strong 'mental reference point' both in media and communication scholarship as well as in media and communication policies. The process of post-communist transformation – 'time of great changes' – formed a distinguishing generational experience and a strong imaginative projection among both scholars and policymakers. Thirdly, new boundaries were set with the fifth accession to the EU. These internally divided the CEE. The new layer of Europeanisation or European harmonisation has set apart – at least in terms of media policy priorities – media landscapes that were linked together by fragile ties of common historical experience.

[1] The CEE countries have participated in the OSCE (Organisation for Security and Co-operation in Europe, formerly the CSCE – Conference on Security and Co-operation in Europe) since the early 1970s, but their involvement was quite limited. The qualitative change came with the collapse of communism and re-arrangement of the organisation into the OSCE.

It is interesting to note, that a substantial part of scholarship originated in the region recognised the collapse of communism and subsequent changes, including accession to the European Union, as a unique, exceptional and quite isolated moment in history. To quote one of many similar assertions: "...CEE societies have been overtaken by a process of change that is perhaps of unprecedented magnitude and complexity in modern world history" (Jakubowicz and Sükösd, 2008: 9). The scale of media system re-invention certainly cannot be compared with more evolutionary developments in other European countries. But the claim of uniqueness largely disregards simultaneous areas of change happening in other parts of the world, involving similar normative goals and questions concerning the media and communication environment, not to speak about globalising processes.

One of the key underlying theoretical assumptions was that the media change in post-communist CEE countries was expected "to mirror the general process of democratic development and create an 'enabling environment' for media freedom and independence" (Price and Krug, 2000; quoted after Jakubowicz, 2012b: 19). Thus, the substantial rearrangement of media environments was not conceived as a force of its own, but largely through the lens of the normative 'other'. It was the Western model – or as Colin Sparks puts it – the model in 'originator countries' (Sparks, 2008: 44) that served as a light house showing the right inevitable direction towards the reforms to be successfully fulfilled. This normativity has for the most part been taken for granted, pushing scholars to frame their questions primarily in terms of how well or how poorly real CEE media models measure up to the norm (Roudakova, 2008: 41). However as it became apparent from comparative studies, and most importantly Hallin and Mancini's (2004) influential work on comparing media systems, the 'liberal model' corresponding mainly with an 'imagined Western model' appeared to be only one abstraction from a relatively rich texture of relations between media and political systems. Moreover, the normative 'Western' model as it has been largely imagined in the bulk of scholarship, has not been, to a great extent, furnished with empirical features, but with constructs – standards and objectives – promoted by international institutions through the number of policy documents, political recommendations and legal provisions.

Thus, it does not come as a surprise that the wave of normatively-directed explanations was confronted with the 'scholarship of disappointment' addressing a problematic applicability of the Western model in CEE post-communist countries. Much of this criticism revolved around the concept of imitation (Splichal, 2001), or mimetic orientation (Jakubowicz, 2007), while other scholars continued to believe that the space for change has been occupied by "more traditional and indigenous CEE media philosophies" (Fabris, 1995). At the same time, several scholars pointed out that the impetus for the fundamental revamping of media environments in CEE was largely exogenous and imitative, given that the CEE post-communist countries copied (with various degrees of success) institutional and regulatory designs from other European and North American countries (Jakubowicz, 2007: viii; Harcourt, 2012). This has been explained in some works through the framework of isomorphism (the tendency 'to become alike'), mainly referring to the concept of institutional isomorphism, that can be further broken into three categories: coercive, mimetic, and normative (Downey, 2012; Harcourt, 2012). Coercive isomorphism occurs when pressure is exerted by one organisation on another, while sometimes this pressure can be very subtle and can manifest itself through the relation of dependency (Downey, 2012: 117). Mimetic isomorphism may be seen as a product of uncertainty, when in new conditions models are applied that successfully function in other environments (2012: 117). Finally, normative isomorphism is largely linked to the adoption of professional norms and standards, and consequently, forms of action. In this regard, a frustrating tone of criticism concerning various forms of policy and institutional imitation brings together all three versions of isomorphism. Some authors focused in their critical account on mechanical copying without an original input from imitators (Sztompka, 2000), others demystified selectivity and superficiality and yet another criticised a 'policy import' without any reflective change (Jakubowicz and Sükösd, 2008).

The field of a media policy, regulation and more broadly, media governance, certainly implies adopting institutions, legal rules, regulatory models and mechanisms. The incentives for this adoption may be both external and internal, while with the changing context of globalisation and raising influence of supra-national forms of governance, external influences gain greater prominence. Alison Harcourt demonstrated that the CEE states have adopted European policy models – on paper – in order to attract resources and interact with policy makers at the European level (Harcourt, 2012: 138). Yet, it should be taken into account, that any attempt of exporting policy models is to be always contextualised to the specific historical, cultural and political circumstances; and will always look differently on paper than on the local ground. Ultimately, the meanings of institutions of public communication change as they travel from one place to another (Voltmer, 2013: 21). A dissonance between media and communication policies 'on paper' and 'on the ground' demonstrates the pitfalls of a mechanistic understanding of how a policy is transposed or should be transposed.

This chapter argues that a superficial harmonisation or synchronicity with the EU media and communication policy resulted not only from inhibiting internal forces inside the consolidating democracies of the young CEE member states but also from the absence of clear benchmarks, formal policy rules and mechanisms (especially in some areas) on the side of the EU. Moreover, simultaneous and lasting problems in the established EU member states (e.g. the concentration of media and political power under the Berlusconi governments in Italy; intervention of the former French President into the nomination procedure of heads of French public service television) prove that the factual harmonisation and adaptation of the common media policy standards remains a continuous challenge for the members of the Union. Moreover, in some respects the EU media and communication policy, has been and is interpreted and practiced in many elastic ways by different member states as the media environments reflect quite specific cultural, geographical, political or historical conditions.

3.2. A policy of conditionality

Needless to emphasise, each of the subsequent waves of the EU enlargement emerged as product of specific historical circumstances. The fifth EU enlargement and pre-accession process followed historical political and economic changes in the CEE, in which the communication media were seen both as catalysts for the process of democratic consolidation as well as the end and objective of necessary policy changes. CEE media environments were not a tabula rasa (with an exception of certain segments) on which completely new and pure media structures could be built from scratch. So was the case of media policy models – the new ones were created as a form of reaction to the old one. This was largely a hybrid process, even though external and exogenous impetus (especially for legal and policy change) dominated over the internal incentives, especially during the initial period of transformation. At the same time, it should not be forgotten that this exogenous influence was generally welcome as an antidote to the 'old system'. Legacies of media censorship and tight media control during the communist era led to a broad political and public acceptance of deregulatory policies after 1989. There was a widespread agreement, that the best media policy is no policy, and that the 'invisible hand' of the market would be a perfect regulator and guarantee for media freedom and pluralism (Klimkiewicz, 2008).

It does not come as a surprise that various international organisations (the Council of Europe at the first place) made it a condition for the CEE states to bring their media legislation into line with European standards and to adopt the European model of PSM (Voltmer, 2013: 155). In addition, there was a great deal of financial aid flowing from Western governments and organisations in order to build democratic media structures (Harcourt, 2003). At the same time, the CEE countries extensively liberalising and deregulating their media environments at the beginning of 1990s, were caught up between the US and European Union over a fundamentally different view on regulation of broadcasting and audiovisual services (Harcourt, 2012: 141). While the 'European' model, promoted through the Council of Europe and the European Union, opted for the 'cultural' protection of European audiovisual works and public support for the PSM, the American option endorsed the liberalisation of audiovisual media services under the General Agreement on Trade and Services.

These two forces of external influences on the domestic media and communication policy have been present in the region already since the mid 1980s. The membership of the CEE countries in the Council of Europe marked an important move towards the 'European' model. The Council of Europe's objectives concerning media and communication were historically linked to the democratisation of media systems in the CEE. One of the fundamental incentives in this respect has been a positive action approach with regard to freedom of expression and the media as guaranteed in Article 10 of the ECHR. European Court of Human Rights has increasingly encouraged member states to ensure a citizen's right to be fully and impartially informed, and to receive the information from diverse and independent sources (Voorhoof, 1998). Also an impressive volume of resolutions, recommendations and declarations adopted by the Parliamentary Assembly and the Committee of Ministers referred repeatedly to the situation in CEE (Klimkiewicz, 2008: 85). The Council of Europe assisted the CEE with the implementation of its crucial legal instrument in the field of media and communication – the European Convention on Transfrontier Television (ECTT) (Council of Europe, 1989). Consequently, the signatories needed to implement rules on: freedom of expression, reception and retransmission; transmission of European works; protection of minors; prohibition of pornography; prohibition of incitement to racial hatred, anti-Semitism and xenophobia; right of reply; advertising standards (limits on advertising time, advertising breaks, prohibition on the advertising of certain products) and others. These provisions were very similar to those of the Television without Frontiers Directive (Harcourt, 2012: 144) transposed by the CEE countries before the EU accession in 2004.

Table 5: Ratification and adoption of the European Convention on Transfrontier Television in the CEE member states

	Ratification	**Entering into Force**
European Convention on Transfrontier Television	1989*	1993
CZECH REPUBLIC	2003	2004
HUNGARY	1996	1997
POLAND	1990	1993
SLOVAKIA	1997	1997

Notes: *opened for signatures.

The Council of Europe actively promoted standards of independence concerning both PSM and regulatory authorities. The activities of the Committee of experts on media concentration and pluralism (MM-CM) established in 1991 to conduct an in-depth examination of media concentrations, coincided with the drafting and adoption of new broadcasting laws in the CEE (Czech Republic – 1991, Slovakia – 1991, Poland – 1992, Hungary – 1996), aiming at the formation of a more diverse and pluralistic media space (Klimkiewicz, 2008). Media pluralism has been recognised as a central pillar of these regulations (2008: 86).

The Council of Europe's involvement in the setting standards and promoting policy solutions was based on political/democratic, cultural, educational and technological functions of the media, and provided an important normative basis for the EU to build on, not only when defining the EU's own membership conditions for the new candidates, but also during the period of EU internal media policy debates preceding the accession negotiations. The EU accession process entailed the adoption of EU rules and media policies (audiovisual *acquis*, competition and state aid policy) as well as incorporation of EU standards (formulated in Copenhagen criteria, Charter of Fundamental Rights of the European Union) on the level of domestic law, political institutions and practices (Klimkiewicz, 2008). The diffusion of common political rules, norms and practices concerning media structures and performance has been secured by the process of conditionality under which the EU provided external incentives for a target government to comply with its conditions (Schimmelfennig and Sedelmeier 2004, 662). Wojciech Sadurski points out that the EU could dictate these conditions and terms because the candidates had a great interest in joining the 'club' (Sadurski, 2003: 43).

The formulation by the European Council of the criteria for membership in Copenhagen in 1993, offered two normative dispositions in the context of media policy: political and economic. These were reinforced by the European Council in Madrid in 1995 by underscoring the implementation and institutional functions (Klimkiewicz, 2008). Fundamentally, however, the role of the EU conditionality at this stage consisted in responding to the rapid change occurring in the CEE and functioned through co-operation and association agreements with CEE states, and by the major assistance programme, PHARE (Sadurski, 2003: 11). Although conditionality would have been most effective and credible when based on a catalogue of succinct criteria, as well as clear enforcement and reward mechanisms, the Copenhagen criteria did not define the benchmarks or the process by which EU conditionality could be enforced and verified (Sasse, 2003: 128). This has been particularly visible in the case of media-related issues where EU conditionality represented a set of more or less vague requirements that had to be met, although it has not always been sure whether it is the state or other institutions that are ultimately responsible for the enforcement of the conditions.

Since 1997, the EU has employed 'carrot and stick' structural levers in the accession process to reward compliance and reprimand resistance (Sasse, 2003: 128). One of such levers was the EU's principal monitoring instrument – annual Regular Reports – that helped the European Commission systematically assess the fulfilment of the membership criteria in the period 1998–2003. In 2003, the Commission issued Comprehensive Monitoring Reports that closed the political component of the assessment and focused solely on *acquis*. By then, the Commision accepted the credibility of commitments made by the candidate countries in the 'political' area and encouraged the candidate states to complete the remaining conditions of *acquis*.

Media-related issues were not recognised and distinguished as an independent category in this evaluation. They were addressed fairly broadly – as a human right (subsumed under 'the freedom of expression' and monitored under the section of 'Human Rights and Protection of Minorities' as part of Political criteria), as an object of regulation, as structures and organisations, as a product of media performance (all in different sections of the reports). Principally though, the media and mediated communication were most frequently assessed in two problem areas: the Copenhagen political criteria (with reference to freedom of expression) and *acquis* (mainly in the section of culture and audiovisual policy). These two areas will be briefly examined in the following sections.

3.3. Monitoring of media-related issues under the political criteria

The political Copenhagen criteria stipulated that the candidate country must have achieved "stability of institutions guaranteeing democracy, the rule of law, human rights and respect for and protection of minorities" (Klimkiewicz, 2008: 87). As these criteria were not based on the *acquis* as such, the Commission had to conduct its monitoring and assessment following a set of values and standards derived from non-EU documents, such as the ECHR (Sasse, 2004). These prerequisites perhaps help to explain why 'freedom of expression' was extracted from a wider and more complex body of communication rights (encompassing also cultural, economic and social rights) and why media-related issues were operationalised within the category of civil and political rights only (Klimkiewicz, 2008: 87). At the same time, the Regular Reports covered a wide variety of issues, which proves that the interpretation of freedom of expression oscillated around various themes, lacking precisely defined criteria for an empirical assessment.[2] In some respects the Reports focused on fundamental matters regarding media freedom as was the case of a high government control over the PSM, criticised by the Commission in the case of Slovakia (Regular Report on Slovakia's Progress Towards Accession, 1998: 11), or legal provisions potentially impeding free speech in the case of Poland (Regular Report on Poland's Progress Towards Accession, 2000, 2001, 2002). In other cases, the Reports raised concerns about the economic and structural issues as was an example of a small number of radio stations in the case Hungary (Regular Report on Hungary's Progress Towards Accession, 1998: 10) or the lack of stability in the television sector in the case of the Czech Republic (Regular Report on Czech Republic's

[2] Following Regular Reports of the European Commission were analysed for this chapter: 1998, 1999, 2001, 2002 Regular Report on Czech Republic's Progress Towards Accession; 1998, 1999, 2001, 2002 Regular Report on Hungary's Progress Towards Accession; 1998, 1999, 2001, 2002 Regular Report on Poland's Progress Towards Accession; 1998, 1999, 2001, 2002 Regular Report on Slovakia's Progress Towards Accession. In addition, the 2003 EC Comprehensive Monitoring Reports on the Candidate Countries' Preparations for Membership were analysed in the case of: the Czech Republic, Hungary, Poland, Slovakia. Finally, two Composite Reports of the European Commission on Progress towards Accession by each of the Candidate Countries were analysed for 1998 and 1999. Since 2000, these reports were restructured into: Enlargement Strategy Papers of the European Commission on Progress towards Accession by each of the Candidate Countries. The four such strategy papers were analysed for: 2000, 2001, 2002 and 2003 (available at: http://ec.europa.eu/enlargement/archives/key_documents/reports_2000_en.htm; retrieved 4.01.2014).

Progress Towards Accession, 2002: 28–29). The Reports also made an impression of a quite particularistic treatment of some countries and some issues. Certain phenomena, for instance, attracted significant attention in the case of a given country (e.g. the development of private media in Hungary), while in other assessed countries these issues remained almost unnoticed (e.g. Slovakia or the Czech Republic).

The media-related issues monitored under the label of 'freedom of speech' and the section of civil and political rights have emerged mainly from four problem areas:

- legal provisions potentially impeding free speech (a legal dimension),
- the extent of demonopolisation and robustness of media environments (a structural dimension),
- political influences on the independence of media regulatory authorities (this area is reflected also in the section on *acquis*) and PSM, constrained conditions of PSM performance (a regulatory and political dimension),
- media performance and coverage (mainly with reference to elections and political communication, and a poor performance of the PSM) (a performance-related dimension) (Klimkiewicz, 2008).

The Regular Reports gave an uneven prominence to these groups of issues. The first category that examined merely a legal dimension of freedom of speech, dominated monitoring in some countries. Poland has been an interesting case in this regard, as most of the Reports paid attention to the slander laws offering politicians a higher level of the protection than would be a case with the general public. The 2000 Regular Report observed that this provision acted in some instances "as an impediment to *free speech*" and that it contradicted "the concept within the jurisprudence of the European Court of Human Rights that the broadest protection against insult is due to the citizen" (2000: 19). At the same time, other problematic practices resulting from the dependency between the media, politics and business remained largely unnoticed. Wojciech Sadurski writes about a generalised sense of frustration concerning the functioning of the institutions in Poland just before joining the EU (so after the monitoring exercise). The media as one of many institutions necessary for democratic consolidation were still seen not functioning particularly well: the public media have been and are controlled by the parties in the government, while private media have been and are vulnerable to manipulations by the state and big business (Sadurski, 2003: 5). The Regular Reports observed similar defamation provisions in other countries (in Hungary, 2002: 29; in Slovakia, 2002: 28), but paid rather marginal attention to them.

Secondly, the Regular Reports employed a relatively selective view on structural development of media environments. Perhaps one of the reasons for this approach was that external investments and foreign ownership (including non-European) have been already present in most of the countries, and the media systems have been largely demonopolised and privatised already since the beginning of the 1990s. The 1999 Composite Paper summarising achievements of all candidate countries, emphasised that "most candidate countries have a robust and lively media" (1999: 15). In the case of Hungary, however, a more detailed account of structural media developments was at place. This can be explained by the fact, that Hungary was the last of the four countries to implement Act I on Radio and Television Broadcasting (1996)[3] revamping and ultimately demonopolising its media system. It is interesting to note, that the criteria evaluating the robustness of the Hungarian media system focused mainly on economic performance factors, such as a competitive pressure and competitiveness of the media market, broadcasting licence allocation to foreign consortia, a number of media outlets operating at different geographical levels of the media system (Klimkiewicz, 2008: 87–88). Other, non-economic, yet quite important aspects of media diversity, such as cultural diversity, view-point diversity, etc. were largely overlooked.

The problem approached in the third group of issues – political influence on media regulatory authorities and the PSM – has already been well known from extensive academic and think-tank research undertaken both before and after the accession (e.g. Sparks, 1998; Price et al., 2002; Sükösd and Bajomi-Lázár, 2003; Jakubowicz, 2004b, Petković et al., 2004, Open Society Institute, 2005; Jakubowicz, 2007). The Commission aimed to investigate in the Regular Reports malpractices of political officials extorting political pressure on both regulatory authorities and the PSM mainly through the procedures of appointment. The 'crisis' of the PSM, as recognised in these reports, has been naturally connected with this area of concern. It should be recalled, that after 1989, the newly established PSM in the CEE were regulated by new broadcasting acts. At least in a normative sense, these aimed at achieving full independence from the State and party politics on the one hand, and partial independence from market forces on the other hand (Klimkiewicz, 2008). These aspirations met many practical difficulties, which were partially reflected in the Regular Reports. In sum, the Reports devoted the most significant space to the crisis of the public service TV in Hungary and the Czech Republic (2008: 88).

---

[3] The Act was adopted on 21st December 1995 by the Hungarian Parliament.

The 2001 Regular Report on Hungary described difficult financial conditions of the Hungarian public service TV (MTV). In particular, the Report observed that the basic capital of the public television "has been reduced to one tenth, outstanding public debts have doubled and numerous staff has been dismissed over the past two years in an attempt to render it more competitive" (2001: 20–21). These circumstances resulted not only in a significant drop in audience share (almost to 10%), but also threatened the fulfillment of public service remit requirements (Klimkiewicz, 2008: 88). Moreover, the abolition of television licence fee in 2002, by a legally questionable procedure (Open Society Institute, 2005: 794), disclosed the vulnerability of the public service television in its relation to ruling political parties (Klimkiewicz, 2008: 88). Although the Report touched upon one of the most vulnerable points in the transformed media environment in Hungary, an eventual remedy largely depended on a political calculus carried out among the ruling elites, and these decided that the political costs of remedy are higher than the costs of the resistance. In the case of the Czech Republic, the 2001 Regular Report reflected on events that started with a strike of the public services television staff in December 2000 and ended with massive protests of the Czech public in January 2001. In December 2000, the Czech Council for Radio and Television Broadcasting dismissed the Director General of the Czech public TV (ČT) and swiftly appointed a new candidate politically affiliated with the Civic Democratic Party (ODS). The employees responded to this situation with a strike and started to produce alternative news programming. The conflict itself was perceived by many citizens as a protest against political interference (Klimkiewicz, 2008: 89). On January 3rd 2001, several thousands of people gathered at the Václav Square in Prague to demand the resignation of the newly nominated Director General and to express support for the journalists on strike. Although some analysts argued that the protests were politically orchestrated, the situation reached the point that could no longer be left without a clear policy response. New legislation has since been adopted, enabling the election of the new Council for Radio and Television Broadcasting. As a result of these legal and institutional changes, the composition of the new Council reflected a relatively wide range of political and civic organisations. The 2001 Regular Report appreciated these changes and stressed that the spirit, in which they were made should be maintained (2001: 16). In the case of Slovakia, the Regular Reports repeatedly argued that the 'public service nature' of the PSM should be ensured and improved (1999; 2000). The Reports did not specify though, what the 'public service nature' of the PSM means; whether it is manifested in PSM performance, management, forms of organisation, financing, accountability or all these aspects together.

Finally, the assessment of media coverage and performance in the Regular Reports has been fairly scarce. The Reports paid attention selectively to some chosen election periods and forms of political communication. The relevant data used for monitoring derived from other international institutions (e.g. OSCE) or NGOs. In most cases, the Reports sought coverage by the PSM rather than private media, and coverage by television rather than print or online. The 2000 Regular Report on Slovakia noted: "monitoring of state-owned television has indicated that the opposition is not given sufficient and objective coverage" (2000: 19). Likewise, the 2002 Regular Report on Hungary observed that "during the election campaign, the presence of Government parties was more evident in the PSM, while private media generally provided a more neutral coverage of events, as underlined by the OSCE..." (2002: 29).

The picture of media-related issues in the CEE emerging from the Commission's Regular Reports under the section of political Copenhagen criteria, was painted rather cautiously (Klimkiewicz, 2008). The technique favoured a lose composition of points rather than drafting coherent territories of a more systematic assessment. The Regular Reports avoided strong criticism in order to sustain progress along the envisaged 'road map' (Sasse, 2004). Under the surface of the official rhetoric, there has been a lack of any comparison, reference to the similar problems and eventually proposed solutions from the established EU member states. Given the fact, that some of the similar problems to those hindering freedom of speech and the media in the CEE countries, remained unresolved in the older member states (e.g. Italy), can explain why the monitoring exercise followed a prescribed pattern rather than immersed deeper into media realities and potential remedies. A milestone, by which candidate countries met the political Copenhagen criteria (2003), stands symbolic rather than pragmatic in the area of freedom of expression and media pluralism (Klimkiewicz, 2008: 89). Many problematic issues indicated in the Reports (most notably an insufficient political independence of regulatory authorities and the PSM) have endured the enlargement momentum and continued to define the reality of media landscapes in the post-accession period (2008: 89).

Table 6: Media-related issues monitored under the political Copenhagen criteria: extracts from country Regular Reports, 1998–2002

	1998	**1999**	**2000**	**2001**	**2002**
CZECH REPUBLIC	– freedom of expression was improved	– no reference to media or freedom of expression	– TV and Radio Council dismissed on grounds that the Czech TV failed to fulfill its public service role – the Council criticised for an ineffective action in addressing an ownership dispute	– concerns of the IFJ about political influence on the Czech TV – the TV and Radio Council replaced the Director of the Czech TV – the staff of the Czech TV on strike	– little progress in transparency and stability in the TV sector – the TV and Radio Council should maintain its political independence
HUNGARY	– freedom of the press continues to be respected – Media Law (1996) broke the monopoly of state TV – competition between commercial TV channels – small number of private radio stations	– concerns about the government's wish to be involved in the operation of the media– the board of trustees of public service TV formed solely by pro-government members	– Hungary respects freedom of the press – the market for news is highly competitive – a wide variety of high quality, uncensored, national and local information – in 1997 national TV licenses granted to two Western private consortia – TV Board of Trustees politically controlled	– 80% of the print media and 70 % of radio and TV stations in private hands – financial situation in public service televi-sion is at risk – the supervision of the public service media not properly ensured – a growing political pressure on the PSM	– equal political representation in the supervisory organs of public service media – election campaign coverage favours government parties in public service media

POLAND	– lively and active press – “slander and abuse” provisions in Penal Code do not cause problems	– Poland fulfills the political Copenhagen criteria – “slander and abuse” provisions in Penal Code do not cause problems for journalists’ rights	– Poland fulfills the political Copenhagen criteria – concerns about the “slander and abuse” provisions of the Penal Code	– continued concerns about the use of the slander laws and stronger protection of politicians than the general public	– slander laws offer politicians a higher level of protection than to the general public
SLOVAKIA	– cases of intimidation of journalists and media reported – the government exercised a high degree of control over public radio and TV	– the public service nature of the PSM should be ensured – changes in the composition of the boards controlling radio and television criticised as politically motivated	– the opposition is not given sufficient and objective coverage in the state-owned TV – the public service nature of the PSM should be ensured and improved	– the freedom of expression enshrined in the Constitution of the Slovak Republic – no particular problems reported in this regard	– ineffective provisions of the Criminal Code concerning defamation of the State President, the Government and the Constitutional Court

3.4. Monitoring of media-related issues under the audiovisual *Acquis*

The 1993 Copenhagen European Council indicated that the ability to take on the obligations of membership requires the adoption and implementation of the *acquis*. In addition, the European Council of Madrid highlighted the importance of ensuring the effective application of *acquis* through appropriate administrative and judicial structures (European Commission, 2000: 21). In the area of media policy, the transposition of *acquis* implied a legislative alignment with the principal legal instrument of the day – the Television Without Frontiers Directive (the TWF Directive) (Klimkiewicz, 2008: 94). Given that most of the CEE countries have ratified and enforced the Council of Europe's Convention on Transfrontier Television (ECTT) and have been involved in the ratification of its amending protocol before the monitoring of the audiovisual *acquis* started, the CEE were bound to succeed with fulfilling the EU conditions in this matter. However, despite easily visible similarities between the two documents, Karol Jakubowicz argued that the ECTT and TWF displayed differences in their fundamental philosophy:

> In one, emphasis was placed on the social, cultural and political function of broadcasting, while the other was geared more to the economic needs of the market, though some of those provisions also had clear cultural implications (Jakubowicz, 2006: 3).

Nevertheless, the Commission deemed the ratification of ECTT by the candidate countries as one of the main benchmarks in their progress towards full transposition of the audiovisual *acquis*. Quite surprisingly, the relevant problem areas exposed in the Regular Reports did not follow particular provisions of the TWF (with some exceptions), but often exposed broader areas of concern, including in particular:

- independence of regulatory authorities and some aspects of adiministrative capacity (e.g. transparency concerning frequency allocation and distribution of support measures),
- media ownership rules,
- promotion of European and independent works and the proportionality of measures promoting works in national languages (Klimkiewicz, 2008).

The monitoring of audiovisual *acquis* generally followed a route towards progress. A cumulative success has been described in a gradual manner – the efforts of each candidate country were evaluated through repeatedly used formulaic expressions: "progress in the audiovisual sector is very limited", "no significant progress", "a moderate level of alignment with the *acquis*", "a substantial degree of alignment with the *acquis*" (Klimkiewicz, 2008: 95). In order to motivate more negligent candidates, the reports praised the diligent ones. The 2002 Regular Report on Slovakia concluded: "Slovakia has made considerable progress, and has reached, overall, an advanced level both in terms of legislative alignment and administrative capacity" (2002: 97). Likewise, the 2001 Report on Slovenia emphasised that the 2001 Mass Media Act brings Slovenian legislation into line with the TWF Directive (2001: 71).

The most problematic in this respect, appeared to be alignment process in Poland. The 2003 Comprehensive Report warned, that "unless rapid action is taken to catch up delays in amending the Broadcasting Act, there is a risk that Poland will not fulfil these requirements and not be able to implement the *acquis* by accession" (2003, 46). The Reports did not explore the political reasons of this serious delay, most likely because the problems have not been unleashed at that time. The Polish legislative alignment with the TWF was seriously hampered by a disclosure of a corruption scandal, widely referred to as *Rywingate*, which ultimately resulted in the resignation of Leszek Miller's government in 2004 (Klimkiewicz, 2008: 95). The scandal revealed legislative manipulations of the National Broadcasting Council (KRRiT) and Ministry of Culture that were backed by political and economic interests of the ruling elite. The proposed Draft Amendment to the Broadcasting Law was designed to prevent owners of the national dailies from cross-media ownership, in particular in the audiovisual sector, while the owners of other periodicals (e.g. weeklies) were allowed to acquire media outlets in other sectors. In such a shape the law strikingly disfavoured one of the largest media companies in Poland – Agora – the owner of the leading national daily *Gazeta Wyborcza*. Agora was approached to pay an immense bribe to 'the group of power' in order to modify the disadvantageous ownership rules. After the disclosure of the scandal, the Parliament appointed a special Investigation Committee that disclosed several "worrying irregularities and manipulations concerning the legislative work on the Draft Amendment". These circumstances led to the withdrawal of the problematic document from the Sejm,[4] but also seriously delayed a legislative transposition of the audiovisual *acquis* as the Draft Amendment contained also provisions implementing the TWF (Klimkiewicz, 2008).

[4] The lower chamber of the Polish Parliament

Rywingate and its political and legal consequences was not mentioned in the Regular Reports on Poland (in 2003 investigations were still pending), but the language of the assessment made it clear that the Commission was concerned: "Poland must pay attention to ensuring a stable, predictable, transparent and effective implementation of the broadcasting regulatory frameworks" (Comprehensive Report on Poland, 2003: 46). The corruption scandal showed the extremely high risks of political interference into the legislative process: hazardous trade-offs that were designed to secure political and economic interests of the ruling elite almost retained the proceeding EU accession. Though the audiovisual policy has not occupied a priority position in a process of conditionality, it presented an important symbolic area focalising the very sense of an advocated change.

Not surprisingly, the Regular Reports devoted substantial space to the media regulatory authorities in the candidate countries, focusing mainly on their administrative effectiveness, capacities, competences, powers and composition (Klimkiewicz, 2008). In some cases the regulatory bodies were praised for their effectiveness (Regular Report on Poland, 1999), independence (Regular Report on Hungary, 2000), whereas in other cases, the Commission suggested that strengthening in terms of staff and equipment (Regular Report on Slovakia, 2000) is needed. A gradual adoption of rules on the European and independent works, as well as proportionality of measures promoting programmes in national languages was quite closely observed in a number of the Reports. The issue was not perceived as a problematic one and it did not raise a contentious policy debate. When introducing new broadcasting laws in the 1990s, many CEE countries have acknowledged that a national presence in the audiovisual sphere (through the contents produced originally in national languages) is crucial and should become a stable component of new regulatory designs. An obligation to adopt audiovisual *acquis* added a European dimension to it, not by replacing the national production quota, but by completing it proportionally (Klimkiewicz, 2008).

To summarise the two sections above: conditionality seemed to work best when it resonated with domestic preferences and political aims (Sadurski, 2003: 14); or when it did not openly entered controversial and 'unwanted' domains. EU conditionality certainly influenced domestic media policies not only 'on paper', but it was, at the same time, essentially complementary and superficial in a process dominated by domestic policy priorities. Two forms of political risks marked the period before and after the EU accession. The focal point of the first risk reflects an ever-present calculus between the political costs of supra-national policy adjustment and the costs of a domestic resistance. The second risk refers to various 'translations' of common policy principles. Policy conditions and principles that are not part of the EU legal system in a comprehensive manner – as is the case of the media and communication field – might not be equally shared by the member states themselves. While conditionality can impose some adjustment to these principles, if the conditions are not succinctly defined, there is a danger that in the post-accession period, practices and mechanism declining from the prescribed 'norm' will quickly reincarnate. Moreover, the credibility of conditionality can be significantly corroborated with 'double standards', especially in terms of what is generally required from the new member, or candidate states on the one hand, and tolerated in the case of the established member states.

3.5. Post-accession developments

After the enlargement, policy harmonisation concerning relevant media issues became guided by accordant units within the Commission (such as the DG INFSO), while freedom and pluralism of the media protected under the EU Charter of Fundamental Rights remained further examined by the EU Network of Independent Experts on Fundamental Rights. The Network was set up by the DG Justice and Home Affairs upon a request of the European Parliament to monitor fundamental rights in the member states in 2002–2006. The Reports (published for the years 2002–2005)[5] covered all actual member states. They focused mainly on cases, where fundamental rights (including the right to freedom and pluralism of the media) were abused or not fully respected, providing also positive instances facilitating the use of these rights. The Reports were prepared on the basis of country reports provided by each member state and a separated report evaluating the activities of the EU institutions. As the Reports have not bound the Commission in terms of policy response, they have mainly offered an analytical value.

Notwithstanding this fact, an attentive reader would easily notice a broad and well-defined scope of issues in the area of freedom of speech and the media, as well as media pluralism. Some of these issues clearly identified areas of concern (the Italian 'Gaspari Law', growing inter-media concentration in Portugal, insufficient impartiality and independence of the Polish regulatory agency – National Broadcasting Council, unequal

[5] Following Reports of the EU Network of Independent Experts on Fundamental Rights were studied for this chapter: 2002, 2003, 2004, 2005 Report on the Situation of Fundamental Rights in the European Union and its Member States.

obligations imposed on foreigners and Slovak citizens with regard to the Slovak Act of Periodic Press), others raised positive aspects and good practices (Reports on the Situation of Fundamental Rights in the European Union 2003, 2004, 2005) (Klimkiewicz, 2008). These included such practices as a requirement of 'internal pluralism' imposed on broadcasters in the Czech Republic, or control of media ownership consolidation in the UK, conducted in order to maintain a sufficient plurality of views (Synthesis Report, 2003). Overall, the Reports demonstrated a human rights perspective – media freedom and pluralism was monitored as the right of an individual to be fully and impartially informed from diverse sources. The coverage of both, old and new member states showed, that despite national specificities, many problem areas are similar and might require harmonised solutions, or at least more formalised monitoring exercise at the European level (Klimkiewicz, 2008).

In the later period, the European Agency for Fundamental Rights (FRA) continued monitoring and reporting on human rights in the European Union, although with a more targeted approach that minimised the evaluation of communication and media-related rights. The FRA had been established in 2007 as an independent expert body for the EU with a role to advise EU institutions and member states on fundamental-rights related issues when implementing EU law. With such a mandate, the FRA perceived its role as institution offering "added value to the EU's institutional and political reality" (FRA, 2012: 27). In the first period of its activities (2007–2010), the FRA focused predominantly on raising rights awareness and the socio-legal assistance on selected fields of issues revolving mainly around the principles of anti-discrimination and equality. The year 2010 marked the first year of the European Union operating on the basis of a legally binding Charter of Fundamental Rights. Not surprisingly, the FRA responding to this development, employed more annual monitoring focused not only on FRA activities, but also human rights in the member states of the Union.

The series started already with the FRA Report covering information, events and developments in the EU for the year 2009 (FRA, 2010). The Report set up the structure and composition of principal areas of focus followed in the next years. These selected and accentuated priority policies of DG Justice rather than corresponded to particular articles of the Charter. Thus, among the issues such as the questions of racial discrimination, child protection, immigrant policies and asylum, the information policy and protection of personal data; freedom of expression and the media, as well as media pluralism have not been distinctively exposed. The 2010 Annual Report of FRA published in June 2011 put the spotlight "on the achievements and challenges of the EU and its member states on fundamental rights". In this way, the logic of monitoring did not seek to detect cases, where fundamental rights were breached, or not respected, but rather to signal broader problem areas requiring further policy response. The 2011 Report examined progress of the EU and member states as regards obligations under the Charter of Fundamental Rights of the EU. The problem area that hints partially on the media and communication (although not from the perspective of media freedom and pluralism) brings into attention one aspect of information policies: the protection of personal data. The Report called for improved protection of personal data mainly in reference to geographical information services on the Internet (Google Street View) and greater sensitivity regarding the publishing of personal information or pictures, especially of younger people (FRA, 2012: 62). The 2012 Report published in 2013 forged ahead the problem of protection of personal data, especially with regard to the role of intermediaries. Although Google has not been directly accused of acting illegally, EU Data Protection authorities have expressed concerns about "insufficient information to its users" and "about the combination of data across services" (FRA, 2013: 86). It was, however, the ACTA international agreement, that gained probably highest exposure among the relevant policy issues covered by the Report. One of the reasons was that the two EU institutions – the Parliament and Commission – exhibited a fairly divergent position on this matter. The Report noticed that the Commission conceived ACTA as fully in line with EU standards and without any interference with citizens' fundamental rights of freedom of expression and data protection. On the other hand, the European Parliament, receiving petitions from more than 2.8 million Internet users against ACTA rejected the agreement in the plenary session in July 2012. The Report quotes a negative recommendation concerning ACTA delivered by the EP's Committee on International Trade: "the intended benefits of this international agreement are far outweighed by the potential threats to civil liberties" (FRA, 2013: 71). In consequence of the EP's rejection of ACTA, neither the EU nor its individual member states can join the agreement.

The year 2012 was also depicted by the FRA as a year of multiple crises in the EU and its member states (FRA, 2013). One of such crises examined briefly as a separate case was 'a wider constitutional crisis' in Hungary. The Report observed that a new constitution which came into force at the beginning of 2012, drew strong criticism both at home and abroad. One of most problematic areas of concern in the respect of this crisis was the exercise of government control over the media (FRA, 2013: 23). The Report did not provide, however, a more detailed analysis of this control, nor did it more broadly reflect on any regulations, practices and mechanisms curtailing freedom of the media in Hungary.

In general, FRA Reports stand in different direction than the Reports produced by the EU Network of Independent Experts on Fundamental Rights, not only because of thematic selectivity. A main intention beneath the FRA's exercise doesn't seem to be a systematic monitoring of the most pertinent cases where fundamental rights of EU citizens were abused, not respected or not protected (including the right to freedom of expression and the media, and the right to receive information from plural sources), and to pair these with an adequate/inadequate reaction from the relevant EU institutions. The FRA Reports are evidently designed to cover the problem areas where the EU or member states institutions *acted,* situations where action was missing, are largely left out of the scope of the analysis. Selective as they are, the Reports are political constructs signaling the progress of the EU institutions in terms of a preoccupation with salient problems and policies employed to tackle these problems. As such, they hardly offer a systematic tool for the assessment of what can be seen as standards of the 'political criteria' (including the media and communication field) in the both established and young member states, and prospective candidate countries. Since 2010, the Commission has prepared annual reports to the European Parliament, the Council, the European Economic and Social Committee and the Committee of the Regions on the application of the EU Charter of Fundamental Rights.[6] The scope of the reports does not seem however to be comprehensive enough, especially with regard to freedom of expression and media pluralism. Other instruments that could tie the monitoring of future with current members, is thus missing. This analytical gap puts under the question maintaining of standards that are politically used as a condition for EU accession.

The post-accession 'Europeanising' effect on the CEE communication and media environments and related changes will be studied more comprehensively in the next chapters focusing subsequently on audiovisual policies, media pluralism, and the independence of media regulatory authorities and PSM. Yet, to provide some reflection on dealing with freedom of expression and the media, as well as with media pluralism, it could be instructive to tackle upon some problematic cases that evolved after the EU accession in selected CEE countries. Given the absence of a comparative and credible tool for tracking and monitoring media freedom and pluralism over a longer period time at the EU

[6] DG Justice (2014) Annual report (information on reports available at: http://ec.europa.eu/justice/fundamental-rights/charter/application/index_en.htm; retrieved 4.01.2014).

level, the dynamics of other indexes will be briefly analysed to extract most salient cases for further investigation. These include the *Freedom of the Press* reports compiled systematically across the world since 1980 by Freedom House and the *Press Freedom Index* produced by Reporters Without Borders globally since 2002. Although these two evaluating indexes were broadly criticised by media freedom experts for their weak methodologies, excessive reliance on experts' views, a Western bias, and a focus on 'old media', they were, at the same time, seen as a valuable and long-term tool with acceptable statistical consistency, reaching often the same general conclusions (CIMA, 2010). Importantly, with no alternative studies reaching the same geographical and diachronic scale, the indexes offer a useful mechanism for comparisons of countries, issues, periods of progress or regress in analysing freedom and pluralism of the media, conditions of journalism and overall media environments mainly with regard to the political function of the media, although other functions are being reflected as well. The table and figure below manifest the ranking of the CEE countries in *Freedom of the Press* index by Freedom House (FH) in years following the EU accession:

Table 7: Freedom of the Press ranking by Freedom House (2005–2013) for the Czech Republic, Hungary, Poland and Slovakia

	2005	**2006**	**2007**	**2008**	**2009**	**2010**	**2011**	**2012**	**2013**
CZECH REPUBLIC	22	20	18	18	18	18	19	19	19
HUNGARY	21	21	21	21	21	23	30	36*	36*
POLAND	20	21	22	24	24	24	25	25	26
SLOVAKIA	21	20	20	22	23	23	22	21	22

Sources: Freedom House: Freedom of the Press (2005–2013) (available at: http://www.freedomhouse.org/report-types/freedom-press; retrieved 19.09.2013).

Notes: * Only Hungary was evaluated as 'partly free' in 2012 and 2013, other CEE countries were perceived as 'free' in 2005–2013.

In the Freedom of the Press methodology, zero or the lowest scores signal the highest level of media freedom. A score of 0 to 30 means that the country has a 'Free' media, while 31 to 60 signals 'Partly Free', and 61 to 100 'Not Free' (CIMA, 2010: 9). As can be seen from the table above and the figure below, the trends observed in the CEE countries, perhaps only with the modest exception of the Czech Republic, do not indicate a linear straightforward and unequivocal progress in freedom of the media after

EU accession. Certainly, the most striking developments were registered by the reports in the case of Hungary that moved from a score of 23 in 2010 to 30 in 2011 and 36 in 2012 and 2013. This led to migration of the country from a category of 'Free' media into the category of 'Partly Free' in 2012. The qualitative jump in the FH's evaluation was evoked by passing and amendment of a new Hungarian law in 2010. The legislation came into force in January 2011 and triggered widespread protests, both within Hungary and across Europe (Voltmer, 2013: 152), mainly due to excessive controlling powers over the media by a new regulatory authority. The second increase of scores can be observed in the case of Slovakia in 2009 and 2010. It stemmed from an enactment of the controversial 2008 Press Act which, among other problematic provisions, required publishers to print responses to any "statement of fact that impinges on the honor, dignity, or privacy of a natural person, or the name or good reputation of a legal entity", regardless of whether the statement in question is accurate (Freedom House, 2011). The law was amended later on, although the controversial framing of 'right of reply' resulted in widespread practice of civil defamation cases where judges, politicians or business elites have claimed excessive damages and often collected overproportional financial compensation. This has not only severely affected

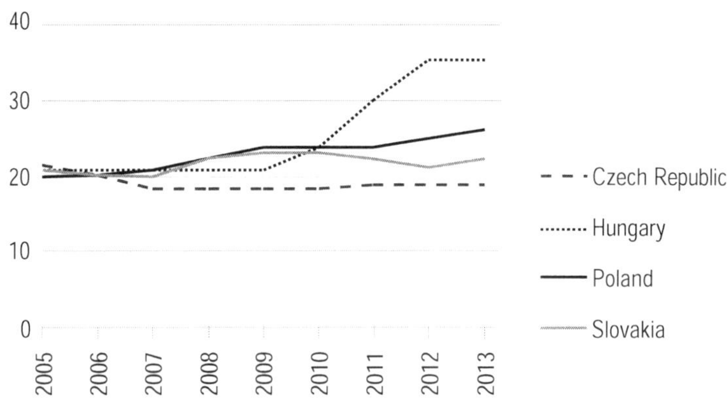

Figure 3: Freedom of the Press ranking by Freedom House (2005–2013) for the Czech Republic, Hungary, Poland and Slovakia

Sources: Elaborated on the basis of Freedom House: Freedom of the Press (2005–2013) (available at: http://www.freedomhouse.org/report-types/freedom-press; retrieved 19.09.2013).

the financial conditions of the Slovak media, but in some cases, also prevented the publication of journalistic material.

The next table and figure show the ranking of the CEE countries in *Press Freedom Index* by Reporters Without Borders (RWB) in years following EU accession:

Table 8: Press Freedom Index by Reporters Without Borders (2005–2013) for Czech Republic, Hungary, Poland and Slovakia

	2005	**2006**	**2007**	**2008**	**2009**	**2010/ 2011**	**2012**	**2013**
CZECH REPUBLIC	9	5	14	16	24	24	14	16
HUNGARY	12	10	17	23	26	23	40	56
POLAND	55	60	57	48	37	32	24	22
SLOVAKIA	8	8	4	10	45	35	27	23

Sources: Reporters Without Borders: Press Freedom Index (2005–2013) (available at: http://en.rsf.org/press-freedom-index-2013,1054.html; retrieved 19.09.2013).

Similarly, as in the Freedom of the Press methodology, also with the RWB's Press Freedom Index, an overall low score for a country is a good score. The total number combines scores from questions about killed, illegally detained, kidnapped and tortured journalists, questions about censorship and self-censorship and others. Likewise with the previous index, trends observed in the CEE countries indicate various fluctuations instead of a steady improvement of media freedom after the EU accession. The developments in Hungary caused very similar score increases than in the case of Freedom House's index: from 23 in 2010/2011 to 40 in 2012 and 56 in 2013. The 2013 Report concluded: "Hungary is still paying the price of repressive legislation that has had a palpable effect on how journalism is practiced" (RWB, 2013). In the case of Slovakia, the Press Freedom Index demonstrated a sharper growth of the score than the FH's index. In 2009, the score increased from 10 to 45. Noteworthy, in 2007, Slovakia with the score 4 occupied one of top positions in the RWB's ranking on a global scale. A quite radical change and the worst rank of Slovakia in the last 7 years, stemmed from the enactment of a controversial press law, discussed briefly above. The RWB's Press Freedom Index also paid more prominent attention than the FH's index, to surveillance of Polish journalists by secret services in 2005–2007. This resulted in as high a score of Poland as 55 in 2005, 60 in 2006 and 57 in 2007.

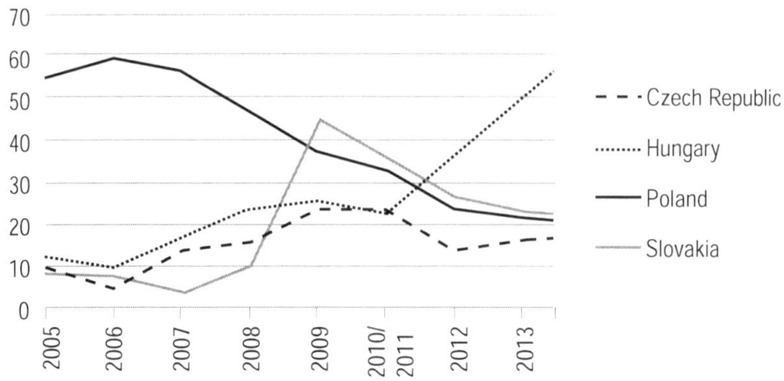

Figure 4: Press Freedom Index by Reporters Without Borders (2005–2013) for the Czech Republic, Hungary, Poland and Slovakia

Sources: Elaborated on the basis of Reporters Without Borders: Press Freedom Index (2005–2013) (available at: http://en.rsf.org/press-freedom-index-2013,1054.html; retrieved 19.09.2013).

A fluctuation of ranking positions, and sometimes even sharp deviations, clearly reflect the buildup of problematic issues as observed by international organisations. Interestingly, some problematic developments occurred in all CEE countries after the EU accession, though they have not been bound by much similarity. This again proves a variety and different outcomes of media policymaking despite the geopolitical and historical commonalities of the region. The two most highly exposed instances in the FH and RWB's indexes stand more symbolic for the process of policy harmonisation. The first considers the decisive role of courts in environments where there is a contrast between what had been envisioned by policy makers and the actual state of law enforcement (Anagnostou et al., 2010: 8–9; quoted after: Školkay and Ondruchová-Hong, 2012: 195). The second points to the decisive role of media regulatory authorities potentially equipped with omnipotent powers by the governments.

3.6. Libel and the Gorilla scandal: The 'silent' case of Slovakia

In recent years, the courts have played a decisive role in affecting both journalistic performance and media and communication policy in Slovakia. Andrej Školkay and Mária Ondruchová-Hong point out that the courts are the final arbiter in defining the limits of freedom of speech and the press (especially regarding libel, defamation, privacy, and breaking the law on government secrets) (Školkay and Ondruchová-Hong, 2012: 195). At the same time, the courts act – though in a more subtle way – as the final arbiter of the media regulatory decisions taken by regulatory bodies (2012: 195). The role of the courts became even more accentuated with the passing of the controversial Press Act on 10 April 2008. The Act, widely criticised by international organisations (including Reporters Without Borders, Freedom House and OSCE), legalised an automatic right of reply to anyone regardless of whether defamation or insult occurred. The Act was amended in September 2011 shortly before the collapse of Iveta Radičová's centre-right government. Most importantly, the amendment eliminated the 'right of reply' in the case of officials where disputed facts pertain to their public lives. Yet, an extensive use of civil defamation suits brought by judges, political and the business elite in recent years, cemented preventive concerns among journalists and media organisations at large.

The 2013 Freedom of the Press Report on Slovakia (Freedom House, 2013) observed that although defamation is not a criminal offense civil defamation suits claim exorbitant damages. Katrin Voltmer observes that even where libel laws are part of the civil code, excessive damage charges can be equally ruinous for the life and career of journalists (Voltmer, 2013: 144). In the case of Slovakia, Prime Minister Robert Fico and the Supreme Court Chairman Štefan Harabin have collected hundreds of thousands of Euro from successful libel lawsuits over the past several years (Freedom House, 2013). These conditions have rendered investigative and politically-critical journalism a difficult challenge. The perception of a severe situation, in which the Slovak media find themselves resonates within the professional environment. Martin M. Šimečka, a prominent Slovak journalist compared in this respect the conditions of the media in the Czech Republic and Slovakia: "Unlike in the Czech Republic, the Slovak courts frequently levy heavy fines for even minor inaccuracies in an otherwise faultless investigative text that a politician or businessman decides to sue over".[7] Voltmer describes this type of state interference into journalistic freedom as a very specific type of libel: seditious libel, or slander laws that criminalise criticism and negative coverage of state institutions and political leaders (2013: 144). Such a damaging practice has a strong and chilling effect especially on economically fragile media companies that cannot afford to cover the expensive costs of professional legal as-

[7] Šimečka, M. Martin (2012) *A Gorilla tearing down the system* [in] Presseurop, 1.02.2012 (available at: http://www.presseurop.eu/en/content/article/1468351-gorilla-tearing-down-system; retrieved 17.09.2013).

sistance and eventually pay extremely high compensations for damages. Among a long list of libel cases, one deserves special attention, as its roots grew from the most explosive political corruption scandal in recent years.

In December 2011, a file coded 'Gorilla' was uploaded on a US-based server. The file was presented as a wiretap document produced by the Slovak Intelligence Service (SIS – Slovenská Informačná Služba)[8] in 2005–2006. The document contained operational transcripts of the conversations allegedly held in 2005 and 2006 between the representatives of the Penta Group – one of the biggest investment companies in Slovakia – and leaders of some political parties as well as important public officials, including e.g. former Minister of Economy and the Head of the National Property Fund. Martin M. Šimečka described the substance of the conversations as "(…) the talk about how many millions which politician or party is to get for the privatisation of enterprises, especially in energy and transport".[9] Politicians invited by the Penta group discussed in detail deals on large privatisation projects, in which 'friendly' committees and selection procedures were agreed upon in an exchange for high paybacks to politicians and political parties. Politically, the files seemed to be most damaging for Mikuláš Dzurinda, the former Prime Minister and leader of the SDKÚ,[10] but also other politicians, including Robert Fico, the leader of the SMER – SD[11] had contacts with the group.

Tom Nicholson, an investigative journalist of Canadian origin working both for Slovak and international media, wrote a book *Gorila* describing his scrutiny of the Gorilla Affair and explaining corruption practices and intricate links between Slovak business and politics. In February 2012, a court in Bratislava ordered Nicholson to abstain from publishing the book and any related investigative material, on the grounds of injunctions brought by Jaroslav Haščák, a co-owner of the Penta group. Again, this was a case in which civil defamation laws were used to stop publishing information about political and business corruption. Numerous organisations condemned the ruling. The Slovak P.E.N. Center considered the court decision as the implementation of censorship and, as

---

[8] SIS (Slovak Information Agency) is a state body with the mandate to defend the constitutional structure, public order and security of the state.

[9] Šimečka, M. Martin (2012) *A Gorilla tearing down the system* [in] Presseurop, 1.02.2012 (available at: http://www.presseurop.eu/en/content/article/1468351-gorilla-tearing-down-system; retrieved 17.09.2013)

[10] SDKÚ – Slovenská Demokratická a Kresťanská Únia (Slovak Democratic and Christian Union) – a liberal conservative party.

[11] SMER – SD – Smer – sociálna demokracia (Smer – social democracy) – a social democratic political party in Slovakia.

such, an overt violation of freedom of expression.[12] In June 2012, a court in Bratislava ruled that the book could be published. The *Gorila* promoted by the publisher as "The most expected book of the year" finally ended up on the bookshop shelves and was sold more than 50 000 copies, a remarkable result for a relatively small book market as Slovakia. Since fall 2012, however, Nicholson has been sued in several defamation suits for libel in relation to the publishing of the book.

The revelation of the scandal spurred citizen demonstrations in January 2012 that were attended by several thousand protesters. Although the numbers might not seem impressive, this has been the first such a significant event of public disapproval against the way democratic politics has been performed in the country since the Velvet Revolution in 1989. Tom Nicholson described the flavour of the protests in his book: "Nobody expected such a common bitterness caused by longstanding theft, deception and falsehood, but also lasting poverty of the country. It was a feeling that the country could long have been prosperous if not led by its fraudulent leaders" (Nicholson, 2012: 181). The protests were expected to have a major impact on the March 2012 election, but the political outcome was not surprising – Robert Fico and Smer-SD came out as winners, securing a healthy majority for governing.

The revelation of the Gorilla scandal and following developments contested the boundaries of Slovak politics, but also shed more light on consequences of a quite extreme use of libel laws on journalism and conditions in which the media operate. The expectations were high, and in addition to more general goals – such as bringing more democracy to Slovakia – they also revolved around a multitude of small actions – such as new web-based investigative projects fulfilling the very ideas of monitory democracy – a surveillance of political, business elites and the judiciary by journalists and ordinary citizens. Tom Nicholson expressed intentions on his part on his blog:

> circumstances have put me in a unique position to continue reporting on Gorilla and other high-level corruption stories: I have your trust and support, as well as a specific set of contacts accumulated through years on the job. With Slovakia's mainstream media eliminating investigative reporting positions and rarely

[12] PEN International (2012) *Slovakia: Bratislava Court prohibits journalist Tom Nicholson from publishing the book on 'Gorilla Affair'*(available at: http://www.pen-international.org/pen-world/centres-news/; retrieved 20.09.2013).

> giving journalists more than a day to spend on stories, I believe that between us, we can come up with important stories that wouldn't otherwise get told.[13]

Collecting financial support from online users and supporters, Nicholson established the association and facebook account *Pod povrchom* (Under the surface) to continue investigative journalism in a de-institutionalised form.[14] Despite the initiation of an official investigation in the 'Gorilla' Affair in 2012, information largely available to the public has not, so far, offered any clear-cut explanations. Instead, in a muddy and dense space of information, contrary arguments and versions of the affair have been constantly fighting for primacy, and Nicholson and his sources continued to be discredited. Perhaps one of the reasons has been the relative silence of the case on the international arena, due to its 'complicated' and 'ambiguous' character. The EU paid little attention to the case and a critical tone of international press freedom index organisations did not translate into a significant assessment critique that could change the status quo.

3.7. The power of regulatory action: The 'loud' case of Hungary

The controversy about Hungary's new media laws that were passed in 2010 and amended in 2011 can be viewed as an instance of more complex regulatory control surrounding journalistic independence, media structures and persisting vulnerability of the PSM (Voltmer, 2013: 151). On the other hand, the high political exposure of the case prevented a more focused debate at the EU level on akin cases from other member countries. Putting the political spotlight on Hungary overshadowed less clear-cut, but still problematic developments limiting either media pluralism or journalistic independence and media autonomy in some other EU countries.

In 2010, the Fidesz[15] party led by Viktor Orbán won the elections with a two-thirds majority. This exceptional majority never experienced since 1989 was instrumental in enforcing a fast amendment to Article 61 of the Constitution on 6 July 2010 that facilitated the adoption of the

---

[13] Nicholson, Tom (2012) Blog: *Hunting Gorillas on the public's dime* (available at: http://nicholson.blog.sme.sk/c/293302/Hunting-Gorillas-on-the-publics-dime.html#ixzz2ekqWWzXo; retrieved 20.09.2012)

[14] Available at: https://www.facebook.com/podpovrchom.sk; retrieved 5.01.2014.

[15] Fidesz – Magyar Polgári Szövetség (Hungarian Civic Union) is the largest national conservative political party in Hungary.

upcoming media laws rearranging substantially the regulation of print, broadcast and online media. The series of these laws started with Act LXXXII of 2010 on the Amendment of Certain Acts on Media and Telecommunication published on 10 August 2010. The law established a new converged regulatory authority and reshaped the institutions governing and supervising the activities of the PSM and of the public service news agency (Lengyel, 2010). The new communications authority NMHH[16] came into shape as a merger of the former telecom regulator, the National Communications Authority (NHH) and the National Radio and Television Commission (ORTT). The pivotal role in the new institution was assigned to the Chairperson appointed by the Prime Minister for a renewable term of nine years. A panoply of powers exercised by the Chairperson has been remarkable: the Chairperson automatically becomes a candidate for the President of the Media Council (Médiatanács), a five-member body which supervises the NMHH; he/she also appoints the Director General of the Broadcast Support and Property Management Fund (with the competence to manage the main body of the properties of the public service media companies) and nominates candidates for the position of CEO of the public service media. Already in September 2010, the OSCE – preceding the actual adoption of remaining media laws – prepared an extensive analysis and assessment of both legislation in force and draft legislation on the media and telecommunications (OSCE, 2010). The document, prepared by Karol Jalubowicz, observed that "the package represents an equally far-reaching effort to put into place a new axiological, legal and institutional framework for media regulation and supervision" (OSCE, 2010: 5). Although the document also analyses the texts of regulation – such as the Bill T/363 on Press Freedom and Basic Rules on Media Content that were never passed – it explains the essence of tenets of media regulation that were finally pushed forward in the 2010 Press and Media Act[17] and the 2010 Mass Media Act.[18] The OSCE criticism emphasised mainly two points: first, that the system for media content regulation (including Internet and ICT media content) reaches beyond the needs of a democratic system of social communication; and second, that a highly

[16] NMHH – Nemzeti Média és Hírközlési Hatóság (National Media and Communications Authority) (http://nmhh.hu/; retrieved 5.10.2013).

[17] Act CIV of 2010 on the Freedom of the Press and the Fundamental Rules on Media Content published on 9 November 2010 in Magyar Közlöny (Official Journal) and amended in March 2011. The Act has been notoriously referred as the 'Press Freedom Act', although the official translation of the Act establishes the abbreviated version: Press and Media Act.

[18] Act CLXXXV of 2010 on Media Services and Mass Media published on 31 December 2010 in Magyar Közlöny (Official Journal) and amended in March 2011.

centralised and politically controlled regulatory institution and regulatory system may have a serious chilling effect on media freedom and independence (OSCE, 2010: 5–6).

Although the Hungarian government maintained that the media legislation conforms to EU standards and its elements are drawn from existing regulations in other European and EU member states (CMCS, 2012), the critical accounts of other supra-national actors, in particular the Council of Europe, European Parliament and the Commission, have steadily resonated in policy documents and statements issued since 2011. These clearly demonstrate a determined willingness of supra-national European actors to influence media law developments in Hungary and change the status quo. In January 2011, Thomas Hammarberg, the Council of Europe Commissioner for Human Rights visited Budapest to discuss the media law package. In the Opinion issued after the visit, the Commissioner expressed concerns about the compliance of some provisions with the CoE's standards on freedom of the media. These included, among others:

- appointments to the National Media and Communications Authority and Media Council (Articles 124–125 of the Mass Media Act),
- appointments to the management of the PSM (Article 102 of the Mass Media Act),
- vague criteria relating to the information and coverage that the media must provide (Article 13 of the Press and Media Act),
- protection of journalists' sources (Article 6 of the Press and Media Act).[19]

Shortly after the Commissioner's initiative, the European Parliament adopted the *Resolution of 10 March 2011 on media law in Hungary* (European Parliament, 2011), in which the Parliament raised concerns about undermining media pluralism by the new legislation, in particular pervasive and centralised governmental and political control over all media through the operation Media Regulatory Authority and Media Council. Interestingly, the Parliament linked the problematic legislative developments in Hungary with EU membership criteria: "...Copenhagen criteria for EU membership, as established in June 1993 at the Copenhagen Euro-

---

[19] Council of Europe (2011) *Opinion of the Commissioner for Human Rights on Hungary's media legislation in light of Council of Europe standards on freedom of the media*, CommDH (2011) 10. Strasbourg 25 February 2011. (available at: https://wcd.coe.int/ViewDoc.jsp?id=1751289; retrieved 6.10.2013). See also: Council of Europe (2011) *Hungary should use Council of Europe's standards to guarantee freedom of expression and media pluralism* (available at: http://human-rights-convention.org/2011/02/28/hungary-should-use-council-of-europe%E2%80%99s-standards-to-guarantee-freedom-of-expression-says-commissioner-hammarberg/; retrieved 6.10.2013).

pean Council, relating to freedom of the press and freedom of expression should be upheld by all EU Member States and enforced through relevant EU legislation" (European Parliament, 2011). The Parliament also called for revisions and reviews of the Hungarian law in order to ensure that it is fully "in conformity with EU law and European values and standards on media freedom, pluralism and independent media governance" (European Parliament, 2011).

The European Commission acted mainly through soft measures, issuing statements and letters calling subsequently for conformity of the problematic provisions with the EU law. In its first letter dated on 23 December 2010, the Vice President of the Commission and Commissioner for DG Connect Neelie Kroes referred mainly to the role of independent media regulatory authority that is expected to ensure the existence of a wide range of independent and autonomous media.[20] The next letter focused on concrete provisions, in particular, an obligation of balanced coverage applicable initially to all media service providers – including print and online press. The Vice President expressed doubts about compliance of the obligation with the fundamental right of freedom of expression and information enshrined in Article 11 of the EU Charter for Fundamental Rights, and with the AVMS Directive with regards to providers of audiovisual media services.[21] The Hungarian government agreed to amend the legislation for the purpose of refining its scope. In March 2011, the amendments were passed following negotiations with the Commission, although some non-governmental organisations claimed the changes did not meet the substance of criticism. In December 2011, Hungary's Constitutional Court made decision 165/2011. (XII. 20.) AB[22] on the constitutionality of the new regulations. Most of the questioned rules were deemed constitutional, however the Constitutional Court annulled several important measures. These led to the exclusion of print and online media from the scope of the sanctioning powers of the NMHH and deleting a provision limiting the confidentiality of journalists' sources to stories serving the public interest (Freedom House, 2013). Still, criticism continued both among non-governmental organisations as well as

[20] The letter of Neelie Kroes, Vice President of the European Commission to Tibor Navracsics, Deputy Prime Minister. 23 December, 2010 (available at: http://cmcs.ceu.hu/resources-new-media-laws-in-hungary-0; retrieved 6.10.2013).

[21] The letter of Neelie Kroes, Vice President of the European Commission to Tibor Navracsics, Deputy Prime Minister. 21 January, 2011 (available at: http://cmcs.ceu.hu/resources-new-media-laws-in-hungary-0; retrieved 6.10.2013).

[22] Decision 165/2011. (XII. 20.) AB of the Hungarian Constitutional Court on the Media Regulation.

European institutions. The critical judgment focused on the one hand on the licencing practices of the Media Council that enabled media outlets owned by Fidesz-lined businessmen to easily expand their local services into regional ones.[23] On the other hand, regulatory and legal issues remained at stake. In one of the numerous reactions – on November 2012 – Neelie Kroes pointed to issues that have not been solved through enforced amendments to the law so far:

> In particular, I want to see immediate action ensuring the real independence of the Media Council; measures to reduce the excessive concentration of powers in the hand of the Media Council and better measures to ensure the effective independent functioning of publicly-funded media. Solutions can be found in co-operation with the Council of Europe – so let's see them. In my view, the Media Council should also reconsider its practices for assigned radio frequencies.[24]

In February 2013, the Hungarian government submitted an Amendment based on negotiations between the Hungarian Government and the Council of Europe. Pursuant to the Amendment, the President of the NMHH is no longer appointed by the Prime Minister but by the President of the Republic on recommendation of the Prime Minister (Nagy, 2013) and the position is limited to a single nine-year term. The amendment has also empowered professional interest groups and self-regulatory interest organisations to make staffing proposals as part of the appointment procedure. Another important aspect of change concerned a provision on the requirement of 'balanced reporting'. Under the previous law, radio and TV broadcasters were required to produce "diverse, comprehensive, factual, up-to-date, objective and balanced" coverage of issues that may be of interest to the general public.[25] The substance of this requirement would perhaps not raise such a broad critique if not connected with the quite omnipotent powers of the regulatory agency. Provisions on balanced reporting are part of regulatory content obligations in various EU countries. For example, the Czech Act on Radio and Television Broadcasting imposes that:

---

[23] Mertek Media Monitor (2013) *Assessment of Media Council's tendering and licencing practices* (available at: http://mediamonitor.ceu.hu/2013/02/report-on-the-frequency-tendering-by-the-media-council-part-2/; retrieved 23.09.2013)

[24] Kroes, Neelie (2012) *My latest thoughts on Hungary and media pluralism* (available at: http://ec.europa.eu/commission_2010-2014/kroes/en/blog/my-latest-thoughts-on-hungary-and-media-pluralism-and-freedom; retrieved 23.09.2013).

[25] Mertek Media Monitor (2013) *Council of Europe and Hungarian Government agree on changes to media laws* (available at: http://mediamonitor.ceu.hu/2013/01/council-of-europe-and-hungarian-government-agree-on-changes-to-media-law/; retrieved 15.10.2013).

> A broadcaster shall provide objective and balanced information necessary for opinions to be freely formed. Any opinions or evaluating commentaries shall be separated from the information having the nature of news.[26]

The amendment of the Act CIV of 2010 on the Freedom of the Press and the Fundamental Rules of Media Content resulted in the following formulation:

> Linear media services engaged in the provision of information shall provide balanced coverage on local, national and European issues that may be of interest for the general public (...).[27]

Krisztina Nagy observes that recent judicial practice has construed the criterion of the "balanced" quality of reporting as a wide umbrella concept, thus it seems unlikely to expect a substantial qualitative shift in the new practical use of the provision (Nagy, 2013). The stance of the Council of Europe, however, became more appreciative. Thorbjørn Jagland, the Secretary-General of the Council of Europe stated in January 2013, that Hungary meets its legal obligations with reference to amendments in media laws. Neelie Kroes continued to point to the remaining problems. At a seminar on media freedom and pluralism held in March 2013 in Dublin, Kroes sustained that "issues on media freedom in Hungary are not yet solved" and that "only a fraction of the Council of Europe's recommendations have been implemented".[28] Although the Hungarian case has been certainly most exposed in current media policy developments in the EU countries, it has not been perceived as a sole and isolated instance. Concerns over media freedom and the need for the EU action echoed at various meetings, seminars, expert groups involving examples from more countries (such as excessive media concentration in Bulgaria, press regulation in the UK). Since 2010, there has been a visible shift to address more comprehensively the citizens' right to free expression and communication. Thus, the Commission criticism although based mainly on the conformity of the Hungarian media law with the AVMS Directive and

---

[26] Act No. 231/2001 of 17 May 2001 on Radio and Television Broadcasting and on Amendment to Other Acts, Section 31 (2) (available at: http://www.rrtv.cz/en/static/documents/act-231-2001/Act-on-RTV-broadcasting-reflecting-AVMSD.pdf; retrieved 5.11. 2013).

[27] Act CIV of 2010 on the Freedom of the Press and the Fundamental Rules on Media Content published on 9 November 2010 in Magyar Közlöny (Official Journal) and amended in March 2011; Article 13.

[28] Mertek Media Monitor (2013) *Kroes calls for more changes to Hungary's media laws* (available at: http://mediamonitor.ceu.hu/2013/03/kroes-calls-for-more-changes-to-hungarys-media-laws/; retrieved 15.10.2013).

the *acquis communautaire* in general (notably in relation to the obligation to offer balanced coverage applicable to all audiovisual media service providers) also transgressed towards the respect for the fundamental right to freedom of expression and information as enshrined in the Article 11 of the Charter, the Council of Europe's recommendations and the very essence of a possible interpretation and use of the new rules.

After a relatively long battle about the substance of media laws, the issue of fundamental rights, including the right to free expression and free media in Hungary returned again to the top of the EU policy agenda. On 11 March 2013, the Hungarian Parliament adopted the Fourth Amendment (CDLREF(2013)014) to the Fundamental Law (CDL-REF(2013)016 – consolidated version) that has been collectively reprimanded by various European institutions. The Venice Commission of the Council of Europe was requested to examine the amendment from the point of view of its compatibility with the Council of Europe's standards (Council of Europe, 2013) and the European Parliament adopted the *Resolution* of 3 July 2013 *on the situation of fundamental rights: standards and practices in Hungary* (European Parliament, 2013c). Both documents raise a number of issues (among others the recognition of churches, communist past, the protection of marriage) that are perceived as non-congruent with European standards on fundamental rights. Among them, the provisions are listed that ban political advertisements on commercial media channels during campaign seasons. These measures introduced by Article 5.1. of the Fourth Amendment to the Hungarian Constitution allow only public service media channels to provide political advertising during the electoral campaigns. Given the high popularity of commercial channels and quite centralised control over the PSM by NMHH, the expert opinions suggest that citizens' access to important and free political information may in this way be limited (Council of Europe, 2013).

Interestingly, the European Parliament framed its reasoning with the importance of "the Union's objective of upholding and promoting its values in its relations with the wider world, as set out in Article 3(4) TEU" and the specific obligation "for the Union's action on the international scene to be guided by the principles which inspired its creation, development and enlargement: democracy, the rule of law and the universality and indivisibility of human rights and fundamental freedoms (21(1) TEU)" (European Parliament, 2013c). A decline from these principles can not only lead to an erosion of internal integrity of the EU, but can possibly corroborate the credibility of the member states and of the Union in terms of its external action.

The 2013 Resolution of the European Parliament on *Freedom of press and media in the world* paralleled this approach stating: "the EU can only be credible on the global stage if press and media freedoms are safeguarded and respected within the Union itself" (European Parliament, 2013b). The EP also acknowledged "the general downward trend in the grading of the press and media freedom environments in various countries both within and outside Europe" and observed that "in recent years some media, notably in the EU, have come under scrutiny themselves for unethical and allegedly illegal behavior" (European Parliament, 2013b). Certainly any potential external action of the EU requires addressing problematic issues internally and demonstrating that the problems can be gradually solved. The Resolution also noticed that, while the EU addresses press and media freedom through several policies and programmes, it lacks a specific overall focus on the issue, as well as a coherent driving vision (European Parliament, 2013b). The DG Connect in response to this claim launched an initiative on *Increased involvement of the European Commission in ensuring respect towards media freedom and pluralism* that presupposes a follow-up action after several consultation processes in the area of media freedom and pluralism in 2014.[29] Both EP's resolutions enacted in 2013 urged the EU to play a more significant role in the candidate countries, as well as in relation to its immediate southern and eastern neighbourhood. The Resolution of 3 July 2013 specifically argued that similar obligations that are imposed on candidate countries under the Copenhagen criteria continue to apply to the member states and should therefore be assessed on a regular basis (European Parliament, 2013c).

3.8. Conclusion: A new approach towards the media and communication rights in the next EU enlargement

In terms of media-related issues, the EU accession process has evolved since 2004 into a more rigorous and comprehensive exercise. The European Commission has admitted that reasons for this shift stem from lessons learned from previous enlargements, in particular when it comes to the need to address the fundamentals first (European Commission, 2013b). 'The lessons' demonstrated certainly the scrappy and underdeveloped nature of benchmarks in the area of freedom of expression and the media,

[29] DG Connect (2013) *Media policy, media pluralism and media freedom* (available at: http://ec.europa.eu/dgs/connect/en/content/media-policy-media-pluralism-media-freedom; retrieved 31.12.2013).

but also a quite passive stance of the EU institutions largely accepting the prescribed and imagined course of action towards the progress ultimately reaching the point of accession. Post-accession developments however proved that the EU found itself in a more turbulent environment challenged by instances of excessive concentration of political and media business power (European Parliament, 2004, referring mainly to Berlusconi and Italian case), unethical media behaviour (European Parliament, 2013b, referring to News International's hacking phone scandal), and also some regressive developments in the new EU member states (e.g. European Parliament, 2013a, referring to the Hungarian media laws). Hence it became quite clear that the ongoing policy of conditionality will need to lay on more solid building blocks, in particular a common institutional blueprint (once missing) and common patterns of practices. To ensure the expected change is rooted deeply in a social environment and not easily corroborated by storms of fast-changing polarised politics, it seems essential that important normative values (including respect for freedom and pluralism of the media) are internalised at various levels of a social system and collectively shared. A corresponding observation can be found in the conclusions of the *Speak-up!2* conference organised by DG Enlargement in co-operation with the European Parliament in June 2013. The document emphasises that improving the situation in the candidate countries calls for the behavioural and cultural change in politics, the judiciary and the media itself (DG Enlargement, 2013c). In other words, equally important as the main policy instruments – the Strategy Papers and Progress Reports – seem to be support policies and soft measures offering solutions that help to remove barriers and improve the quality of free media performance.

Certainly, freedom of expression and the media has been more explicitly and intensely recognised by the EC and other EU institutions in the recent enlargement policy as a right and quality through which the political function of the media can be fulfilled. The geopolitical scope seems to be even more challenging than with the previous enlargements as the EU attempts to incorporate Turkey and the countries of the Western Balkans (including Albania, Bosnia and Herzegovina, Kosovo, Montenegro, Serbia, and the Former Yugoslav Republic of Macedonia) to complete the Stabilisation and Association Process. To this extent, the DG Enlargement has perceived freedom of expression as a key indicator of a country's readiness to become part of the EU. Independent and healthy media have been seen as vital watchdogs of political systems that are expected in turn to create the right conditions for operation of such media. Freedom of expression and the media has found various manifestations in problem areas echoed in several enlargement policy documents, including Communication from the Commission to the European Parliament and the Council *Enlargement Strategy and the Main Challenges* (European Commission, 2011, 2012c, 2013b). These are summarised in the table below:

Table 9: Media-related issues referred in selected DG Enlargement documents and Commission's Enlargement Strategy Communications under 'freedom of expression and the media'

Media-Related Issues Referred Under 'Freedom of Expression and the Media'	Selected DG Enlargement Documents (abbreviated titles)	Commission's Enlargement Startegy Communications
Impartiality and independence of the MRA	– EU Enlargement: Speaking out – EU Enlargement Fact Sheet: Safeguarding Freedom of Expression	– 2013–2014 Enlargement Strategy
Decriminalisation of defamation/ Avoiding prosecutions of journalists	– EU Enlargement: Speaking out	– 2012–2013; 2013–2014 Enlargement Strategy
Stronger and independent journalism	– EU Enlargement: Speaking out	– 2011–2012 Enlargement Strategy
Reform of public service broadcasting	– EU Enlargement: Speaking out – *Speak-up!2.* Conclusions – EU Enlargement Fact Sheet: Safeguarding Freedom of Expression	– 2011–2012; 2013–2014 Enlargement Strategy
Investigative reporting	– EU Enlargement: Speaking out – EU Enlargement Fact Sheet: Safeguarding Freedom of Expression	– 2011–2012; 2013–2014 Enlargement Strategy
Avoiding political interference into the media	– *Speak-up!2.* Conclusions	– 2011–2012; 2012–2013; 2013–2014 Enlargement Strategy

Addressing economic challenges (lack of ownership transparency and lack of fair completion)	– *Speak-up!2*. Conclusions – EU Enlargement Fact Sheet: Safeguarding Freedom of Expression	– 2011–2012; 2012–2013; 2013–2014 Enlargement Strategy
Protection of journalists	– *Speak-up!2*. Conclusions	– 2011–2012; 2012–2013; 2013–2014 Enlargement Strategy
Implementation of media regulation	– *Speak-up!2*. Conclusions	– 2011–2012; 2012–2013 Enlargement Strategy
Developing self-regulation	– *Speak-up!2*. Conclusions – EU Enlargement Fact Sheet: Safeguarding Freedom of Expression	– 2011–2012; 2013–2014 Enlargement Strategy
Avoiding self-censorship of journalists		– 2011–2012; 2012–2013; 2013–2014 Enlargement Strategy
Improving internal governance of media outlets	– *Speak-up!2*. Conclusions	

Sources: Elaborated on the basis of European Commission, 2011, 2012c, 2013b; DG Enlargement (2013a, 2013b, 2013c).

The studying of these documents opens a quite different perspective of the EU's assessment of freedom of expression and media-related issues, and thus also expectations from the candidate countries. One of the central points in these assessments is the institutional blueprint conceived through the values of impartiality and independence of the media regulatory authorities (MRA). In the previous monitoring exercise, the Commission paid attention mainly to the effectiveness, strength and capacities of the MRA which was closely connected with the implementation of audiovisual *acquis*. Various instances observed by the Commission and other institutions in the region, and a Hungarian regulatory approach in particular, resulted in paying closer attention to the MRA status, appointment procedures, and forms of political control and values that justify the MRA's special status among state institutions.

Defamation and libel laws were closely observed also before the 2004 enlargement, however greater attention was paid to legal measures and provisions themselves than a practice in courts. The DG Enlargement has drifted more towards ensuring that judges do not use state or political power to silence or self-censor journalists as has been already the case in some countries, including member state – Slovakia, for example. The reform of the PSM in transitional and post-transitional media systems has been a standard flag theme in the EU and pan-European media policies since the 1990s, while in the newest enlargement strategy a greater emphasis was put on the involvement of the EBU and co-operation with other PSMs in the EU to transfer the best practices and solutions, in particular financial autonomy and sustainability. The accentuation of a stronger, independent journalism and the role of investigative reporting has partly resulted from weak safeguards of journalistic autonomy in the region (including a lack of mature professional organisations), and partly from a broader flow of crisis in professional journalism generally, caused mainly by a drain of financial sources towards technological and legal investments.

Political interference and control of media performance has been of major importance in monitoring, as some media developments both in established and young member states, exposed deficiencies limiting the democratic functions of the media. Among various gates of such interference, the DG Enlargement considers the role of public and state-related advertising that may potentially support politically subservient media. Thus, transparent and non-discriminatory rules are needed to govern procuring public sector advertisements (DG Enlargement, 2013c). An interesting switch in comparison with previous enlargement assessments can be observed in the area of the economic performance of the media. While pre-2004 reports focused on the robustness of media landscapes, number of actors, and instruments encouraging foreign investments, the new approach emphasises challenges of informal economic pressure that can possibly silence the media and spread self-censorship (European Commission, 2013b; DG Enlargement, 2013c). These include at foremost the lack of media ownership transparency and lack of effective competition.

Again, the map of media-related issues covered by the DG Enlargement seems quite large and varied, yet the course of navigation focuses more clearly on the political and pro-democratic functions of the media, and where other values are tested (such as the economic competitiveness of the media), these are approached through the logic of the political system performance in which the communication media are seen to play a fundamental role. This transformed strategy is both outward and inward looking: externally, it sends the message that freedom of expression and the media belongs to fundamentals in terms of standards and rights to be fulfilled before EU accession. Internally, it poses a requirement of instant and constant self-observation of the EU member states themselves in order to maintain credibility in the politics of conditionality and with respect to improvement.

4. SHAPING A EUROPEAN AUDIOVISUAL LANDSCAPE: TWO DIMENSIONS OF AVMSD

4.1. An Introduction: eroding boundaries of 'audiovisual'

The EU has attributed a significant importance to the audiovisual sector for most than 30 years. The audiovisual policy was singled out from the broader media field for two reasons: first, justifications for regulating audiovisual media space were built on the Council of Europe's approach manifested in Article 10 of the ECHR. Second, it has been recognised that other media sectors (e.g. print and online press) could potentially develop their services without relying on publicly owned frequencies and regardless of boundaries, as long as member states did not impose limits on their activities. In addition however, audiovisual services and television in particular, were seen as strategic channels of communication practices that have a potential to generate a more cohesive European identity, European information space, and most importantly stimulate the cross-border internal market. Thus, the 'audiovisual strand' in the media policy is characterised by hard legal instruments (directives – TWF, AVMS) and clearly defined implementation and monitoring procedures.

The critics of harmonisation through the EU audiovisual policy however argue that the hard instruments aimed to 'commodify and commercialise' democratic, political and cultural functions of the media (Kaitatzi-Whitlock, 2008); while others more cautiously sustain that the audiovisual policy was underpinned also by cultural, political and democratic values (Ward, 2002; Humphreys, 2008). Moreover, in addition to recognising multiple media functions (although with various proportions), the EU audiovisual policy has amalgamated an external and internal EU dimension combined with national preferences. Jakubowicz (2011) observed that the EU audiovisual policy gradually evolved as a compromise between contrasting tendencies: for both economic and cultural reasons, the EU has sought in the WTO and GATS negotiations a safeguard for the ability of member states to protect their audiovisual markets. These external incentives resonated with internal objectives, as described above.

In response to the convergence and evolution of digital media landscapes, the adoption of the AVMS Directive widened and diversified the scope of the audiovisual regulation. At the same time, its primary focus has not been remodelled. In its first report on the application of the Directive, the Commission states: "The AVMSD is an internal market instrument that combines the right to provide audiovisual services with the right to freedom of expression and information and the protection of important public interest objectives" (European Commission, 2012d: 4). Thus, the AVMS Directive remains, at the foremost, the hard legal instrument for a free circulation of audiovisual media services, including on demand services. Its main objective is to harmonise the internal market for audiovisual media services, while the extent of harmonisation varies among specific problem areas that are designed in a complementary manner and synchronised. For instance, the rule of 'one member state jurisdiction' is promoted as a contribution to media pluralism in the Recital 34:

> In order to promote a strong, competitive and integrated European audiovisual industry and enhance media pluralism throughout the Union, only one Member State should have jurisdiction over an audiovisual media service provider (...) (European Parliament and the Council, 2010a).

Analogous complementary links may be identified in the case of media literacy (Recital 47), selfregulation and co-regulation (Recital 44), the right to information and wide access by the public to events of major importance for society (Recital 49), the right of persons with a disability and of an elderly to participate and be integrated in the social and cultural life of the Community (Recital 46). These examples demonstrate that the AVMS Directive not only accommodated various partial issues under the frames of the audiovisual policy, but integrated multiple rationales in one regulatory framework. Another question is however, how these 'added values' function in the Directive. The document certainly offers differentiated degrees of regulation combining rhetoric recognition (media literacy, media pluralism) with regulatory encouragement (promotion of European works by non-linear services) and regulatory obligation (broadcasting of European works by linear services). In addition, the AVMS Directive harmonises some concepts (e.g. advertising spot), whereas in other cases it does not significantly affect the ability of member states to define specific requirements concerning national circumstances and traditions (e.g. content harmful for minors) (European Commission, 2012d).

Hence hard economic and cultural (e.g. European quota) provisions are combined with soft instruments and measures responding to educational function of the media (media literacy), political/democratic function (media pluralism), cultural function (cultural diversity). It should be remembered that the Directive mainly serves to regulate the content, not audiovisual media structures and performance, although the content regulation might affect the latter. For example, thanks to the provision on free circulation of audiovisual media services, relevant providers may decide to register in another country of origin, than the country targeted with their offers.

In the convergence era the familiar policy framing building on the strategic importance of the audiovisual media has been extended to the converged media services. The change in language signals a change in the perception of a media reality: for decades, broadcasting has been heavily institutionalised and thus also more easily captured by policy thinking and regulation. In the elusive and ever-changing digital landscape, converged media services go out of a hand both in terms of conceptualisation and regulation. In this regard, the Commission sees its role in embracing and defining the services that are expected to meet certain qualities to satisfy European users' needs. On this point, the Green Paper: *Preparing for a Fully Converged Audiovisual World: Growth, Creation and Values* asserts: "The Commission's vision is to seize the opportunity of this changing technological environment to ensure the widest possible access to European diversified content for all Europeans and, the widest choice of high quality offers" (European Commission, 2013a: 3).

While convergence and technological progress generate greater media choice, they also induce critical challenges. The audiovisual media constitute a complex landscape, access to which is increasingly navigated through digital intermediaries affecting the findability of the audiovisual content with particular characteristics. Thus, the findability very much depends on the users' ability to identify the appropriate access website/platform allowing them to retrieve the audiovisual content which meets the users communication needs, including an appetite for diversity and quality. How much these reflect a public value or balance various functions the media play in societies, is an open question. Various forms of knowledge inequality (e.g. political, cultural) may rise as a result of voluntary consumption decisions, or contractual conditions the users encounter with providers. To what extent these should be subject to corrective regulatory policies, will be reflected in the forthcoming policy considerations of the EU on the converged audiovisual world.

Yet, in the converged media landscape it seems increasingly difficult to delineate and define audiovisual media services that fall under the scope of the AVMS Directive. The Recital 22 of the Directive specifies that these are the services that "cover mass media in their function to inform, entertain and educate the general public, and should include audiovisual commercial communication but should exclude any form of private correspondence" (European Parliament and the Council, 2010a). In addition Recital 23 states that "the term 'audiovisual' should refer to moving images with or without sound, thus including silent films but not covering audio transmission or radio services" (European Parliament and the Council, 2010a). With regards to non-linear or on-demand audiovisual media services, the Directive however provides further explanation emphasising a 'TV-like' character of these services:

> It is characteristic of on-demand audiovisual media services that they are 'television-like', i.e. that they compete for the same audience as television broadcasts, and the nature and the means of access to the service would lead the user reasonably to expect regulatory protection within the scope of this Directive (European Parliament and the Council, 2010a, Recital 24).

Although a vast number of audiovisual media services can be more or less easily identified according to these categorisations, proliferating developments of hybrid offerings constantly erode the boundaries between 'press-like' and 'TV-like' services. What makes them fundamentally different? And if the difference is diminishing, why do 'press-like' services fall under divergent regulatory patterns? And why e.g. couldn't the PSM offer 'press-like' services? The Directive provides plenty of examples of services that are excluded from the scope of the regulation listing among them: "all services the principal purpose of which is not the provision of programmes, i.e. where any audiovisual content is merely incidental to the service and not its principal purpose" (Recital 22); "websites that contain audiovisual elements only in an ancillary manner" (Recital 22); "audio transmission or radio services" (Recital 23); "electronic versions of newspapers and magazines" (Recital 28). Thus, the boundaries in the definition are rather provided through enumerating examples than the definition itself. The inner boundary between linear and non-linear services falling under a different degree of the regulation, may raise similar concerns (Woods, 2008: 150).

The potential gaps and uncertainties stem very much from the changing and converging nature of the audiovisual sector. Though embracing constantly a larger territory of overlapping issues, the EU audiovisual policy – for the most part of its history – concentrated on two axes: on the one hand – free circulation of audiovisual media services within the EU internal market; on the other hand – cultural protection of the EU audiovisual media services. These two dimensions will be studied in the next sections of this chapter with respect to policy harmonisation in the CEE countries.

4.2. European and independent works

Despite a relatively weak cultural proximity within the EU and an anemic transnational dimension of the media systems, the EU has shown a firm regulatory determination in the protection of European cultural expressions and cultural diversity through European audiovisual contents. Governed by the logic of competitiveness in a global environment, cultural diversity has mainly been conceptualised and operationalised as the competitiveness of European ideas, cultures, languages – and most crucially – the media and communication industries as a whole, on the global scene. Thus, supra-national content rules have been defined and used to protect the common European media space from foreign (mainly US) imports and to support European dominant media players. In this sense, the concept of cultural diversity justified measures concerning European works and independent production in the AVMS Directive. The promotion of European works, co-productions and works made by independent producers has been increasingly perceived and interpreted as an essential contribution to nurturing of the cultural diversity both within and outside Europe, as a pertinent way of correcting the proportions between media representations of cultures on a global scale (Klimkiewicz, 2009b).

In regulatory terms, the defining concept under which the European cultural expressions and representations are protected in the audiovisual media is European works. What does this expression mean? What makes the works European – the place of production or other distinctive characteristics? The AVMSD (and earlier TWF Directive) in the Article 1 (n) recognises these services as works originating in one of the member states. Works originating in states which are not members of the EU but are party to the Council of Europe's Convention on Transfrontier Television (ECTT) can also be considered 'European works'. Works have to be "mainly made with authors and workers residing in one or more of the States referred to in those provisions" (European Parliament and the Council, 2010a). In addition, also works co-produced within the framework of agreements related to the audiovisual sector concluded between the Union and third countries can be acknowledged as 'European works'. Finally, works that are produced within

> the framework of bilateral co-production agreements concluded between Member States and third countries shall be deemed to be European works provided that the co-producers from the Union supply a majority share of the total cost of production and that the production is not controlled by one or more producers established outside the territory of the Member States (European Parliament and the Council, 2010a).

Though this rich definition deals with multiple categories of works, the main criterion by which they are perceived as 'European' is the place of their production or a location of residence of their authors and workers involved. No other distinctive characteristics are involved, no any specific conditions refer to a European dimension in the content itself. Shalini Venturelli observes that "Clearly, none of these provisions accounts for the crucial distinction between audiovisual programming integrated into the multinational production and distribution chain, and programmes that are independent of this structure" (Venturelli, 1998: 205). In other words, the protection of what is defined as 'European works' in the AVMS Directive does not ensure by definition the desired representation of European cultures. Such a representation can indirectly result from the cultural embeddedness of producers and expectation of audiences, but is not conditionally linked with the definition per se.

The Recital 32 of the Directive enables member states to establish a more detailed definition of European works for media service providers under their jurisdiction, in compliance with Union law and the objectives of the Directive. Consequently, e.g. France further specifies the concept of 'European work' (Decree n° 90–66) by stating that, there is required, for each film, a minimum proportion of authors and workers to be residing in the European States concerned (Attentional, 2011a: 21). In addition, under French law, the producer not only needs to be established in one of those States, but also to have managers and a majority of its directors being nationals from those States (Attentional, 2011a: 21). Even with all these qualifications, the 'European' dimension of European works refers mainly to the nationality and place of residence of media professionals involved in the content production. In this way, it seems to protect not the cultural expressions of the European works per se, but the organisational and professional framework of their production.

With an exception of the Czech Republic, the other Central European countries introduced provisions on European works in their media or broadcasting laws before the formal start of pre-accession monitoring in 1997. The AVMSD was designed already within the EU in a new geographical shape with young members states from Central and Eastern

Europe. Although nothing signalled possible implementation problems, already in the pre-accession monitoring, the Regular Reports underlined repeatedly the institutional weakness of regulatory bodies responsible for implementation and monitoring of the Directive. Insufficient capacities of the regulatory bodies, political pressures and communication deficit led to serious delays in the implementation of the AVMS Directive in the case of Poland and Slovakia (in Poland at the end of 2012 and Slovakia at the beginning of 2013), while in the case of Hungary concerns were raised by the Commission about the political control over the National Media and Communications Authority that was established on basis of media laws passed in 2010. The communication deficit in the case of Poland led to the weak ability of the regulatory body (KRRiT – National Broadcasting Council) to translate successfully the objectives of the Directive to the mainstream media, some of which reported the implementation of the Directive as an "attempt to regulate the Internet". On the other hand, the implementation of the consolidated version of AVMSD served the Hungarian policy-makers as a strong argument for imposing the controversial practice of media outlets registration which has later been abandoned. Ultimately, the rules on registration and authorisation of media service providers were amended to comply with the Directive, allowing media service providers to register with the regulatory agency within 60 days of launching their services, rather than prior to doing so (Freedom House, 2013). These mismatches of reasons behind the national implementation of the EU regulation prove that in addition to simple transposition of rules within a given time frame, a decisive role has been played and continues to be played by political culture and political involvement, as well as by the ability or inability of regulatory bodies to build more durable and closer ties with media users.

4.2.1. A majority proportion of European works: Article 16

A quota system for European works was established in Article 4 of the Television without Frontiers Directive (European Council, 1989). The AVMS Directive maintained largely the wording of this Article in Article 16 (1):

> Member States shall ensure, where practicable and by appropriate means, that broadcasters reserve for European works a majority proportion of their transmission time, excluding the time allotted to news, sports events, games, advertising, teletext services and teleshopping. This proportion, having regard to the broadcaster's informational, educational, cultural and entertainment responsi-

bilities to its viewing public, should be achieved progressively, on the basis of suitable criteria (European Parliament and the Council, 2010a).

Although the quota system was quite contentious from its onset (McGoonagle, 2008: 187), a gradual consensus on the rules evolved among stakeholders and the Commission asserted a satisfactory progress in its following reports on the application of EU works promotion. Yet the widening of the AVMS Directive's scope to non-linear audiovisual media services brought far less agreement both among the stakeholders and member states. Peter Humphreys noticed that "France sought for the quotas to be extended to on-demand services, while others like the UK resisted such change" (Humphreys, 2008: 163). Ultimately, a compromise has been reached among the member states entailing that providers of on-demand services shall promote the production of and access to European works (Article 13, European Parliament and the Council, 2010a). As will be shown in the next section of this chapter, many countries, among them all the CEE member states studied empirically in this volume, opted for quotas in the case of on-demand services, thus, in fact applying the 'French solution'.

The member states are obliged to report on the implementation of Article 16 and 17 within their jurisdictions biannually. The reports on the application of Article 13 are due in each four years. The largest body of data generated in the reporting process is primarily statistical, although other factors influencing different national outcomes of implementation are also taken into consideration. These include: a legal analysis, monitoring and sanctions. In its First Report on the Application of the AVMS Directive, the Commission demonstrated that throughout the EU the average broadcasting time for European works increased from 62.6% in 2007 to 63.2% in 2008. Between 2005 and 2008 it remained stable at a satisfactory level (European Commission, 2012d: 6). In 2009, the average transmission time dedicated to European works by all reported channels in the EU-27 slightly increased to 63.8% and in 2010 – to 64.3% (European Commission, 2012e). Comparing the situation in particular member states, the average share of transmission time devoted to European works during the reference period varied between 44% (Ireland) and 83% (Hungary) in 2009 and between 47.4% (Slovenia and UK) and 81% (Hungary) in 2010 (European Commission, 2012e: 9). Interestingly, young CEE member states are both among the countries with the lowest score (Slovenia) as well as among the countries with the highest score (Hungary). Václav Štetka observes that in 2004, just after the accession, the new member states achieved comparable results to those reached by the EU-15 countries (Štetka, 2010). It seems, however, important to observe the dynamics of the average share of transmission time devoted to European works in the CEE countries. The table and figure below present the dynamics of these data between 2005–2010 in the Czech Republic, Hungary, Poland and Slovakia.

Table 10: The average share of transmission time devoted to European works in the CEE member states between 2005–2010 (in %)

	2005	2006	2007	2008	2009	2010
CZECH REPUBLIC	62.9	79.9	64.3	65.9	64.1	58.1
HUNGARY	71.9	76.9	68.5	75.3	83.0	81.0
POLAND	80.2	81.1	85	83.1	78.4	78.4
SLOVAKIA	63.8	62.3	66.5	67.3	71.7	68.2

Source: European Commission (2008; 2012g).

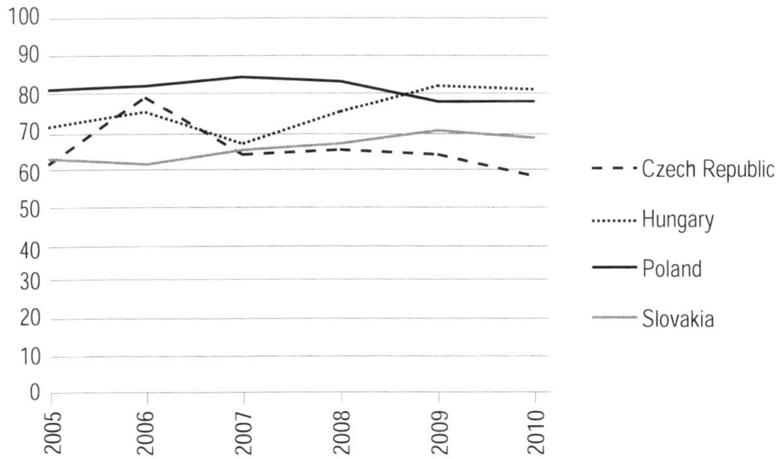

Figure 5: The average share of transmission time devoted to European works in the CEE member states between 2005–2010

Source: Elaborated on the basis of the European Commission (2008; 2012g).

As can be seen from the table and figure presented, there is no unilateral trend of progress or decrease among the countries studied. Two countries – Slovakia and Hungary witnessed a growth of transmission time devoted to European works, while Poland experienced a slight drop and the Czech Republic also a more visible decrease. In comparison to the average EU-27 shares in 2009 and 2010, all CEE countries demonstrated a higher share than the EU average in 2009 and only the Czech Republic displayed a lower share in 2010 (58.1%). The high and relatively stable share of European works especially in Poland and Hungary (around 75–80%) gives an impression that a crucial portion of audiovisual production offered by the channels covered in the monitoring originates in the EU countries.

These satisfactory results have to be put in a broader context of media structural developments, legal prerequisites and regulatory choices. First of all, it is worth seeing, how many channels have surpassed the required threshold of 50% and how many failed to reach that level. The table below illustrates the number of channels in these two opposite categories.

Table 11: The number of channels failing to achieve and complying with the Article 16 in 2010

	Identified channels	**Channels covered by Article 16 (% of identified channels)**	**The number of TV channels failing to achieve the majority proportion required by Artitcle 16 (in %)**	**The number of channels complying with the majority proportion required by Article 16 (in %)**
CZECH REPUBLIC	77	67 (87%)	32 (47.9%)	35 (52.1%)
HUNGARY	39	25 (64.1%)	3 (12%)	22 (88%)
POLAND	73	58 (79.1%)	10 (17.0%)	48 (83%)
SLOVAKIA	34	26 (82.3%)	5 (19.2%)	21 (80.8%)

Sources: European Commission (2012h).

The table demonstrates that in 2010, in the two countries with the highest shares of European works (Poland and Hungary) the number of channels failing to achieve the required threshold was relatively low (in the case of Poland – 17%, in the case of Hungary – 12%). On the contrary, in the Czech Republic the number of channels elapsing the required portion of the European production reached a remarkable high level (32 channels; 47%). Interestingly enough, many of these channels do not target Czech audiences, but rather viewers in neighbouring countries (e.g. in Hungary: *Comedy Central Hungary, HBO HU, MTV Hungary*; in Poland: *Comedy Central Poland, HBO2 PL, HBO Comedy Poland, HBO PL, MTV Polska*) (European Commission, 2012h). A brief look at these data reveals that more open TV landscapes and liberal approach to granting licences to foreign broadcasters tend to be associated with lower shares of transmission time devoted to European works.

Another important aspect to mention in this regard are legal prerequisites, such as the definitions of European works in terms of inclusion or exclusion of particular programme types. Total transmission time qualifying for the application of the European quota excludes in the AVMS Directive "the time alloted to news, sports events, games, advertising, teletext services and teleshopping" (Article 16 (1); the European Parliament and the Council, 2010a). Many member states have transposed the definition directly into the national legislation in a form identical or equivalent to the Directive. These include Poland, Slovakia and the Czech Republic. On the contrary, Hungary has opted in the past for a broader definition (more programmes included). This had a direct impact on the results achieved in measuring the share of European works, because the programmes excluded from narrow definitions are usually produced domestically, making it more difficult for broadcasters to comply (Attentional, 2011a: 22). Hungary did not exclude any programmes from the annual transmission time in 2009 and 2010, and it is worth recalling in this context that Hungary reached the highest shares of European works in 2009 and 2010 among all 27 EU member states. In these cases – the 50% requirement was based on the total amount of broadcasting time, making it easier for broadcasters to achieve a majority proportion of European works (Attentional, 2011a: 23). Substantial changes in this practice were introduced with the enforcement of the Act CLXXXV on Media Services and Mass Media.[1] Under Article 22 (7) the qualifying transmission time excludes: "news programmes, sports programmes, games, advertisements, teleshopping, political advertisements, public service announcements, sponsorship communications, public service advertisements and the noninteractive teletext".

Another affecting provision is the 'where practicable' clause.[2] Despite attempts to modify and clarify the obligations of broadcasters through

[1] Act CLXXXV of 2010 on Media Services and Mass Media published on 31 December 2010 in Magyar Közlöny (Official Journal) and amended in March 2011.

[2] "Member States shall ensure, where practicable and by appropriate means, that broadcasters reserve for European works a majority proportion of their transmission time (...) (Article 16 (1), European Parliament and the Council, 2010a).

removing the phrase 'where practicable', the main institutional players involved in the following modernisations of the Directive opted for essentially unchanged wording (McGoonagle, 2008). This has resulted in various practices among the member states opening the possibilities for the more or less flexible approach used by the national regulatory agencies. Some of the countries decided to define under what conditions a lower proportion will be accepted. In the case of Poland, a lower proportion for the first transmission year of a new broadcaster, and lower thresholds for pay-TV and thematic channels were established in Article 15 (4) of the 1992 Broadcasting Act. In addition, a possibility of lower shares applies also to programme services that are intended for national or ethnic minorities and a community using a regional language, as well as programme services transmitted solely via information and communication technology systems.[3] Likewise, in Slovakia, national legislation allows the regulator to set a lower proportion in licences for the first-time holders of licence and for broadcasters of monothematic (special interest) programme services (Attentional, 2011a: 25).[4] The regulatory agency can also determine a gradual increase of the required share depending on the economic situation of the broadcaster and accessibility of European works.[5] In Hungary, the provisions on European quotas do not apply to "the local media service with the exception of community media service"[6]; "the media service which broadcasts its service exclusively in a language other than the languages of the Member States of the European Union"[7] and "the media service which is exclusively broadcasted in countries outside of the European Union".[8] The Czech Republic seems to offer the most flexible rules in this regard as the 2001 Act on Radio and Television Broadcasting contains only a general reference to 'where practicable' and in addition, provides categories of broadcasters that are exempted from an obligation to reserve a majority of transmission time

[3] 1992 Broadcasting Act (Ustawa o Radiofonii i Telewizji) adopted on 29 December, 1992, Official Journal 1993, No. 7, item 34, as amended (available at: http://www.krrit.gov.pl/Data/Files/_public/Portals/0/angielska/Documents/Regulations/broadcasting_act_28022013.pdf; retrieved 29.07.2013).

[4] Act No 308 of 14 September 2000 Coll. on Broadcasting and Retransmission (as amended), Article 23(2). (available at: http://www.rvr.sk/_cms/data/modules/download/1364909855_zakon_308-2000_ucinny_2013-01-01.pdf; retrieved 5.11.2013).

[5] Ibidem.

[6] Article 22 (1) d, Act CLXXXV of 2010 on Media Services and Mass Media published on 31 December 2010 in Magyar Közlöny (Official Journal) and amended in March 2011.

[7] Article 22 (1) c, Act CLXXXV of 2010 on Media Services and Mass Media published on 31 December 2010 in Magyar Közlöny (Official Journal) and amended in March 2011.

[8] Article 22 (1) e, Act CLXXXV of 2010 on Media Services and Mass Media published on 31 December 2010 in Magyar Közlöny (Official Journal) and amended in March 2011.

to European works. In addition to operators of local broadcasting, also broadcasters primarily aiming at non-Czech and non-EU audiences are exempted from the European quotas:

> The obligations of the television broadcaster set out in Sections 42 to 44 hereof shall not apply to television broadcasters whose broadcasting is intended exclusively for reception outside the Czech Republic and outside the territory of the Member States of the European Communities, which television broadcasting is not directly or indirectly received by the public in the Czech Republic or in any of the Member States of the European Communities[9]

It is worth mentioning that the application of European quotas by linear broadcasters is also affected by schedule time requirements. For example, in Hungary, the broadcasters must ensure that relevant proportions of European works are broadcasted during the transmission time of the different media services between 5.00 a.m. and 12.00 p.m.[10]

Analysing the European quota policy in context of the television scene in the Czech Republic, Václav Štetka (2010) argues that the fact that the Directive does not distinguish between domestic and non-domestic European programmes in its definition of European works, enables the broadcasters to comply with the provisions of Article 16 without devoting even a minute to programmes from another European country. Accordingly, the Commission's report *Promotion of European works in EU scheduled and on-demand audiovisual media services* (European Commission, 2012e: 9) observes that although the rule on promotion of European works in linear services is generally working well, it has "a limited effect on the circulation of programmes throughout the EU as it does not ensure the distribution of non-domestic European works".

This challenge is strengthened by the fact that some national regulatory models use quotas for national production or works produced originally in a national language, while any provisions on non-domestic European production are relatively rare. The Recital 70 of the AVMS Directive invites member states to implement Article 16 in such a way that broadcasters are encouraged to include an adequate share of co-produced European works or of European works of non-domestic origin (European Parliament and the Council, 2010a). Notwithstanding, the proportion of non-domestic European works has still been low and made up only 8.1 %

[9] Act No. 231/2001 of 17 May 2001 on Radio and Television Broadcasting and on Amendment to Other Acts, Section 45 (2) (available at: http://www.rrtv.cz/en/static/documents/act-231-2001/Act-on-RTV-broadcasting-reflecting-AVMSD.pdf; retrieved 5.11.2013).

[10] Article 22 (5), Article 22(1) e, Act CLXXXV of 2010 on Media Services...

of the total qualifying transmission time in 2010 (Attentional, 2011a: 11). Even though in the young EU member states non-domestic European works seem to be represented more prominently than in old member states (13.5% vs. 6.4%) (Attentional, 2011a: 11–12), legal implementation of Article 16 is in some countries paired with the protection of nationally produced content, but not a requirement of a relevant proportion of non-domestic European works. In 2009, the European Court of Justice confirmed that member states may adopt measures to defend and promote one or several official languages as part of their cultural policy.[11] The table below offers comparison of rules promoting national works or works in national languages as implemented in national broadcasting laws in the Czech Republic, Hungary, Poland and Slovakia.

Table 12: Legal provisions in national broadcasting laws aiming to protect national works or works produced in national languages in the Czech Republic, Hungary, Poland and Slovakia

Country	**Existence of quota system**	**Protection/promotion of national works**	**Definition of national works**	**Legal basis**
CZECH REPUBLIC	NO	–	–	–
HUNGARY	YES	Article 20 (1): The media service provider – shall allocate over one-third of its transmission time to broadcasting Hungarian works; – shall allocate at least eight percent of its transmission time to broadcasting Hun. works that were ordered from an independent production company.	Article 203 (37) 'Hungarian works' shall mean: – works originally made in the Hungarian language in their entirety; – works originally made in the majority in Hungarian.	Act CLXXXV of 2010 on Media Services and Mass Media, as amended

[11] Case C-222/07, UTECA, 5.03.2009. (European Commission, 2012d: 6).

HUNGARY	YES	Article 20 (2) At least ten percent (of the total length of the programmes made available in a given calendar year in the form of on-demand audiovisual media services) shall be Hungarian works. Article 20 (3) The public media service provider shall be obliged to allocate over half of its annual transmission time to broadcasting Hungarian works.	– works in which subject matter concerns the life or culture of the given nationality in Hungary.	
POLAND	YES	Article 15 (1) TV broadcasters shall reserve at least 33% of their quarterly transmission time for programmes originally produced in the Polish language, excluding news, advertising, teleshopping, sports events, teletext services and games	Article 4 (14) ‘Programmes originally produced in the Polish language’ shall mean: a programme which meets the criteria of ‘European work’, which has been produced on the basis of a script written originally in the Polish language and first registered in the Polish language	1992 Broadcasting Act adopted on 29 December, 1992, as amended
SLOVAKIA	NO (other measures at place)	Article 16 (3) The broadcasters are required to ensure the use of a national official language, the languages of national minorities and foreign languages in accordance with special provisions	–	Act No. 308 of 14 September 2000 Coll. on Broadcasting and Retransmission (as amended)

Sources: Elaborated on the basis of national broadcasting laws in the Czech Republic, Hungary, Poland and Slovakia as quoted in the table.

The table demonstrates that national provisions with the effect of promoting national works decidedly vary from a country to country. The Czech Republic does not impose any such measures in its broadcasting law, while Slovakia requires from broadcasters to use the official national language in accordance with other special provisions. Both Poland and Hungary apply a fairly similar quota system to promote national works. The broadcasters are obliged to reserve one third of their transmission time to national works in Hungary, while 33% in Poland. The differences can be observed with regards to the definition of 'Hungarian works' in Hungary (these may also include works produced in other languages provided that they concern the life and culture of nationalities in Hungary) and 'programmes originally produced in the Polish language' (referring to 'European works' originally registered in the Polish language and produced on basis of the script in the Polish language). Although implying a direct causal link between the legal promotion of national works and significant share of European works may be too far-reaching, the statistical data show that the largest share of European works in 2005–2010 was achieved in Poland and Hungary – the countries that used the quota system for the support of national works.

The European Commission has repeatedly proclaimed that the effort to promote European culture through the policy on European works has been successful. To the certain extent, this success materialises in statistical results and the lasting (although not necessarily enthusiastic) support of stakeholders. The CEE countries have proved to meet the quota requirements comfortably above the EU average, but varied country outcomes seem to depend on additional factors: licencing policies, definition of European works, more or less flexible treatment of the 'where practicable' clause, and measures on national works. The positive trends – reported in various EU policy documents – have been clearly constrained by several limits. First, Karol Jakubowicz (2011: 306) notices that despite the quota policy, there has been greater preference for US-originated content than non-domestic European works, and a clear preference for domestic and national over non-domestic content. Second, Tarlach McGoonagle pays attention to drawing general conclusions without analysing the substance of content. In other words, the statistical and quantitative data offer comfortable generalisations, but tell us little about the effectiveness of the quota policy at the level of content and stimulation of cultural creativity (McGoonagle, 2008: 202). The new reporting template being used since 2010, has included also "linear and non-linear content analysis" (Attentional 2011a; 2011b), but this did not provide a comprehensive pattern for studying the content in terms of its focus, cultural dimension, and cultural representation, but instead offered a quantitative viewing data and reference to a genre category. Actual viewing preferences (use, exposure) is certainly an important dimension completing the data on a mere transmission (supply), and should be part of the regular monitoring. But sufficient understanding of how the cultural aims of the audiovisual policy have been met through the implementing of a quantitative quota needs an analysis of qualitative characteristics of the content.

4.2.2. European works created by independent producers and recent works: Article 17

In addition to promotion of European works at a general level, the AVMS Directive protects European works produced by independent producers. Under Article 17 of the Directive

> Member States shall ensure, where practicable and by appropriate means, that broadcasters reserve at least 10% of their transmission time, excluding the time allotted to news, sports events, games, advertising, teletext services and teleshopping, or alternately, at the discretion of the Member State, at least 10% of their programming budget, for European works created by producers who are independent of broadcasters (European Parliament and the Council, 2010a).

Such a proportion must be achieved by earmarking an adequate proportion for recent works – that are the works transmitted within 5 years of their production. The Directive does not explain how the term "adequate proportion" has to be understood by member states. In consequence, some of the member states have merely transposed the AVMSD wording without interpretations (among them Slovakia), some defined the minimum proportions that broadcasters are obliged to reserve for recent works (among them Poland and Czech Republic) and some have required the entire proportion of works created by independent producers to be recent (among them Hungary). The table below summarises this large variety among the CEE member states.

Table 13: Provisions on European works created by independent producers in the Czech Republic, Hungary, Poland and Slovakia

Country	Provisions on independent works	Provisions on recent works	Legal basis
CZECH REPUBLIC	10% of Qualifying Transmission Time or 10% of programming budget	At least 10% of the amount of transmission time dedicated to Independent Production shall be recent	Section 43 Act No. 231/2001 of 17 May 2001 on Radio and Television Broadcasting and on Amendment to Other Acts
HUNGARY	10% of Qualifying Transmission Time	All recent works	Article 20 (1) Act CLXXXV of 2010 on Media Services and Mass Media, as amended
POLAND	10% of Qualifying Transmission Time	Majority of recent works	Article 15a 1992 Broadcasting Act adopted on 29 December, 1992, as amended
SLOVAKIA	Choice between 10% of Qualifying Transmission Time or 10% of programming budget Public Service Broadcaster: 20%	Appropriate share of recent works	Article 25 (1), (2) and (3) Act No. 308 of 14 September 2000 Coll. on Broadcasting and Retransmission (as amended)

Sources: Elaborated on the basis of national broadcasting laws in the Czech Republic, Hungary, Poland and Slovakia as quoted in the table.

Article 17 of the Directive establishes two alternative conditions for European works created by independent producers: broadcasters may reserve at least 10% of either transmission time or programming budget for independent productions. For the reason that the member states can deliberately choose between these two alternatives, the national regulatory responses have varied again. Some of the member states have chosen to apply the 10% proportion of transmission time (among them Hungary and Poland), some offered a choice between transmission time or programming budget (among them the Czech Republic and Slovakia). Until 31 December 2010, Hungary was the only country to apply both criteria to all channels (Attentional, 2011a: 32). This has changed, however, with the adoption of the 2010 Act CLXXXV on Media Services and Mass Media.

Some divergence can also be observed with regard to the definition of ‘independent producer’. Recital 71 of the Directive proposes member states to take into consideration certain criteria that enable to define ‘independent producer’. These include: “the ownership of the production company, the amount of programmes supplied to the same broadcaster and the ownership of secondary rights” (European Parliament and the Council, 2010a). Although some member states did not introduce any definition and some used in their definition only one criterion proposed in the AVMS Directive, all CEE member states employed more than one criterion to define ‘independent producer’. As can be seen from the table below, most commonly used criterion for the definition is ownership and ability to control the producer through various forms of ownership ties. All country definitions refer to this criterion. In addition, the Czech Republic adopted the criterion of the programme supply, Poland and Hungary the criterion of executive employees bounds and Slovakia the criterion to exercise creative control over production.

Table 14: Definitions of ‘independent producer’ in the Czech Republic, Hungary, Poland and Slovakia

Country	Terms applied	Capacities of ‘Independent producer’	Legal basis
CZECH REPUBLIC	INDEPENDENT PRODUCER	– not interconnected with a TV broadcaster in property terms, or – whose supply of works to a single television broadcaster does not exceed 90% of its total production over 3 years – not interconnected through a person holding voting rights or an ownership interest	Section 43 Act No. 231/2001 of 17 May 2001 on Radio and Television Broadcasting and on Amendment to Other Acts

HUNGARY	INDEPENDENT PRODUCTION COMPANY	– no interconnectedness over the owner with a qualifying holding (direct or indirect shareholding) – executive employees or any of their close relatives not be bound by a work-related relationship	Article 203 (12) Act CLXXXV of 2010 on Media Services and Mass Media, as amended
POLAND	PRODUCER INDEPENDENT OF A GIVEN BROADCASTER	– not bound by employment relation with the given broadcaster – not a broadcaster itself – holds no stake in the broadcaster's organisation, and in which neither the broadcaster nor any of its subsidiaries nor any companies associated in the same group hold a stake – governing board members are not bound by employment relation with the given broadcaster and are not broadcasters themselves	Article 4 (26) 1992 Broadcasting Act adopted on 29 December, 1992, as amended
SLOVAKIA	INDEPENDENT PRODUCTION/ INDEPENDENT PRODUCER	– has capacity to exercise control over authors, production and equipment facilities used in the production and not influenced by the broadcaster – not interconnected through ownership with the broadcaster – independent production are not programmes linked directly to broadcasting activities such as news, live transmissions of sporting events, games, advertising, teletext and teleshopping	Article 24, Article 26 Act No. 308 of 14 September 2000 Coll. on Broadcasting and Retransmission (as amended)

Sources: Elaborated on the basis of national broadcasting laws in the Czech Republic, Hungary, Poland and Slovakia as quoted in the table.

The EU-average proportion reserved for independent productions broadcast by all reported channels in the member states was 34.1% in 2009 and 33.8% in 2010 (European Commission, 2012e:10). This represents a visible decrease in comparison with the previous period. Independent works seem to be more prominent in old and large member states than in young and small (Attentional, 2011a). The table and figure below show that the share of independent works varies also across the CEE member states. In 2010, Hungary achieved the highest proportion – 42.5%, while the Czech Republic the lowest share – 26%.

Table 15: The average share of transmission time devoted to European works by independent producers in the CEE member states between 2005–2010 (in %)

	2005	**2006**	**2007**	**2008**	**2009**	**2010**
CZECH REPUBLIC	33.9	35.0	32.2	40.7	30.9	26.0
HUNGARY	43.4	53.9	39.7	41.8	42.9	42.5
POLAND	26.7	26.0	25.0	29.0	31.0	30.8
SLOVAKIA	25.4	26.0	24.0	23.8	29.0	27.6

Source: European Commission (2008; 2012g).

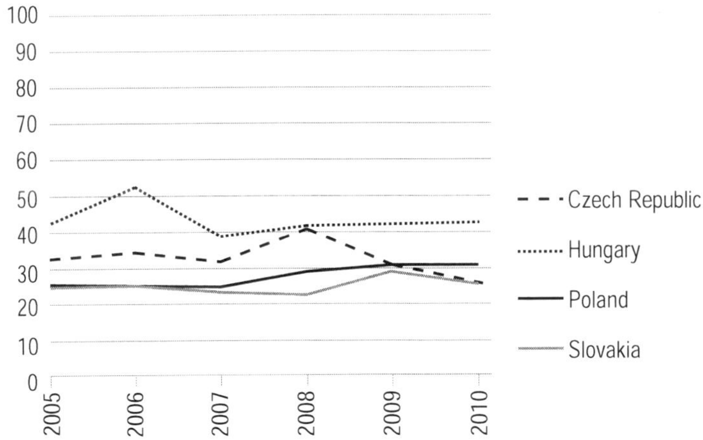

Figure 6: The average share of transmission time devoted to European works by independent producers in the CEE member states between 2005–2010

Source: Elaborated on the basis of the European Commission (2008; 2012g).

The share of independent works slightly increased in Poland and Slovakia; decreased in the Czech Republic and diverged in Hungary between 2005–2010. Given that a declining trend with respect to the level achieved in 2007 was reported by the Commission (European Commission, 2012e: 12) for the EU, only the Czech Republic represents a congruent trend with these developments. On the other hand, only Hungary demonstrates a proportion of independent works above the EU average, the remaining countries (the Czech Republic, Poland and Slovakia) do achieve lower shares than the EU average.

4.2.3. Promotion of European works in on-demand audiovisual services: Article 13

The promotion of European works has always been seen as one of the essential AVMSD provisions, that needs to be extended to on-demand audiovisual services. Recital 69 of the Directive provides justification for this extension claiming that "on-demand audiovisual services have the potential to partially replace television broadcasting", therefore they should promote the production and distribution of European works (European Parliament and the Council, 2010a). On the other hand, Recital 58 states that "on-demand audiovisual services are different from television broadcasting with regard to the choice and control the user can exercise (...)". This justifies requirement of a lighter regulation of audiovisual media services (European Parliament and the Council, 2010a). These two regulatory guidelines are reflected in the Article 13 (1):

> Member States shall ensure that on-demand audiovisual media services provided by media service providers under their jurisdiction promote, where practicable and by appropriate means, the production of and access to European works. Such promotion could relate, inter alia, to the financial contribution made by such services to the production and rights acquisition of European works or to the share and/or prominence of European works in the catalogue of programmes offered by the on-demand audiovisual media service (European Parliament and the Council, 2010a).

Article 13 (2) sets reporting obligations for member states to report every four years on the application of Article 13. The deadline for the first reporting period was established as of 19 December 2011 in the AVMSD. Although by 2010, a majority of the member states have transposed Article 13 into their national legislation, some CEE member states did so later (Poland and Slovakia). Thus, the data on on-demand audiovisual services collected from national authorities for the *Study on the implementation of the provisions of the Audiovisual Media Services Directive concerning the promotion of European works in audiovisual media services* (Attentional, 2011a; 2011b) and the Commission Staff Working Document (European Commission, 2012f) are fairly uneven and description of relevant promotion practices in some member states virtually missing. Moreover, the legal analysis concerning the national implementation of obligations for the on-demand media services to promote European works seems to be very incomplete. The table below seeks to fill these gaps and offer a comparison of relevant measures in the CEE member states on the basis of the most recent legal rules.

Table 16: Legal obligations of providers of on-demand audiovisual services with regard to promotion of European works in the Czech Republic, Hungary, Poland and Slovakia

Country	Type of obligation	Obligations of providers of on-demand audiovisual media services	Legal basis
CZECH REPUBLIC	*PROGRAMME QUOTAS *CONTRIBUTION TO THE PRODUCTION OR THE ACQUISITION OF EUROPEAN WORKS	– the obligation to devote at least 10% of the total number of qualifying programmes of the catalogue to European works or to spend at least 1% of revenues to the production or the acquisition of European works	Section 7 Act No. 132/2010 of 13 April 2001 on On-Demand Audiovisual Media Services and amending certain laws (the On-Demand Audiovisual Media Services Act)
HUNGARY	*PROGRAMME QUOTAS (EUROPEAN AND NATIONAL WORKS) *PROMINENCE IN THE CATALOGUE	– the obligation to devote over one-quarter of the total length of the programmes made available in a given calendar year in the form of on-demand audiovisual media services to European works, and at least ten percent to Hungarian works	Article 21 (2) Act CLXXXV of 2010 on Media Services and Mass Media, as amended

POLAND	*IDENTIFICATION AND SEARCH OPTIONS *PROGRAMME QUOTAS (EUROPEAN AND NATIONAL WORKS) *VISIBILITY OF EUROPEAN WORKS	– the obligation to promote European works, including works produced originally in the Polish language (by proper identification of the programmes available in the catalogue or placement of materials promoting European works) – the obligation to allocate at least 20% of the content in their catalogue to European works including works originally produced in the Polish language – the obligation to provide adequate visibility to such programmes in the catalogue	Article 47f (1), (2), (3) and (4) 1992 Broadcasting Act adopted on 29 December, 1992, as amended
SLOVAKIA	*PROGRAMME QUOTAS	– the obligation to reserve at least 20% of the total time of all programmes to European works	Article 27a Act No. 308 of 14 September 2000 Coll. on Broadcasting and Retransmission (as amended)

Sources: Elaborated on the basis of national broadcasting laws in the Czech Republic, Hungary, Poland and Slovakia as quoted in the table.

Similarly as in the previous section, it would be instructive to reflect upon these regulatory obligations in the context of exemptions or reductions of the requirements by the national authorities. In Slovakia, national legislation allows the regulator to set a lower proportion of European works "taking into account the economic situation of an on-demand audiovisual media service provider, the availability of European works or the focus of an on-demand audiovisual media service".[12] In Poland, the requirement of the programme

[12] Act No. 308 of 14 September 2000 Coll. on Broadcasting and Retransmission (as amended), Article 27a(2). (available at: http://www.rvr.sk/_cms/data/modules/download/1364909855_zakon_308-2000_ucinny_2013-01-01.pdf; retrieved 5.11.2013).

quotas does not apply to "the catalogues, in which only audiovisual programmes other than European works are provided to the general public".[13]

By 2010, only the Czech Republic fully implemented AVMSD regulations concerning on-demand services, and thus was the only country among the CEE member states that provided factual data on the implementation of Article 13 for the Commission's First Report on the Application of Articles 13, 16 and 17 of Directive 2010/13/EU for the period 2009–2010 (European Commission, 2012e). In 2010, 29 on-demand services were reported in the Czech Republic, among which the quota obligation applied to 24. The proportions of European works offered in the catalogues ranked from 10% to 100%, the average share being 51.3%. All services complied with the quota obligation set out in the legislation (European Commission, 2012f: 12).

Generally, the CEE member states have opted for the quota system in promotion of European works by on-demand services rather than requiring financial contribution to the production or acquisition of European works (with the exception of the Czech Republic). The quotas vary from 10% in the Czech Republic to 25% in Hungary. So far, the information on adopting the quota system by on-demand service providers has been scant. Observing the results achieved by the Czech providers of on-demand services, one can assume that meeting the quota conditions depends very much on a specific character of the service, and thus, compliance may largely differ among providers.

4.3. Country of origin, free circulation of audiovisual media services and internal market

While the promotion of European production has mainly been perceived as guided by cultural objectives, free circulation of audiovisual media services certainly fulfills economic objectives of audiovisual media policy, and is seen to contribute to the development of the internal market. Free circulation of media services supported by internal market rules finds practical application in the country of origin principle of Article 2 of the AVMSD (European Commission, 2012d: 4). Article 3 (1) requires from member states to ensure freedom of reception and no restrictions on retransmissions on their territory of audiovisual media services from other

[13] 1992 Broadcasting Act adopted on 29 December, 1992, Official Journal 1993, No. 7, item 34, as amended; Article 47f (4) (available at: http://www.krrit.gov.pl/Data/Files/_public/Portals/0/angielska/Documents/Regulations/broadcasting_act_28022013.pdf; retrieved 29.07.2013).

member states (European Parliament and the Council, 2010a). This fundamental principle of free circulation of broadcasts has been implemented by national broadcasting laws in the CEE countries in a quite differentiated way as the table below demonstrates.

Table 17: Provisions on free circulation of audiovisual media services the in the Czech Republic, Hungary, Poland and Slovakia

Country	Provisions on free circulation of audiovisual media services	Legal basis
CZECH REPUBLIC	"A broadcaster and rebroadcaster shall be entitled to broadcast programmes in a free and independent manner. Any intervention in the contents of the programmes is only admissible on the basis of law and within the limits thereof".	Section 31 (1) Act No. 231/2001 of 17 May 2001 on Radio and Television Broadcasting and on Amendment to Other Acts
HUNGARY	"Media services may be provided and press products may be published freely, information and opinions may be transmitted freely through the mass media, and Hungarian and foreign media services intended for public reception may be accessed freely in Hungary (...)".	Article 3 Act CLXXXV of 2010 on Media Services and Mass Media, as amended
POLAND	"Reception of domestic and foreign programme services and on-demand audiovisual media services, intended by media service providers for reception by the general public, shall be free subject to compliance with the requirements set forth by the applicable law".	Article 1 (2) 1992 Broadcasting Act adopted on 29 December, 1992, as amended
SLOVAKIA	"A broadcaster shall be entitled to broadcast programmes in a free and independent manner. Any intervention in the contents of the programmes is only admissible on the basis of law and within the limits thereof".	Article 15 (1) Act No 308 of 14 September 2000 Coll. on Broadcasting and Retransmission (as amended)

Sources: Elaborated on the basis of national broadcasting laws in the Czech Republic, Hungary, Poland and Slovakia as quoted in the table.

As can be seen from the table above, none of the studied countries incorporated the Article 3 (1) in an identical or equivalent manner with the Directive in the national broadcasting laws. The closest wording to the

AVMSD was adopted in Poland. Article 1 (2) recognises free reception of domestic and foreign programme services and on-demand audiovisual media services, but does not refer to the absence of restrictions on re-transmissions on their territory from other member states.[14] Hungarian law accordingly provides the legal safeguards for a free transmission and reception of Hungarian and foreign media services.[15] The relevant provisions in the Czech[16] and Slovak[17] laws rather tend to entitle broadcasters to broadcast their programmes in free and independent manner, but do not explicitly ensure freedom of reception and lack of restrictions on re-transmissions from other EU countries.

It has to be added though, that the principle of free circulation of audiovisual media services derives its legal endorsement from Article 26 (TFEU) (ex article 14 TEC) that equips the EU with competencies to adopt measures establishing or ensuring the functioning of the internal market (European Union, 2010). Moreover, Articles 49 to 55 (TFEU) lay down the fundamental right to freedom of establishment (European Union, 2010). Referring to these legal grounds in the Treaties, Recital 40 of the AVMSD recognises that media service providers should in general be free to choose the member states in which they establish themselves. Acknowledging that the member states should be able to apply more stricter rules, the Recital 41 encourages the states to co-operate with one another in cases where a broadcaster under the jurisdiction of one member state provides a television broadcast which is wholly or mostly directed towards the territory of another member state (European Parliament and the Council, 2010a).

In order to briefly asses how the provisions enabling the free circulation of audiovisual media services translate to structural conditions in the CEE countries, the table below presents a number of broadcasting channels targeting domestic and non-domestic markets in the EU.

---

[14] Article 1 (2), 1992 Broadcasting Act...

[15] Article 3, Act CLXXXV of 2010 on Media Services and Mass Media...

[16] Section 31 (1) Act No. 231/2001 on Radio and Television Broadcasting...

[17] Article 15 (1) Act No. 308 on Broadcasting and Retransmission...

Table 18: The number of broadcasting channels according to targeted countries in the Czech Republic, Hungary, Poland and Slovakia in 2013

Country	The number of registered broadcasting channels	The number of local and regional channels (%)	The number of registered broadcasting channels targeting other countries (%)	Other countries targeted
CZECH REPUBLIC	297	84 (28.3%)	100 (33.7%)	Hungary (15) Poland (19) Slovakia (4) Slovenia (11) Romania (10) Croatia (9) Serbia (9) Bulgaria (8) Netherlands (5) Others (10): Russian Federation, the Arab world, The former Yugoslav Republic of Macedonia, Germany, France, UK
HUNGARY	561	504 (89.8%)	4 (0.7%)	Romania (2) Czech Republic (2)
POLAND	350	211 (60.3%)	3 (0.9%)	Belarus (1) France (1) North America (1)
SLOVAKIA	108	69 (63.9%)	none	none

Sources: Elaborated on the basis of European Audiovisual Observatory (2013) The MAVISE database: mavise.obs.coe.int (retrieved 13.11.2013).

In 2013, the largest number of channels was registered in Hungary – 561. Many of these, however, are local and regional channels (89.8%). At the same time, the proportion of channels established in Hungary, but targeting non-domestic markets, has been very small – 0.7%. A similar situation can be observed in Poland (0.9% of channels), while the share of regional channels is less significant and accounts for 60.3%. Slovakia represents the only country with channels established to target solely the domestic market.

The largest number of channels targeting other countries was registered in the Czech Republic (100 – 33.7%). Many of these, are however, not part of the EU broadcasting/media groups, but belong to US corporations: *Cinemax HBO* (25); *CBS Action* (3); *Comedy MTV* (3); *Disney Children's* (8); *HBO 2* and *3* (10); *HBO Comedy* (13); *HBO HD* (9); *MTV* (4). As can be seen from these examples, the most represented group is HBO (a subsidiary of Time Warner, the owner of *TV Nova* in the Czech Republic and *TV Markíza* with a controlling share on the market of commercial terrestrial television in the Czech Republic and Slovakia[18]). It would be interesting to add in this context that the Czech Republic was the first CEE country to attract the US TV investment in the beginning of the 1990s and by then, developed into a 'regional center' of the US-based television industry (at that time owned mainly by the CME – Central European Media Enterprises). The EU accession and transposition of the *aquis* in the area of audiovisual policy has not fundamentally changed this setting. Shalini Venturelli (1998: 209) argued that the integrative function of the Directive facilitated the further domination of the audiovisual and broadcast markets by the multinational audiovisual industry originating primarily in the USA. In relation to the Czech Republic, and its role as a regional center for the integrated transnational circulation of audiovisual services connected to US corporations; this observation holds true with certain reservations. While in structural terms, the Czech TV landscape seems integrated better than its neighbours with other (mostly CEE) EU countries through transnational circulation of audiovisual media services, the content dimension is characterised by lower compliance in the area of protection of European works. Thus, while structures seem to be better integrated in a transnational EU setting, the content does not offer an integration through the European dimension and most of the non-domestic channels demonstrate lower prominence of the European production than is the case of the domestic channels.

4.4. Legal implementation and compliance with the AVMS Directive in the CEE countries: conclusions

The area of audiovisual policy belongs to policies covered by 'traditional methods' referring to legislation initiated by the Commission – the directive – ratified by the Council of Ministers and the European Parlia-

[18] See more on this issue in the Chapter 5.

ment (Harcourt, 2008). One of the Commission's role in this mechanism is to oversee the implementation, and as a part of this process, to submit every three years to the European Parliament, to the Council and to the European Economic and Social Committee, a report on the application of the Directive (Article 33, European Parliament and the Council, 2010a). A systematic approach to monitoring the implementation allows the Commission to constantly observe national models of application against the changing conditions in the field of audiovisual media services, in particular in the light of new technological developments, the competitiveness of the sector and levels of media literacy.

In an attempt to better understand evolving models of implementation in the four CEE countries, the section below compares the legal implementation in the area of protection of European works and free circulation of audiovisual media services with the levels of compliance as measured within the standard frames of reporting on the AVMSD application (protection of European works) and structural characteristics of the national audiovisual landscapes (broadcasting channels targeting domestic and non-domestic markets). The first table summarises the legal implementation of the AVMSD in the four CEE Member States in the area of protection of European works:

Table 19: Legal implementation of the AVMSD in the area of the protection of European works in the Czech Republic, Hungary, Poland and Slovakia

Country	Definition of qualifying time	Majority of EU works	Rules for lower shares of EU works	Schedule time requirements	No-apply rules***	Protection of national works	Criteria for definition of independent producers	Quota requirements regarding independent works	Requirements regarding recent works	Obligations of providers of on-demand audiovisual services
CZECH REPUBLIC	Equivalent**	Equivalent	No	No	Yes	No	Ownership and programme supply	More flexible: choice between quota on transmission time (10%) and contribution to the production (10%)	Slightly more prescriptive (10% of independent works)	More prescriptive (choice)

HUNGARY	Equivalent	More prescriptive	Yes	Yes	Yes	Yes (quota system)	Ownership and executive employment	More prescriptive: quota on transmission time (10%)	Significantly more prescriptive (all indep. works)	More prescriptive (no choice)
POLAND	Equivalent	More prescriptive	Yes	No	Yes	Yes (quota system)	Ownership and executive employment	More prescriptive: quota on transmission time (10%)	More prescriptive (a majority of indep. works)	More prescriptive (no choice)
SLOVAKIA	Equivalent	More prescriptive	Yes	No	Yes	Other qualitiative measures	Ownership and control over creative production	More flexible: choice between quota on transmission time (10%) and contribution to the production (10%)	Equivalent	More prescriptive (no choice)

Notes:
* The rules described in the first nine columns from right refer to linear audiovisual services; the rules described in the last column refer to on-demand services
** Equivalent or identical to the AVMSD's definition
** No-apply rules refer to provisions excluding certain types of channels/broadcasters from compliance with the rules protecting European works

The table above uses various terms to indicate how selected provisions of the Directive correspond with relevant measures in the national legislation. The term 'equivalent' denotes identical or equivalent transposition of the AVMSD's rules or definitions. The term prescriptive indicates that national provisions are more specified, and thus may also include more limitations than the measures of the Directive. The term flexible illustrates a greater extent of flexibility in application of the provisions than prescribed by the Directive.

As can be seen from the table, there is a visible variety among the CEE member states considering the legal implementation of the AVMSD in the area of the protection of European works. Moreover, the CEE countries have rarely implemented provisions of the AVMSD in an identical or equivalent manner with the Directive. The few exceptions confirming this rule include: the definition of the qualifying time in all countries, the reference to the majority of European works in the case of the Czech Republic (with use of 'where practicable' clause) and provisions on recent works in Slovakia. In most cases, the studied rules seem to be slightly more or more prescriptive than required in the AVMSD. The most flexible rules were introduced in the Czech Republic (the lack of schedule time requirements, no protection of national works, a choice of obligation in a definition of the 'independent producer', a relatively low quota for the share of recent works, a choice of obligations applicable to providers of on-demands services).

On the contrary, the most prescriptive rules were implemented by Hungary that has opted for schedule time requirements, a relatively high quota on national works, a relatively high quota on recent works (all independent works) and more prescriptive and quota-based obligations set for providers of on-demand services. Poland, although less prescriptive than Hungary, seems to share many similar solutions with Hungary. For example, both countries do not use the 'where practicable clause' when defining the requirement of a majority of European works. Both countries also use a similar mechanism of protection of national works (around 33% of transmission time) and prefer a more prescriptive than flexible definition of 'independent producer'. Slovakia, on the other hand, shares more similar settings with the Czech Republic, although slightly more prescriptive. The Slovak broadcasting law does not impose, for instance, a quota of national works, but requires that broadcasters ensure the use of a national language, languages of national minorities and foreign languages in accordance with special provisions.

The legal implementation of the AVMSD in the area of free circulation of audiovisual media services also demonstrates differences from country to country in the CEE:

Table 20: Legal implementation of the AVMSD in the area of free circulation of audiovisual media services

Country	**Implementation of Article 3 (1)**	**Recognition of free reception of audiovisual media services from other countries**	**Rules applicable to services registerd in other EU country but targeting the country in question**
CZECH REPUBLIC	Flexible (no reference to free reception)	No	Yes, with some limitations
HUNGARY	Less prescriptive (indirect reference to free reception)	Yes	Yes
POLAND	Less prescriptive (direct reference to free reception)	Yes	Yes, to a limited extent
SLOVAKIA	Flexible (no reference to free reception)	No	Yes

Sources: Adopted and calculated on the basis of previous tables used in this chapter.

All studied countries have transcribed the provisions on free circulation of audiovisual media services (Article 3 (1) of the Directive) in a more flexible way than the AVMSD. While Hungary and Poland did include the recognition of free reception of audiovisual media services from other countries, the Czech Republic and Slovakia merely entitled broadcasters to broadcast their programmes in a free and independent manner. The Czech Republic, Hungary, Poland and Slovakia also designed the rules applicable to services registered in other EU country, but targeting their national audiences. Finally, the next table summarises compliance with the AVMSD in the area of the protection of European works and free circulation of audiovisual media services:

Table 21: Compliance with the AVMSD in the area of the protection of European works and free circulation of audiovisual media services

Country	Share of European works (2010) (in % and trend)	Share of independent works (2010) (in % and trend)	Share of recent works (in %) (2010)	Share of channels targeting non-domestic markets (in %) (2013)
CZECH REPUBLIC	below the EU average (58.1% – decreasing)	below the EU average (26 % – decreasing)	below the EU average (56.8% – decreasing)	33.7%
HUNGARY	highly above the EU average (81% – slightly decreasing)	above the EU average (42.5% – slightly decreasing)	above the EU average (67.9% – decreasing)	0.7%
POLAND	highly above the EU average (78.4% – slightly decreasing)	below the EU average (30.8% – slightly decreasing)	above the EU average (70.3% – slightly decreasing)	0.9%
SLOVAKIA	above the EU average (68.2% – slightly decreasing)	below the EU average (27.6% – slightly decreasing)	no data	none

Sources: Adopted and calculated on the basis of previous tables used in this chapter.

As all of the CEE countries complied with the content obligations promoting European works in 2005–2010, the table above presents a comparison of the compliance at the national level with the EU average. The results for 2010 demonstrate that there is a large variety among these countries. Hungary reached the highest level of compliance almost in all categories (with the exception of the share of recent works). Also Poland manifests a high level of compliance with the only exception of its share of independent works (below the EU average). On the other hand, the Czech Republic reaches the lowest level of compliance, in all categories – below the EU average. The Czech Republic can be perceived at the same time as the only country with visible structures supporting transnational circulation of audiovisual media services due to a significant share of channels targeting non-domestic markets.

Table 22: The model of legal implementation and level of compliance in the area of protection of European works and free circulation of audiovisual media services in the Czech Republic, Hungary, Poland and Slovakia

Country	Model of legal implementation	Level of compliance
CZECH REPUBLIC	Flexible	Moderate
HUNGARY	Highly prescriptive	High
POLAND	Prescriptive	High
SLOVAKIA	Semi-flexible	Moderate

Sources: Adopted and calculated on the basis of previous tables used in this chapter.

We can observe some correlation between the model of legal implementation and the level of compliance. Countries with more flexible models of legal implementation tend to achieve moderate levels of compliance, translating to achieving the required proportions of European works below the EU average. At the same time the conditions facilitating the free circulation of audiovisual services seem to be best performed in the case of the Czech Republic with most flexible regulatory environment. Thus, quite logically, broadcasters established in various EU members states seem to seek the most flexible legal environment to offer their services in the internal market. On the other hand, the countries with more prescriptive modes of legal implementation (Hungary and Poland) achieve higher compliance in the area of protection of European works that includes also a significant share of national works or works in national languages. In both these countries, the share of channels targeting non-domestic markets is fairly tiny (in both cases less than 1%).

These considerations continue to support the view on the significance of the national dimension. Although the CEE countries proved quite successful in implementing the legal and empirical-content dimension of the Directive, they demonstrate that the compliance is highest when supported by national measures (e.g. protection of national works). Moreover, the models of implementation do not lead to greater harmonisation among the countries, as almost each of them uses different national standards.

In its Resolution on the *Implementation of the Audiovisual Media Services Directive covering the period 2009–2010* the European Parliament observed that "the Member States have implemented the AVMSD in a *particularly diverse manner*" and that "the 'country of origin' principle, when properly applied, gives broadcasters important clarity and certainty about their operational arrangements" (European Parliament, 2013a). The Parliament also noticed that even though most member states comply with the rules regarding the promotion of European works, priority is still given to national works, whilst the percentage of independent works on TV is on the decline (European Parliament, 2013a). Both these remarks are reflected in legal implementation and application of the AVMSD rules in given areas, by the CEE countries.

In the past, the requirement of the promotion of European works in the TWF Directive has been viewed to a certain extent as an alienated provision not synchronised well with the main objective of the Directive – support for the internal market and circulation of audiovisual services across national borders. This argument was justified by the lack of explicit rudiments in the EU Treaty law for the Union to take action in the field of culture (deWitte, 1995; Craufurd Smith, 2004; McGoonagle, 2008). On the other hand, these two axes of the EU audiovisual policy guiding the Directive seem perfectly logical at the conceptual level as explained above: both (protection of European production guided by cultural values and the internal market – guided by economic values) support the competitiveness of European creativity, cultures, languages and media industries on the global scene. Why then does a brief analysis of legal implementation and compliance in the CEE countries seem to offer a quite ambiguous picture? Why do countries performing well in the area of protection of European production not employ structures supporting the free circulation of audiovisual media services? And vice versa: why do countries supporting more open audiovisual landscapes achieve lower shares of European works?

The answer is self-explanatory: in both cases (the protection of European production and free circulation of audiovisual services) the results do not refer primarily to the *European* dimension: countries attracting transnational broadcasters with channels targeting other countries and linguistic communities (the Czech Republic) actually appeal to US-based corporations (most channels targeting non-domestic markets are of US origin). Likewise, countries achieving the highest share of European production and demonstrating the most supportive legal implementation in this regard (Hungary, Poland) mostly protect national works. Thus in the case of the CEE countries, both of these described sets of measures have been less effective in promoting the *circulation* of *European* works.

Whereas the CEE countries shared obvious and long standing connections based on a common historical experience, path dependency and in some cases, cultural affinities, significant varieties can be observed in current policy landscapes. In the case of media and audiovisual policy, for example, solutions tend to be shared between Poland and Hungary; and the Czech Republic and Slovakia. This seems to be dictated not only by the market size and history of common geopolitical and cultural relations, but also by consequences of political choices made during the first period of media system transformation.

Finally, it needs to be mentioned that the Treaty of Lisbon entering into force in 2009, strengthened the legal basis for taking culture, as well as freedom of expression and media pluralism, into account in the EU actions, including the audiovisual policy under the AVMSD. Article 4 of the TFEU confirms that shared competence between the Union and the member states applies to such principal areas as the 'internal market' and the 'area of freedom, security and justice'. Article 6 entitles the Union to carry out actions to support, co-ordinate or supplement the actions of the member states in areas such as 'culture'. This competence is further described in Article 167 (4) of the Treaty on the Functioning of the European Union under which the Union takes cultural aspects into account in its actions, in particular in order to respect and to promote the diversity of its cultures (European Union, 2010). The consolidated version of the TEU and TFEU contains also the Charter of the Fundamental Rights of the EU. By virtue of the first subparagraph of Article 6(1) of the Treaty on the European Union, the Charter has the same legal value as the Treaties (European Union, 2012). In this light, the Union's actions in the area of audiovisual policy are to be in line with the Article 11 protecting freedom of expression and stating respect for freedom and pluralism of the media.

All this represents a much broader legal ground for incorporating multiple values into the audiovisual policy and its main legal instrument – the AVMSD. Accordingly, the Recital 16 of the AVMSD confirms that the Directive enhances compliance with fundamental rights and is fully in line with the principles recognised by the Charter (European Parliament and the Council, 2010a). In addition, the Directive refers to safeguarding various public interests, including: cultural diversity, the right to information, media pluralism, the protection of minors and consumer protection, and to enhance public awareness and media literacy (Recital 12, European Parliament and the Council, 2010a). In turn, the protection of European works has been more frequently viewed not only as an exclusive area of audiovisual policy and one of the key objectives of the Directive, but also the crucial element of other thematic policy parcels such as media pluralism. The Media Pluralism Monitor, for instance, includes content-related indicators that refer explicitly to the protection of European works.[19] These encompass e.g. the proportion of European works in TV broadcasting (C 1.1.), regulatory safeguards for European works in TV broadcasting (C 1.2.), promotion of European works in non-linear AVMS (C 1.3.), proportion of non-domestic European works in top TV programmes in the linear AVMS (C 1.6) and others.

This exemplifies that value grounds for the EU audiovisual policy have differentiated and became composite in an ongoing architecture of rules and principles built in a complementary manner through the modernisation of the Directive and other evolving instruments. Yet, what seems less represented in this polyvalent melting, is coherence and primary focus on shared – *European* – communication needs. As follows, more relevant now than before seems to be the question how to transmute a reactive and protective policy strand into a more proactive approach representing the conscious and meaningful choice supporting the combined synergy of values instead of prioritising some at the expense of others.

[19] Media Pluralism Monitor is an integral part of the *Independent Study on Indicators for Media Pluralism* (K.U.Leuven et al., 2009) The Media Pluralism Monitor contains the indicators embedded in a risk-based scoring system. (http://ec.europa.eu/digital-agenda/en/independent-study-indicators-media-pluralism#the-research-team; retrieved 23.11.2013).

5. MEDIA PLURALISM: PUTTING ENDS AND MEANS AT THE RIGHT PLACE

5.1. Crystallising the normative view on media pluralism in European media policies: An introduction

For a relatively long period of time, media pluralism has been perceived as a complex and elusive issue both in media studies and media policies. At the same time, it has often been used in selective ways that edit out its important and relevant dimensions. This chapter aims to shed some light on the conceptualisation and operationalisation of media pluralism as a policy rationale. In particular, it will explore the regulatory framework for media pluralism and the dynamics of the changing conditions of structural media pluralism in the CEE countries.

First of all, it would be helpful to explore the conceptual frame of media pluralism. Notions of media pluralism, plurality, and diversity have been used in many contexts – as empirical ends to be achieved with certain policies, as normative principles, as a set of characteristics applicable to media systems at various levels, as communication needs and rights. Dietrich Westphal (2002) argues that the notion of diversity is characterised by its neutral and thus general meaning, whereas the notion of pluralism is related and confined primarily to the media. Other authors emphasised a more value-free and empirically oriented meaning of media diversity, and evaluative and normative framing of media pluralism (Klimkiewicz, 2004b; Karppinen, 2013). Yet, in the course of recent years, media pluralism has been more prominently exposed as a policy rationale with a clearly normative and value-ridden angle. This normative layer is manifested in the belief that a condition of media pluralism is socially desirable and beneficial for the sake of functioning democracy, generating knowledge from diverse sources, the formation of a cultural identity, and the effective and competitive operation of markets. In other words, the normative view of pluralism does not encompass 'everything' or 'any kind of diversity' but such arrangement of diversity in a media system that facilitates performing the key functions which the media play in societies. In Karppinnen's view (2013: 129) the argument that the notion of media pluralism only serves as a smokescreen for deregulation and marketisation, underestimates the importance of alternative thinking in media policy. As described in Chapter 2, these strands at the EU level currently encompass protection against new configurations of media power, independence of media regulators from state and industry, defence of the PSM, public support for enabling technological structures, support for community and minority media, media literacy, and others.

A debate about media pluralism in the media policy is not a new phenomenon. At the pan-European level, one of the long-standing and developing vectors of action has been a positive approach to the interpretation of Article 10 of the ECHR. In this sense, Article 10 has functioned not only as a guarantee against interventions by states in the field of freedom of expression and freedom of the media, but it has also encouraged ensuring the citizen's right to be fully and impartially informed, and to receive the information from diverse and independent sources (Voorhoof, 1998: 35–57). This approach has been supported by a large number of documents, many of which stressed the importance of the active implementation of Article 10 of the ECHR for the appropriate development of media pluralism and access to diverse sources of information. Most of these documents are not legally binding, but they do set down a number of principles and strategies suggested to member states for further implementation (Klimkiewicz, 2009b). The Council of Europe has gradually broadened its agenda on media pluralism since the 1970s, when the media landscapes in Europe underwent the first wave of major mergers and business failures in the press sectors. From the time of, the periods of the CoE's involvement in media pluralism have been marked by several milestones articulated in the following recommendations:

- Recommendation of the Committee of Ministers No. R (94) 13 on Measures to Promote Media Transparency (adopted on 22 November 1994),
- Recommendation of the Commitee of Ministers No. R (99) 1 on Measures to Promote Media Pluralism (adopted on 19 January 1999),
- Recommendation Rec of the Committee of Ministers (2007) 2 on Media Pluralism and Diversity of Media Content (adopted on 31 January 2007).

It has to be mentioned in this respect that the CoE's activities in this matter aimed to respond not only to the media market and technological developments, but were linked to historical circumstances most importantly articulated in the process of democratisation (including media systems) in Central and Eastern Europe. Sustained democratic premises induced both the Committee and Assembly to repeatedly call member states' attention, in order to adopt recommended measures protecting various aspects of media pluralism, and ultimately unfreeze implementation idleness (Klimkiewicz, 2009b).

With the successive waves of the EU enlargement and entry of the CEE countries into the legal and policy space of the EU, the CoE's role in promoting media pluralism has diluted to a certain extent, while the role of the European Parliament came to the forefront, especially after the adoption of the Lisbon Treaty. However, going back, intensified Parliament's activities on pluralism can be observed already in the mid 1990s. At that time, the Parliament pushed forward the idea to harmonise national restrictions on media concentration, and in consequence, to enable the Community to intervene in acts of concentration which endanger pluralism on a European scale. After the double rejection of the draft directive by the College of Commissioners, parliamentarians themselves admitted that media pluralism is 'without doubt the biggest failure of the EP' (Sarikakis, 2004: 132). A new opening of media pluralism issue by the EP came with the fifth wave of the EU enlargement and Berlusconi case in 2004. In its *Resolution on the risks of violation, in the EU and especially in Italy, of freedom of expression and information* (European Parliament, 2004) the Parliament examined the situation in selected member states (including new members) and Italy in particular, to underline the necessity to refocus media pluralism policies, taking into account the principle of democracy and the conception of EU citizenship. Finally, the new Parliament's and non-governmental actors' initiatives on media pluralism described in Chapter 2 demonstrate that the newest wave of interest has been prompted by some problematic cases in the member states (Hungary's 2010 media law; the UK's hacking phone scandal and the following debate on media reform), a need to strengthen EU credibility in its external actions (regarding new enlargement process and global actions), and last but not least – technological and economic developments leading to the reconfigurations of media power.

The protection of media pluralism proved to be a difficult task especially with regards to EU competencies and developing hard policy instruments (directives) by the EU in the 1990s. On the one hand, political and economic interests of some member states diverged, on the other hand, highly varied media market conditions (population, size, regional and cultural diversity, languages spoken, etc.) made it difficult to come up with one scheme of rules. Moreover, the recent enlargements of the Union incorporating the CEE countries with relatively young media markets and policy models shaped by intense reforms in a compressed time frame (Klimkiewicz, 2009a) made it even more challenging to implement harmonising rules. Karppinen observes that the malaise of diversity (interests, actors, states, views and approaches) in dealing with media diversity actually leads to nonpolicy or silent policy (2013: 139). This however seems to apply only to hard policy instruments as soft policy concerning media pluralism has been in place for some time at the EU. The next sections will reflect on these initiatives and will test national policies in the CEE countries in respect to media system developments following three crucial dimensions of structural media pluralism.

5.2. Structures of control, function and space

Both in policies and media studies, media pluralism has been approached at various levels: a macro level of media systems (diversity media structures, ownership patterns, entry costs and conditions), a meso level of media institutions and performance (diversity of professional practices, employment structures, transparency), and a micro level of media contents (diversity of sources, genres, viewpoints, representations) (Klimkiewicz, 2009b). Media pluralism has also been interpreted through conceptual dichotomies or alternatives such as proportional/open, organised/spontaneous, polarised/moderate, evaluative/descriptive or reactive/interactive/proactive, but most significant in terms of policy development has been the distinction on external and internal pluralism. 'External' stands for diversity located outside a particular media entity (and thus may be generated through various media outlets each expressing a different point of view), while 'internal' is seen to reside inside the media organisation or unit, and basically reflects differentiation of contents and services offered (including diversity of values, interests, representations and views expressed). Although a direct causal link between the external and internal pluralism has not been unanimously proved (e.g. Ward, 2006), in media policies various initiatives on media pluralism revolved mainly around its structural domain (including ownership in particular). Katrin Voltmer (2000: 5) argues that

> the relevance of structural diversity derives from the assumption that it is closely related to performance diversity in that particular structural conditions of media systems guarantee or, at least, foster the production of a diverse and generalistic information quality, whereas other institutional settings impede the public representation of a broad plurality of political viewpoints.

Structural pluralism, very generally speaking, refers to a condition where diverse independent media entities exist within a system and are arranged together in a particular way. This has most often been exemplified by the existence of a wide range of media outlets, organisations and services reflecting various points of view and information, recognising diverse cultural representations and values, and offering different ways of social interests' formation, interaction and use. Such framing also implies an existence of diverse ownership and forms of control, not only in terms of various entities owning media outlets, but also presupposing different 'types' of media ownership naturally linked with different media functions, such as public, private, non-profit, minority, etc. (Klimkiewicz, 2010b).

For a few years now, however, basic assumptions about structural media pluralism have been losing conceptual clarity, and some even argue – *raison d'être*. A rapidly changing media environment extended with the Internet (not only as a platform of delivery but a universe of its own) has become fluid, fragmented, abundant in communication flows. An excessive diversity, and at the same time, opaque or superficial diversity of media structures and contents reaches users through their choice, filtering, navigation, participation, networking. This does not make the users, though, immune from new configurations of media control and gate keeping. Forms of limitations revolve around contractual conditions of operators offering various media services, lack of comprehensive information about the choice the users can enjoy, technical incompabilities, the commercial use of personal data etc. Natali Helberger argues that diversity of supply does not automatically translate into diversity of exposure; quite the contrary – more supply can also result in less diversity (Helberger, 2012: 69).

Likewise, the traditional view on structural media pluralism becomes more complicated. Some analysts argue that structural policies are becoming quite obsolete in fluid media environments. Mara Einstein analysing US media diversity policies argues that structural regulation of the media is simply inadequate to produce an abundance of varying voices available through the media (2004: 211). In short, if the aim is to create diverse content and make it more accessible to users then the content should be regulated, "not everything around it" (2004: 211). Steven Barnett warns that in current technical and industrial circumstances, well-resourced journalism is under threat and there is little point in promoting structural solutions, when the very structures themselves are in danger of extinction (2010: 8). In other words, monopolistic or oligopolistic media structures might be perfectly acceptable if these are tied to content regulations which ensure that the civic and democratic values of journalism will be prioritised above the interests of share-holders and corporate profits.

All these concerns and observations clearly show that policy thinking about structural media pluralism reaches new avenues and the issue remains substantive both at national and EU levels. The Commission's Staff Working Document *Media pluralism in the Member States of the European Union* (European Commission, 2007a: 5) endorses a 'broad understanding' of media pluralism: "Although pluralism of ownership is important, it is a necessary but not sufficient condition for ensuring media pluralism. Media ownership rules need to be complemented by other provisions". The Document further observes: "Ensuring media pluralism, in our understanding, implies all measures that ensure citizens' access to a variety of information sources, opinion, voices etc. in order to form their opinion without the undue influence of one dominant opinion forming power (2007a: 5)". The Commission recognises among these measures voluntary rules for media to ensure the independence of journalistic output; rules preventing politicians to influence media coverage; control mechanisms for media concentration; programme requirements of broadcasters (especially PSM); and others. At the same time, the Commission observes that media pluralism analysis has most often been limited to external pluralism, in particular media ownership rules (2007a: 12). For all that, the document does not offer any concrete policy position, nor does it signalise possible rules that could mark new areas of the Commission's involvement. The initiative clearly sets up analytical and monitoring tools, but does not envisage hard policy follow-up.

The recent conclusions of the European Council on media freedom and pluralism in a digital environment (Council of the European Union, 2013) demonstrate that the Council does not support a visible and decisive shift in the current soft policy approach performed by the Commission. The role of the member states is much more clearly promoted by the Council. It encompasses ensuring independence of media regulatory authorities, media transparency, protection of journalistic sources and preventing the possible negative effects of excessive concentration of media ownership (2013: 3). In a different manner, the role of the Commission, as seen by the Council, is merely limited to support of the projects protecting journalists and media professionals, and monitoring media pluralism. Interestingly, the conclusions also emphasise 'non-legislative' actions concerning the operations of audiovisual regulatory authorities. Unlike in the case of the member states, the Council does not mention the issue of independence of the regulatory authorities, although the Commission has been increasingly active in this field, not only due to the situation in Hungary. In 2013, the Commission opened public consultation on the independence of audiovisual regulatory bodies with a purpose to collect views and possible options for strengthening independence through policy instruments, including a possible revision of Article 30 of the AVMS Directive. This issue will be more broadly discussed in Chapter 6.

Independence of media regulatory authorities, media transparency, protection of journalists from various kind of pressures as well as prevention against excessive economic control over the media, are certainly important conditions of the structural media pluralism. All of these are reflected in the number of indicators developed by the *Independent Study on Indicators for Media Pluralism in the Member States: Towards a Risk-Based Approach* (K.U. Leuven et al., 2009) announced in the Staff Working Document. The study offers legal, economic and socio-demographic indicators for pluralism of media ownership and control, pluralism of media types and genres, political pluralism, cultural pluralism, geographical pluralism and pluralism of distribution (K.U. Leuven et al., 2009). In 2013, the Commission decided that the study together with accompanying monitoring tool (Media Pluralism Monitor) will be implemented by the Centre for Media Pluralism and Media Freedom established at the European University Institute. This will provide a good opportunity to implement enormously complex and large-scale measurement methods to follow, among others, the structural conditions of media pluralism.

Such a broadly defined scope of media pluralism certainly extends the possibility of empirical assessment in this book. Yet, as will be argued in the following sections of this chapter, three dimensions play a principal role in the understanding the structural trends in pluralism, especially in media landscapes that underwent a profound transformation in a relatively short time as has been the case of the CEE countries. If, as is generally assumed, structural pluralism refers to the way diversity is organised on a macro-level of the media environment, then the three dimensions with a crucial role for differentiation of media structures include: the diversity of media control, diversity of media functions and geographical/cultural diversity.

First of all, structural media pluralism may be generated through a balance between multiple centres of media control. These may not be necessarily identical with the ownership structures, although the ownership and financial control over the production and operation choices (including complex technological conditions and investment needed) definitely play the most influential role as it comes to the development of media networks. The centres of control crystallise inside the ownership structures (in particular around a power to make strategic decisions), but are also dependent on delivery platforms, journalistic and content producer autonomy, and more generally, regulatory constraints. It might therefore be useful in this context to focus on what degree the multiple competing centres of media control mutually balance themselves. For example, a strong tendency of ownership consolidation in the press system may be balanced by regulatory constraints, and subsidy mechanisms for alternative press and editorial independence safeguarded by self-regulatory measures.

Second, structural media pluralism combines different functions the media play in a society. These are linked with media activities generating economic profit, public value, well-informed citizenship and opinion formation, entertainment, cultural representations and expressions. Understanding how different functions evolve in time and how they balance or complement each other in the overall media system helps to paint the whole picture of structural pluralism. For example, the declining strength of public service media vis-à-vis commercial and private media financed predominantly from advertising can demonstrate an increasing inclination towards commercial and entertainment functions.

The third important dimension is one of geographical/cultural diversity. Commonly, it combines spatial structures (organisation of media operations and institutions at transnational, national, regional and local levels) and cultural and societal structures (response of media contents and services to the unique needs and interests of local and regional communities, nations, transnational audiences). The geographical dimension of structural media pluralism can help to understand how media structures balance themselves at different geographical levels (e.g. local and regional vis-à-vis national media structures), whether the strength of the structures at one level increases in comparison over the others and what is the general trend either in terms of centralisation or decentralisation of the media environment.

Media regulation plays a crucial role in harmonising various forms of control, media functions and geographical levels. Structural regulation seems to generate the most complex type of media pluralism, because it attempts to engineer the whole environment within which media as institutions, outlets and services, operate (Hitchens, 2006: 65). It should also be noted in this context that 'structural media pluralism' as a concept used within the framework of 'structural regulation', especially in American tradition, was adapted from the economic and competition law perspectives to media market analysis (Klimkiewicz, 2010b: 907). As such, it has often been analysed and described through the lens of economic operation and competition policy. Economic prerequisites (e.g. multiple owners as defined by competition law) do not necessarily guarantee media pluralism ready-to-be-used by potential media users (2010b: 908).

All in all, media control and hegemonic influences are not only exercised through ownership patterns and structures, but a whole set of dependencies (e.g. political) that cannot always be translated into a marketable value. Rachel Craufurd Smith et al. (2012: 7) observes that it is recognised in Europe that the media not only need protection from state control and influence but that citizens, media users and governments may need protection from powerful private media companies. The fact that structural media regulation cannot be simply identified with a narrowly understood protection of economic competition on media markets, does not seem to raise much disagreement in the media policy environment and certainly, media-specific approaches have been used widely in many European countries. There, however, seems to be also another visible trend in the media and communications policy discourse, calling increasingly for empirical proof and metrics (especially quantitative methods of measurement) that would justify and clearly demonstrate the need to sustain or implement media-specific regulation to control media ownership structures (and concentration in particular) (Napoli, 2007; Just, 2009). Several such measurements and policies have been implemented recently in the USA (Diversity Index in 2003); UK (the public interest or plurality test, 2003); Italy (measuring the integrated communications market, 2004) and Germany (new approach to weighing the influence of various media by the KEK, 2006). None of the CEE countries implemented a formalised index for the measurement of structural media diversity, although the protection of media pluralism has taken a variety of, often hybrid, forms. This issue will be examined in the next section.

5.3. Protecting media pluralism in the CEE countries

The notion of media pluralism played an essential role in re-arranging media systems in the CEE after 1989. New regulatory frameworks that have come into effect largely in the 1990s varied in their responses to this objective. Most commonly, novelised or amended national press laws have not addressed structural media pluralism in any particular or explicit way, nor were press specific measures introduced to measure ownership concentration in a media system. The common approach was to rely simply on the operation of general competition rules as the previous forms of the press control (licencing, censorship) have been legally abolished. In addition, most countries of the region (Poland was the only exception), did not introduce a regulatory basis for the press privatisation that would imply some differentiated forms of ownership or subsidies strengthening, e.g. small or local newspapers. There were virtually no instruments other than the general competition rules to influence the takeovers, mergers and acquisitions that followed the first press privatisation period (Klimkiewicz, 2009a: 145). In a different vein, the radio and television landscapes have been subject to more complex forms of regulation, and basically all broadcasting laws inscribed gradually the goal to protect or promote media pluralism. The CEE countries subsequently employed composite rules that allow structural plurality/diversity considerations to be envisaged in company with general competition rules when reviewing mergers of broadcasters holding licences or ownership conditions of licence applicants. In addition, the laws have required some forms of ownership and financial transparency, provided for monitoring measures, included must curry rules and preferential treatment (in some cases even financial support) of community, minority or social broadcasters. In some cases, cross-media ownership rules were introduced. The section below will offer a comparative analysis of these composite measures protecting media pluralism in national broadcasting laws.

As described in Chapter 3, the issue of media pluralism in the CEE was exposed relatively high on the political agenda during the 5th EU enlargement, and it defined media policy discourse in the post-accession period as well. The CEE-specific problems related with media pluralism resonated in various EU policy documents. The Final Report summarising the debate of the Group on Media Pluralism at the Liverpool Audiovisual Conference devoted to revision of the TWF Directive, observed: "New member states tended to have different notions of what pluralism means than the older members of the Union. There is a danger of applying double standards when dealing with media pluralism issues" (Working Group 5, 2005: 1). The Staff Working Document (European Commission, 2007a) paid attention in particular to the intercommunity dimension of transnational investment arguing that various sectors of media markets in CEE are dominated by large transnational companies. The document addresses concerns that such undertakings may use their market power to the detriment of small, national publishers and broadcasters (2007a: 10).

The AVMS Directive (European Parliament and the Council, 2010a) refers to media pluralism directly or indirectly in various parts of the document (e.g. Recitals 5, 8, 34 and 94). Relevant provisions are linked to relatively different ends of media pluralism. Recital 5 underlines diverse functions and importance of media services for societies, in particular ensuring diversity of opinion and media pluralism. Recital 8 deems to prevent a dominant position and undue media power that may be ultimately detrimental to media pluralism. Recital 34 refers to pluralism of information as a fundamental principle of the Union. Finally, Recital 94 recognises that instruments chosen by member states in the process of implementation of the Directive should contribute to the promotion of media pluralism. Thus on the one hand, the end is to stimulate content and service diversity, on the other hand, prevention of controlling media power. As Craufurd Smith et al. (2012) observe, these may call for an incompatible course of action. However, in the normative sense, *any* content diversity is not the primary goal of pluralism policies as is not the prevention of *any* controlling media power. The point is to limit such media power that potentially leads to biased coverage or bypassing certain issues for commercial or political reasons, or that seeks to influence politicians to secure particular private interests at the expense of public interest. The media power mobilising civic interest in order to e.g. protect the environment or promote a healthy diet in schools, responds to public concerns and hence, does not pose a direct risk to media pluralism. As it stands, the Directive does not impose any form of media pluralism measurement/monitoring by the member states. Reference to media pluralism reinforces other provisions such as content provisions, jurisdiction by one member state, etc. The AVMSD implementation process has not normally included pluralism considerations, but the context of the enhanced debate at the EU level, many accompanying activities and new measures introduced in some EU countries, put the issue of pluralism into a new light of policy interest.

In the CEE countries, media pluralism measures have resulted from a cumulative recognition, and subsequent amendments to the initial broadcasting laws. These do not bring clear-cut answers to the question *what kind* of media diversity would be best tailored to the media landscapes in the region, and respond with differing angles to observed developments in national media markets. In general, media pluralism provisions can be divided into three large categories:

- general recognition of media pluralism as an important value justifying regulatory decisions,
- internal pluralism provisions,
- external pluralism provisions.

The table below summarises provisions belonging to the first category.

Table 23: General recognition of media pluralism as a regulatory rationale in national broadcasting laws in the Czech Republic, Hungary, Poland and Slovakia

Country	Type of provision	Provisions concerning media pluralism	Legal basis
CZECH REPUBLIC	*TASK OF THE COUNCIL (RRTV)	Section 4 (2) "The Council (…) supervises the maintaining and further development of plurality in the programme portfolio and information offered in the field of radio and television broadcasting…"	Act No. 231/2001 of 17 May 2001 on Radio and Television Broadcasting and on Amendment to Other Acts
HUNGARY	*RECOGNITION OF DIVERSITY AS A FUNDAMENTAL PRINCIPLE	Article 4 "The diversity of media services is a particularly important value. The protection of diversity shall also include the avoidance of the formation of ownership monopolies and any unjustified restriction of competition on the market. The provisions of this Act shall be interpreted in consideration of the protection of diversity".	Act CLXXXV of 2010 on Media Services and Mass Media, as amended
POLAND	*TASK OF THE COUNCIL (KRRiT)	Article 6 (1) KRRT shall "…ensure an open and pluralistic nature of radio and television broadcasting"	1992 Broadcasting Act adopted on 29 December, 1992, as amended
SLOVAKIA	*TASK OF THE COUNCIL (RRTV)	Article 4 (2) The Council takes care of maintaining plurality of information in news services of broadcasters…"	Act No. 308 of 14 September 2000 Coll. on Broadcasting and Retransmission (as amended)

Sources: Elaborated on the basis of national broadcasting laws in the Czech Republic, Hungary, Poland and Slovakia as quoted in the table.

The table demonstrates quite varied approaches in general recognition of media pluralism. Principally, media diversity is recognised as a fundamental principle in the 2010 Hungarian Act on Media Services and Mass

Media.[1] The Act does not only acknowledge the particularly important value of the 'diversity of media services', it also suggests that all provisions of the Act will be interpreted in consideration of the protection of diversity. The Act refers to "the avoidance of the formation of ownership monopolies and any unjustified restriction of competition on the market" but suggests that other aspects of diversity are included as well. With a lack of more precise definition of 'diversity of media services', the concept remains quite evasive and vague, and as such leaves a wide discretion to the National Media and Communications Authority (NMHH) in interpreting this value for the purpose of the regulatory intervention.

In the case of other countries (the Czech Republic, Poland, Slovakia), media pluralism is seen as a possible end of regulatory policies and a concrete task of the national media regulatory authorities. This task is though framed quite differently from country to country. In the Czech Republic, the Council is expected to cater for "plurality in the programme portfolio and information offered", which accents the connectedness between structural decisions on licensing with the 'internal dimension' of a variety of programmes and services offered by broadcasters. In Poland, the Council should ensure the "open and pluralistic nature" of broadcasting which may afford a relatively large discretion in interpreting its 'pluralistic nature' through various possible dimensions – content, genre, ownership, function, etc. In Slovakia, the Council is expected to take care of maintaining "plurality of information in news services" of broadcasters, thus plurality more narrowly relates to news and current affairs content.

Although internal media pluralism does not stand for the main focus of this chapter, the table below summarises measures concerning the media content dimension in order to contextualise these with structural measures.[2]

[1] Act CLXXXV of 2010 on Media Services...

Table 24: Internal pluralism measures in national broadcasting laws in the Czech Republic, Hungary, Poland and Slovakia

Country	Type of provision	Provisions concerning internal media pluralism	Legal basis
CZECH REPUBLIC	*PROVISIONS ON BALANCED NEWS	Section 31 (2) "A broadcaster shall provide objective and balanced information necessary for opinions to be freely formed (…)". Section 31 (3) "A broadcaster shall ensure that principles of objectivity and balance are complied with in news and political programme units (…)".	Act No. 231/2001 of 17 May 2001 on Radio and Television Broadcasting and on Amendment to Other Acts
	*CONDITIONS IN LICENCE-GRANTING PROCESS	Section 17 (1) The programme structure proposed by the licence applicant with regards to existing diversity of programmes is to be assessed in the process of granting the licence.	
HUNGARY	*PROVISIONS ON BALANCED NEWS	Article 13 "Linear media services engaged in the provision of information shall provide balanced coverage on local, national and European issues that may be of interest for the general public (…)".	Act CIV of 2010 on the Freedom of the Press and the Fundamental Rules on Media Content as amended
	*NEWS PROVISION	Article 38 (1) an obligation to broadcast news by linear audiovisual media service providers with significant market power.	Act CLXXXV of 2010 on Media Services and Mass Media, as amended

SLOVAKIA	*DIVERSITY OF NEWS PROVISION	Article 16 (3) "A broadcaster should ensure comprehensiveness of information and plurality of views in broadcasting its service".	Act No 308 of 14 September 2000 Coll. on Broadcasting and Retransmission (as amended)
	*PUBLIC INTEREST PROVISON	Article 18 (1) "A broadcaster is obliged to ensure a diverse programming output, especially with regard to a majority proportion of programmes in the public interest, in all services provided the broadcaster".	
	*CONDITIONS IN LICENCE-GRANTING AND EXTENDING PROCESS	Article 47 (d) A balance of programming output is taken into account in decisions about licence granting. Article 52 (3) Contribution to the cultural development and the well-informed public, as well as the development of original production, is taken into account in the process of extending the licence term.	

Sources: National broadcasting laws in the Czech Republic, Hungary, Poland and Slovakia as quoted in the table.
Note: The table does not cover the specific rules concerning PSM. The table does not include content rules on European and national works covered in Chapter 4, and does not cover other content rules that are not directly relevant for internal media pluralism.[2]

[2] Poland has not been included in the table as the relevant internal pluralism provisions are only reflected in Article 36 (1) (4) of the 1992 Broadcasting Act, and these refer to a consideration of declared proportion of European works, described in Chapter 4.

The internal pluralism provisions are based on the premise that all relevant viewpoints, opinions are to be represented in the programming offer of a broadcaster. These might require certain content conditions e.g. proportional representations of certain types and genres of programming that will support an exposure of views and opinions (news, public interest content). In Hungary, the broadcasters with significant market power are obliged to broadcast news programmes, seen as important contribution to supply diversity. In Slovakia, broadcasters are expected to ensure diverse programming output, consisting in particular from contents and services important for the public interest. Both these obligations stem from the assumption that news and public interest content might be underrepresented by broadcasters without preventive regulatory safeguards.

In media regulatory policies, the premise of balanced news and information has often been associated with the claim for internal diversity (e.g. fairness doctrine). In journalistic practice, however, a mere technical confrontation of opposing views and claims does not necessarily generate valuable internal diversity. Article 13 of the 2010 Hungarian Act on Freedom of the Press and the Fundamental Rules on Media Content[3] obliges the linear media services engaged in the provision of information to provide balanced coverage. As shown in Chapter 3, this provision in its former wording raised many objections from various international organisations, especially due to the large scope for interpretation by the regulatory agency. A very similar measure applies to all broadcasters under the 2001 Czech Act on Radio and Television Broadcasting[4] that obliges the broadcasters to "provide objective and balanced information necessary for opinions to be freely formed" and to ensure that "principles of objectivity and balance are complied with in news and political programme units".

In terms of possible regulatory interventions, the most feasible are measures on internal pluralism that help to finalise decisions on granting or extending the licence. In the Czech Republic, the regulatory authority is expected to asses the proposed programme structure, while considering available content diversity in the broadcasting landscape. In Slovakia, the regulatory authority takes into account both "a balance of programming output" and "contribution to the cultural development and a well-informed public, as well as the development of original production".

External pluralism measures are usually more complex than rules on internal diversity and may employ various considerations concerning media ownership, transparency, must-carry rules, and support for community and socially valuable media. The table summarises sets of these provisions in the Czech Republic, Hungary, Poland and Slovakia.

[3] Act CIV of 2010 on the Freedom of the Press and the Fundamental Rules...

[4] Act No. 231/2001 of 17 May 2001 on Radio and Television Broadcasting...

Table 25: External and structural pluralism measures in national broadcasting laws in the Czech Republic, Hungary, Poland and Slovakia

Country	Type of provision	Provisions concerning external and structural media pluralism	Legal basis
CZECH REPUBLIC	*CROSS-MEDIA OWNERSHIP AND CONCENTRATION	Section 55 one licence only rule for nation-wide analogue TV or radio broadcasting; limits on ownership interests and consolidation, Section 55a one licence only rule for nation-wide digital TV or radio broadcasting; limits on ownership interests and consolidation Section 56 limits on the audience reach of local and regional TV and radio broadcasters Section 57 formation of programme networks (limits on audience reach by TV and radio broadcasting of programme networks) Section 58 consolidation of broadcasters or rebroadcasters (pre-consolidation notification obligations; definition of a substantial influence)	Act No. 231/2001 of 17 May 2001 on Radio and Television Broadcasting and on Amendment to Other Acts
	*MUST-CARRY RULES	Section 54 must carry rules to allocating free of charge one channel for an unpaid local information system serving exclusively to meet the needs of the local community must carry rules to offer PSM	
	*MEDIA TRANSPARENCY	Section 17 (1) the transparency of ownership in the applicant's company is taken into account in the process of decision-making for granting the licence by the Council	

HUNGARY	*CROSS-MEDIA OWNERSHIP, CONCENTRATION AND EXCESSIVE CONTROL	Article 68 setting the threshold of 35% of an average audience annual share for linear media service providers and 40% of a joint audience share for linear radio and media service providers, in order to limit further activities related to media services Article 69 definition of media service providers with significant market power Article 70 rules of procedures aimed at the preventing media market concentration and identifying media service providers with significant power Article 71 rules governing media service providers of analogue media linear services Article 64 (1) rules on connecting to a network, expansion of the reception Area Article 72 thresholds on the number of media services distributed on the given transmission system	Act CLXXXV of 2010 on Media Services and Mass Media, as amended
	*MUST-CARRY RULES	Article 73 'must carry' obligations Article 74 media service distributors obliged to carry media services of the PSM free of charge Article 75 media service distributors obliged to contract regional or local audiovisual community media services Article 78 rules on the obligation to offer media services	

	*RULES ON COMMUNITY MEDIA	Article 66 (1) definition of linear community services, the procedure of recognition Article 136 rules on the operation of a Media Service Support and Asset Management Fund, established to promote and support public service and community media services Article 137 forms of support and conditions of tendering overseen by the Media Council	
	*MEDIA TRANSPARENCY	Article 41 rules on general notification applicable to providers of media services Article 41 (6) rules on public access to the data collected in the registers Article 42 rules on media transparency (including ownership data) applicable to providers of linear services	

POLAND	*MEDIA OWNERSHIP AND CONCENTRATION	Article 36 (2) preventing the awarding of licences to applicants that may achieve a dominant position in the mass media in a the given area Article 38 (2) a possibility to revoke a licence if a broadcaster achieves a dominant position mass media on the given relevant market or if another person takes over control over the activity of the broadcaster Article 38a(3) assessment of merger cases in terms of transferring licence rights to transformed entities	1992 Broadcasting Act adopted on 29 December, 1992, as amended
	*MUST-CARRY RULES	Article 43 must carry rules for the PSM	
	*RULES ON SOCIAL BROADCASTERS	Article 4 (10) definition of a social broadcaster Article 39b entities eligible for the status of social broadcasters; exemption of social broadcasters from fees payable for awarding or altering the licence	
	*MEDIA TRANSPARENCY	Article 37a media service providers required to deliver financial statements to the National Broadcasting Council on an annual basis	

SLOVAKIA	*CROSS-MEDIA OWNERSHIP AND CONCENTRATION	Article 42 (1) the publisher of a daily newspaper distributed in at least 50% of Slovak territory cannot hold a licence for national or multi-regional broadcasting Article 42 (2) a physical or legal entity can have ownership share only in one broadcaster with a national or multi-regional coverage Article 42 (3) a physical or legal entity can have ownership share in more broadcasters with local or regional coverage but target audience cannot exceed 50% of all inhabitants Article 43 the TV or radio broadcaster cannot have ownership shares in or be the publisher of, a nationally distributed daily newspaper	Act No. 308 of 14 September 2000 Coll. on Broadcasting and Retransmission (as amended)
	*MUST-CARRY RULES	Article 17 (1) must carry rules (e.g. for carrying at least one locally oriented channel)	
	*MEDIA TRANSPARENCY	Article 52 (3) media ownership transparency is taken into account in the process of extending the licence term, as well as the contribution to the development of a media market Article 54 the Council may withdraw a licence due to substantial ownership changes without prior notification	

Sources: Elaborated on the basis of national broadcasting laws in the Czech Republic, Hungary, Poland and Slovakia as quoted in the table.

Katrin Voltmer (2013: 46) argues that externally diverse media often compensate for the structural barriers of mainstream media to provide alternative discourses and serve those groups of users that seem to be less attractive to affluent advertisers. The table above demonstrates that the measures incorporated in the national broadcasting laws in the CEE countries can be divided into four groups. The largest category of measures includes those provisions that tend to limit media power and control of dominant players in broadcasting markets. Rachel Craufurd Smith et al. (2012: 12) point out that "the greater the degree of sophistication and discretion involved, the greater the likelihood of uncertainty for industry and 'agency capture'". Thus, the best methods avoiding these risks involve establishing fixed ownership limits. Among the countries studied, only Hungary introduced such media specific ownership thresholds, in addition to competition law and policy. Major linear media service providers cannot initiate a new media service or acquire a share in a company providing media content if their annual audience share exceeds 35% or 40% of a joint audience share for linear radio and media service providers.[5] However, in comparison with the former Act I of 1996 on Radio and Television Broadcasting which was in force until 2010, the scope of cross-ownership limitations has shrunken. The previous Act did not permit cross-ownership involving the press sector: the owner of a national newspaper could not have a controlling share in a media provider operating in national broadcasting and vice versa. The change in the 2010 Act is considered as an indirect consequence of digitisation (OSF, 2012b: 66). It is important to add in this respect, that unlike in the Czech Republic, Poland and Slovakia, the Media Council (*Médiatanács*) of the NMHH is authorised to monitor media market concentration, eventual distortions on the media markets and abuses of a dominant position. The measurement involves mainly audience shares.

The Czech Republic and Slovakia introduced limits on cross-media ownership setting a restriction on the number of operating licences. Under the Czech broadcasting law, the broadcaster can hold only one licence for a nation-wide analogue or digital TV or radio. The law also prevents cross-ownership between the operator of an electronic communications network and the holder of a broadcasting license.[6] At the same time, there are no restrictions on cross-media ownership involving potential mergers between print and broadcasting sectors (OSF, 2013a: 62). In Slovakia, the rule of granting one licence only to a broadcaster of a national or multi-regional TV or radio, is paired with limits on cross-ownership pertaining to eventual

[5] Act CLXXXV of 2010 on Media Services and Mass Media…

[6] Act No. 231/2001 of 17 May 2001 on Radio and Television Broadcasting…

mergers or cross ownership between broadcasters and publishers "of a daily newspaper distributed in at least 50% of Slovak territory".[7] With the digital switchover process, broadcasters with nationwide coverage were allowed to operate thematic channels under the 2007 Act on Digital Broadcasting.[8]

In comparison with other CEE countries, Poland seems to employ the most relaxed rules on cross-media ownership and concentration. Actually, the 1992 Broadcasting Act[9] limits only monomedia or horizontal concentration.[10] A broadcasting licence may not be awarded if transmission of a programme service by the applicant results in achieving a dominant position by the applicant in a given area. Also, the broadcasting licence may be revoked on the same grounds. Yet, the Broadcasting Act does not explicitly define "a dominant position in the mass media in a given area". It is the Act on Competition and Consumer Protection,[11] which provides for an interpretation of such a position. This is understood as a position that allows an entrepreneur to prevent efficient competition on the relevant market, entailing that the market share exceeds 40%. In compliance with the 1992 Broadcasting Act, the National Broadcasting Council (KRRiT) evaluates, whether a particular applicant may achieve such a dominant position considering above all the main goals of the Act, that is the open and pluralistic nature of broadcasting.

Craufurd Smith et al. (2012: 13) note that companies that attract more than 30% of the television audience are presumed to exert too great an influence on public opinion. The thresholds set up in the national broadcasting laws (in some cases in combination with competition laws) in the CEE countries surpass this limit. This only proves that while certain media specific ownership rules are in place, these are largely more permissive than the rules used in many EU countries. Moreover, the current regulatory regimes seem to support the status quo on the broadcasting landscapes that took shape during the first licence-granting processes in 1993–1996. These enabled some major broadcasters to safely divide broadcasting markets and control their significant shares, practically from their onset at the beginning of the 1990s. Although the issues of preventing media concentration have been discussed repeatedly with introducing or considering new policies,

[7] Act No. 308 of 14 September 2000 Coll. on Broadcasting...

[8] Act No. 222 of 29 March 2007 Coll. on Digital Broadcasting of Programme Services and Providing other Content Services by Digital Transmission.

[9] 1992 Broadcasting Act adopted on 29 December, 1992...

[10] Mono-media or horizontal media concentration refers to integration of capital or ownership within a single media sector activity such as the print press, TV broadcasting, online news, etc.

[11] Act on Competition and Consumer Protection adopted on 15 December 2000, Official Journal, 2000, No. 122, item 1319, as amended.

these hardly led to a greater certainty to offering clearer definitions, less discretion on part of regulatory authorities, simpler procedures and thresholds adjusted to the converged media landscapes. In Hungary for example, the cross-media ownership rules (previously involving publishers of newspapers) were eased with the 2010 media law, but at the same time, the Media Council was equipped with greater competence to decide on matters of media concentration. Accordingly, the recommendations and opinions of the Media Council bind the Hungarian Competition Authority (GVH) under the 2010 Act on Media Services and Mass Media. In Poland, the policy document *Polish State Strategy for the Electronic Media for 2005–2020* prepared by the National Broadcasting Council (KRRiT), proposed limits of maximum 30% of market share for those broadcasting licence holders and publishers of daily newspapers (both on national and local markets) that apply for new licences (both on local and national markets) (KRRiT, 2005: A5). This proposal was never implemented due to opposition from commercial broadcasters. Thus, the new *Regulatory Strategy for 2011–2013* of the National Broadcasting Council (KRRiT, 2011:26) merely lists among the objectives of the Council support for the pluralism of media ownership (existence of diverse, autonomous and mutually independent media, financed from various sources) without specifying conditions concerning the media (including cross-media) consolidation and mergers.

The second important category of rules relevant for structural media pluralism concerns specific media types financed from non-commercial sources. These are recognised as 'community media' in Hungary and 'social broadcasters' in Poland. The Hungarian 2010 Act on Media Services and Mass Media defines community media as services provided to satisfy the special needs for information and to enable access to cultural programmes for a certain social, national, cultural or religious community, or for residents of a given settlement or region. Also the services providing most of their programming in accordance with the objectives of the PSM are understood as community media.[12] The community media are eligible for funding from the Media Service Support and Asset Management Fund. In Poland, the 1992 Broadcasting Act exempts social broadcasters from fees payable for awarding or altering the licence. A social broadcaster is defined as a broadcaster who promotes learning and educational activities, charitable deeds, and respects the Christian system of values and strives to preserve national identity in the programme services. Such a broadcaster cannot transmit advertising and teleshopping and spon-

[12] Act CLXXXV of 2010 on Media Services and Mass Media… Article 66.

sored programmes and may not charge any fee for transmission, retransmission or reception of the programme service.[13]

Must carry rules were introduced in national broadcasting laws of all studied CEE countries, often in combination with digital acts or digital switchover acts. These stipulate usually the obligation to carry public service channels and locally-oriented channels. Last, but not least are provisions on media transparency that can be seen as an essential component of structural media pluralism. Stolte and Craufurd Smith note that the availability of accurate and up-to-date data on media ownership lies at the very heart of any media pluralism regulation, as it would be impossible to limit excessive media concentrations without the tools to transparently identify them (Stolte and Craufurd Smith, 2010). Yet, media ownership transparency has also an important public dimension: not only should the specialised public agencies (such as media regulatory authorities) be equipped with a mandate to access the relevant ownership data, also media users should be able to know who owns the media they use. This would oblige media companies to publicly disclose and share such data in a clear, easily accessible and free-of-charge form. As table 24 demonstrates, media transparency rules in the CEE countries mainly revolve around an obligation to notify media regulatory authorities about broadcasters' ownership, eventual changes, financial situation and plans for concentration and mergers.

In Poland, the Chairman of the National Broadcasting Council may require a broadcaster to provide materials, information and documentation to the extent necessary for the purpose of supervising the broadcaster's compliance with the provisions of the Act and the terms of the broadcasting licence.[14] Under Article 37a of the 1992 Broadcasting Act, media service providers are required annually, to deliver to the National Broadcasting Council their financial statements prepared in a form specified by the Act on Accounting (1994).[15] The purpose of this requirement is to review the financial and economic conditions of broadcasters including advertising revenues, financial results (profits and loses), ownership structure and capital concentration. In practice, a detailed analysis of financial statements by the National Broadcasting Council may appear to be problematic as the quote from the annual report of the National Broadcasting Council shows: "(the financial statements) do not always give complete knowledge on the economic and financial situation of broadcasters and about the achieved

[13] 1992 Broadcasting Act..., Article 4 (1).

[14] 1992 Broadcasting Act..., Article 10 (2).

[15] 1994 Act on Accounting (Ustawa o Rachunkowości) adopted on September 29, 1994, Official Journal, 1994, No. 121, item 591, as amended.

results of their broadcasting activity" (KRRiT, 2003: 10). In Slovakia, media ownership transparency is taken into account in the process of extending the licence term. The purpose of this process is to consider the contribution to the development of a media market.[16] Likewise, in the Czech Republic the transparency of ownership in the applicant's company is taken into account in the process of decision-making leading to granting the licence by the Council. In Hungary, media transparency rules are an integral part of the process of notification. The providers of media services are subject to registration by the Office of the National Media and Communications Authority (NMHH). Under Article 41(6) the data recorded in the registers concerning "the names, contact information of media service providers, press product founders and publishers, as well as the names and titles of the media services and press products" are publicly available.[17] It is worth mentioning though, that this publicly available information does not include data on ultimate ownership. The Mapping Digital Media report on Hungary concludes: "Most of the major media outlets' websites indicate the owner. Thus citizens can learn through publicly available information who the owners of the media are" (OSF, 2012b: 71). It should be noted though that the name of the company does not always indicate the ultimate owner and other important information that may be relevant in the context of media ownership such as active political involvement of the owner. Under the Hungarian media law, different rules of disclosure apply to providers of linear services and providers of on-demand services and press products. The providers of linear services are required to provide

> data on the size of direct or indirect ownership stake held by the notifier or by any other person with a qualifying holding in the notifier undertaking, in any undertaking providing media services, or applying for media service provision rights, within the territory of Hungary.[18]

Thus, even though the providers of linear services have to disclose more detailed data on media ownership, these are merely collected by the NMHH and not automatically disclosed to the public in an easily accessible form.

As can be seen from this brief analysis, the broadcasting laws in the CEE seem to be relatively permissive in ownership policies and consolidation. They also allow for too much discretion on the side of regulatory authorities to limit eventually the size of media companies, mergers or decide about revoking licences. Media ownership details are often opaque and do not allow an automatic disclosure or identification of the ultimate

[16] Act No. 308 of 14 September 2000 Coll. on Broadcasting..., Article 52 (3).
[17] Act CLXXXV of 2010 on Media Services and Mass Media...
[18] Ibidem, Article 42 (1)e.

owner of particular media outlets. Besides, the changes in ownership are constant and complex. The transparency rules largely function within the media regulatory authorities, but do not automatically ensure the access of the public to the full datasets free of charge.

The next section of this chapter will focus on three dimensions of structural media pluralism: diversity of media control/patterns of media ownership; diversity of media functions and geographical diversity.

5.4. Diversity of media control: patterns of media ownership

An important precondition of structural diversity is a diversity of players – newspapers (both print and online), TV channels, radio stations and other media services that users identify as distinct entities offering different types of content services. Media entities (usually institutions) and their operations are most often aggregated according to ownership links and controlled by the owners. Relatively similar ownership patterns might however result in various levels of service diversity: some owners invest in media outlets that reflect a broader range of viewpoints and cultural representations, others make specific uses of their media to achieve political and economic benefits (Klimkiewicz, 2010b: 908). Ownership patterns intersect with horizontal levels of media sectors (such as print, broadcasting and Internet) and vertical production and distribution chains (news production, advertising, distribution). Current media business structures make it more difficult to paint ownership borders of media entities as most influential players engage in manifold alliances, joint ventures, networks and forms of co-operation that lead to diffusion of control and require a reconciliation of multiple interests (2010b: 908).

The interrelation between politics and economic interests of the media is seen as one of the most serious threats to media pluralism. The Commission in the Staff Working Document on Media Pluralism observed: "Given the important role that the media play in disseminating information about the economy and political actors and their activities, there is no European Member State where political and/or economic actors do not try to influence media coverage according to their own interest" (European Commission, 2007a: 6). Thus, diversity of ownership is seen not only as a condition ensuring a diverse range of information sources and various forms of organisational structures, but also as a condition preventing an excessive political power and political influence of the media owners. The next two sections of this chapter will elaborate on the question of foreign ownership in the CEE countries and media ownership types, with a particular consideration of the question of media ownership consolidation.

5.4.1. Foreign and domestic media ownership: does it matter?

Very few media scholars and professionals in the region would probably claim that the new media structures that developed after 1989 decreased media pluralism and diversity in general. But an interpretation of empirical currents, especially as it comes to power of media structures, do not offer clear-cut views of steady progress. This refers particularly to the question of foreign media ownership. It has been common knowledge that one of the most distinguishing features of the media systems in the CEE is foreign ownership, especially in the sector of the print press. Foreign capital brought to Central and Eastern Europe the necessary investment needed for revamping media landscapes and old production routines. Foreign investors also helped to assimilate Western managerial practices in CEE sister companies and improved production technology (Jakubowicz, 2007). This has been seen as 'a natural course' of media development that could eventually be reproduced in other parts of the world. John Downey observes that transnational capital in the CEE media sector can be characterised by the theory of mimetic isomorphism (2012: 117). Uncertainty of the CEE media environments resulted in copying successful business models from Western countries. Indeed, transnational owners proved to be very cautious in experimenting with genuinely new projects. They have rather tended to 'clone' and bring to Central European markets the types of products that met commercial success in their respective countries. But explaining this by the high uncertainty in the region might be exaggerated. The CEE countries implemented relatively permissive regulatory frameworks to attract rather than discourage, foreign investors. Bound by membership in the Council of Europe, EU pre-accession negotiations and the significant proximity to the Western part of Europe, the fresh and unfurnished media environments constituted a relatively attractive ground for foreign capital and innovation in media services. The CEE countries did not impose any limitations on foreign ownership in the sector of the print press, and some constraints in broadcasting markets have been gradually lifted in order to comply with the premises of the internal market.

Indeed, from the perspective of EU internal market, division on 'foreign' (EU based) and domestic ownership becomes pointless. After EU accession, not only did all CEE countries lift barriers on EU non-domestic ownership, but some decided to lift or considerably weaken rules on foreign (non-EU) ownership as well (Klimkiewicz, 2009a). At the same time, Katrin Voltmer observes that foreign ownership is felt as a form of cultural domination in countries of the region, which – for better or worse – are beginning to develop their national identities by distancing themselves from the West (Voltmer, 2013: 172). The issue of 'foreign media ownership' has also gradually gained greater political exposure in national political discourses, signifying economic and cultural influence. The Commission's Staff Working Document: *Media Pluralism in the Member States of the European Union* (2007a: 9–10) paid attention to the issue of cross-border concentration distinguishing its two dimensions: an international dimension and intercommunity dimension. While the first is related to the increasing influence of non-European investors in Europe (mostly US-based), the second refers mostly to Western companies significantly investing in "the countries that joined the Union in 2004 and 2006". Although the Document notes that non-domestic owners do not necessarily pose a threat to media pluralism, the lack of legal safeguards at place and insufficient editorial independence from the owner may effectively curtail freedom of expression and information. In addition, the vast presence of transnational conglomerates may be seen as detrimental to domestic media businesses, may lead to growing commercialisation and may also make national competition regulation more harder to enforce against foreign undertakings.

The table below presents the rules on foreign ownership in the audiovisual sector before and after EU accession.

Table 26: Rules on foreign ownership in the broadcasting sector in the Czech Republic, Hungary, Poland and Slovakia

Country	Restrictions on foreign ownership before 2004	Restrictions on foreign ownership after 2004	Applies to	Legal basis
CZECH REPUBLIC	NO	NO	–	–
HUNGARY	YES (partial) Persons with Hungarian citizenship residing in Hungary and legal persons established in Hungary must hold at least 26% of the voting rights in a private company with national program provision	2004–2010 Persons with Hungarian citizenship residing in Hungary and legal persons established in Hungary must hold at least 26% of the voting rights in a private company with national program provision	broadcasting	Article 122, Act I of 1996 of Radio and Television Broadcasting
		Since 2010 NO	–	–

POLAND	YES Article 35 foreigners may not hold more than 33% in the opening or share capital of the company	YES Article 35 (2) companies having foreign (non-EU) shareholders may be awarded a licence under the condition that foreign shares in the equity stake or the capital do not exceed 49%; share of votes does not exceed 49% or if Polish persons constitute a majority in its top decisive bodies	broad-casting	1992 Broadcasting Act adopted on 29 December, 1992, as amended
SLOVAKIA	YES (partial) Article 46 there are obligations to inform about the foreign activities of broadcasters Article 47g In making a decision about granting the licence, the Council shall be obliged to evaluate and take into account: the fact that it is necessary to ensure adequate ownership participation of the Slovak persons and their representation in bodies of the company provided that the applicant for the licence is a legal person with foreign (non-EU) capital participation	YES (partial) Article 46 there are obligations to inform about foreign activities of broadcasters Article 47g In making a decision about granting the licence, the Council shall be obliged to evaluate and take into account: the fact that it is necessary to ensure adequate ownership participation of Slovak persons and their representation in bodies of the company provided that the applicant for the licence is a legal person with foreign (non-EU) capital participation		Act No. 308/2000 Coll. of 14 September, 2000 on Broadcasting and Retransmission as amended

Sources: Elaborated on the basis of national broadcasting laws in the Czech Republic, Hungary, Poland and Slovakia as quoted in the table.

Before EU accession, the most restrictive regulation concerning foreign ownership had been implemented in Poland. The share of capital of foreign owners on broadcasting markets could not exceed 33% until 2004. This threshold in fact resulted in a prominent presence of domestic TV owners, two of which built successively their media businesses around the flagship TV channels – *Polsat* (Polsat Media group owned by Zygmunt Solorz) and *TVN* (owned by the ITI group originally established by Mariusz Walter and Jan Wejchert). After EU accession, Poland maintained limits for foreign non-EU ownership and Slovakia kept provisions encouraging an adequate ownership participation of persons with Slovak citizenship.

Studying the dynamics between foreign (transnational) and domestic (national) structures in the CEE countries demonstrates how self-sustainable a media system is in its particular environment and how much it depends on external resources (financing, know-how, human capital). The lack of self-sustainability can be enhanced or counterbalanced by appropriate policy approaches and choices. These have been used to a very limited extent by the CEE countries as regards the print press sector, and in some countries – the Czech Republic in particular – also in the broadcasting sector. The dominance of foreign ownership in the press markets can be exemplified by the lists of the top press companies (measured by the level of revenues) in the CEE countries. In Hungary, in 2011 the top six media companies were foreign, including a Finish publishing group Sanoma, and the Swiss-owned Ringier. In the Czech Republic, in 2011 the top positions among publishing companies were occupied by Ringier Axel Springer, MAFRA (Rheinisch Bergische Verlagsgeselschaft – RBV) and Passauer Neue Presse (Verlagsgruppe Passau), in Slovakia by Ringier Axel Springer and RBV.[19] In the audiovisual field, significant revenues were generated by US-owned CME (Central European Enterprises), now a subsidiary of Time Warner, which controls the top commercial TV channels in the Czech Republic and Slovakia. The top positions of the two leading broadcasting companies in Hungary – *RTL Klub* (owned by Bertelsmann) and *TV2* (previously the US-owned and Luxembourg based MTM-SBS company, now ProsiebenSat1) resulted from the opening the Hungarian market to commercial broadcasting in 1996, thus establishing a three-tier structure involving two commercial TV channels with foreign ownership and the public service broadcaster *MTV*. In Poland, one of the top positions among media companies is occupied by *Canal+* (owned by the French Vivendi) developing operations through its leading digital platform.

---

[19] WAN (2012) World Press Trends (available at: http://www.wan-ifra.org/microsites/world-press-trends; retrieved 23.12.2013).

The asymmetric development of the ownership structures in the 1990s has gained more fluctuating dynamics in last 10 years. Szabolcs Tóth observes that "The level of foreign ownership in Hungarian media has been unhealthily high since the mid 1990s. This started to change in the last couple of years" (Reuters Institute for the Study of Journalism, 2012). Certainly, some shifts in media ownership signal the rise of domestic resources both in terms of financing and know-how. Václav Štetka even argues that domestic tycoons are back on the ground and local business elites looking to influence politicians, are buying into the media sector (2013). A number of media ownership changes or initiatives in the region epitomise this trend. One of them was the entry of the Slovak investment group J&T (established by Patrik Tkáč and Ivan Jakabovič) into the ownership of the second most popular private TV channel TV *Joj* and in 2010 into control of the daily *Pravda* (previously owned by the Daily Mail group). At the end of 2013, Patrik Tkáč with the Czech businessman Daniel Křetínský acquired the business activities of Ringier Axel Springer in the Czech Republic, including the Czech press wholesaler *První novinová společnost a.s. (PNS)*, and a leading tabloid *Blesk*.[20] In Poland, similar developments represent a takeover of Axel Springer's daily *Dziennik* by the Infor company in 2009 and the daily *Rzeczpospolita* by the Polish businessman Grzegorz Hajdarowicz in 2011. In the Czech Republic, the coal baron Zdeněk Bakala acquired the weekly *Respekt* in 2006 and a financial daily *Hospodářské noviny,* together with the weekly *Ekonom* in 2008. In addition, the owner of the largest media buying agency in the country, Jaromír Soukup, controls a media empire which includes several news and lifestyle magazines as well as the fourth largest television channel, TV Barrandov (Štetka, 2013). In Hungary in 2005, the businessman Gábor Széles launched a commercial cable television channel *Echo TV* and the *Echo News Agency,* and purchased the liberal daily newspaper *Magyar Hírlap,* and converted it into a conservative newspaper (OSF, 2012b: 68).

By contrast, there have been other examples that illustrate a contrary development – the growing ownership participation of large scale transnational media groups in some media activities in the region. In 2007, the TV market leader *Markíza* became wholly owned by the U.S. conglomerate Central European Media Enterprises (CME – now ultimately owned by Time Warner), which had previously controlled 50% of the channel.

[20] Press Release: *Ringier Axel Springer Media AG: Entrepreneurs Daniel Křetínský and Patrik Tkáč take over activities in the Czech Republic* (2013) Axel Springer 20.12.2013 (available at: http://www.axelspringer.de/en/presse/Ringier-Axel-Springer-Media-AG-Entrepreneurs-Daniel-K-etinsky-and-Patrik-Tka-take-over-activities-in-the-Czech-Republic_19709787.html; retrieved 22.12.2013)

Before that, *Markíza* had been heavily influenced by the unofficial Slovak co-owner and politician Pavol Rusko (OSF, 2013b: 63). Following a series of collusions with the Czech partner and protracted arbitration between the CME and the Czech State, CME settled its 100% of ownership in the leading private broadcaster *Nova* in the Czech Republic in 2005 (Downey, 2012: 120). In Poland, the largest radio network *RMF* was bought by the German publishing giant Bauer in 2006 from its Polish owner. In 2012, the largest news portal in Poland *onet.pl* (owned before by the ITI group) was acquired by Ringier Axel Springer. Finally in 2013, Canal+/Vivendi merged its digital platform *Cyfra+* with the competitive digital platform *n* owned before by the ITI group. These shifts exemplify that the dynamics between foreign (transnational) and domestic (national) media ownership structures in the CEE countries is brisk and uneven, dictated by a growing self-sustainability of national media environments on the one hand, and refocusing priorities of the transnational media companies on the other hand.

Although research has not offered a clear diagnosis of the influence of foreign ownership on structural media pluralism, three different ways may be mentioned in which transnational companies are likely to modify the diversity of media structures or services. Firstly, the takeover of media companies by foreign owners may more easily lead to reaching transactions among large transnational entities with prioritising the supranational and regional interests rather than paying due respect to the communication needs of national audiences. Secondly, transnational media networks and entities tend more often than domestic companies to multiply the same business models and products across national boundaries, thus reducing the type of structural diversity being rooted in a specific national, cultural and geographical space (Klimkiewicz, 2009a). Thirdly, in the search for greater precaution, conformity and synergies with activities in other national markets, the transnational companies may tend to avoid contents that bear political risks or more ambitious journalism.

With regard to transnational takeovers and strategic alliances, the transnational owners have gradually invested in particular sectors of media markets to acquire controlling positions. In 2007, among the seven largest paid-for daily newspapers in the Czech Republic, foreign companies controlled 90% of circulation, and in 2013 88% of the circulation.[21] This high proportion was largely shared between the three German

[21] This share will certainly decrease since December 2013, as the leading Czech tabloid Blesk together with other Czech media businesses of Ringier Axel Springer were bought by Czech businessman Daniel Křetínský and Patrik Tkáč, the co-owner of the Slovak J&T investment group.

publishing groups: Ringier Axel Springer, Rheinisch Bergische Verlagsgesellschaft (RBV) and Verlagsgruppe Passau (Passauer Neue Presse), each specialising in a different type of the press (tabloid, quality daily, regional press). In Slovakia, foreign owners controlled 70% of print press circulation among the top seven paid-for dailies in 2011. This share was divided between two German publishing groups – Ringier Axel Springer and RBV. In Hungary the proportion of foreign ownership among the top seven paid-for dailies reached 83% in 2011 and 82% in 2013. Two publishing groups – Ringier and the Hungarian subsidiary of the Daily Mail Group (Lapcom)[22] shared this high proportion. Poland seems to be the only country where the share of foreign owners measured through the sold circulation of the seven largest paid-for dailies reached 45% in 2013 which accounts for less than a majority. This proportion was shared between Ringier Axel Springer and Verlagsgruppe Passau.

Strategic partnerships and acquisitions can be well illustrated by the case of Ringier and Axel Springer. Ringier AG established in 1833 in Switzerland entered the CEE press markets in 1991. The company quickly acquired a position of the market leader in the segment of dailies in the Czech Republic, Slovakia and later Hungary. Axel Springer established in Germany in 1946, entered the CEE press markets in 1989 starting operations in Hungary and in 1994 in Poland. Both companies focused on various segments of the press markets, but reached greater competitive proximity with the launch of the tabloid *Fakt* in Poland in 2003 and the tabloid *Reggel* in Hungary in 2004. Changing media business models and the necessity of digital investments led to consideration of a strategic partnership in the CEE. In 2010, Springer and Ringer finalised a large merger that aimed to integrate their CEE activities and generate synergies across Poland, Hungary, Slovakia, the Czech Republic and Serbia. The combined operating potential of the company became immense: the joint venture started to control the leading tabloid in each country, as can be seen from the table below:

Table 27: Leading companies in the sector of paid-for daily newspapers

	Before 2010	**After 2010**
CZECH REPUBLIC	Ringier	Ringier Axel Springer
HUNGARY	Ringier	Ringier
POLAND	Axel Springer	Ringier Axel Springer
SLOVAKIA	Ringier	Ringier Axel Springer

[22] In January 2013, Lapcom was sold by the Daily Mail Group to the Eliott Group.

John Downey notices that within such a structure each national subsidiary harnesses the power of the other to cement their dominance in press markets in the CEE (2012: 132). The merger between Ringier and Axel Springer was accepted in Poland, the Czech Republic and Slovakia, but in 2011 was stopped by the Hungarian Media Council. The opinion of the Media Council is binding for the Hungarian Competition Office under Act CLXXXV of 2010 on Media Services and the Mass Media. Article 70 of the Act entitles the Media Council to examine the facts concerning media markets in order to prevent media market concentration and identify media service providers with significant market power.[23] The Media Council justified its decision stating that the merger would significantly infringe upon the right to diverse sources of information. In comparison with the Czech Republic, Slovakia and Poland, Hungary represented the only press market where both companies enjoyed a high presence in similar press segments before the merger: Axel Springer has published eight regional dailies and the business daily *Világgazdaság*, as well as a number of women's, home, cooking, puzzle and youth magazines altogether amounting to more than 60 print and online titles. Ringier's portfolio has comprised more than 30 titles including the broadsheet *Népszabadság*, tabloid *Blikk* and sports daily *Nemzeti Sport*. Despite the merger was blocked, both companies still plan the combination of activities in Hungary. It is worth mentioning in this context that Hungary is seen as one of the strategic CEE markets together with Poland and Slovakia, where the merged Ringier Axel Springer intends to further develop their operations. As mentioned earlier in this section, Axel Springer sold its Czech print businesses to the Czech and Slovak businessmen, in order to refocus its further expansion on a digital fundament that has not been well developed in the Czech Republic.[24]

The multiplication of the same business models and products has been manifested by several transnational companies operating in the region. Ringier acting before the 2010 merger in Hungary, the Czech Republic and Slovakia, succeeded in launching or acquiring leading national tabloids. Although the tabloids have appeared under different titles (*Blikk* in Hungary; *Blesk* in the Czech Republic and *Nový Čas* in Slovakia), they were tailored to replicate the Swiss model – *Blick*. All of them provide

[23] Act CLXXXV of 2010 on Media Services and Mass Media...

[24] Press Release: *Ringier Axel Springer Media AG: Entrepreneurs Daniel Křetínský and Patrik Tkáč take over activities in the Czech Republic* (2013) Axel Springer 20.12.2013 (available at: http://www.axelspringer.de/en/presse/Ringier-Axel-Springer-Media-AG-Entrepreneurs-Daniel-K-etinsky-and-Patrik-Tka-take-over-activities-in-the-Czech-Republic_19709787.html; retrieved 22.12.2013).

akin content categories, and follow an entertainment-oriented logic, thus resulting in the same format and style of journalism. Similar examples are represented in the Polish tabloid *Fakt* published by Axel Springer since 2003, and modelled after the AS flagship title *Bild Zeitung*, or numerous cloned magazines printed mostly by Bauer, Ringier Axel Springer and Burda in Poland, Hungary, Czech Republic and Slovakia (Klimkiewicz, 2009a). Verlagsruppe Passau operating mainly on local and regional press markets in the Czech Republic and Poland reproduced chaining of newspaper titles under one brand, thus offering sections with unified content. Central European Media Enterprises owning commercial TV stations with a national coverage across the region 'transplanted' the model of an entertainment-focused TV from the US ground. In terms of contents offered, these TV channels predominately focus on US entertainment production, complementing it with other domestically produced genres – such as the news. It would be wrong, however, to assume that transnational companies multiply only commercial/entertainment media models. In 2006, Axel Springer established in Poland a quality daily newspaper *Dziennik* (modelled after the AS quality daily *Die Welt*) to compete with a successful and domestically owned *Gazeta Wyborcza*. The daily survived only three years though, compelled to merge with another daily *Gazeta Prawna* (published by Infor) in 2009. It seems understandable that at the dawn of the 21st century the copying of media business models and types of services presented a cheaper and safer option than experimenting with more risky online and digital services (at that time many successful activities were introduced by relatively small or medium size domestic groups). Yet, a few years later the necessity of investing in cross-media activities and appropriate bridging of content production with digital distribution became unavoidable. Transnational companies attempted to respond to these trends through various forms of cross-media expansion. Several examples can be mentioned in this respect. In Poland, the German press publisher Bauer stepped into the radio and online sector through the acquisition of the major commercial radio station *RMF FM* in 2006 and the subsequent acquisition of the *RMF*-related horizontal portal *interia.pl* in 2008. As Poland was the only country in the region where the publisher of daily newspapers could potentially acquire TV stations (other countries of the region introduced limits on cross-ownership in the print and broadcasting sector as discussed above), Axel Springer took the necessary steps in 2007 to buy 25.1% of shares in *TV Polsat* owned by Zygmunt Solorz. The Polish Office for Competition and Consumer Protection (UOKiK) however rejected the application arguing that despite acquiring only 25.1% of the shares, the influence of Axel Springer deems to be more significant due to the fact that without the approval of the FMV (a subsidiary of Axel Springer) important decisions concerning *TV Polsat* could not be taken. In 2012, the largest news portal in Poland *onet.pl* (owned before by the ITI group) was acquired by Ringier Axel Springer. In terms of popularity of use, only *google* achieves better results in Poland than *onet.pl.*

It would be interesting in this respect to reflect on structural and ownership changes in the sector of telecommunication and follow some initiatives introduced by the telecom operators. As in other EU countries, the telecom field underwent a process of internationalisation – both in terms of the outlook and strategies of its key commercial protagonists (Simpson, 2008). CEE's telecom markets were historically highly national-centric and foreclosed markets due to the monopolistic positions of state operators. After the wave of privatisation, Central European telecom markets became largely restructured. Again, strong transnational corporations helped to increase productivity, efficiency, and most importantly build the necessary infrastructure for converging telecom services. The new structures cemented leading positions of two principal players: France Telecom/Orange (controlling through TP S.A. the fixed telecommunication market in Poland) and Deutsche Telekom (controlling through Magyar Telecom the fixed telecommunication market in Hungary and through Slovak Telecom the market in Slovakia). Both companies also control the leading mobile operators in the region – Orange and T-mobile co-operating on the use of LTE technology. The incumbents i.e. the former monopolist operating telecom infrastructures succeeded also in offering a range of new audiovisual and content services, most importantly IPTV (under such brands as T-Home in Hungary, Magio in Slovakia or Neostrada with TV in Poland), thus positioning themselves to challenge the interests of cable and digital platform operators mostly owned by transnational competitors such as UPC or Canal Plus. In addition, the telecom operators more actively immerse in the online content production, thus moving steadily from an exclusive operation of distribution networks. In 2005, Slovak Telecom (subsidiary of the Deutsche Telekom Group) bought the information and news portal *zoznam.sk* enjoying a high degree of popularity among Slovak Internet users. The website attracts the second-highest monthly traffic in Slovakia (OSF, 2013b: 59). In 2005, Magyar Telecom as part of a rebranding strategy (full introduction of T-brand in Hungary) established the web portal T-online (Axelero's successor) that was renamed in 2007 as *origo.hu.*[25] According to the measurement of the

[25] Magyar Telecom (2013) *Company History* (available at: http://www.telekom.hu/about_us/about_magyar_telekom/company_history; retrieved 25.12.2013).

Medián web audit company *origo.hu* has been the most popular online news and current affairs provider in Hungary in 2007–2011 (OSF, 2012b: 25). In Poland, Telekomunikacja Polska/Orange has operated the web portal *wp.pl* (Wirtualna Polska) since 2001, although in October 2013 the portal was sold to the another web portal *o2* owned by the private equity company Innova Group.[26] In 2013, Wirtualna Polska was the second most popular news and current affairs portal.[27] At the EU level, the incumbents are advocating for more national consolidation to strengthen their competitive potential transnationally. The European Commission however prefers cross-border consolidation. The CEE telecom markets may be seen as a practical epitome of this view.

Finally, transnational companies may tend to avoid contents that bear political risks and uncertainties. In this sense the question of 'foreign' media ownership has been politically sensitive in Central and Eastern Europe. Again, research has not offered unambiguous answers to the question as to how significant political influence of transnational owners is. Certainly, there is no evidence to suppose that political links made foreign owners more keen to exert pressure on news production than is the case of domestic owners. There may be obvious commercial rationales for that: greater political polarisation and more clearly defined political interests and preferences in media contents might result in a decline of sales (Klimkiewicz, 2009a: 52). Thus, economic factors largely dictate high political discretion and prudence. Karol Jakubowicz observed that

> (...) on the whole, foreign owners have not been as involved in political infighting as local media players and this also presents a potential that they promote impartiality in news coverage, thus frustrating their journalists who consider local political issues important (2007: 222).

This view comes up with perceptions of staff journalists in some newspapers (acquired by transnational owners) that criticised the transformation of opinion-forming dailies into 'light' titles filled with information lacking deep analysis and reflection.[28] At the same time, some political leaders – such as Jarosław Kaczyński in Poland – dared to address

---

[26] Forbes (2013) *O2 kupuje Wirtualną Polskę za 375 mln złotych* 23.10.2013 (available at: http://www.forbes.pl/o2-pl-kupuje-wirtualna-polske-za-375-mln-zlotych, artykuly,165259,1,1.html; retrieved 25.12.2013).

[27] Measurement by Gemius in October 2013 (available at: http://www.wirtualnemedia.pl/artykul/najpopularniejsze-serwisy-tematyczne-w-pazdzierniku-2013-roku; retrieved 25.12.2013).

[28] Świątek, K. (2004) „Sprasowana prasa" (Pressed Press) in *Tygodnik Solidarność* 16.01.2004 No. 3.

foreign ownership in the political discourse and namely – as a political problem, that is derived from the economic and symbolic colonisation of the national public sphere by foreign media owners. This view resonates with e.g. Czech media experts that expressed their skepticism with regard to the consequences of foreign ownership for the national media landscape after the second great wave of concentration on the Czech daily press market (Waschková Císařová, 2007) and defended the legitimacy of the last Czech-owned media (Klukan, 2007). Political prudence and the discretion of transnational owners manifests itself mainly during the momentous regulatory/political changes as was the case of an enforcement of the Hungarian media law package in 2010. The transnational media companies, including Ringier, Axel Springer and RTL, remained relatively silent about the changes and did not bring up their stance on controversial issues (such as the omnipotent power of the regulator) into the forefront of the public discussion.

5.4.2. Patterns of media ownership and ownership consolidation

Referring to the strategies and goals of the owners, Voltmer (2013: 168) distinguishes between two types of ownership: profit-seeking and policy-seeking ownership that lead to different kinds of biases. Profit-seeking owners are mainly concerned with the economic profits and in consequence, they can take on any political stance or pursue a relatively impartial editorial line, but would take decisive steps when their business interests are affected by particular policy proposals. This type of ownership can be illustrated in the CEE countries by large transnational companies such as Ringier Axel Springer, CME, RTL/Bertelsmann, and Verlagsgruppe Passau. In contrast, policy-seeking owners use their media to promote a particular political idea or party, occasionally even when this is against their economic interests (Voltmer, 2013: 168). This type of ownership can be characterised by media groups that are keen to support certain political options, which does not automatically mean they stick to them forever. In practice, some policy-seeking owners act with greater discretion as is the case of the ITI group in Poland (supporting the Civic Platform party[29]), others articulate their political endorsement more stoutly. The group of policy-seeking owners also includes media ownership by foundations or private persons under the strong control or influence of political parties or movements. Among these, there are the

[29] Civic Platform – Platforma Obywatelska – PO – a center-right political party in Poland.

examples of Hungarian daily newspapers with various political orientations including a leftist daily *Népszabadság*[30], or the rightist daily *Magyar Nemzet*, supporting the Fidesz party. In Poland, the media belonging to the network of *Radio Maryja* (radio *Maryja*, TV *Trwam*, the daily *Nasz Dziennik*) are formally owned by the Catholic Foundation Lux Veritatis, but controlled by a Catholic priest Tadeusz Rydzyk supporting the right-wing Law and Justice party[31].

In addition to these, a third type of owners can be defined as warranty-seeking owners that aspire to establish or buy media outlets in order to hold 'politicians in check' with regard to other businesses they control. These owners treat their media instrumentally and as a possible political leverage. Such strategy might result in promoting views that may be contradictory to the economic interests of the media, but are fully congruent with the economic interests of their owners. There are numerous examples illustrating this category. In Hungary, Gábor Széles, the owner of powerful industrial Ikarus group owns cable *Echo TV,* the *Echo News Agency,* and daily newspaper *Magyar Hírlap.* Two other businessmen Zsolt Nyerges and Lajos Simicska, controlling – among other businesses – the diversified holding construction company Közgép are active on the advertising market, and Simicska bougth the daily *Metropol* from the Swedish Metro International Group in 2011. The growing media structures of the Czech coal baron Zdeněk Bakala, the Polish businessman Grzegorz Hajdarowicz and the Slovak investment group J&T were just discussed in the previous section. In addition, the case of Slovak businessman Ivan Kmotrík can be mentioned. Kmotrík owns the printing company Grafobal, the football club Slovan and has various shares in energy-related businesses. In the media sector, Kmotrík acquired a news channel TA 3 and a press distribution network.

Finally, the last category can be distinguished as connection-seeking owners. This group is represented by large incumbent companies or digital platform operators predominantly focusing on building infrastructures and economic solutions boosting the dissemination and distribution of content. These owners quite recently started to invest in the production of content mainly to compete with the media networks that in turn more increasingly invest in technologies or get into partnerships with

[30] In 2006, the Ringier Publishing House acquired a majority interest (67.7%). Today, Ringier owns a 70.77% stake in *Népszabadság*. Ringier (2013) *Népszabadság* (available at: http://www.ringier.com/en/products/hungary/newspapers/nepszabadsag; retrieved 25.12.2013).

[31] Law and Justice – Prawo i Sprawiedliwość – PIS – a national conservatice political party in Poland.

independent delivery systems. The media content production is secondary to distribution activities – the main purpose is to connect through as many platforms as possible. The entities that represent this group include Orange, T-mobile, Slovak Telekom. Some instances manifest that the category of connection-seeking owners overlaps with all other categories as is the case of Slovak Towercom cotrolled by the J&T group. Towercom was the dominant analogue terrestrial operator in Slovakia, and later was awarded with all three terrestrial multiplexes by the Telecommunication Office of the Slovak Republic (TÚSR – Telekomunikačný Úrad SR) (OSF, 2013b: 54), thus becoming in fact a monopolist in the area of digital broadcasting distribution.

The report of the High Level Group on Media Freedom and Pluralism *A free and pluralistic media to sustain European democracy* (HLGMFP, 2013: 16) recognises as one of the challenges to media freedom and pluralism in member states "the concentration of ownership of commercial media and the influence this might have in the political space". Especially three such conditions are mentioned in the Report:

- ownership in the hands of ruling politicians,
- concentration of all media in a country within the hands of a single owner,
- or (especially in small countries) concentration of all media in the hands of foreign owners (2013: 16).

The conditions of media concentration defined in this way may seem quite exceptional, but as guidelines – they detect the main vectors of threats to media pluralism derived from structural and ownership developments, and in particular, media ownership consolidation.

Justin Schlosberg points out that one of the stumbling blocks in dealing with threats to media plurality concerns "the inherent difficulties in measuring media market shares in a converged environment with print news markets facing structural decline" (Schlosberg, 2013: 5). The *Feasibility Study for the Preparatory Action "Erasmus for journalists"* (Economisti Associati et al.,2011) uses three indexes to measure concentration on national media markets in different media (press and TV) sectors. The C4 refers to the concentration ratio, which aggregates the share in the market of the largest companies. The C4 stands for the widely used four-firm concentration which represents the market share of the top four companies. In the table below, the variables have been calculated on the basis of the number of existing titles and their average circulation level per issue (2011: 80). The second index applied in the study is most frequently used Herfindahl-Hirschman Index (HHI). It calculates a company's share of a market as its percentage of the total revenue generated by all firms serving the market. However, shares may be also measured in other ways. Each company's share is squared and the sum of the squared shares for all companies in a given market represents the HHI (Wildman, 2007: 153). An amount between 1000 and 1800 indicates a moderate concentration, and above 1800 the highly concentrated market. The Noam Index is derived from HHI, but in addition to market power, it also takes into account the available diversity manifested in the number of alternative voices available (Economisti Associati, 2011: 80).

Table 28: Concentration in the press and TV markets of selected CEE countries

	Concentration in the circulation of paid-for-dailies (2009)			**Concentration in the audience share of TV channels (2009)**		
	C4	**HHI**	**NOAM**	**C4**	**HHI**	**NOAM**
CZECH REPUBLIC	77%	1791	199	79%	2113	116
HUNGARY	35%	560	101	–	–	–
POLAND	57%	801	130	67%	1210	44
EU AVERAGE	43%	793	129	60%	1196	60

Sources: Adapted from Economisti Associati et al., 2011.

The table shows that the level of concentration in the press markets is higher in the two studied CEE countries – the Czech Republic and Poland (Slovakia was not included in the sample) than the EU average. The highest concentration characterises the Czech market (77%, HHI – 77%), while the lowest can be observed in the case of Hungary (35%, HHI – 560). As regards the TV market, both Poland and the Czech Republic exhibit higher levels of concentration than the EU average. The HHI index measured for the purpose of the study suggests that the press market in the Czech Republic is moderately concentrated, while the TV market is highly concentrated. In the case of Poland, the HHI value shows the relatively competitive press market, and the moderately concentrated TV market. The report commissioned by the Polish Broadcasting Council (KRRiT) (Indicator, 2012) *Pluralism in the Polish electronic media* (Pluralizm w polskich mediach elektronicznych) uses the calculation of revenues shares, audience shares and advertising shares. The findings lead to slightly different conclusions than in the Feasibility Study – the authors emphasise that Polish TV market is highly consolidated, the concentration though does not significantly influence the development of the TV market (2012: 21). The study conducted by Marína Urbániková demonstrates different values for the HHI in the case of the Czech Republic and Slovakia.[32] The study reaches the conclusion, that both the Slovak and Czech daily press markets are highly concentrated with the amount of 2390 for Slovakia and 2829 for the Czech Republic. Likewise, the TV markets in both countries achieve a significantly high concentration amounting in the case of the Czech Republic to 3172 and Slovakia 3500.[33] The different values produced by both studies show how important and decisive role in application of measurement methodologies is played by the defining of a relevant product market, choice of calculation indicating market shares (share in the total revenues, audience shares, share in production capacities, share in advertising, etc.) and finally, the available data.

To examine the issue of consolidation from a slightly different angle it would be instructive to reflect on recent developments and changes in the print press and TV markets in the region and contextualise these data with the dynamics of media ownership changes and reflection on other media sectors.

Table 29: Average daily circulation (in 000) of the top paid-for dailies in the Czech Republic

	Founded (Year)	**Ultimate Parent Company**	**2006**	**2007**	**2008**	**2009**	**2010**	**2011**	**2012***	**2013***
Blesk	1992	Ringier Axel Springer	477	460	436	412	385	348	297	282
MF Dnes	1945	MAFRA (RBV)*	303	302	292	256	240	222	206	185
Deník	2001	Passauer Neue Presse	–	322*	287*	248	224	204	181	163
Právo	1921	Borgis	161*	152*	144*	138	128	120	111	104
Aha!	2006	Ringier Axel Springer	101*	125*	114*	107	100	89	82	64
Sport	1953	Ringier Axel Springer	72*	79*	65*	60	54	50	45	43
Lidové Noviny	1992	MAFRA (RBV)*	73	70	70	59	50	43	42	38

[32] Slovak Press Watch (2010) *Je koncentrácia vlastníctva slovenských médií problémom?* (available at: http://spw.blog.sme.sk/c/244151/Je-koncentracia-vlastnictva-slovenskych-medii-problemom.html; retrieved 26.12.2013).

[33] Ibidem.

Sources: Elaborated from WAN, World Press Trends 2012, 2011, 2010, 2009, 2008, 2007 (available at: http://www.wan-ifra.org/microsites/world-press-trends; retrieved 26.12.2013), and Czech Audit Bureau of Circulation ABC CR (available at: http://www.abccr.cz/en/; retrieved 26.12.2013).
Notes: * The data refer to September circulation in given years
** Rheinisch Bergische Verlagsgesellschaft

The average sold circulation of top-paid-for dailies has been significantly decreasing in the Czech Republic. The sale of paid-for-dailies in all specific groups (tabloids, quality and regional dailies) has declined proportionately, at the same time the group of most affected newspapers includes the tabloids *Blesk*, regional chain *Deník* and quality daily *Lidové Noviny*. Paradoxically, *Právo* displays one of the most moderate decline, remaining so far the Czech-owned newspaper in the control of Zdeněk Porybný, its former and current editor-in-chief. In terms of ownership, the Czech Republic press market resembles a classic oligopoly. Three main owners Ringier Axel Springer, RBV and Verlaggruppe Passau control the respective shares. The next table demonstrates the proportion of sold circulation (indicating ownership consolidation) controlled by each of these groups in 2007 and 2011:

Table 30: Proportions of circulation shares controlled by the three largest publishing companies in the Czech Republic

	2007	**2011**
TOTAL CIRCULATION OF PAID-FOR DAILIES (in 000)	1,672	1,138
RINGIER AXEL SPRINGER (% of circulation)	39.7%	42.8%
RBV (% of circulation)	22.2%	23.2%
VERLAGSGRUPPE PASSAU (% of circulation)	19.3%	17.9%
PROPORTION OF THE THREE LARGEST PUBLISHING COMPANIES (% of circulation)	81.2%	83.9%

Sources: Calculated on the basis of the data from WAN and ABC CR (as quoted above).

As can be surmised from these calculations, the combined proportion of the three top publishing companies slightly increased – achieving an exceedingly a high level of consolidation at 84% in 2011. Between 2007 and 2011, the shares of Ringier Axel Springer increased most significantly reaching 43% in 2011. The shares of RBV rose to 23%, while the proportion of Verlagsgruppe Passau decreased to 18%. In this vein, the level of consolidation by the three largest publishing groups increased in the Czech Republic, with Ringier Axel Springer leading the group and cementing its dominant position even stronger.

Table 31: Average daily circulation (in 000) of top paid-for dailies in Hungary

	Ultimate parent company	**2006**	**2007**	**2008**	**2009**	**2010**	**2011**	**2012**	**2013***
Blikk	Ringier	246	233	232	210	196	183	164	147
Bors	Lapcom/ Hid Radio	62	67	76	89	86	83	74	71
Népsza-badság	Ringier	152	128	112	94	78	66	57	50
Kisalföld	Lapcom	78	77	76	73	70	69	68	66
Nemzeti Sport	Ringier	83	77	78	69	67	61	57	51
Magyar Nemzet	NEMZET Lapés Könyvkiadó	72	66	60	53	50	46	41	39
Vas Népe	Pannon Lapok Társasága	57	56	54	53	50	47	46	44

Sources: Elaborated from WAN, World Press Trends 2012, 2011, 2010, 2009, 2008, 2007 (available at: http://www.wan-ifra.org/microsites/world-press-trends; retrieved 26.12.2013), Hungarian Audit Bureau of Circulation MATESZ (available at: http://matesz.hu/).
Notes: *Mid-year data.

Hungary has not been an exception in the overall trend of declining circulation of print daily newspapers. It is worth noticing though, that this process has a diversified impact on particular titles, and even segments. The most affected newspaper has been *Népszabadság*. The sold circulation of this newspaper decreased from 152,000 in 2006 to 50,000 in 2013. Other national quality dailies have also been exposed to severe declines. At the same time, ownership in this segment has been more varied than in the case of the Czech Republic, though linked to political interests. The circulation of tabloids diminished gradually with less extreme results. Finally, leading regional daily newspapers preserved the most stable position in comparison with other titles. Paradoxically, these represent the segment of the daily press market that is usually perceived as the most fragile. As the Feasibility Study (Economisti Associati et al., 2011) observed, the Hungarian daily press market seems least concentrated from all the CEE countries studied in this work. Relatively significant shares in sold circulation are controlled especially by three publishing groups – Ringier, Lapcom and Axel Springer (operating mainly on the regional dailies' market).

Table 32: Proportions of circulation shares controlled by the two leading publishing companies in Hungary

	2007	**2011**
TOTAL CIRCULATION OF PAID-FOR DAILIES (in 000)	1,331	1,237
RINGIER (% of circulation)	32.9%	25.0%
LAPCOM (% of circulation)	10.8%	12.3%
PROPORTION OF THE TWO PUBLISHING COMPANIES (% of circulation)	43.7%	37.3%

Sources: Calculated on the basis of the data from WAN and MATESZ (as quoted above).

The table comparing the proportions of circulation controlled by Ringier and Lapcom shows that the level of consolidation generally decreased from 43.7% to 37.3% between 2007–2011. The share of Ringier decreased from 32.9% to 25%, while Lapcom achieved a higher concentration in 2011 than in 2007 amounting to 12.3%.

Table 33: Average daily circulation (in 000) of top paid-for dailies in Poland

	Founded (Year)	**Ultimate Parent company**	**2006**	**2007**	**2008**	**2009**	**2010**	**2011**	**2012**	**2013***
Fakt	2003	Ringier Axel Springer	514	515	495	467	437	394	374	325
Gazeta Wyborcza	1989	Agora	434	448	411	370	336	306	256	202
Super Express	1991	Murator S.A.	200	198	204	192	184	174	162	152
Rzeczpospolita	1982	Presspublika	173	164	157	142	141	129	108	91

*Dziennik*** *Gazeta Prawna*	2009	Infor Biznes	–	–	–	81	100	92	82	63
Polska Dziennik Zachodni	1945	Polska-presse	97	91	82	79	70	64	57	48
Przegląd Sportowy	1921	Ringier Axel Springer	72	62	64	58	51	48	43	40

Sources: Elaborated from WAN, World Press Trends 2011, 2010, 2009, 2008, 2007 (available at: http://www.wan-ifra.org/microsites/world-press-trends; retrieved 26.12.2013); Polish Audit Bureau of Circulation – ZKDP – Związek Kontroli Dystrybucji Prasy (available at: http://www.zkdp.pl/index.php?option=com_content&view=category&layout=blog&id=8&Itemid=4&lang=pl; retrieved 26.12.2013).

Notes: * The data refer to September circulation in given years
** The daily *Dziennik* and *Gazeta Prawna* were merged in 2009, thus creating a new consolidated title *Dziennik Gazeta Prawna*.

The size of the Polish print press market is larger than all the markets of the other CEE countries examined in this book together. These empirical conditions shape more diversified ownership patterns and a greater presence of domestic owners in the case of Poland. Yet, the decline of sold circulation of paid-for-dailies is significant especially in the sector of quality daily newspapers. The circulation of *Gazeta Wyborcza* dropped from 434,000 in 2006 to 202,000 in 2013 and *Rzeczpospolita* from 173,000 in 2006 to 91,000 in 2013. The dramatic developments in the segment of quality daily newspapers urged a merger between *Dziennik-Europa-Polska-Świat*, owned by Axel Springer, with *Gazeta Prawna*, owned by Infor in 2009. Both titles tough maintained different news websites – *dziennik.pl* and *gazetaprawna.pl*. The decline in tabloids' circulation proved less profound, albeit Ringier Axel Springer – the publisher of the most popular tabloid in Poland *Fakt* – decided to invest in the most popular news website *onet.pl* in 2012 to prepare for a future remodeling of content production. The Polish Office for Competition and Consumer Protection (UOKiK) approved the acquisition although, should the relevant market be defined as news market regardless of platform delivery, the transaction might raise concerns: Ringier Axel Springer controls the largest circulation share in the daily press market and *onet.pl* shares among news portals fluctuated between 40–30% in recent years. It is worth noticing in this respect, that unlike in Hungary, the segment of regional daily newspapers experienced a relatively high decline in circulation between 2006–2013. This issue will be further examined in the next sections of this chapter.

Table 34: Proportions of circulation shares controlled by the leading publishing companies in Poland

	2007	2011
TOTAL CIRCULATION OF PAID-FOR DAILIES (in 000)	3,946	2,810
RINGIER AXEL SPRINGER (% of circulation)	14.6%	15.7%
AGORA (% of circulation)	11.4%	10.8%
POLSKAPRESSE (% of circulation)	11.5%	11.4%
MURATOR S.A. (% of circulation)	5.0%	6.1%
PRESSPUBLIKA (% of circulation)	4.1%	4.6%
PROPORTION OF THE THREE LARGEST PUBLISHING COMPANIES (% of circulation)	37.5%	37.9%
PROPORTION OF THE THREE LARGEST PUBLISHING COMPANIES (% of circulation)	46.6%	48.6

Sources: Calculated on the basis of the data from WAN and ZKDP (as quoted above).

The proportions of shares controlled by the largest publishing groups in Poland do not indicate such a high level of consolidation as was the case of the Czech Republic, and all the more, the position of the leading owner in the segment of daily newspapers – Ringier Axel Springer (amounting to 15.7% in 2011) is less dominant in terms of shares than the position of Ringier in Hungary (amounting to 25% in 2011). The combined share of the three largest publishing groups – Ringier Axel Springer, Agora and Polskapresse reaches around 37% – a similar proportion than the one achieved by the two leading publishing groups in Hungary. Recognising that 15% circulation share by one player in a particular market represents a limit above which ownership concentration may be viewed as potentially detrimental to media pluralism (Craufurd Smith et al., 2012; Schlosberg, 2013), the Polish daily press market stands as quite a balanced and moderately diverse daily press landscape.

Table 35: Average daily circulation (in 000) of top paid-for dailies in Slovakia

	Founded (Year)	**Ultimate Parent company**	**2006**	**2007**	**2008**	**2009**	**2010***	**2011**	**2012***	**2013***
Nový Čas	1990	Ringier Axel Springer	185	179	172	150	145	136	118	107
SME	1993	Petit Press/ RBV[34]	76	65	60	59	58	53	47	41
Pravda	1920	FLORENA	76	67	63	51	54	54	51**	–
Plus 1 Den	2006	Spoločnosť 7 Plus	65	59	64	58	60	55	54	48
*Új Szó****	1948	Petit Press/ RBV	25	25	25	24	23	21	21	20
Korzár	1998	Petit Press/ RBV	33	30	27	25	23	20	18	16
Šport	1953	Šport Press	55	55	25	25	–	20	–	–

Sources: Elaborated from WAN, World Press Trends 2011, 2010, 2009, 2008, 2007 (available at: http://www.wan-ifra.org/microsites/world-press-trends; retrieved 26.12.2013); Slovak Audit Bureau of Circulation ABC SR (available at: http://abcsr.sk/; retrieved 26.12.2013).

Notes: * The data refer to September circulation in given years

** The data refer to July 2012

*** The daily published in the Hungarian language for the Hungarian national minority composing almost 10% of the Slovak population.

Contrary to Poland, Slovakia represents the smallest press market in the region. The decline of circulation affected mainly the largest daily newspapers – both the tabloid *Nový Čas* and the quality daily *SME*. The most stable position and smallest losses characterise the daily *Új Szó* published in the Hungarian language for the Hungarian minority. This can be partly explained by the fact that *Új Szó* has strong links with the community it

[34] RBV owns 50% in the Petit Press group, the other half is controlled by the Slovak owner.

Table 36: Proportions of circulation shares controlled by the two leading publishing companies in Slovakia

	2007	2011
TOTAL CIRCULATION OF PAID-FOR DAILIES (in 000)	513	381
RINGIER AXEL SPRINGER (% of circulation)	34.9%	35.6%
PETIT PRESS (% of circulation)	23.4%	24.7%
PROPORTION OF THE TWO PUBLISHING COMPANIES (% of circulation)	58.3%	60.3%

Sources: Calculated on the basis of the data from WAN and ABC SR (as quoted above).

targets, and is also supported by subsidies from the Slovak Ministry of Culture along with other press titles serving national and ethnic minorities in Slovakia.

The position of two leading publishing companies – Ringier Axel Springer and Petit Press (owned by RBV) – indicates a slight increase of consolidation on the daily press market between 2007–2011. In 2011, Ringier Axel Springer controlled a high share of 36% in that market, while Petit Press 25%. The proportion of both companies exceeds 60% in a market which stands for high concentration as proved in the study of Marína Urbániková, mentioned earlier in this section.[35]

Analysisng media ownership consolidation, it is important to reflect on the extensions of activities of legacy media outlets and owners into the Internet and digital world, including delivery platforms. The provision of news migrated (although not exclusively) to the Internet and online services. Barnhurst and Nerone observe that in times, when professional designers construct entire pages on a computer screen, the ultimate control of the newspaper resides in corporate ownership (Barnhurst and Nerone, 2002: 10). Thus, a reflection on online media structures helps to contextualise the structural analysis of legacy media. An important precondition of the fast development of online newspapers and news websites is Internet penetration. The Gemius report *Do you CEE? The overview of the Central and Eastern Europe internet market in 2011* points out that although the most advanced CEE markets could be considered as saturated with respect to Internet penetration, there is still a long way to go to reach the

[35] Slovak Press Watch (2010) *Je koncentrácia...*

highest European standards (Gemius,2011). The table below shows internet penetration in the CEE countries studied and online adspend share in comparison with the EU average in 2013 and 2012.

Table 37: Internet penetration and adspend share in the Czech Republic, Hungary, Poland and Slovakia in 2013

	Internet penetration (2013)	**Adspend share per internet user in EUR (2012)**	**Adspend share (2012)**
CZECH REPUBLIC	69%	45%	17%
HUNGARY	57%	19%	23%
POLAND	59%	26%	19%
SLOVAKIA	67%	19%	6%
EU AVERAGE	69%	55%	26%

Sources: Adapted from Gemius (2013).

The table suggests that although Internet penetration increases steadily, it is still lower than the EU average. In terms of adspend per Internet user, only the Czech Republic can be compared with the EU average, while the adspend share generally seems to be significantly lower in all the other CEE countries than the EU average. This shows, that the CEE online markets still bear a lot of possibilities in investment and modifications, which certainly resonates with some expansion strategies of the legacy media owners. The table below summarises top online news providers and the most popular newspaper sites in the region.

Table 38: Top online news providers and most popular newspaper websites in the Czech Republic, Hungary, Poland and Slovakia in 2011

	Most popular online news providers	**Most popular newspaper websites**
CZECH REPUBLIC	*novinky.cz* (news portal) *Idnes.cz* (online daily) *lidovky.cz* (online daily) *aktualne.cz* (news portal) *tn.cz* (news portal)	*novinky.cz; pravo.cz* *Idnes.cz* *blesk.cz* *denik.cz* *lidovky.cz* *hn.ihned.cz* *ahaonline.cz*

HUNGARY	*origo.hu* (news portal) *index.hu* (news portal) *hir24.hu* (news portal) *portfolio.hu* (economic news portal) *hvg.hu* (online weekly) *blikk.hu* (online tabloid) *borsonline.hu* (online tabloid)	*expressz.hu* *blikk.hu* *nepszabadsag.hu* *nemzetisport.hu* *borsonline_.hu* *napi.hu* *nepszava.hu*
POLAND	*onet.pl* (news portal) *wp.pl* (news portal) *gazeta.pl* *interia.pl* (news portal) *o2.pl* (news portal)	*gazeta.pl* *fakt.pl* *naszemiasto.pl* *se.pl* *rp.pl*
SLOVAKIA	*azet.sk* (news and information portal) *zoznam.sk* (news and information portal) *sme.sk* (online daily) *atlas.sk* (news and information portal) *aktuality.sk* (news portal) *topky.sk* (news portal) *cas.sk* (online tabloid)	*cas.sk* *sme.sk* *korzar.sme.sk* *ujszo.com* *pravda.sk* *pluska.sk* *HNonline.sk*

Sources: Elaborated from WAN, World Press Trends 2011, 2010, 2009, 2008, 2007 (available at: http://www.wan-ifra.org/microsites/world-press-trends; retrieved 26.12.2013); Gemius (2011), OSF (2012b, 2012c, 2013a, 2013b).

From the comparison of these categories it may be inferred that online newspaper sites lost dominant positions in the provision of news via the Internet and there are, in most cases, news/information portals without their print counterparts that occupy leading positions. In some cases, these are connected to publishing companies in their ownership structures as is the case of *onet.pl* owned by Ringier Axel Springer or *novinky.cz* belonging to the Borgis group, thus consolidating their ownership control. Other cases – such as *origo.hu* – show that new actors in the news content production represented in this case by the incumbent Magyar Telecom might prove successful. In terms of most popular online newspapers, the data do not unequivocally point to the group of tabloids or quality dailies, the visiting of titles from both categories seems quite proportionality distributed. At the same time, it is worth adding that top positions of newspapers with the highest circulation are more or less reproduced in their online editions with one reservation: the dominance of tabloids does not seem so strong.

The available studies on media concentration discussed above signal that the consolidation of broadcasting markets in the CEE region is more profound than is the case of print press markets. The table below illustrates the share of the three top broadcasters in the CEE countries, including public service broadcasters.

Table 39: The share of the three top TV broadcasters in the Czech Republic, Hungary, Poland and Slovakia (in %)

	2003	2004	2005	2006	2007	2008	2009	2010
CZECH REPUBLIC	93.2	93.8	93.8	92.8	90.5	86.5	82.5	77.6
HUNGARY	78.2	75.9	73	71.3	65.7	60.9	56.4	54
POLAND	84.9	85.4	86.5	86.5	85	81.7	78.4	75.9
SLOVAKIA	78.6	71.9	70.9	74.1	73.7	73.8	70.7	68.7

Sources: Elaborated on the basis of European Audiovisual Observatory (2011) 2011 Yearbook – Television in 37 European States, Strasbourg; 2009 Yearbook; 2006 Yearbook.

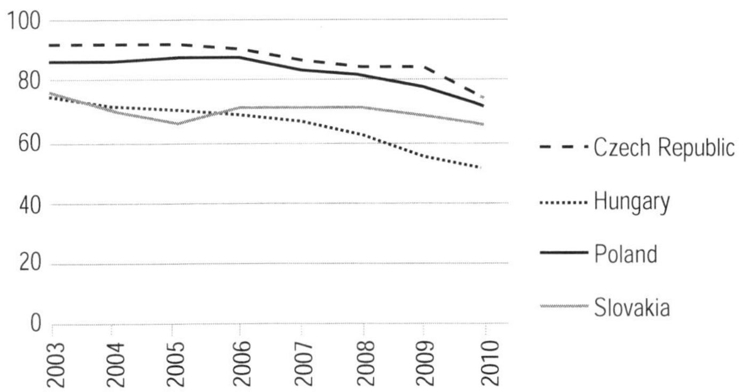

Figure 7: The share of the top three TV broadcasters in the Czech Republic, Hungary, Poland and Slovakia

Sources: Elaborated on the basis of European Audiovisual Observatory (2011) 2011 Yearbook – Television in 37 European States, Strasbourg; 2009 Yearbook; 2006 Yearbook.

The calculation of the proportion in the audiovisual markets includes the audience share of all channels operated by one broadcaster. Thus, the share of public service TV broadcaster combines the shares of all channels operated by the broadcaster. The share of the three dominant broadcasters aggregates the shares of all channels offered by these broadcasters to audiences.

As can be seen from both the figure and the table, the audience share of the three top TV broadcasters seems to be relatively high in all countries, although we may observe varied dynamics of decline depending very much on the position of public service television and its ability to adapt to the new digital environment with the offer of thematic digital channels. Practically, in all CEE countries, the three largest broadcasters control the market, in Poland and the Czech Republic (where public service TVs enjoy greater popularity) reaching around 76%, in Hungary 54% and Slovakia 69% in 2010.

In the Czech Republic, the television market continues to be dominated by the private channel TV *Nova* (belonging to CME), which achieved an audience share of 28.9% in 2011 (*Nova* experienced a 13% decline since 2006). The public service broadcaster Czech Television (*Česká Televize – ČT*), had a total audience share of 27% (*ČT1*, *ČT2*, *ČT24* and *ČT4*). The private channel TV *Prima* (owned by the Modern Times Group) occupied third place with a share of 17.4% in 2011 (*Prima* experienced a decline from 20.2% in 2006).[36] It is worth noticing though, that the combined share of all three broadcasters in fact increased in 2011 reaching 83.76% and increased also in 2012 amounting to 84.2%. This can be explained by the launch of additional thematic channels by all broadcasters (e.g. *Fanda* for women by *Nova* in 2012, or *Prima* Cool for men by *Prima*).

The Hungarian market has been dominated by two private channels: *RTL Klub* (RTL Group) and *TV2* (ProsiebenSat1), that have continued to control the biggest audience shares since the second half of the 1990s. *RTL Klub* remained the market leader in 2011 with 27.9% while *TV2* had 19.5%. The public channels *M1* and *M2* had a combined market share in 2011 of 11.6% (down from 18.6% in 2006) in 2011.[37]

In Poland, the public service broadcaster *TVP* continues to occupy a strong position in the audiovisual market, although recent years marked significant losses. All the *TVP* channels reached 36% of audience share in

[36] MAVISE (2013) (available at: http://mavise.obs.coe.int/country?id=9#section-10; retrieved 27.12.2013).

[37] MAVISE (2013) (available at: http://mavise.obs.coe.int/country?id=16; retrieved 27.12.2013).

2011. The three most popular TV channels mirror the market positions of the three leading broadcasting groups to which they belong: the most popular channel *TVP1* achieved a share of 17.4%, *TVN* (belonging to the ITI group) a 15% share and *Polsat* (the flagship channel of the Polsat group) a share of 14.5%. All the dominant broadcasters offer a variety of thematic and specialised channels. In 2012, *TVP* operated 12 national channels altogether (including three HD channels) and 16 regional services.[38] The *TVN* group provided 12 channels (including 4 HD channels), while the ITI group (the owner of *TVN*) controlled a total of 24 channels.[39] The group Polsat Cyfrowy fully controls one of the digital platforms in Poland with the same name and 14 channels (including 2 HD channels). Polsat Cyfrowy also bought the Info-TV-FM company owned by NFI Magna Polonia in 2011 to become the only operator of a mobile TV multiplex in Poland. This significantly strengthened the position of the group vis-à-vis its competitors both on the market of digital broadcasting and mobile telephony as the Polsat group controls also the mobile telecom operator Polkomtel. The Canal+ group (a subsidiary of the French group Vivendi) controls 24 channels (of which 13 are HD) and the second digital platform *nc+* that was formed from the merger of *Canal+* and the digital platform *n* sold from the ITI group in 2013. Finally, it is worth adding that the combined share of the three leading broadcasting groups – *TVP*, *TVN* and *Polsat* – dropped in 2012 in comparison with the previous years and reached a level of 66.6%.

The television structures in the Slovak Republic resemble the Hungarian model in which the public service television controls significantly smaller shares than commercial broadcasters. The leading channel TV *Markíza* and TV *Doma* (both belonging to CME) reached a 34% of audience share in 2011. The second commercial channel, TV *Joj* (and allied channel *Joj Plus*) had a combined audience share of 23.8% in 2011.[40] It is noteworthy in this respect, that the J&T group owning TV *Joj* also controls the operator of all digital multiplexes in Slovakia – Towercom. In addition, through a subsidiary company it runs the daily *Pravda*, and currently became involved in the acquisition of the Ringier Axel Springer activities in the Czech Republic. The public service channels of *STV* had a combined share of 12.2% (approximately half of the audience share

[38] MAVISE (2013) (available at: http://mavise.obs.coe.int/country?id=24; retrieved 27.12.2013).

[39] Ibidem.

[40] MAVISE (2013) (available at: http://mavise.obs.coe.int/country?id=28; retrieved 27.12.2013).

they held in 2004).[41] The launch of some digital thematic channels proved relatively successful, while others failed to attract a sufficient audience.

The patterns of media ownership in the CEE countries – with few exceptions – demonstrate a high or moderate concentration in various segments of media markets that has been a product of more profound concentration waves and takeovers, as well as clustering of business activities in the pre-EU-accession period. The dynamics of consolidation seems to be quite stable (the calculations do not display significant increase or decrease of concentration), at the same time, changes of ownership are fast and often not fully transparent. Various vectors of these changes may be detected – such as increasing takeover of media activities in various sectors by domestic business elites or entry into cross ownership involving online media or digital platforms by large transnational owners. So far, the scarce policy responses focused only on some disapprovals of mergers (e.g. Hungary in the case of a merger between Axel Springer and Ringier or Poland in the case of the takeover of shares in the TV *Polsat* by Axel Springer), or licencing, but have not covered more systematically media transparency, questions of the political influence of the owners or remedies preventing the owners from influencing editorial independence. As Justin Schlosberg notices: "measures such as independent boards with powers over editorial appointments have a track record in media merger conditions" (Schlosberg, 2013: 8).

5.5. Diversity of media functions: genres and policy measures

Functional pluralism is generated by different functions the media fulfill in a society, reflected most explicitly in various models of performance and financing mechanisms. The way how the media are financed, to whom they are accountable, what performance objectives they follow and what is the main purpose of their operation, set the defining lines between commercial entertainment oriented structures (e.g. tabloids, commercial/entertainment TV channels), the PSM, private news and information oriented media (e.g. quality daily newspapers, news websites, TV news channels), community media and thematically specialised media (e.g. thematic TV channels or websites focusing on history, travel, fashion, etc.). In the debates about media pluralism, there are views that principal premise of media plurality is to provide diverse, alternative

[41] MAVISE (2013) (available at: http://mavise.obs.coe.int/country?id=28; retrieved 27.12.2013).

viewpoints and information, and this is generally a domain reserved for news and current affairs genres. Thus, functional media diversity should focus on the diversity of the news media, while other genres and thematic fields should be left out of the scope of media policies. The counter argument is that other forms of content, entertainment, religious or cultural programmes, for example, can be equally important in conveying political and social information and that we require access to diversity across all programme genres (Craufurd Smith et al., 2012: 9). Then, as discussed above, media pluralism is a concept that unites response to, and an acknowledgement of, various communication needs – also those that affect the construction of individual and collective identities. These may certainly lead to an expression of divergent political interests and forms of political involvement.

Summarising the functional change in media structures over the past decades, Jens Lucht and Linards Udris (2010: 15) point to the decline of quality newspapers, tabloidisation, and changing media structures that negatively affect media content, including a growing occurrence of scandals, strategies of personalisation and entertainment, capture of political coverage. To briefly examine these functional changes in the CEE countries, it would be instructive to pay attention to these proportions among media structures offering more entertainment – focused content and news and current content. This can help also to understand (to a certain extent) whether market imperatives and high ownership concentration in particular resonates with the growing significance of the tabloid media.

In the domain of the print press, a possible indicator that can be used in this respect, is a comparison of the circulation shares of national tabloids and quality daily newspapers over a certain period of time.

Table 40: The proportion of circulation of tabloids and quality daily newspapers in the Czech Republic, Hungary, Poland and Slovakia

	Total circulation of paid-for dailies (in 000) 2007	Share of national tabloids (in %) 2007	Share of national quality dailies (in %) 2007	Total circulation of paid-for dailies (in 000) 2011	Share of national tabloids (in %) 2011	Share of national quality dailies (in %) 2011
CZECH REPUBLIC	1,672	34.3	31.3	1,138	38.4	33.8
HUNGARY	1,331	23.2	16.2	1,237	21.5	11.3

POLAND	3,946	18.0	22.2	2,810	20.2	18.7
SLOVAKIA	513	46.4	25.7	381	50.2	28.4

Sources: Calculated on the basis of WAN 2011, 2010, 2009, 2008, 2007 (available at: http://www.wan-ifra.org/microsites/world-press-trends; retrieved 26.12.2013) and national Audit Bureau of Circulations (ABC CR, MATESZ, ZKDP and ABC SR).

The table above demonstrates that in 2007, the circulation share of tabloids surpassed the share of quality dailies in all the CEE countries with the exception of Poland. This can be explained by the fact, that in 2006 a new quality daily was launched – *Dziennik-Europa-Polska-Świat* – by Axel Springer. In 2011, when the daily was already merged with *Gazeta Prawna*, the proportion of tabloids (20.2%) exceeded quality dailies (18.7%). Between 2007 and 2011, the market shares of tabloids increased slightly in all countries with the exception of Hungary. At the same time, national quality dailies registered even a greater loss in the circulation share in Hungary between 2007 and 2011. This proves the relative popularity of regional dailies that exhibit less significant losses in the sold circulation than is the case of the other two categories. To sum up, tabloids seem to be less vulnerable to a general trend of circulation decline than the quality papers, also because they are less affected by the decline in advertising. The double decrease – in sales and advertising – has made quality newspapers more fragile vis-à-vis advertising from the state, state companies or political parties. In terms of policy remedies, such structural changes invite a reconsideration of public support for the print/online press. Publishers and newspaper associations, especially in West-European countries, have called recently to maintain a zero or reduced VAT rate for printed newspapers, and their digital formats as well (ENPA, 2011). A brief scrutiny over the public support for the press in the CEE region shows that while direct subsidies are almost exclusively limited to ethnic and national minority press and some specialised titles (for instance with educational goals), the indirect subsidies practically imply a reduced VAT for the sale of newspapers, and are used in all the CEE countries with the exception of Slovakia that introduced a flat VAT rate. Albeit in comparison with the Western part of the EU where the public support for the print/online press sector takes many different forms (Nielsen and Linnebank, 2011), the approach in the CEE region seems rather minimalistic.

One of the most commonly used structural arrangement supporting functional diversity, especially across the EU, has been the provision of the public service media. This issue will be discussed more closely also with consideration of the role of commercial broadcasters in the chapter six.

5.6. Geographical diversity

The geographical dimension of structural media pluralism can be attributed to a balance of media structures at different geographical levels. The dynamics between local/regional and national media structures indicates what is the position of the structures at both levels over some period of time. It might also reveal how centralised/decentralised a particular media system is and what is the vector of these forces. A prominent role of the regional media, and the press in particular, in preserving and fostering media pluralism has been recognised in numerous scholarly works (Drok 1998, Alger 1998, Hallin and Mancini, 2004). The segment of regional and local press often serves as a primary source for other regional media (TV, radio, online). Rich and well-developed regional media may compensate for a lack of external diversity on the highly concentrated national markets.

Regional and local press had a long and lively history in the CEE region before World War II. Its reconstruction after 1989, became marked by a challenge of fragility, especially in some countries of the region. This has not only been gradually caused by the declining role of the regional press in a new media ecosystem offering online local and community services, but also because of the fact that traditional local and regional press markets appeared to be relatively vulnerable to ownership concentration, structural chaining and syndication of the content (Klimkiewicz, 2009a). In most CEE countries a significant number of regional newspapers was sold to foreign owners in large packages at the beginning of the 1990s (in Poland to the French Socpresse company, at that time owned by Robert Hersant, in the Czech Republic and Slovakia mainly to VGP, in Hungary to Axel Springer and WAZ). During the second half of the 1990s, regional press markets gravitated towards consolidated structures (Klimkiewicz, 2009a). These structures have been gradually cemented through the acquisition and subsequent merging of competing titles and the ultimate chaining of newspapers belonging to one or two groups.

Verlagsgruppe Passau (VGP) operating in all the CEE countries studied in this volume with the exception of Hungary stands out as an instructive example in this respect. In the Czech Republic, the group gradually absorbed daily newspapers in the regions of Bohemia (1992–2000), Moravia and Silesia (2001), thus virtually dominating not only news production, but also print services (through the network of its own print plants) and distribution system (Klimkiewicz, 2009a: 54). The consolidation strategy implied in the first wave takeover of structures, and in the second run content syndication under the common chain brand – *Deník* (The Daily). In this way, VGP became a monopolist publisher on the regional daily press market in the Czech Republic. A similar strategy was applied in Poland, though the Polish regional press market ended with two publishing groups dividing the segment geographically (Polskapresse and Media Regionalne). In the fall of 2007, (several months after the birth of the *Deník* chain in the Czech Republic), Polskapresse (the Polish subsidiary of VGP) introduced a new product named *Polska* (Poland), combining six previous and 12 new editions in a unified national project with injections of varied regional, and unified international content provided by the British *Times*.[42] Slovakia also experienced chaining of regional titles. Economic necessities and market size urged the Petit Press group[43] to come up with two options – the regional weekly *MY* (published in 22 local editions) and the daily *Korzár* (published in various local editions). Vlasta Hochelová emphasises that regional and local newspapers chained by the Petit Press are probably of the best journalistic quality when compared with other titles in the same segment, but the dailies are strongly affected by an unification of content (Hochelová, 2007: 29). In comparison with the other CEE countries, Hungary represents the most diverse market of regional and local daily press. The number of publishers is higher than in the other countries, although the largest shares of circulation are controlled by two transnational groups – WAZ and Axel Springer.

Table 41: The level of press decentralisation in the Czech Republic, Hungary, Poland and Slovakia (measured as a proportion of paid-for regional dailies' circulation and paid-for national dailies' circulation)

	2000	**2001**	**2002**	**2003**	**2004**	**2005**	**2006**	**2007**	**2008**	**2009**	**2010**	**2011**
CZECH REPUBLIC	22.2	22.1	26.7	27.8	25.8	23.2	20.6	19.4	19.0	18.2	18	17.9
HUNGARY	52.5	52.9	52.0	51.3	51	49.3	51.4	53.4	52.7	53	54	60.7

[42] Polskapresse (2013) *Polska* (available at: http://www.polskapresse.pl/kat/79.html?ses_pp=519f98c026fb7eb6492500786d5fe9a4; retrieved 28.12.2013).

[43] Petit Press was previously owned by VGP (50%), currently by RBV (50%).

POLAND	59	48.8	48.3	39.3	36.4	31.8	29.8	34.7	33.8	35.7	34.2	32.3
SLOVAKIA	13.5	9.3	10.2	12	11.5	9.3	8.1	7.3	7.4	7.4	13.2	11.3

Sources: Calculated on the basis of WAN, World Press Trends 2012, 2011, 2010, 2009, 2008, 2007, 2006, 2005, 2004, 2003, 2002 (available at: http://www.wan-ifra.org/microsites/world-press-trends; retrieved 26.12.2013).

The relative strength and sustainability of the regional daily press in a particular media system displays its decentralisation and potential to offer information from diverse sources for local and regional communities. The table and figure below provide a measurement of decentralisation calculated as a proportion of circulation of paid-for regional dailies and paid-for national dailies during the period 2000–2011.

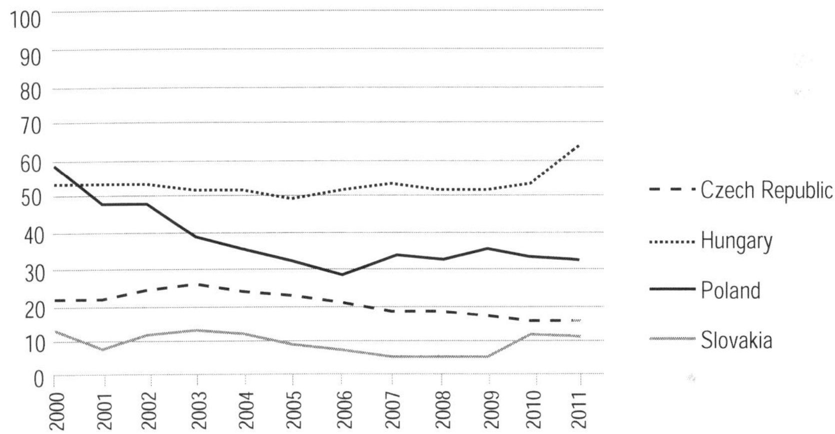

Figure 8: The level of press decentralisation in the Czech Republic, Hungary, Poland and Slovakia

Source: Calculated on the basis of WAN, World Press Trends 2012, 2011, 2010, 2009, 2008, 2007, 2006, 2005, 2004, 2003, 2002 (available at: http://www.wan-ifra.org/microsites/world-press-trends; retrieved 26.12.2013).

The highest level of centralisation characterises the Slovak daily press market. Slovakia is undoubtedly the smallest market in the studied region – exposed more as other countries in the group – to a shortage of resources, more costly media production, dependence on external forces and vulnerability (Puppis, 2009: 10–11). In 2009, regional daily newspapers comprised only 7.4% of the total circulation of daily newspapers published in Slovakia. This small share started to increase in two recent years which stems mainly from a relatively stable position of the fifth largest daily *Új Szó* published for the Hungarian minority. On the other hand, in Hungary the proportion between regional and national dailies seems to be quite balanced, and in recent years even leaning towards a stronger position of the regional dailies (amounting to 60.7% of the regional dailies' share in 2011). The Czech and Polish daily press markets, experienced particularly increasing centralisation between 2000–2011. This process seemed to be most intense in the case of Poland, where in 2000 the circulation of regional and local dailies (59%) surpassed the circulation of national dailies (41%). In 2006, the share of regional dailies stood only for 30%, then slowly increased and again decreased reaching 32% in 2011. The presented data manifest that the regional press markets are fluctuant in the region, while the centripetal drives prevail over centrifugal, with the exception of Hungary. The centripetal tendencies include a decreasing number of regional daily newspapers, decreasing circulation of regional dailies, and most importantly, an increasing level of centralisation, concentration of media ownership and chaining. The CEE countries are not an exception in comparison with some other West-European counterparts, where ownership concentration among local news publishers is advancing more rapidly than is the case of national press publishers. What is different though, rests on the proportionality. In the CEE region, the fast pace of mergers at the regional level led to a geographical dominance exploiting given possibilities with a very minimal focus on new inventions. On the other hand, due to economic reasons, the only financially-viable alternative revolves around a quite rich system of municipal press that is bound by high political dependency on the local politicians.

The policy responses to this course of developments have been scattered and in terms of tactics, varied across the countries. The lack of media-specific regulations (with the exception of Hungary) aside from the broadcasting laws, has limited interventions to reviews of mergers and chaining by national competition authorities. These sometimes used different approaches to relevant market definitions that led to divergent outcomes in relatively similar cases. In the Czech Republic, the National Competition Authority (ÚOHS) scrutinised the cases after two merger waves of the Vltava-Labe-Press (a subsidiary of VGP) in 1992 and 2001. The proof of the abuse of a dominant position on a relevant market could not be found, as the relevant media market was basically conceived as a geographical wholesale – in other words comprised of both – national and regional dailies (Šmíd, 2004). In Poland however, the Office of Competition and Consumer Protection (UOKiK) approached differently the case of the VGP merger between the regional dailies published in Wrocław in 2003. The definition of a relevant market favoured the regional dimension. A sound application of competition law can certainly serve as a precondition, but not a guarantee for a diverse regional media landscape. Therefore, it is often emphasised that competition and media concentration law has a complementary nature (Institute of European Media Law, 2005: 15). At the same time, the harmonisation of competition approaches towards the media markets at the EU could bring a common normative ground in determining pluralism measures in the CEE region. Justin Schlosberg (2013) argues that the most effective means of regulating the geographical dimension of pluralism might be a cross-market share limit combined with a series of subsidiary policies aimed at promoting local plurality. These can include provisions preventing local media owners from engaging actively in politics, subsidies to support entry-level journalism jobs, co-operative and alternative news start-ups and legislative amendments to enable local newspapers to acquire charitable status (Schlosberg, 2013: 10–11).

5.7. Searching the right means for complex ends: Conclusions

The shaping of media structures by policy means represents one of the most demanding aspects of media policymaking. A proportional deployment of possible corrections relies heavily on the hurdles of empirical metrics and assessment. Philip Napoli argues that difficulty in translating complex concepts such as diversity or pluralism into empirical measures may ultimately produce results that undermine the role of these principles in media policymaking rather than support them, and moreover, there are limits to what research can effectively capture (Napoli, 2007: xviii). This proved more than apparent at the EU level of policymaking, concerning media pluralism.

Arguably, also at the national level, matching principles with measures brought highly varied priorities and different results. In the area of policies, the broadcasting and media laws in all CEE countries generally recognised the importance of media pluralism. In Hungary, the pursuit of media diversity is acknowledged as essential in justifying the interpretations of the media law. In other countries (the Czech Republic, Poland, Slovakia), media pluralism stands for a possible end to regulatory policies and concrete task of national media regulatory authorities. At the same time, regulations differ in terms of translating these premises into legal rules covering the various areas of media pluralism. As regards internal pluralism measures, Hungary and the Czech Republic introduced provisions on balanced news that in the case of Hungary, evoked reactions from international institutions.[44] In addition, the Hungarian media law contains a requirement of news provision applicable to providers of linear media services with significant market power, and the Slovak broadcasting law stipulates a diversity of news provision and public interest provision in the case of all linear broadcasters. In Poland, similar measures apply only to the PSM. Most of external pluralism measures are reactive in their character and relatively permissive especially as regards media ownership policies and consolidation. The Czech Republic and Slovakia introduced limits on cross-media ownership setting a restriction on the numbers of operating licences. In Hungary, the cross-media ownership rules were relaxed in the 2010 media law, but concurrently, the Media Council was equipped with a stronger competence to decide on matters of media concentration. In comparison with these solutions, Poland seems to employ the most permissive rules on regulation of media ownership and concentration. At the same time, Poland applied the most restrictive rules on foreign ownership in the broadcasting market before the EU accession. Some of these country specific settings translate into shapes and structures of media landscapes.

Foreign media ownership remains relatively dominant in the CEE region and media sector markets display a relatively high consolidation (in comparison with their Western counterparts), albeit there are important differences among the particular CEE countries. For instance, the Czech market represents a classical oligopoly where the market of daily newspapers is divided among three strong transnational press groups. Hungary is characterised by the most diverse ownership, especially with regards to the segment of regional and local newspapers. Poland's media sector markets display the strongest presence of domestic owners and in the broadcasting sector, Poland has been the only country in the group that lacked strong foreign competitors on the television market. Still and all, the media ownership tapestry modifies constantly and rapidly, becoming often opaque for ordinary users. Some shifts in ownership patterns signal the rise of domestic resources both in terms of financing and know-how. By contrast, there have been other changes that illustrate a contrary development – the growing ownership participation of large scale transnational media groups in the region.

What is interesting for our purpose comes with defining the end of policies focusing on media pluralism: what do we expect from remedies correcting media diversity? Is it the increased choice of media services for consumers? Or is it a creation of an environment free of structural imped-

[44] This issue is discussed in the Chapter 3.

iments that might favour media capture and lead to serious imbalances in media functions, forms of control and geographical levels on which and through which media operate? Who are the primary beneficiaries of media pluralism? Consumers, citizens or media users? Media pluralism is directly linked with communication needs that cannot be conceived only in economic and commercial terms. Thus, the crucial aspect in a process of policymaking is putting the ends and means at the right place: the ends should ultimately determine the use of means, not be adjusted to the available and most comfortable means.

This also impacts setting priorities: in some countries, policymakers might be concerned about the growth of foreign media ownership as the media system is becoming more vulnerable and dependent on external sources. Other countries may pay more attention to a high level of centralisation, depriving media structures of original and locally produced content. Yet, other countries might pay less attention to concentration on their internal markets in order to let their companies maintain competitiveness on transnational markets, and as long as other measures are at place that might balance a growing structural consolidation. In Germany for instance, mergers are being allowed between publishing companies in the case of market dominance, as long as editorial independence is guaranteed (Just, 2009: 102). The problem is however that such accompanying measures might not necessarily be used in other countries where these companies operate. The harmonised EU approach towards media pluralism should allow for an integration of various country priorities and at the same be firm in the principles on which the notion of media pluralism is built.

Regulating poor or endangered media diversity only by ex-post interventions (following e.g. mergers or chaining) might be as limited in terms of effectiveness as handling ex-post with decreasing biological or cultural diversity. Critics of preventive measures however claim that ex-ante actions can put media companies at risk of unduly penalising innovation and competitiveness, and would lead to immediate divestment (Schlosberg, 2013: 5). Such arguments sound highly convincing in media environments that experienced profound and radical transformation in a compressed period of time as is the case of the CEE. On the other hand, organic growth can be just as damaging to the public interest (Craufurd Smith et al., 2012: 19). Ellen P. Goodman proposes proactive instead of reactive policy enactments, considering subsidies and various kind of support that should work to promote demand as well as supply (2007: 375). The demand side of media pluralism necessarily points to an involvement and empowerment of media users, and the adoption of media literacy.

Media users are often challenged by fast-changing markets (Tambini, 2011: 11), and for various reasons, they might not explore the whole variety of media offerings. In this sense, a more comprehensive and profound approach to media transparency could offer the very first step in structural pluralism policies.

The three dimensions of structural media pluralism studied in this chapter (control-related, functional, geographical) demonstrate, on the one hand, trends in the CEE media landscapes, on the other hand, these dimensions present features of a *potential* diversity. Full usage of pluralism depends on multiple factors such as users' ability to access different platforms and contents, to receive and critically digest contents and services, to contextualise, to meaningfully use the knowledge about media ownership, media functioning in a society, and to interact with media services in various ways (Klimkiewicz, 2010b). Thus, putting the ends and means at the right place, opens the question what media structures would facilitate the use of potential media pluralism.

6. INDEPENDENCE OF MEDIA REGULATORY AUTHORITIES AND PUBLIC SERVICE MEDIA

6.1. A dynamic relationship between independence and external dependency: An Introduction

Media regulatory authorities (MRA) and the public service media (PSM) constitute important 'defining centres' in the infrastructure of public communication (Klimkiewicz, 2013). In normative terms, MRA are perceived as 'operational' or 'assisting' in the process of developing an autonomous media system that gains independence from its social environments, and thus can facilitate deliberative legitimation process (Habermas, 2006). The PSM are expected to provide universal access, diversity of perspectives in which the common world presents itself, and to offer a space of constant bargaining over the definition and common understanding of social reality (Arendt 1958; Keane 1991). The concepts of independence and autonomy play a crucial role in this respect: they serve as principal rationales justifying a specific status of the MRA and PSM. The principles of independence and autonomy ensure that an influence of the state and market, as well as their institutions (including e.g. government, parliament, commercial entities), are reduced to the minimum so that both the PSM and regulatory agencies are allowed to fulfill their mission with full professional autonomy (Klimkiewicz, 2013: 189).

Manuel Puppis and Martino Maggetti (2012: 77) argue that the MRA became key policy actors in media and communication governance especially following privatisation of state-owned companies in telecommunications and broadcasting markets in Europe. In the CEE, the MRA were created in the 1990 most often in a way of cloning the chosen West European model. In both cases, the regulatory authorities have accumulated increasing responsibility in governing broadcasting landscapes and the operation of both private and public broadcasters. A significant share of policymaking in the field of media and communication has thus been carried out by and delegated to organisations that are not democratically elected, at the same time that are not expected to be directly accountable to elected politicians (Puppis and Maggetti, 2012: 77). The current strands of the EU media policy hint at this institutional reinforcement with greater recognition of the role of MRA (e.g. in the AVMSD) and especially, with the emphasis on the concept of MRA independence. In a similar vein, the concept of PSM autonomy, especially with regard to remit and financing, has been used to delineate areas of EU policy concerning the PSM and state aid.

Autonomy can be seen as a form of independence from external control, influence, sources, support, etc. More precisely, both autonomy and independence would refer to a capacity of the MRA and PSM to achieve their goals regardless of the influence and resources of the external domains, including the political realm, media market (with a special role of advertising) and a socio-cultural environment (in particular articulated through claims and support of various social groups) (Klimkiewicz, 2013: 190). On the contrary, external dependency would define conditions under which the capacity of the MRA and PSM to achieve their goals is contingent upon the influence and resources of external domains (2013: 190). When linked with practical actions and operations, the close relation between the two binary oppositions is tested against the normative and evaluative views of the institutions in question. For example, the PSM are perceived as institutions that are best equipped to fulfill their mission when they are professionally autonomous and independent from external pressures. At the same time, the PSM are highly dependent on support from audiences – both in terms of viewing and contribution to its very existence through the system of licence fees. Puppis and Maggetti argue (2012: 78) that the MRA represent public sector institutions that are disaggregated from the public administration and enjoy a degree of autonomy even though they cannot be fully independent. As observed in the study on *Indicators for independence and efficient functioning of audiovisual media services regulatory bodies for the purpose of enforcing the rules in the AVMS Directive* (hereafter the INDIREG study), independence can be understood as a dynamic variable in relation to various possible dependences stemming from particular interests (Hans Bredow Institute for Media Research et al., 2011: 19).

Most obviously, the MRA and PSM do not operate in a cultural vacuum, hence the way how autonomy and external dependency function in a given society does not depend only on technical dimensions (appointment procedures and management, accountability, financing mechanisms and performance), but also on cultural precepts: these include collective perceptions, attitudes and behavior (Klimkiewicz, 2013). In other words, actual fulfillment of MRA and PSM autonomy is strongly shaped by cultural values and practices, including the political culture (Humphreys, 1996). Moreover, global media and policy flows generate some commonalities and interdependencies, in a normative understanding of independence for example. Here especially, the role of the EU seems important as will be discussed in the next section of this chapter.

The autonomy of the MRA implies that they – as devices of media governance – are created and given responsibilities by legitimate public institutions proportionally representing a given society (Klimkiewicz, 2013). Their status should be constituted in such a way, that it guarantees independence from governments and other political institutions (for example political parties), and media and communication entities (such as AVMS providers). The MRA are expected to carry out their work in full autonomy, impartially and transparently, in accordance with their professional remit (defined by the administrative, supervisory, rule-making and monitoring functions), eliminating a potential risk of political or economic interference (2013: 191). There are, however, various limitations in these normative expectations. First of all, autonomy and independence can never be absolute, but have to constitute themselves against the limits set by e.g. socio-cultural, historical, political factors. The MRA accommodate manifold interests in society, therefore they would hardly achieve factual independence from individually or collectively formulated values. For example, deciding about the eventual programming sanctions to be imposed on the grounds of broadcasting insulting certain ethnic groups or ridiculing religious practices, the MRA have to take into account two conflicting rights – the right to freedom of speech and expression, and the right not to be discriminated. An eventual decision will, in most cases, reflect such cultural factors as the ethnic and religious composition of a society and its cultural tradition (Klimkiewicz, 2013).

The PSM's special status might be conceptualised through competitive and complementary relationship with other actors in the media landscape. The competitive function arises with respect to the amount and share of viewing, but also from other aspects of PSM operation such as quality, innovation, professionalism, standards of performance, social relevance, serving a variety of interests, etc. (Blumler and Hoffmann-Reim, 2002: 202). In a competitive relationship, autonomy is compromised by what is expected by audiences, and also by the extent to which the PSM have to rely on mass audience (when they are e.g. co-financed from the advertising). The complementary function arises from the narrowing imperatives of the market, and on the other side, from the significance for a society at large of preserving the values that other actors (private broadcasters in particular) tend to neglect (Blumler and Hoffmann-Reim,

2002). In other words, a side-effect of the operation of media markets is that they fail to produce and offer the overall quality of media services that users would desire. The two most important reasons why this happens are first, that broadcasting can have adverse 'external effects' (e.g. amplifying violence in society) and second, that good broadcasting is a 'merit' good (just as education) (Graham 1999: 19). In addition, an important complementary dimension stems from a basic principle of democracy. The creation and sustenance of 'common knowledge' is a vital element in the functioning of a democracy. In order to be agreed solutions have to be derived from a common understanding (Graham 1999: 6) and 'enlarged' opinion-forming that involves incorporation of other people's views and preferences (Arendt, 1969). In normative terms, autonomy is compromised in a complementary relationship, by this 'enlarged mentality' that validates public opinion, and in consequence also the representation of collective interests. Organised pressure groups are only one aspect of these limits, others might be illustrated by indirect formulation of claims, interests and preferences of various identity groups defined by e.g. ethnicity, gender, language, social position, etc. (Klimkiewicz, 2013). The next section of this chapter will elaborate more closely on the issue of independence of MRA in EU media policy.

6.2. Independence of MRA in the EU media policy

In a wider context of the EU policy, the independence of the MRA finds its legal grounds in contributing to the safeguards of Article 11 (Charter of Fundamental Rights of the EU) and enactment of Article 288 TFEU (European Union, 2012) that sets the directives binding to the member states but leaves the choice of form and method of implementation to the national authorities (Hans Bredow Institute for Media Research et al., 2011: 7). Most obviously, the regulatory bodies are responsible for the implementation of the AVMSD, and in addition, also in authority to incorporate non legally binding policy standards and principles. The AVMSD refers to the role of the MRA in two Recitals and Article 30. Recital 94 stipulates that member states are free to choose the appropriate instruments for the implementation of the Directive according to their legal traditions and established structures, including the form of their competent independent regulatory bodies, in order to carry out their work impartially and transparently (European Parliament and the Council, 2010a). Recital 95 encourages close co-operation between competent regulatory bodies. The condition of co-operation is guaranteed more explicitly in Article 30 of the Directive:

> Member States shall take appropriate measures to provide each other and the Commission with the information necessary for the application of this Directive, in particular Articles 2, 3 and 4, in particular through their competent independent regulatory bodies (European Parliament and the Council, 2010a).

Article 30 does not specifically acknowledge the independence of audiovisual regulators, and does not require from member states to guarantee this independence. It is worth noting in this respect that the draft version of the Directive prepared by the Commission in 2005 included Recital 47 which addressed explicitly the independence of regulatory bodies:

> Regulators should be independent from national governments as well as from audiovisual media service providers in order to be able to carry out their work impartially and transparently and to contribute to pluralism. Close cooperation among national regulatory authorities and the Commission is necessary to ensure the correct application of this Directive (European Commission, 2005b).

This wording was however questioned by some member states that perceived it as a form of an ungrounded intervention stepping over EU competencies. As a result, a moderate version of Article 30 was agreed upon. The solution nonetheless, has not cleared up limitations that have become already apparent in pre-accession negotiations, where the Commission lacked a binding instrument to require the independence of media regulatory bodies established in the CEE countries.[1] As described in Chapter 3, the pre-accession Regular Reports devoted substantial space to media regulatory authorities in the candidate countries, focusing on various aspects such as administrative effectiveness, capacities, competences, powers and composition, often referring to the issue of independence. At the same time, the Commission could not use a legal leverage to demand the MRA's independence more formally. The Commission had to deal with the same obstacle in the case of expressing an opinion on the new Hungarian media law and the establishment of a regulatory authority controlled by the Prime Minister. Instead of relying on a legal tool, the Commission had to use soft policy instruments and political pressure – as noted in Chapter 3.

These practical cases led to a reconsideration of possible policies and broadening the scope of policy knowledge on the issue. In 2009, the Commission commissioned the *Study on Indicators for independence*

---

[1] DG Connect (2013) *Public consultation on the independence of the audiovisual regulatory bodies: the questionnaire* (available at: http://ec.europa.eu/digital-agenda/en/public-consultation-independence-audiovisual-regulatory-bodies; retrieved 31.21.2013).

and efficient functioning of audiovisual media services regulatory bodies, conducted by the Hans Bredow Institute, in order to collect a detailed legal description and analysis of the MRA, an analysis of the effective implementation of the legal framework and the identification of key characteristics constituting an independent regulatory body (Hans Bredow Institute for Media Research et al., 2011: 5). The study found out that in some EU countries either the legal set-up does not guarantee that regulatory bodies exercise their powers independently or that regulatory bodies are formally independent, but not in practice.[2] Other studies or reports emphasised the importance of a pan-EU approach harmonising standards of MRA independence. The Report of the High Level Group on Media Freedom and Pluralism highlighted – as part of its recommendations – that regulators should be independent, with appointments being made in a transparent manner, with all the appropriate checks and balances. In addition the Report proposed the creation of a network of national audio-visual regulatory authorities similar to the model established by the electronic communications framework (HLGMFP, 2013: 7). The Study on *European Union competencies in respect of media pluralism and media freedom* by the Centre for Media Pluralism and Media Freedom (CMPF), emphasised in a similar vein that a lack of harmonisation in this area contrasts strongly with the electronic communications framework. An agreement on harmonised solutions would be justified by the fact that some member states already have a single body supervising both electronic communications and audiovisual media services (CMPF, 2013).

As mentioned in the previous chapter, in March 2013, the DG Connect launched a public consultation on the independence of audiovisual regulatory bodies. The main objective of the consultation was to collect views and opinions from various stakeholders and reconsider an eventual possibility of strengthening the condition of independence through policy measures, including a possible revision of Article 30 of the AVMSD. The consultation process was closed in June 2013.[3] The DG Connect prepared a form of questionnaire in which the background of the initiative was explained. The Commission received 68 responses from various actors including citizen, producers' associations, the PSM, media regulatory authorities, NGOs, media companies, and ministries. Among these, only one

[2] DG Connect (2013) *Public consultation on the independence of the audiovisual regulatory bodies: the questionnaire* (available at: http://ec.europa.eu/digital-agenda/en/public-consultation-independence-audiovisual-regulatory-bodies; retrieved 31.12.2013).

[3] DG Connect (2013) *Public consultation on the independence of the audiovisual regulatory bodies* (available at: http://ec.europa.eu/digital-agenda/en/public-consultation-independence-audiovisual-regulatory-bodies; retrieved 31.12.2013).

response was submitted from CEE regulatory authorities – from the Polish National Broadcasting Council (KRRiT). Following the completion of the public consultation, the European Council published *Conclusions on media freedom and pluralism in the digital environment* (Council of the European Union, 2013). The document clearly divides the role of member states and the Commission as regards the independence of the MRA. While member states are invited to ensure the independence of their regulatory bodies, the Commission is encouraged to strengthen, through non-legislative actions, cooperation between member states' audiovisual regulatory authorities (2013: 3). This formulation (to which the Commission reported reservation) clearly signaled disagreement of the Council on possible legislative initiatives by the Commission. Hence, the future of the initiative proposed by the Commission seems rather uncertain.

6.3. Independence of the MRA in CEE

An empirical assessment of MRA independence is built on the conceptual distinction between *formal* and *de facto* independence (Hans Bredow Institute for Media Research et al., 2011: 28) or *formal* and *informal* independence (Puppis and Maggetti, 2012: 80). Formal independence derives from prescriptions constituting the MRA in law, in particular from defining its status (including establishment, appointment procedures, and accountability), organisational design and procedures of operation (including management, tasks and competences, financing, performance). Formal independence needs to be completed by de facto independence which refers to the practical implementation of all safeguards for formal independence as well as the overall compliance with formal provisions (Hans Bredow Institute for Media Research et al., 2011: 28). This section of the chapter aims at an empirical assessment of formal MRA independence in selected CEE countries in line with current EU policies seeking harmonisation in this particular field. The assessment will examine the dynamic relationship between independence and external dependency in a given historical, cultural and geopolitical context, thus also the conditions of practical – informal – implementation will be briefly described. Two 'technical' dimensions of this particular relationship were chosen as a primary focus: appointment procedures and accountability.

The current position of the MRA in the selected CEE countries has crystallised along specific historical currents and the growing importance of shared regulatory trends in Europe. The establishment of new MRA in CEE countries took place at the unique historical juncture in which democratic transition met with successive membership in the Council of Europe and European Union. The creation of the MRA among many other institutions building the administrative skeletons of transitioning states, was largely inspired by exogenous forces. The theory of institutional isomorphism suggests that if an apparently successful model of a regulator exists, it is likely to be copied (Hans Bredow Institute for Media Research et al., 2011: 14). In the CEE countries, the French model proved to be most successful in this regard. In Poland, the National Broadcasting Council – *Krajowa Rada Radiofonii i Telewizji* – KRRiT) was established by the 1992 Broadcasting Act. One of the main prerequisites for revamping the regulatory structure was the decomposition of former dependencies and relations of control between institutions of political power, regulatory units and the media. The National Broadcasting Council was designed according to the French model of *Conseil supérior de l' audiovisuel* (CSA) to reflect the institutional components of representative democracy: four of the KRRiT's nine members were to be appointed by the Sejm (the Lower House of the Polish Parliament), two by the Senate and three by the President. Since then, the KRRiT's competencies have encompassed granting and revoking broadcasting licences, participating in broadcasting policy formation, nominating members of the Supervisory and Program Councils who oversee the operations of the PSM, and scrutinizing the activity of broadcasters (content and audience in particular) (Klimkiewicz, 2013: 197). In the Polish Constitution enacted in 1997, the National Broadcasting Council has been recognised as one of the organs of state control and protection of rights.[4] The Constitution defined the tasks and competences of the KRRiT in general terms, and also outlined its composition and incompatibility rules. Thus any potential future change in the law would have had to respect and be adjusted in accordance with constitutional provisions.

The institutional model in the Czech Republic and Slovakia has roots in the first Federal Council for Radio and Television Broadcasting (*Federální Rada pro rozhlasové a televizní vysílání – FRRTV*) established in 1991 by the 1991 Act on Radio and Television Broadcasting.[5] Milan Šmíd argues that following foreign models was a common method used by politicians in the transitional period. Likewise in Poland, the new Czechoslovak regulatory authority was designed according to the prototype of the French CSA (Šmíd, 2011). The Federal Council was composed of nine members

[4] The Constitution of the Republic of Poland (Konstytucja Rzeczypospolitej Polskiej) adopted on 2 April, 1997, Official Journal, 1997, No. 78, item 483, Articles 213–215, (http://www.sejm.gov.pl/prawo/konst/angielski/kon1.htm retrieved 3 January, 2014).

[5] Act No. 468/ 1991 of 22 November 1991 on Radio and Television Broadcasting.

who were appointed by three bodies: three by the Federal Assembly, three by the Czech national parliament and three by the Slovak Parliament. In this way, the plurality of appointment aimed at reflecting diverse interests in the operation of the Council. In 1993, Czechoslovakia was split into two independent states and the Federal Council was dissolved at the end of 1992. Its competencies were transposed to the Czech Council for Radio and Television Broadcasting (*Rada pro rozhlasové a televizní vysílání – RRTV*) and Slovak Council for Broadcasting and Retransmission (*Rada pre vysielanie a retransmisiu – RVR*[6]). Contrary to the Federal Council, however, both national bodies have been since then appointed by one source – the Czech national parliament (Česká národní rada) and the Slovak national parliament (Národná Rada SR). Accordingly, the representation of diverse interests in society has been channeled only through the parliamentary structure. In Hungary, the regulatory body for radio and television broadcasting was established by the 1996 Broadcasting Act.[7] Between 1996 and 2010 the Hungarian National Radio and Television Authority (*Országos Rádió És Televízió Testület – ORTT*) was appointed from nominations delegated by various political parties. The 1996 Act stipulated that the Authority is comprised of at least 5 members nominated by the Parliament factions. Moreover, Article 32 (1) explicitly stated that the Authority is an independent legal entity under the supervision of the Parliament. With the 2010 Act on Media Services and Mass Media, the former activities of the ORTT and NHH (*Nemzeti Hírközlési Hatóság* – National Communications Authority) were merged under a newly created body – the National Media and Communications Authority (*Nemzeti Média és Hírközlési Hatóság – NMHH*). As described in Chapter 3, this regulatory change leading to significant centralisation of powers over the overall media landscape and political control over the appointment procedures by the governing party and Prime Minister, evoked a decisive reaction from the Council of Europe, the OSCE and the European Commission.

The table below summarises provisions concerning general recognition of the independence of the MRA in the CEE countries.

---

[6] The Council was first established under the name The Council of the Slovak Republic for Radio and Television Broadcasting.

[7] Act 1 of 1996 of Radio and Television Broadcasting.

Table 42: General recognition of the independence of media/audiovisual regulatory authorities in the Czech Republic, Hungary, Poland and Slovakia (emphasis in extracte added below – B.K.)

Country/ MRA	Relevant area	Provisions concerning independence	Legal basis
CZECH REPUBLIC/ The Council for Radio and Television Broadcasting (RRTV)	Activities of Council members	Section 6 (13) The Council members should carry out activities besides their capacity in the Council in a way which could not damage or challenge the trust in the **independence and impartiality of the Council**	Act No. 231/2001 of 17 May 2001 on Radio and Television Broadcasting and on Amendment to Other Acts
HUNGARY/ The National Media and Communications Authority (NMHH)	General	Article 109 (1) The National Media and Infocommunications Authority is an **independent regulatory** body solely subject to the law	Act CLXXXV of 2010 on Media Services and Mass Media, as amended
	Tasks of MRA	Article 109 (6) The Authority performs its tasks and **exercises its powers independently**, in compliance with applicable legislation Article 123 (2) The Media Council and its members shall be **solely subject to laws** and may not be instructed with respect to their activities	
POLAND/ National Broadcasting Council (KRRiT)	No relevant area	No explicit recognition of independence	1992 Broadcasting Act adopted on 29 December, 1992, as amended
SLOVAKIA/ Council for Broadcasting and Retransmission (RVR)	No relevant area	No explicit recognition of independence	Act No. 308 of 14 September 2000 Coll. on Broadcasting and Retransmission (as amended)

Sources: Elaborated on the basis of national broadcasting laws in the Czech Republic, Hungary, Poland and Slovakia as quoted in the table.

The legal and general recognition of MRA independence does not guarantee factual autonomy in achieving the goals and ends without external interferences. It does though provide a useful indication how the principle of independence is valued by policy makers, and how much is it exposed in legal acts and attached to the concept of regulatory bodies. As can be seen from the table above, the principal recognition of independence of the MRA in broadcasting and media laws in the region has not been an automatic and universally shared safeguard protecting the regulators from external influences. Polish and Slovak broadcasting laws do not contain an explicit recognition of MRA independence. It should be added though, that the Slovak Statute of the Council for Broadcasting and Retransmission (RVR) defines the Council as a "collective and independent body (...)".[8]

The 2001 Czech Act on Radio and Television Broadcasting links the issue of independence with the activities of the Council and in particular, the trust of the general public. Thus independence and impartiality is seen as an important condition of public trust that should be maintained by the practical activities of the Council's members. In comparison with other countries in the region, it is the 2010 Hungarian Act on Media Services and Mass Media that accords the greatest prominence to the principle of independence. First, independence is recognised generally as a feature of the National Media and Communications Authority defined by Article 109 (1). Secondly, independence refers to the performance of tasks by the Authority. Moreover, the Act also sustains that the Media Council may not be instructed with respect to their activities. At the same time, it is important to contextualise these safeguards with the appointment procedures and the control of political institutions to understand the full scope of regulatory autonomy and its limitations. Moreover, the concentration of powers in the hands of the Authority's chair has a strong effect on the operation of the whole body, as will be discussed below.

The next aspect of independence studied in this section is the appointment of the MRA. In normative terms, such procedures should guarantee a composition of membership that will be independent from political and business interferences, and at the same time, will "represent collectively the interests of society in general" (Council of Europe, 1996). Thus, on the one hand, the MRA membership mandate requires autonomy, on the other hand external dependency in terms of the pluralistic representation of social interests. The table below summarises five elements of appointment procedures in the selected CEE countries including membership (number, composition of the body), appointment and selection procedure, term, the position and election/nomination of the Chairperson and conflict of interests rules.

---

[8] Štatút Rady pre vysielanie a retransmisiu No. 1114, 4 May 2001, (available at: http://www.rvr.sk/sk/spravy/index.php?aktualitaId=429; retrieved 4.01.2014).

Table 43: Appointment procedures concerning media/audiovisual regulatory authorities in the Czech Republic, Hungary, Poland and Slovakia

Country/ MRA	Relevant areas	Appointment procedures	Legal basis
CZECH REPUBLIC/ The Council for Radio and Television Broadcasting (RRTV)	Membership	Section 7(1) 13 members	Act No. 231/2001 of 17 May 2001 on Radio and Television Broadcasting and on Amendment to Other Acts
	Appointment and selection	Section 7 (1) Members are appointed and removed by the Prime Minister on the basis of a proposal made by the Chamber of Deputies	
	Term	Section 7 (2) six years	
	Chairperson	Section 9 (1) The Council elects its Chairperson and 3 Vice-Chairpersons from among its members	
	Conflict of interests	Membership in the Council is incompatible with: Section 7 (9) top state offices, membership in the Councils: of the Czech Press Agency, the Czech TV and Czech Radio Section 7 (11) positions in political parties or movements and acting in their favour Section 7 (12) positions in media companies	

HUNGARY/ The National Media and Communications Authority (NMHH)	Membership	Article 124 (1) President and four members	Act CLXXXV of 2010 on Media Services and Mass Media, as amended
	Appointment and selection	Article 124 (1) elected by the Parliament – with a two-thirds majority of the votes of Members of Parliament present	
	Term	Article 124 (1) nine years	
	Chairperson	Article 111A/ (1) The NMHH President is to be appointed by the President of Hungary for a period of nine years, on the recommendation of the Prime Minister Article 111A (5) The requested organisations shall make their nominations in writing Article 111A (6) The Prime Minister shall name his/her candidate after considering the nominations made in the course of the consultations	
	Conflict of interests	The positions of NMHH President, Vice-President, Director General and Deputy Director General are incompatible with: Article 118 (1) top state and municipal offices, MPs, MEPs, working relationship with the PSM, Public Foundation for the PSM and other relevant councils for media and communications, government and local-level offices, working relationship with political parties, top offices in the media and communication services, ownership in companies providing media and communication services, ownership in business associations Membership in the Media Council is incompatible with: Article 127 (2) the categories defined by the Article 118 (1)	

POLAND/ National Broadcasting Council (KRRiT)	Membership	Article 7 (1) five members	1992 Broadcasting Act adopted on 29 December, 1992, as amended
	Appointment and selection	Article 7 (1) two members are appointed by the Sejm, one by Senate and two by President	
	Term	Article 7 (4) six years	
	Chairperson	Article 7 (2b) elected by the National Broadcasting Council from amongst its members and also dismissed by the Council members	
	Conflict of interests	Membership in the Council is incompatible with: Article 8 (3) membership in governing bodies of associations, trade unions, employers associations, as well as in church or religious organisations Article 8 (4) holding an interest or shares, or with any other involvement, in an entity which is a media service provider or a radio or television producer, as well as with any other gainful employment Article 214 (2)[9] members of the KRRiT may not belong to a political party, a trade union or perform public activities incompatible with the dignity of his function	

[9] The Constitution of the Republic of Poland (Konstytucja Rzeczypospolitej Polskiej) adopted on 2 April, 1997, Official Journal, 1997, No. 78, item 483, (http://www.sejm.gov.pl/prawo/konst/angielski/kon1.htm retrieved 3.01.2014).

SLOVAKIA/ Council for Broadcasting and Retransmission (RVR)	Membership	Article 6 (1) nine members	Act No. 308 of 14 September 2000 Coll. on Broadcasting and Retransmission (as amended)
	Appointment and selection	Article 6 (1) and 6 (2) The members are appointed and recalled by the National Council of the Slovak Republic on the basis of nominations delegated by MPs, professional and civic associations in the fields of: media, culture, science, education, sport, religion, etc.	
	Term	Article 8 (1) six years	
	Chairperson	Article 6 (3) The Council elects its Chairperson and Deputy Chair from amongst its members	
	Conflict of interests	Membership in the Council is incompatible with: Article 7 (2) top state and municipal offices Article 7 (3) holding a function in a political party or political movement; being a publisher of a periodical press or broadcaster, operator of retransmission; having shares of voting rights in a broadcasting or retransmission company; providing the broadcasters or operators of retransmission with expertise or a specialist service	

Sources: Elaborated on the basis of national broadcasting laws in the Czech Republic, Hungary, Poland and Slovakia as quoted in the table.

To grasp the role of appointment procedures in shaping the MRA's autonomy, it is worth starting from the composition of the membership. As the table demonstrates, the number of members varies highly – from five in Hungary and Poland to 13 in the Czech Republic. Interestingly, the Czech Republic and Poland started from the same level – nine members – using the CSA model. A higher number of members might better reflect various interests in a society that can be defined more broadly than solely in political terms. On the other hand, a lower number of members might guarantee a higher degree of efficiency and internal cohesion. In both cases, advantages highly depend on the appointment and selection procedure itself. The key roles in this process are in all the studied countries played by national parliaments. There are however, important nuances.

In Poland, the nomination of the KRRiT members by the Parliament and President, both elected through general elections, potentially creates a balance of powers. In practice, appointment decisions relating to the regulatory body have raised turbulent disputes and often, criticism. Puppis and Maggetti argue that regulators tend to be more independent in countries where political uncertainty is higher (Puppis and Maggetti, 2012: 80). In Poland on the contrary, a relatively fast circulation of political power and subsequent changes in the central administration proved to bring about an appetite for a more direct control over the composition of the regulator. Although the constitutional provisions protect the representative composition of the National Broadcasting Council and eliminate party membership of the KRRiT members,[10] the Constitution does not sharply define the number of the Council members and the length of their terms. This has been used by politicians not only to change the number of the KRRiT members, but also its very composition (especially in the case of the 2005 law change and subsequent attempts to re-arrange the composition and competencies of the KRRiT).[11]

In the case of the Czech Republic, the tasks, performance and composition of the Council for Radio and Television Broadcasting (RRTV) are

---

[10] Constitution of the Republic of Poland 1997..., Art. 214

[11] In December 2005, the newly elected right wing government prepared the Act on transformations and modifications to the division of tasks and powers of state bodies competent for communications and broadcasting (adopted on 29 December 2005, Official Journal 2005, No. 267, item 2258), which reduced the number of KRRiT members from nine to five. Although the rationale behind the Act was the establishment of a new super-regulatory body – the Office of Electronic Communications (*Urząd Komunikacji Elektronicznej – UKE*), most critics of the project underlined that the Act merely changed the composition of the National Broadcasting Council, Supervisory Councils of the Polish Television and Radio, and in consequence, management boards of both PSM institutions.

stipulated by the 2001 Act on Radio and Television Broadcasting.[12] The Council's competencies encompass granting and revoking broadcasting licences, overseeing the operation of retransmission and monitoring compliance with the law and conditions of the licences. The current appointment procedures have been in place since the pre-accession period and demonstrate a departure from the initial model inspired by the French solution of balancing political powers. The 13 members of the RRTV are formally appointed by the Prime Minister but nominated by the Chamber of Deputies. Thus, the Council membership continues to reflect the distribution of power in the Chamber of Deputies (OSF, 2013a: 79). Although the RRTV has in the past couple of years been considered less politically biased, the procedures for the appointment leave room for political interference (2013a: 79). In the case of Slovakia, the Council of Broadcasting and Retrasmission (RVR) has been composed of nine members appointed by the National Council of the Slovak Republic. The law guarantees that nominations for membership may be delegated by MPs, and professional and civic associations in the fields of: media, culture, science, education, sport, religion, etc.[13] In practice, however, many members have indirect links to political parties (OSF, 2013b: 76).

While the MRA in Poland, Czech Republic and Slovakia are responsible for the regulation of broadcasting and on-demand audiovisual services, and structurally they are accompanied by relevant bodies responsible for electronic communications, the Hungarian case presents the only converged regulator among the studied CEE countries. Merging of structures and responsibilities resulted in the creation of an institution that covers a remarkably large field of supervision. Its main tasks comprise ensuring the functioning and development of the communications market, safeguarding the interests of the users, fostering the development of fair and efficient competition within the electronic communications sector, and compliance with the law and licence conditions. Thus, the scope of supervision covers communication and media services as well as press products. The National Media and Communications Authority (NMHH) has a fairly complex structure: it is comprised of the NMHH President, the Media Council (Médiatanács) and the Office.[14] Among these, the Chairperson enjoys overarching powers, covering appointments of the Director General of the Office, two Vice-Presidents, Director General and Deputy Director of the NMHH. In addition, the Chairperson appoints the Director

[12] Act No. 231/2001 of 17 May 2001 on Radio and Television...

[13] Act No. 308 of 14 September 2000 Coll. on Broadcasting and...

[14] Act CLXXXV of 2010 on Media Services..., Article 109 (3).

general of the Broadcast Support and Property Management Fund and nominates candidates for the position of CEO of the public service media. As a result of the compromise reached with the Council of Europe, the amended version of the 2010 Act stipulates that the Chairperson is appointed by the President of Hungary for a period of nine years, on the recommendation of the Prime Minister who considers the nominations made in the course of consultations with various organisations.[15] The members of the Media Council are elected by the Parliament – with a two-thirds majority of the votes.[16] Even after changes, these procedures still continue to transpose centralised political control into the structure and operation of the regulatory body.

The conflict-of-interests rules constitute an important aspect of the appointment procedures as they paint the contours of public expectations towards the regulators. The provisions in all the CEE countries generally demonstrate that active politicians are excluded from appointment to media regulatory councils. Many examples of nominations to the MRA, however, prove that MRA members have been politically active before or after the terms, or co-operated actively with those political parties that pushed forward their nominations (OSF, 2012b; OSF, 2012c; OSF, 2013a; OSF, 2013b; Hans Bredow Institute for Media Research et al., 2011). The second large group covered by incompatibility rules includes media owners, top media management, and in some cases, also experts advising media companies. This category also appears among conflict-of-interest rules in all studied laws.

The next section of this chapter will reflect on mechanisms of accountability. Normative prerequisites with this regard are related to a simple question: to whom are the MRA accountable? What kind of accountability (administrative, legal, political, social) plays a leading role? Does this role in turn, define specific features of MRA appointment procedures and management? While administrative accountability involves answerability to superiors, legal accountability is directly linked to the rule of law (Goetz and Gaventa, 2001: 7). Political accountability can be defined as the elected officials' obligation to answer to the public, and of public servants to the elected officials (Blind, 2011: 7). Social accountability is generally seen as a bottom-up process, encapsulated in a variety of initiatives of direct and indirect civil society and citizen engagement in public affairs aiming to exact accountability (Ackerman, 2005: 16).

---

[15] Act CLXXXV of 2010 on Media Services..., Article 111A.

[16] Act CLXXXV of 2010 on Media Services..., Article 124 (1).

Table 44: Accountability of media/audiovisual regulatory authorities in the Czech Republic, Hungary, Poland and Slovakia

Country/ MRA	Relevant areas	Accountability procedures	Legal basis
CZECH REPUBLIC/ The Council for Radio and Television Broadcasting (RRTV)	Reporting obligations	Section 6 (1) The Council submits every year to the Chamber of Deputies an annual report on its activities and on the situation in the field of radio and TV broadcasting and in the field of the provision of on-demand audiovisual media services Section 6 (2) The Council submits the Report to the Chamber of Deputies for approval and simultaneously to the Prime Minister for expressing an opinion, and to the public	Act No. 231/2001 of 17 May 2001 on Radio and Television Broadcasting and on Amendment to Other Acts
	Dismissal	Section 6(3) In case that the Council repeatedly and seriously infringes on the obligations laid down in Sections 5 and 6 or if the Annual Report fails repeatedly to be approved due to serious faults, the Chamber of Deputies may propose to the Prime Minister to remove the Council.	

HUNGARY/ The National Media and Communications Authority (NMHH)	Reporting obligations	Article 109 (4) The President of the Authority reports to the Parliament on the activities of the Authority once every year. Article 133 (1) By 31 May of each year, the Media Council submits a report to the Parliament to give account of its activities for the previous year. The information includes the state of freedom of speech, changes in ownership status, etc.	Act CLXXXV of 2010 on Media Services and Mass Media, as amended
	Dismissal	Article 109 (7) The communications regulatory powers of the Authority cannot be withdrawn in any way Article 113(2) The President of the Republic shall dismiss the President, if he/she fails to eliminate the conflict of interest or the President is placed under guardianship affecting his/her legal capacity Article 129 (5) The mandate shall be terminated by dismissal, if the President or member of the Media Council is placed under guardianship affecting his/her legal capacity	

POLAND/ National Broadcasting Council (KRRiT)	Reporting obligations	Article 12 (1) By the end of March each year, the Council submits to the Sejm, the Senate and the President, an annual report on its activities during the preceding year, as well as information concerning key issues in radio and television broadcasting Article 12 (2) Each year, the Council presents to the Prime Minister an annual account of its activities as well as information on key issues in radio and television broadcasting	1992 Broadcasting Act adopted on 29 December, 1992, as amended
	Dismissal	Article 12 (4) In case of rejection of the report by both the Sejm and the Senate, the term of office of all the members of the Council shall expire within 14 days but only if: Article 12 (5) approved so by the President	
SLOVAKIA/ Council for Broadcasting and Retransmission (RVR)	Reporting obligations	Article 5 (3) The Council is obliged to submit to the National Council of the Slovak Republic information on the situation in broadcasting and about its own activities Article 6a Describes the content of the annual report	Act No. 308 of 14 September 2000 Coll. on Broadcasting and Retransmission (as amended)
	Dismissal	Article 6 (1) The members of the Council can be recalled by the National Council	

Sources: Elaborated on the basis of national broadcasting laws in the Czech Republic, Hungary, Poland and Slovakia as quoted in the table.

The table above examines two aspects of accountability: reporting obligations and procedures of dismissal. Although reporting obligations clearly involve answerability to superiors (thus manifesting administrative accountability), the fact that in all studied countries, the MRA annual reports are to be submitted and also accepted by the Parliaments, proves that the process is dominated by political accountability. In Poland, the President is also involved in this process. In case of rejection of the annual report by both the Sejm and the Senate, the term of office of the KRRiT members expires, but only if this decision is approved by the President. In Polish political practice, with its relatively fast pace of exchange of political power in the past, political affiliation of the President often differed from the parliamentarian majority. However recently, since the President has represented the same party as the government, the annual report was rejected in 2010 and the whole regulatory body dismissed. In the case of Hungary and Slovakia, the procedure of the MRA dismissal is not directly related to the acceptance of the annual report. In Hungary, the Chairperson (President) or members of the Media Council may be dismissed if they are placed under guardianship affecting their legal capacity albeit the law does not specify the term 'guardianship'. In Slovakia, the RVR members can be dismissed only under the circumstances of a conflict of interest as defined by law, or when they are convicted of a crime or they cannot fulfill their duties for more than six months. The measures collected in Table 43 and examples given reveal a clear asymmetry between a strong preference for political, rather than legal, administrative or social accountability.

To summarise: although the issue of MRA independence comprises many aspects of the MRA's status and performance (e.g. appointment, use of powers, accountability, financing), two dimensions seem to be particularly important. Puppis and Maggetti (2012: 80) define them as political and economic independence. While political independence refers to the ability to select policy objectives without influence from the government, economic independence points to the ability to use instruments of policy without economic restrictions and industry influences. Against this background, especially political independence has been limited in various ways in the studied CEE countries, most notably through appointment procedures and accountability measures.

6.4. The EU policies concerning the PSM

In normative terms, PSM has long been perceived as a constitutive element of functional diversity in classical Europe-born media system arrangements. This type of structural diversity is generated by different functions, the way in which they are balanced and complement each other. It is important to add in this respect that Recital 13 of the AVMSD acknowledges the co-existence of private and public audiovisual media service providers as a feature which distinguishes the European audiovisual media market (European Parliament and the Council, 2010a). PSM integrating competitive and complementary functions, are to offer a set of qualitative priorities, differing from the market-driven media. This difference is not so much congruent with genres and areas of programming, as with functions, gratifications, standards and quality, as well as with its reputation for accessibility to public concerns and responsiveness to public needs (Blumler and Hoffmann-Reim, 2002). In addition to genre provisions (information, entertainment, education), qualitative priorities should reflect such important social and cultural functions like cultural self-determination, innovation, trans-national appeal, imaginativeness, and an ability to illuminate controversy, authenticity, social relevance, expressive richness and integrity (Blumler and Hoffmann-Reim, 2002: 207).

These functional attributes delineating performance and remit of the PSM paint contours of autonomy. In other words, conditions under which the PSM operate determine quality and autonomy of performance and fulfilling the special functions generating public value. One of such pivotal conditions are financing mechanisms. Financing in particular, should reflect independence from the political environment and especially the government, as well as the market. It should guarantee accordingly managerial and professional autonomy. As regards the PSM, longstanding practice in various European countries contributed to a broad acceptance (not without controversy) of various forms of funding including a flat broadcasting licence fee, taxation, state subsidies, subscription fees, advertising and sponsoring revenue, specialised pay-per-view or on-demand services, the sale of related products such as books, videos and films, and the exploitation of the PSM's audiovisual archives (Council of Europe 2009b). At the same time, being a public institution in law and governance, the PSM are seen to best preserve their managerial and professional autonomy through primary funding from public sources – in particular a flat broadcasting license fee (Klimkiewicz, 2013: 194). This type of funding does not only prevent an undue influence of the government in terms of establishing a direct amount to be transferred in a form of subsidies, grants or other similar forms, it also secures a long-term approach to the PSM's future planning, which annual funding from state budgetary sources would not allow (2013: 194).

In this sense, the question of PSM funding conceptually captured by the state aid policy regime supervised by DG Competition, became one of the long-term themes underpinning the EU's policy with a growing significance for the future of the PSM. EU policy concerning the PSM has been briefly discussed in Chapter 2. This section will describe more closely issues that resonate with the question of autonomy and subsequent analysis of the position and strength of the PSM in the selected CEE countries. Mark Wheeler points out that in applying state aid rules, wherein public subsidies are seen to unfairly distort the market, to the audiovisual sector, DG Competition has become an increasingly active player in intervening in European television markets (Wheeler, 2010: 51). In doing so, the policy perception of the PSM in audiovisual landscapes, has progressively been filtered through economic values and competition rules guided by economic logic. As observed in the chapter one, media systems and environments fulfil various functions (including economic) that respond to communication needs. Normatively, these are not all subordinated to the economic function. In EU media and communications policy, however, certain strands show that prioritising economic values and functions transgresses into the domain of institutions that were set in the past to operate outside economically defined markets. In ideal terms, the PSM were not perceived to be part of the market, but as a complementary structure correcting a failure of the market. In practice however, competitive functions have grown from the PSM's general appeal and popularity among audiences especially with the development of the private broadcasting sector.

As mentioned in the chapter two, the 1997 Protocol of Amsterdam ensured funding for the fulfilment of the public service remit but under the condition, it does not distort market competition and the competitive balance between public and commercial broadcasters is preserved. As the Protocol referred explicitly to 'broadcasting', not the 'media' or 'media services', the interpretation of PSM activities on new platforms brought by technological advancement stood under question. *The resolution of the Council and of the Representatives of the Governments of the Member States, meeting within the Council of 25 January 1999 concerning public service broadcasting*, reaffirmed that the fulfilment of the mission of public service broadcasting requires that it continues to benefit from technological progress (Council of the European Union, 1999). The subsequent communications from the Commission on this issue reaffirmed this approach (European Commission, 2001; 2009a). But already in the 2001 Communication the limits and areas were mentioned where public funding should not be used to support certain new media services. In the 2009 Communication, the Commission encourages the member states to implement clearer instruments – such as tests – to weigh the impact of new media services launched by the PSM on the economic market against the public or social value of this service for society. Thus, the states are supposed to introduce mechanisms that will enable identify when public value (supported by public funding) surpasses economic values of effective competition.

The European Commission has become involved with several state aid cases concerning the funding of the PSM. Mark Wheeler argues that DG Competition hardened its stance against the PSM and their anti-competitive effect in terms of market distortion (Wheeler, 2010). In the case of Danish *TV 2* and the Dutch *NOS DG* Competition required the re-payment of funding received by the PSM; in the case of the German *ARD* and *ZDF* and the Irish *RTE* and *TG4*, the PSM were subjected to refined commitments requiring them to define more strictly their public service obligations and be responsive to proportionate financial regimes. As regards the CEE countries, in February 2008, Poland's largest commercial broadcaster the TVN group consulted the European Commission in order to suggest an examination of the use of state aid by the Polish public service television (*TVP S.A.*) and compliance of *TVP's* operation with the EC competition rules. The main argument used in the claim was grounded on the fact that the legal definition of the public remit is not precise enough and *TVP S.A.* can finance commercial activity as if this were a public mission (Masłowska, 2008). The *TVP S.A.* established separate accounts for the task of fulfilling the public service mission and for commercial activities. The National Broadcasting Council (KRRiT) has reported on these mechanisms in its annual reports (e.g. KRRiT, 2003). Nevertheless, the TVN group maintained that the realisation of the public mission by *TVP S.A.* is not sufficiently monitored and the KRRiT is merely limited to analysing statistical data (Masłowska, 2008). *TVP S.A.* in its letter to the Commission, submitted on the occasion of the Commission's review of the communication on state aid to PSM, explained the conditions and competition on the audiovisual media market in Poland, referred to the dual system of financing introduced in Poland at the beginning of 1990s and extracted tasks and duties forming public service mission (Telewizja Polska, 2008). With regard to the TVN claim, *TVP S.A.* expressed the opinion that complains of commercial broadcasters confirm that they "aim at weakening the position of public media in Poland and in doing so, they would try to involve European institutions to support them" (Masłowska, 2008). As a consequence of the EC examination, the KRRiT in co-operation with the *TVP* has started to work on a Charter of TVP's duties with a more precise listing of audiovisual services for the next 5 years. The Charter is expected to be publicised in 2014.

All these cases prove, that the operation, financing and in consequence also autonomy of the PSM have been conceptualised in more technocratic terms. As Mark Wheeler notices, the rigid employment of state aid, however, fails to take into account the social, cultural and democratic functions of the PSM and the need to separate these areas in media and communication environments which have become increasingly defined by competitive commercial services (Wheeler, 2010: 60).

6.5. Changing conditions of the PSM in the CEE

The current state of the PSM in the CEE region has resulted from a specific historical juncture and increasingly important converging of pan-European trends. Recently, these trends have accentuated the decline in normative certainties, especially as regards the function of the PSM in a new communication environment (Klimkiewicz, 2013: 195). Moreover, new challenges have arisen around growing regulatory pressure from the European Commission in terms of clarifying the PSM remit and financial mechanisms (Meier 2003; Bardoel and d'Haenens 2008; Ward 2008), and new political choices inspired by commercial incentives (removal of advertising in Spain and France) or populist reasons (abolition of the licence fee in Hungary and a policy debate about similar solutions in Poland and the Czech Republic).

In CEE, the PSM have been created more than 20 years ago as part of a far-reaching media system reform in conditions of 'compressed' time. This compression was caused by the fact that the PSM were exposed relatively early to competition with their private counterparts (Klimkiewicz, 2013). The period of 'inventing' and 'reinventing' the PSM appeared to coincide with a development of commercial broadcasters imposing their own commercial logic and way of action. At the same time, three limitations can be extracted that affected conditions of autonomy and independence of the PSM in the CEE countries.

First, the 'new' PSM preserved the institutional continuity of the former state media. Katrin Voltmer (2013: 153) describes them as huge bureaucratic organisations that were hopelessly overstaffed, inefficient and governed by an attitude of subservience to their political masters. To quote the Mapping Digital Media Report on the Czech Republic, the public service radio (*Český rozhlas* – ČRo) and television (*Česká televize* – ČT) are still perceived to a certain extent as "legatees of the communist state-administered institutions" and as "institutions trying to lose their reputation as politically manipulated, inefficient media giants" (OSF, 2013a: 31). Second, although there was a CEE domestic option to create a three-level broadcasting system composed of the public, private/commercial and social/civic media, a solution inspired by the will to copy the legal and institutional framework of the West-European dual model prevailed (Ociepka 2003). Third, the starting point of PSM institutional birth in the CEE countries (1990–1995) coincided with an enhanced criticism and PSM crisis in the Western part of Europe. Karol Jakubowicz argues that the internal reform and adoption of the normative West European PSM pattern has been put under question before successfully completed and before an alternative self-regeneration option was conceived. In the given historical circumstances, the West European pattern has appeared obsolete, born in a quite different historical time and different social, political, cultural and technological conditions – and now in acute need of a redefinition of its rationale and purpose (Jakubowicz 2004: 67).

These three circumstances determined quite a specific course of action, in which the PSM has not developed as a formally autonomous system (as in the case of the professional model described by Humphreys 1996: 155–158), but a more inclusive system combining a 'Western' normative model as a point of reference with political control (mainly over appointments in management structures), legal norms granting professional autonomy and commercial prerequisites (Klimkiewicz, 2013: 196). As the legal embeddedness of the PSM shows, legal measures describing status of the PSM are more or less satisfactory, but political culture and the way rules are used and implemented in practice generates a whole set of political dependencies, in particular when it comes to the appointment procedures of the PSM boards, management and supervisory bodies, and political decisions about sources of finding.

One of the dimensions exposing the strength of public service television over a longer period of time is audience share in the whole audiovisual landscape. Once monopolist broadcasters, nowadays public service TVs occupy a much smaller proportion of the market. There are, however, significant differences among the countries studied and course of changes in this respect. The table below shows the average daily share of public service channels in the region. It may be added in this respect, that the proportions of average daily share do not substantially differ from the proportions reflected in prime time audience share.

Table 45: Proportion of public service TV channels in audience share (%) in the Czech Republic, Hungary, Poland and Slovakia between 1999–2010

	1999	**2000**	**2001**	**2002**	**2003**	**2004**	**2005**	**2006**	**2007**	**2008**	**2009**	**2010**
CZECH REPUB-LIC	32.1	31.2	29.2	29.4	29.7	30.5	29.8	30.8	31.8	30.6	27.9	27.8
HUN-GARY	18.1	15.2	16.9	16.9	19.2	19.1	17.6	18.6	16.6	15.0	13.4	13.5
POLAND	51.1	46.2	48.1	50.5	52.5	51.1	51.6	49.8	46.6	44.5	43.1	42.2
SLOVA-KIA	18.1	18.0	20.2	21.0	21.8	24.6	25.0	24.7	22.6	22.0	20.8	17.4

Sources: Calculated on the basis of European Audiovisual Observatory (2011) 2011 Yearbook – Television in 37 European States, Strasbourg; 2009 Yearbook; 2006 Yearbook.

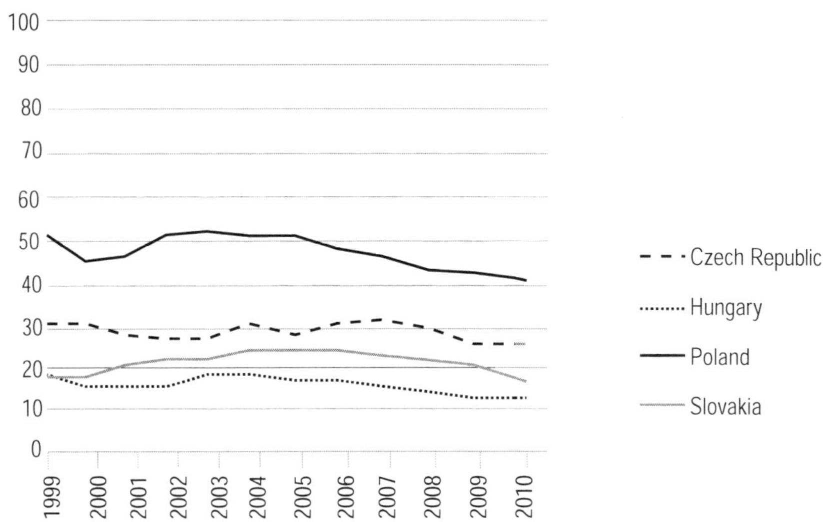

Figure 9: Proportion of public service TV channels in audience share (%) in the Czech Republic, Hungary, Poland and Slovakia between 1999–2010

Sources: Calculated on the basis of European Audiovisual Observatory (2011) 2011 Yearbook – Television in 37 European States, Strasbourg; 2009 Yearbook; 2006 Yearbook.

As can be seen from both the table and figures, two groups can be distinguished among the countries studied. The first is represented by public service TV in Poland. The second group is comprised of countries with a weaker position of public service TV channels including the Czech Republic, Slovakia and Hungary. In Poland, *TVP* became a cardinal player in the national advertising market and leader in television audience share, thus posing itself as a main rival to commercial channels, at the beginning of the 1990s. This superior position has ensued from two reasons. First, *TVP* enjoyed a relatively high audience loyalty. Second, unlike in the case of the press, the broadcasting regulation imposed limits and control on the broadcasting market (Klimkiewicz, 2013). As explained in the chapter five, until 2004, foreign investors were allowed to hold only minority shares (up to 33%) in the Polish broadcasting media. In consequence, the absence of influential foreign investors contributed to a division of the television market into two parts: one covered by the strong public broadcaster and the other dominated by two strong private companies – *Polsat* and *TVN*, each owning several channels. In recent years however, the share of other companies (offering mostly thematic channels) significantly increased. It has to be also emphasised that the most recent results depicting the annual audience share of *TVP* demonstrate a significantly weaker position in the market and amount only to 32%.[17] Most recently, Slovak public service broadcaster *STV* also experienced heavy losses in audience share at the expense of private commercial and thematic channels attaining only 12% of audience share.[18] The Mapping Digital Media Report on Slovakia observed that the main reason for this decreasing viewership has been the successful strategy of the commercial broadcasters, and namely extending the main news programmes in time slots controlled earlier by the *STV* (OSF, 2013b: 27). The pressure from commercial broadcasters has certainly been more evident in the CEE region, as the advertising market has shrunk and migrated to other platforms, mainly the Internet. Albeit the pressure also took other forms than marketing and programme strategies as the case of the examination of state aid to *TVP* by the European Commission illustrated.

To fully understand the strength of public service TV in an overall audiovisual landscape, attention has to be paid to autonomy in terms of financing schemes. The next figure shows the proportion of funding from the license fees – as a source – independent both from commercial mechanism as well as from the government subsidies.

---

[17] MAVISE (2013) (available at: http://mavise.obs.coe.int/country?id=24; retrieved 27.12.2013).

[18] MAVISE (2013) (available at: http://mavise.obs.coe.int/country?id=28; retrieved 27.12.2013).

Table 46: Proportion of licence fees in revenues of public service channels (%) in the Czech Republic, Hungary, Poland and Slovakia between 1999–2010

	1999	**2000**	**2001**	**2002**	**2003**	**2004**	**2005**	**2006**	**2007**	**2008**	**2009**	**2010**
CZECH REPUBLIC	65	60.5	51.4	64.7	66.7	67.2	61.3	65.1	72.6	73.9	79.2	80.4
HUNGARY	19.5	19.7	15.9	28.5	–	–	34.5	33.6	31.2	30.9	32	44.5
POLAND	29.2	29.2	30.1	30	32.4	32.1	28.0	27.0	24.6	20.5	16.9	12.2
SLOVAKIA	55.5	66.5	62.1	65.6	–	–	–	43.6	44.2	52.6	54	–

Sources: Calculated on the basis of the European Audiovisual Observatory (2011) 2011 Yearbook – Television in 37 European States, Strasbourg; 2009 Yearbook; 2006 Yearbook.

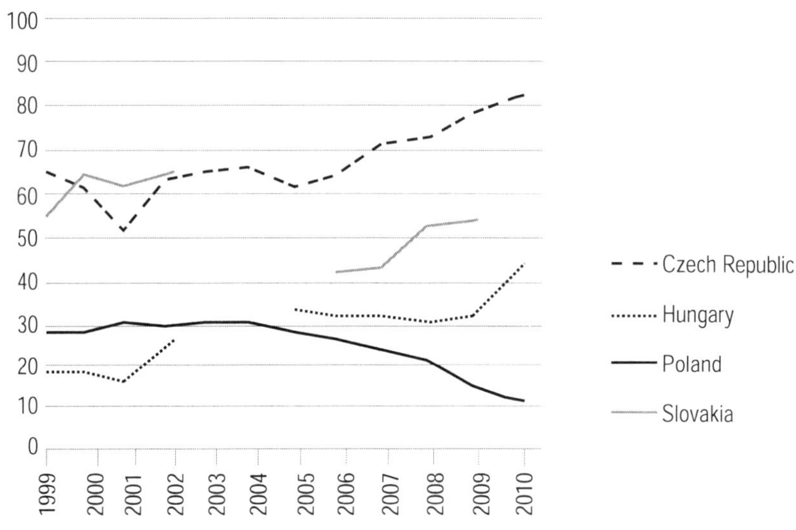

Figure 10: Proportion of licence fees in revenues of public service channels (%) in the Czech Republic, Hungary, Poland and Slovakia between 1999–2010

Sources: Calculated on the basis of European Audiovisual Observatory (2011) 2011 Yearbook – Television in 37 European States, Strasbourg; 2009 Yearbook; 2006 Yearbook.

Again, two groups of countries emerge from this comparison: the first group includes the Czech Republic and Slovakia. The public service TVs in these countries, have seemed to enjoy relatively stable and continuous funding from the licence fees. In the case of the Czech Republic, the proportion of licence fees has been comparable with financial mechanisms in some West European countries – such as France, the UK, and Germany. The stable and relatively sufficient funding also contributed to a balanced although not highest audience share in the period of 1999–2010. The Slovak *STV* underwent several reforms, both in terms of financing and organisational structure, most recently leading to the institutional merger of three *STV* channels and nine *SRo* (*Slovenský rozhlas* – Slovak Radio) stations under one brand. In January 2011, a single public service broadcaster was created under the name of Radio and Television of Slovakia (*Rozhlas a televízia Slovenska,* RTVS) (OSF, 2013b: 26). All these changes so far, however, have not contributed to better *STV* performance in a viewership.

The second group is represented by – Poland and Hungary – two quite opposite cases demonstrating practical difficulties in terms of achieving financial autonomy. In Poland, license fee revenue has oscillated between 30%–17% of TVP's total revenues during the last 20 years. Thus, most of its activities were financed from advertising, sponsoring and other commercially related sources. The advertising funding encourages the PSM to spend only the minimum required to keep the largest possible audience watching, and to successfully compete with private commercial counterparts (Graham et al., 1999). In the case of Poland, this situation resulted in a vicious circle: the viewers have not opted for paying licence fees, because public service television has spent too much time on advertising and programmes similar to what commercial broadcasters offer; public service television, on the other hand, has not succeeded in collecting substantial revenues from licence fees to make itself independent from advertising sources (Klimkiewicz, 2013: 202). In consequence, the pure pressure to achieve ratings has eroded the ability of public service television to secure its professional autonomy. In the case of Hungary, the change of financial mechanism was caused by the political choice. The abolition of the television license fee in 2002 led to the implementation of financing directly from the state budget. Consequently, annual state allocations to the *MTV* budget rendered *MTV* performance dependent on political decision-making and choices. Moreover, political and financial vulnerability contributed to a drop in audience share (to around 10%).

It is worth acknowledging that these trends weakening the position of the PSM correlate, to a certain extent, with challenges the European PSM are undergoing at the moment. However, public service media and especially TV seem to be still in a worse position in some CEE countries. This is not only due to commercial pressures, difficulties with defining the PSM remit but also due to political choices and sometimes populist reasons (the abolition of licence fee in Hungary and the policy debate about similar solutions in Poland, the Czech Republic and Slovakia).

6.6. Conclusions

A policy theme integrating in this chapter two separate and at the same time normatively interrelated fields – the independence of the MRA and autonomy of the PSM – has been one of the most challenging in terms of harmonising the EU and national approaches. Unsuccessful efforts of the Commission to legally recognise the value of MRA independence demonstrated a strong willingness of the states to control this institution and its embeddedness in national media environments. An empirical assessment of selected technical dimensions of MRA independence in the CEE countries has shown a range of varied arrangements. Although many of these originated in the adoption of West European models (most notably the French CSA), the evolving picture drifted towards nationally specific solutions often reflecting the political system and cultural and historical context. As regards general recognition of MRA independence and appointment procedures, legal safeguards varied largely from a country to country. In all cases however, the MRA have been interwoven into a complex set of relations with the political system, determined by political culture, democratic consolidation and political manners. The accountability dimension has been heavily dominated by political accountability, not providing parity or stability between administrative, legal and social accountability.

In the area of the autonomous operation of the PSM, the European Commission has championed a technocratic approach to the PSM mainly through state aid policies administered under DG Competition. This prevailing approach settled frames of debates about the PSM (and also about their future) in economic and competition field, thus weighing PSM output in terms of palpable social and public values, against 'market impact'. PSM financing has been a crucial element of the negotiated autonomy of the PSM which have more frequently been perceived as a complementary rather than competitive structure in the media environment as a whole. An empirical assessment of the changing conditions of the PSM in the CEE has demonstrated an overall trend of a weakening the PSM both in terms of audience share and financing. Bardoel and d'Haenens (2008) describe a growing critical attitude among governments and politicians towards the PSM resulting from a frustration and inability to build a more clientelistic partnership. "The forced tango that national politics and public broadcasters have danced for many decades" is being discreetly replaced by partnership with private media promising "to be less critical and cynical towards politics than PSB" (Bardoel and d'Haenens 2008: 339). Yet CEE experience shows that politicians were relatively successful in building clientelistic relationships with the PSM, at the same time they tended to weaken the PSM generally and reduce their autonomy, especially through financing mechanisms. This can be illustrated by the example of the abolition of licence in Hungary, or inaction concerning licence fees by the Polish politicians who seemed to accept the PSM financing from advertising. Overreliance on the advertising sources of financing, however, has created tensions with the fulfillment of the public service provision and led to complaints by commercial broadcasters to the European Commission.

Closer and more symmetric relations between the PSM and their audiences will be an important condition in the process of regaining the PSM's symbolic capital and their relative weight in entire media environments in the CEE region. A part of the problem lies in the fact that relations between the PSM and society could hardly be institutionalised and that society is not an established actor as such (Bardoel and d'Haenens, 2008). At the same time, only with greater inclusion and participation of audiences and media users in various aspects of PSM performance and policy, can the PSM equip themselves with a stronger functional legacy, more balanced accountability and autonomy against political and economic influences. Moreover, this can also empower the PSM at the EU level where increased tensions between the PSM and commercial media are moving from the national levels. Without a clear strategy seeking support and alliance with PSM users, the considerable changes which the PSM will have to undergo, can bring an unpredictable result.

The role of national political systems and the EU will be crucial in this process, especially as regards the questions of PSM and MRA autonomy. There is certainly a demand for more autonomous and transparent institutions occupying central positions in the infrastructure of public communication. This does not pose a new demand but a demand centered around those aspects of public communication that have long been neglected for various reasons (Klimkiewicz, 2013: 208). 'Classical' public service purposes and regulatory expectations are still valid. But they have to meet the communication needs of new media users and respond to the new social conditions of increasing mobility, virtual networking, social fragmentation, growing uncertainty, global competitiveness, including competitiveness of cultures and ideas (2013: 208).

7. BETWEEN AN ORGANIC GROWTH AND GARDENING: HARMONISATION OF THE POLYVALENT MEDIA POLICY. CONCLUSIONS

A rise of new forms of communication and new media architecture once again in history dramatically changes the way the media function in societies. The new media have a tremendous potential to create a universe of their own, pervading more profoundly into community and individual lives. In these new communication environments, the users simultaneously switch among platforms, services, and ways of interactions, in search of contents meeting various communication needs. Depending on the available media structures, their accessibility and conditions of use, users gain more autonomy in choice and control over the services they select. At the same time new media systems and environments, through their resources and relations with other fields of social actions, play important roles and functions determining what communication needs, and – in what ways – will be met. This constitutes a most fundamental challenge in media and communication policy that seeks to shape the structures and practices of the media. Following these observations the questions emerge: What media functions are most beneficial for the harmonious development of societies? What functions should be given priorities over the other? How can a right media balance and sustainable environment be achieved? Through an organic growth or gardening?

The normative model of the polyvalent media policy presented in this work aims to explain the process of balancing and harmonising various functions which the communication media play in contemporary societies. It proposes a reconsideration of normative grounds for policymaking in a wider context of the interplay of policy arguments and rationales (technological, cultural, educational and knowledge-generating, economic and political) rooted in various social fields rather than seeing policy as a battlefield between economic and cultural/political values. This implies extracting various policy strands affecting macrostructures – media systems or media environments – that are arranged in particular ways. As such structures are always deeply rooted in a particular historic, cultural, economic, political context and path dependencies, revealing common grounds and regularities often lacks a clear approach. Instead of capturing specific policy outcomes through large sets of statistical data, this book sought to comprehend the processes and mechanisms of media-policy being made at the EU level and their harmonisation at the national level.

In this respect, EU policy scope concerning the media and communications grew considerably in the areas of audiovisual policy (TWF and AVMS Directives), pan-European media, EU support for audiovisual production, the public service media, media pluralism, convergence and the digital agenda, media literacy and digital divide, community and minority media, international trade and cultural diversity and others. In addition to a proliferation of thematic areas, policy processes also became more complex. The symptoms of this complexity include: policy actors' interdependence, polyvalent rationality, complementarity anf functional convergence and knowledge and data asymmetries. In other words, the polyvalent character of media policy has implied an involvement of multiple values in policy reasoning and justification, diffussion and growth of interdependent policy actors and a constant complementing and attunement of various functional fields. The symptoms of complexity result from the fact that various strands in EU media and communication policy developed along distinct phases, thematic clusters and media levels (structural, content and performance-related policies). At the same time, an overarching media policy rationale grounded on the principle of freedom of expression and media pluralism became more profoundly anchored in the EU normative framework, as with the Lisbon Treaty coming into force on 1 December 2009, the Charter of Fundamental Rights of the European Union was made legally binding.

While acknowledging the polyvalent character of the EU media and communications policy an important question appears about harmonisation. In this respect, the contours of harmonising efforts strike one as being elastic and adaptable to national reservations. On the one hand, the EU accomplished synchronised standards and procedures in such areas as the internal market, common rules on audiovisual media services, support schemes for EU audiovisual production and for pan-European media projects (although these were quite unsuccessful). On the other hand, nationally specific approaches blocked EU initiatives on media pluralism, the independence of media regulatory authorities, support to other media sectors such as the print press or community and minority media, and a more complex approach towards the PSM. The specificity of supranational versus national policy-making certainly implies varied and subsidiary levels of the policy enactment. Ideally, these should be built on the anchored core of norms that are not nationally negotiable, and secondly on country-adaptable priorities. In the media and communication policy field, the core norms would most probably be based on general principles of communication rights. The negotiable principles might be adapted to country-specific needs and characteristics such as size, geographical location, ethnic and demographic structure, cultural and historical tradition.

Yet, one of the most challenging aspects of harmonisation has been the extracting of these levels from the polyvalent character of the media and communications policy, and in particular an uncertainty as how to balance, these sometimes contradictory values. Thus, the least contentious policy options have paved the way to prioritising economic values and recently – the digital agenda – which became the main pillar in the array of EU thematic policies. The use of the term 'agenda' is not accidental. It demonstrates the seriousness and principal place of digital communication in the hierarchy of post-Lisbon EU policies, and also a dominant vector for redirecting media policies diffused across various thematic fields. Experiencing a profound economic crisis, the EU is placing hope in policies and visions that could restore a sense of collective purpose and would not necessarily require a more sophisticated reconciliation of societal needs and interests.

Interestingly, the EU enlargement has been one of the areas where the EU media and communication policy could be tested quite comprehensively in a condensed period requiring a transposition of EU standards and fulfillment of EU conditions by the candidate countries. This process could verify a normative integrity and balance of values, potential media policy choices rooted in various media functions as well as responsiveness to communication needs and rights. The CEE countries selected for the assessment in this volume (the Czech Republic, Hungary, Slovakia and Poland) present an intriguing case. The scale of media systems re-invention after 1989 in conditions of compressed time stands as relatively unique in comparison with more evolutionary developments in other European countries. Yet the impetus for the fundamental revamping of media environments in CEE was largely exogenous, leaning towards the adoption of foreign institutional and policy designs. Although membership in the European Union and Council of Europe, and gradual transposition of accession standards, played a quite important although not ultimate role in democratic transitions and media change, an assessment of the pre-accession EU policy on media-related issues showed that the CEE countries accomplished a superficial harmonisation. This resulted not only from inhibiting internal forces inside the consolidating democracies of the young CEE member states but more importantly, from an absence of clear formulation of core values in media policy and benchmarks on the side of the EU. The transformation of media structures in the CEE did not follow a linear route where subsequent steps logically build on each other. A number of relatively recent cases in CEE (the controversial use of a libel law by judges in Slovakia, the Hungarian media law, lack of independent media regulatory authorities) demonstrate that national responses may corrode transnational attempts when the collective purpose becomes weak. This has been reflected in media freedom indexes demonstrating that the situation of media freedom and pluralism has not fundamentally improved in the CEE countries after the EU accession. Moreover, problematic developments occurred in all CEE countries after the EU accession, though they have not been bound by much similarity.

These lessons exposed the scrappy and underdeveloped nature of benchmarks in the area of freedom of expression and the media in the EU enlargement policy. The EU institutions, and the EP in particular, realised that a quite passive stance in the pre-accession period may later lead to more turbulent developments showing signs of regress in the field of media freedom and pluralism. The experience from the 5th enlargement also made it clear that essentials – such as media freedom and pluralism – should be anchored at the core of the EU polyvalent media policy and not merely substituted by a focus on economic criteria. Hence it became quite clear that the ongoing policy of conditionality will need to lay on more solid building blocks, in particular a common institutional blueprint (once missing) and common patterns of practices.

The EU audiovisual policy continues to form a core media policy strand singled out from a broader media field by the fact of implementing hard policy instruments – the TWF and AVMS Directives. It also stands for the longest history in comparison with other thematic fields. Guided by various rationales including economic, cultural, political and technological (although with different proportions), the audiovisual policy integrates, in addition, an internal and external EU policy dimension leaving room for maneuver by member states. Though embracing constantly a larger territory of overlapping issues, the EU audiovisual policy – for the most part of its history – concentrated on two axes: on the one hand – free circulation of audiovisual media services within the EU internal market; on the other hand – cultural protection of the EU audiovisual media services. These two dimensions were assessed with respect to policy harmonisation in the CEE countries. It should be emphasised in this context that the process of implementation of the AVMSD found its locus in the heart of the audiovisual policy, becoming at the same time more systematically driven.

Whereas the CEE countries shared obvious and long standing connections based on common historical experience, path dependency and in some cases, cultural affinities, the current policy landscapes, including audiovisual policy and implementation of AVMS rules, bring to light significant differences. In general, all of the CEE countries complied with the content obligations promoting European works in 2005–2010, albeit there has been a large variety among the countries. Hungary reached the highest level of compliance above the EU average, while the Czech Republic demonstrated the lowest level of compliance below the EU average. Concurrently, the Czech Republic appeared to be the only country in the group with visible structures supporting the transnational circulation of audiovisual media services due to a significant share of channels targeting non-domestic markets. These differences seem to be dictated not only by market size and a history of common geopolitical and cultural relations, but also by consequences of political choices made during the first period of media system transformation.

The area of media pluralism, unlike audiovisual policy and the implementation of the AVMSD, has constituted a complex and elusive territory for EU media policy mainly due to the difficulty in reconciling and balancing various rationales under one commanding and coherent premise. The issue of media pluralism demonstrated that the visions and directions in policies very much depend on how complex media environments are perceived, conceptualised, and what values and functions are prioritised. New configurations of media power have not fundamentally challenged the structural dependencies between the media and political and economic system described by Sandra Ball-Rokeach. These relations are relatively symmetrical in the sense that the survival and welfare of the media system is as contingent upon the resources of the political and economic systems as the survival and welfare of the economic and political systems are contingent upon the resources of the media (Ball-Rokeach, 2006: 4). The interdependencies that give rise to the necessity of co-operation between the media, political and economic system also give rise to conflicts as each party in these relations tries to maximise its power position vis-à-vis the other by increasing exercise of its control in areas that make the other parties more dependent (Ball-Rokeach, 2006: 5). This has been apparent in many problematic cases that developed in Europe in recent years including the case of Silvio Berlusconi and the concentration of political and media power in Italy, the UK's hacking phone scandal revealing the enormous influence of Murdoch's New International on the UK's political system and also the implementation of new media law in Hungary in 2010, in which the media regulatory authority became subordinated to the Prime Minister and governing political party. In all these cases, symmetrical relations between the political, and economic systems and the media have been infringed as one of these domains (in the case of UK the media, in Hungary the government) pursued to increase its control over the others.

It is important to add that the media users' domain has not developed the same symmetrical relations with the media as the users participated in communication structures mainly *through* the political or economic system. A new media architecture brings the potential of change in these structural patterns although it should be recognised that increased media choice, possibilities of filtering, navigation, participation and networking, as well as an excessive diversity and content abundance bear serious limits, These revolve around the contractual conditions of operators offering various media services, lack of comprehensive information about the choice the users can enjoy, technical incompabilities, the commercial use of personal data etc. Thus, the normative view of pluralism should not encompass 'everything' or 'any kind of diversity' but such an arrangement of diversity in a media system that generates symmetrical relations not only between the media, political and economic system but also media users and facilitates performing the key functions the media play in societies in a sustainable way.

In media policy this certainly implies incorporation of such policy strands that contribute to a sustainable diversity of the media systems such as the independence of media regulatory authorities, media transparency, protection of journalists from various kinds of pressures as well as prevention against excessive economic control over the media. Chapter five demonstrated that the EU policy in these regards has been limited to monitoring and soft measures as well as promotion of standards. To understand how the CEE countries resonate with these policy standards and how media structures changed over time, the empirical assessment involved studying the three dimensions with a crucial role for the differentiation of media structures: the diversity of media control, diversity of media functions and geographical/cultural diversity. A comparative analysis showed that outcomes both in terms of policies, as well as media structures, are different in the studied countries.

In the field of policies, this variety manifests itself in diverging approaches to media ownership concentration (e.g. the use of cross-media ownership limits in the Czech Republic and Slovakia, while in Poland monomedia concentration limits apply), recognition and support for the community media or social broadcasters, and rules on internal pluralism. At the same time, it is worth mentioning that the broadcasting and media laws in CEE seem to be relatively permissive in ownership policies and consolidation. They also allow for too much discretion on the side of regulatory authorities to limit eventually the size of media companies, mergers, or decide about revoking licences. Media ownership details are often opaque for media users and do not allow an automatic disclosure of the ultimate owner of particular media outlets. Besides, the changes in ownership are constant and complex. The transparency rules largely function within the media regulatory authorities, but do not automatically ensure the access of the public to full datasets free of charge.

In the field of media structures, the CEE countries employed varied approaches to foreign media ownership and transnational investment that presents one of the most distinguishing features of CEE media landscapes. Although the foreign ownership prevails in various CEE media sectors, in some countries domestic owners dominate particular media segments (e.g. the segment of quality daily press or TV broadcasting market in Poland, digital delivery systems in Slovakia). The patterns of media ownership in the CEE countries – with few exceptions – demonstrate high or moderate concentration in various segments of media markets that has been a product of more profound concentration waves and takeovers, as well as the clustering of business activities in the pre-EU-accession period. In recent years, the dynamics of consolidation seems to be quite stable (the measurement did not display a significant increase or decrease of concentration), at the same time, changes of ownership are fast, brisk and often not fully transparent. Various vectors of these changes may be detected – such as the increasing takeover of media activities in various sectors by domestic business elites or entry into cross ownership involving online media or digital platforms by large transnational owners.

In terms of functional diversity, the media which is focusing on entertainment financed from commercial sources, seem to perform better and be less vulnerable to current economic challenges than is the case of the quality daily press or public service media. This double decrease – in sales and advertising – has made quality newspapers more fragile vis-à-vis advertising from the state, state companies or political parties. Finally, an assessment of geographical diversity showed that there are significant differences among the countries regardless of market size. For instance, the highest level of decentralisation in the market of daily newspapers characterises Hungary, not Poland as could be expected from the difference in market size. The regional press markets proved to be fluctuant in the region, while centripetal drives prevail over centrifugal, with the exception of Hungary. The centripetal tendencies include a decreasing number of regional daily newspapers, decreasing circulation of regional dailies, and most importantly, an increasing level of centralisation, concentration of media ownership and chaining.

The media policy strands integrated in the chapter six seem to be one of the most challenging in terms of harmonising EU and national approaches. The legal recognition of MRA independence that could contribute more formally to a structural rebalancing of political and economic influences on media structures proved to be too contentious. A strong willingness of the national states to control this institutional setting for media regulation hampered the Commission's efforts. An empirical assessment at the level of the CEE countries showed a range of arrangements concerning the legal recognition of MRA independence, although in terms of the appointment procedures and accountability, a strong dependency on the political system was identified in all countries. The EU approach to the PSM has been dominated by the economic and competition perspective, setting the frames of action and debate in weighing PSM output by palpable social and public values against 'market impact'. A more strict application of financing in relation to the public service remit has increasingly been demanded from private commercial broadcasters trying to secure their positions against a fragmented advertising market. An empirical assessment of changing conditions of the PSM in the CEE has demonstrated an overall trend of weakening the PSM both in terms of audience share and financing mechanisms. This trend, stimulated very much by political choices, can only be balanced by empowering PSM users. Only with a greater inclusion and participation of audiences and media users in various aspects of PSM performance and policy, can the PSM equip themselves with a stronger functional legacy, more balanced accountability and autonomy against political and economic influences. Moreover, this can also empower the PSM at the EU level where increased tensions between the PSM and commercial media, are moving to from the national levels.

New forms of communication and new media architecture not only fundamentally transform the functions media play in various fields of social life, they also rearrange dependencies and interrelations within these fields. In addressing the new conditions in making the polyvalent media policy faces a challenge of putting the ends and means at the right place. This will require redirecting and rebalancing the current strands of policy-making and rationales towards a more prominent recognition of communication needs in perspective of media users as opposed to the interests of actors representing the economic and political domains. In such a process an organic growth of the media should be carefully combined with non-intrusive gardening – so that the diversity and survival of the most valuable media 'species' is protected. Normative concerns continue to be valid in this respect. The imposing of 'one media policy size' to highly varied national media landscapes would be misplaced. Yet in terms of standards and meaningful guidelines it is worth acknowledging that we are certainly able to distinguish between better and worse quality, between media systems that better respond to the communication needs of a country's citizens and those that do not allow users' demands and needs to be met or limit them for various economic and political reasons. Thus, the art of policy harmonisation is to follow the route from one of exercising control, to building social trust.

GLOSSARY

Accountability of MRA – See p. 268, 272

ACTA International Agreement – See p. 123

Appointment of MRA – See p. 261, 266, 267

Audiovisual media services – See p. 147, 148

AVMSD – Audiovisual Media Services Directive, adopted in 2007 – See p. 65, 66, 67, 146

BEREC – Body of European Regulators for Electronic Communications – See p. 87

CCD – Convention on the Protection and Promotion of the Diversity of Cultural Expressions, adopted by UNESCO in 2005 – See p. 98

CEE – Central and Eastern Europe

CoE – Council of Europe – See p. 108

Communication media – integrated networks of structures, technologies, institutions, forms of performance and contents that enable a mediation of multilateral communication as well as dissemination and exchange of information

Communication needs – See p. 41

Communication policy – See p. 38, 39

Communication rights – See p. 41

Communicative abundance – See p. 10, 24

Community media – See p. 93, 94, 95, 208

Convergence – See p. 85, 86

Cultural diversity – See p. 97, 98

DAE – Digital Agenda for Europe – See p. 87, 88

DG COMP – Directorate General for Competition – See p. 54, 60, 61, 62

DG CONNECT – Directorate General for the Communications Networks, Content and Technology – See p. 53, 60, 61, 62

DG EAC – Directorate General for Education and Culture – See p. 54, 60, 61, 62

DG INFSO – Directorate General for Information Society and the Media (2005–2012) – See p. 53

DG MARKT – Directorate General for Internal Market and Services – See p. 60, 61, 62

DG JUST – Directorate General for Justice – See p. 60, 61, 62

Digital switchover – a gradual process by which analogue TV broadcasting is being replaced by digital TV broadcasting – See p. 88

EBU – European Broadcasting Union – established in 1950 in order to facilitate co-operation between member organisations – public service broadcasters – See p. 69

EC – European Commission

ECHR – European Convention on Human Rights (the Convention on Human Rights and Fundamental Freedoms), adopted by the Council of Europe in 1950 – See p. 63, 186

ECTT – European Convention on Transfrontier Television adopted by the Council of Europe in 1989 – See p. 109

EP – European Parliament

European works – See p. 149, 150, 151

EU communication deficit – See p. 52

EU democratic deficit – See p. 51

EU enlargement – See p. 103, 107

EU identity deficit – See p. 51, 52

EU legitimation deficit – See p. 51, 52

EU media deficit – See p. 52

EU media policy deficit – See p. 52

External media pluralism – See p. 206, 207

Findability – See p. 147

Foreign media ownership – See p. 212, 213

FRA – the European Agency for Fundamental Rights, established in 2007, p. 122

Freedom of expression and the media – See p. 108

GATS – General Agreement on Trade in Services – See p. 97, 98

GATT – General Agreement on Tariffs and Trade – See p. 97, 98

Geographical media diversity – See p. 243

Information society – See p. 85

Internal market – an area that enables and facilitates the free movement of capital, goods, services labour and people, with some common policies and product regulation. In the EU, it is intended to generate economic integration

Internal media pluralism – See p. 200

Internet universality – See p. 13

Legacy media – traditional or 'old' media (such as newspapers, TV, radio) that have functioned before the advent of the Internet and digital technologies

Mass media – Technologies, institutions, contents and services as well as forms of performance with a primary aim to disseminate and mediate communication to/between large scale audiences – See p. 26

Media and communication policy – See p. 38

Media environment – the surroundings, configurations, settings and conditions, in which media use and mediated communication is taking place

Media governance – See p. 37, 38

Media literacy – See p. 17, 91, 92

Media ownership – See p. 211

Media pluralism – See p. 185, 186, 187

Media policy – See p. 36, 37

Media regulation – See p. 36, 37

Media systems – macrostructures in which media entities, functions and performances are arranged together in a particular way due to various sets of conditions: endogenous (e.g. historical, cultural), exogenous (e.g. globalising forces), empirical (e.g. population size) and normative (e.g, cultural values, social imaginaries, legal principles) – See p. 27, 28, 29

Media transparency – See p. 209, 210

Minority media – See p. 94, 95, 96

MRA – Media Regulatory Authorities – See p. 251, 252

MRA autonomy – See p. 252

MRA independence – See p. 252, 253

Must carry – regulations that oblige operators of a cable, satellite or digital platform to carry selected channels in order to protect specific kinds of contents and services (e.g. local, public service) – See p. 209

OECD – Organisation for Economic Co-operation and Development

OSCE – Organisation for Security and Co-operation in Europe

Policy actors – See p. 41, 42

Polyvalent media policy – See p. 41, 42, 43

Polyvalent rationality – See p. 56, 57

PSB – Public Service Broadcasting – See p. 74, 75

PSM – Public Service Media – See p. 16, 73, 74, 75, 273, 274

PSM autonomy – See p. 252

PSM competitive function – See p. 253, 254

PSM complementary function – See p. 253, 254

PSM independence – See p. 251, 252

Structural media pluralism – See p. 191, 192

Technological neutrality – the principle under which a regulation should not favour one technology over an other and be attentive to ongoing technological changes – See p. 86

TWF – Television Without Frontiers Directive, adopted in 1989 – See p. 65, 66

Veto players – See p. 42

WTO – World Trade Organisation

BIBLIOGRAPHY

Ackerman, John M. (2005) „Social Accountability in the Public Sector: A Conceptual Discussion" [in] *Social Development Papers, Participation and Civic Engagement*. March 2005/No. 82. The World Bank. (available at: http://siteresources.worldbank.org/INTPCENG/214574-1116506074750/20542263/FINALAckerman.pdf; retrieved 6.01.2014).

ACT, AER, EPC (2004) *Safeguarding the Future of the European Audiovisual Market: A White Paper on the Financing and Regulation of Publicly Funded Broadcasters* (available at: http://www.aereurope.org/images/PolicyPDFs/public%20sector%202004.pdf ; retrieved 1.06.2013).

Alger, Dean (1999) *Megamedia: How Giant Corporations Dominate Mass Media, Distort Competition, and Endanger Democracy*. Lanham: Rowman and Littlefield Publishers.

Ansell, Chris (2000) „The Networked Polity: Regional Development in Western Europe" [in] *Governance* 13 (3): 303–333.

Arendt, Hannah (1958) *The Human Condition*. Chicago and London: The University of Chicago Press.

Arendt, Hannah (1969) "Truth and Politics" pp. 104–133 [in] Laslett, P. and Runciman, W.G. (eds.) *Philosophy, Politics and Society: Third Series*. Oxford: Basil Blackwell.

Ariño, Monica (2011) "Which Frontiers for EU Media Policy? An Assessment in the Context of the European Project" pp. 321–344 [in] Sükösd, M. and Jakubowicz, K. (eds.) *Media, Nationalism and European Identities*. Budapest-New York: CEU Press.

Ariño Monica and Llorens, Carles (2008) "Back to the Future: New Media, Same principles? Convergence Regulation Re-visited" pp. 125–144 [in] Ward, D. (ed.) *The European Union and the Culture Industries: Regulation and the Public Interest*. Aldershot: Ashgate.

Attentional et al. (2011a) *Study on the implementation of the provisions of the Audiovisual Media Services Directive concerning the promotion of European works in audiovisual media services: Final Study Report*. Smart No. 2010/0002. (available at: http://ec.europa.eu/avpolicy/docs/library/studies/art_13/final_report_20111214.pdf; retrieved 28.10.2013).

Attentional et al. (2011b) *Study on the implementation of the provisions of the Audiovisual Media Services Directive concerning the promotion of European works in audiovisual media services: Final Study Appendix*. Smart No. 2010/0002. (available at: http://ec.europa.eu/avpolicy/docs/library/studies/art_13/final_report_app_20111214.pdf; retrieved 28.10.2013).

Bagdikian, Ben H. (1997) *The Media Monopoly*. Fifth Edition. Boston: Beacon Press.

Baisnée, Oliver (2007) „The European Public Sphere Does Not Exist (At Least It's Worth Wondering...") [in] *European Journal of Communication* 22 (4): 493–503.

Baker, Edwin (2002) *Media, Markets and Democracy*. Cambridge: Cambridge University Press.

Baker, Edwin (2006) *Media Concentration and Democracy: Why Ownership Matters*. New York and Cambridge: Cambridge University Press.

Baldi Paolo and Hassebrink, Uwe (2007) *Broadcasters and Citizens for Europe. Trends in Media Accountability and Viewer Participation*. Intellect Books: Bristol and Chicago.

Ball-Rokeach, Sandra J. (2006) "The Origins of Individual Media-System Dependency: A Sociological Framework" pp. 1–18 [in] McQuail, D. (ed.) *Mass Communication. Volume I: Theories, Basic Concepts and Varieties of Approach*. London: Sage Publications.

Bardoel, Jo and d'Haenens, Leen (2008) "Reinventing public service broadcasting in Europe: prospects, promises and problems" [in] *Media, Culture and Society*. 30 (3): 337–355.

Bardoel, Jo and Vochteloo, Marit (2012) "Conditional Access for Public Service Broadcasting to New Media Platforms: EU State-aid Policy vis-à-vis Public Service Broadcasting – the Dutch Case" pp. 301–315 [in] Puppis, M. and Just, N. (eds.) *Trends in Communication Policy Research: New Theories, Methods and Subjects*. Bristol: Intellect.

Barnett, Steven (2010) "What's wrong with media monopolies? A lesson from history and a new approach to media ownership policy". *MEDIA@LSE Electronic Working Papers*. (available at: http://www.lse.ac.uk/media@lse/research/mediaWorkingPapers/pdf/EWP18.pdf; retrieved 5.01.2014).

Barnhurst, Kevin G. and Nerone, John (2002) *The Form of News: A History*. New York: The Guilford Press.

Basić-Hrvatin, Sandra and Thompson, Mark (2008) "Public Service Broadcasting in Plural and Divided Societies" pp. 8–40 [in] Basić-Hrvatin, S. et al. (eds.) *Divided They Fall: Public Service Broadcasting in Multiethnic States*. Sarajevo: Mediacentar.

Baumgartner, Frank R. and Jones, Bryan D. (1993) *Agenda and Instability in American Politics*. Chicago and London; University of Chicago Press.

BBC Trust (2007) *Public Value Test (PVT) Guidance on the Conduct of the PVT*. (available at: http://www.bbc.co.uk/bbctrust/assets/files/pdf/regulatory_framework/pvt/pvt_guidance.pdf; retrieved 23.03.2013).

Benson, Rodney et al. (2012) "Media Systems Online and Off: Comparing the Form of News in the United States, Denmark, and France" [in] *Journal of Communication*. 62 (1): 21–38.

Blind, Peril K. (2011) "Accountability in Public Service Delivery: A Multidisciplinary Review of the Concept" prepared for the *Expert Group Meeting Engaging Citizens to Enhance Public Service Accountability and Prevent Cor-*

ruption in the Delivery of Public Services, 7–8 and 11–13 July 2011, DMB/DPADM/UNDESA, Vienna, Austria.

Blumler, Jay and Hoffmann-Reim, Wolfgang (2002) "New Roles for Public Service Television" pp. 201–210 [in] McQuail, D. (ed.) *McQuail's Reader in Mass Communication Theory*. London: Sage Publications.

Bourdieu, Pierre (1998) *On Television*. New York: The New Press.

Bourdon, Jérôme (2007) "Unhappy Engineers of the European Soul: The EBU and the Woes of Pan-European Television" [in] *International Communication Gazette* 69 (3): 263–280.

Boyer, Dominic and Sükösd, Miklós (2011) "European Media and Culture of Europeaness' pp. 223–246 [in] Sükösd, M. and Jakubowicz, K. (eds.) *Media, Nationalism and European Identities*. Budapest-New York: CEU Press.

Castells, Manuel (2009) *Communication Power*. Oxford: Oxford University Press.

Čelovský, Bořivoj (2001) *Konec českého tisku?* Šenov u Ostravy: Tilia.

Centre for Media Pluralism and Media Freedom (CMP) (2013) *European Union competencies in respect of media pluralism and media freedom: Policy Report*. European University Institute: Florence (available at: http://ec.europa.eu/digital-agenda/sites/digital-agenda/files/CMPFPolicyReport2013.pdf; retrieved 1.01.2014).

Chalaby, Jean K. (2002) "Transnational Television in Europe: The Role of Pan-European Channels" [in] *European Journal of Communication* 17 (2): 183–203.

CIMA (Center for International Media Assistance) (2010) *Evaluating the Evaluators: Media Freedom Indexes and What They Measure*. (available at: http://cima.ned.org/publications/research-reports/evaluating-evaluators-media-freedom-indexes-and-what-they-measure; retrieved 20.09.2013).

CMCS (Center for Media and Communication Studies) (2012) *Hungarian Media Laws in Europe: An Assessment of Consistency of Hungary's Media Laws with European Practices and Norms*. Budapest: CMCS (available at: http://www.eui.eu/Documents/General/DebatingtheHungarianConstitution/HungarianMediaLawsinEurope.pdf; retrieved 5.10.2013).

CMPF (The Centre for Media Pluralism and Media Freedom) (2013) *European Union Competencies in Respect of Media Pluralism*. Florence: European University Institute/Robert Schuman Centre (available at: http://cmpf.eui.eu/Documents/CMPFPolicyReport2013.pdf; retrieved 2.01.2014).

Collins, Richard (1990) *Culture, Communication and National Identity*. Toronto: University of Toronto Press.

Collins, Richard (2007) *Media and Identity in Contemporary Europe: Consequences of Global Convergence*. Bristol: Intellect.

Commission of the European Communities (1992), *Pluralism and Media Concentration in the Internal Market: An Assessment of the Need for Community Action*, Commission Green Paper, COM (92) 480 final, Brussels, 23.12.1992.

Commission of the European Communities (1994), *Follow-up to the Consultation Process relating to the Green Paper on "Pluralism and Media Concen-*

tration in the Internal Market – an Assessment of the Need for Community Action", COM (94) 353 final, Brussels, 5.10.1994.

Cooper, Mark (2007) "When Law and Social Science Go Hand in Glove: Usage and Importance of Local and National News Sources – Critical Questions and Answers for Media Market Analysis" pp. 193–224 [in] Napoli, P.M. (ed.) *Media Diversity and Localism: Meaning and Metrics*. Mahwah, New Jersey and London: LEA Publishers.

Cormack, Mike and Hourigan, Niamh (eds.) (2007) *Minority Language Media: Concepts, Critiques and Case Studies*, Multilingual Matters: Clevendon.

Cottle, Simon (ed.) (2000) *Ethnic Minorities and the Media: Changing Cultural Boundaries*. Buckingham and Philadelphia: Open University Press.

Council of Europe (1989) *European Convention on Transfrontier Television* (ECTT) ETS No. 171.

Council of Europe (1994) *Recommendation of the Committee of Ministers No. R (94) 13 on Measures to Promote Media Transparency*.

Council of Europe (1996) *Recommendation No. R (96) 10 of the Committee of Ministers to Member States on the Guarantee of the Independence of Public Service Broadcasting*.

Council of Europe (1999) *Recommendation No. R (99) 1 of the Committee of Ministers to Member States on Measures to promote Media Pluralism.*

Council of Europe (2000) *Report on Media Pluralism in the Digital Environment* adopted by the Steering Committee on the Mass Media in October 2000, Strasbourg, CDMM (2000) pde.

Council of Europe (2002) *Media Diversity in Europe*. Report prepared by the AP-MD, H/APMD (2003)001.

Council of Europe (2004) *Transnational Media Concentrations in Europe*. Report prepared by the AP-MD, AP-MD (2004)7.

Council of Europe (2007) *Recommendation Rec (2007)2 of the Committee of Ministers to Member States on media pluralism and diversity of media content.*

Council of Europe (2009a) *Recommendation of the Parliamentary Assembly 1855 (2009) on the Regulation of Audiovisual Media Services*.

Council of Europe (2009b) *Recommendation of the Parliamentary Assembly 1878 (2009) on Funding of Public Service Broadcasting*.

Council of Europe (2013) *Opinion on the Fourth Amendment to the Fundamental Law of Hungary Adopted by the Venice Commission at its 95th Plenary Session, Venice, 14–15 June* 2013 CDL-AD(2013)012-e (available at: http://www.venice.coe.int/webforms/documents/?pdf=CDL-AD%282013%29012-e; retrieved 31.12.2013).

Council of the European Union (1999) *The resolution of the Council and of the Representatives of the Governments of the Member States meeting within the Council of 25 January 1999 concerning public service broadcasting*. O.J. 5.02.1999 C 30/ 1–77 (available at: http://eur-lex.europa.eu/LexUriServ/LexUriServ.do?uri=OJ:C:1999:030:0001:0001:En:PDF; retrieved 5.01.2014).

Council of the European Union (2009) *Council conclusions on media literacy in the digital environment*. 2978th Education, Youth and Culture Council meeting 27.11.2009, Brussels (available at: http://ec.europa.eu/culture/media/media-content/media-literacy/council_adoption_ml_27112009.pdf; retrieved 17.07.2013).

Council of the European Union (2013) *Council conclusions and of the representatives of the Governments and Member States, meeting with the Council, on media freedom and pluralism in the digital environment,* Education, Youth, Culture and Sport Council meeting 25–27.11.2013, Brussels (available at: http://www.consilium.europa.eu/uedocs/cms_data/docs/pressdata/en/educ/139725.pdf; retrieved 1.12.2013).

Coyer, Kate and Hintz, Arne (2010) "Developing 'The Third Sector': Community Media" pp. 275–298 [in] Klimkiewicz, B. (ed.) *Media Freedom and Pluralism: Media Policy Challenges in the Enlarged Europe*. Budapest: CEU Press.

Craig, Geoffrey (2004) *The Media, Politics and Public Life*. Crows Nest: Allen & Unwin.

Craufurd Smith, Rachel (ed.) (2004) *Culture and European Union Law*. Oxford: Oxford University Press.

Craufurd Smith, Rachel et al. (2012) "Regulating Media Plurality and Media Power in the 21st Century" [in] *Media Policy Brief* No. 7 (available at: http://www.lse.ac.uk/media@lse/documents/MPP/Policy-Brief-7-Media-Pluralism.pdf; retrieved 7.12.2013).

Croteau, David and Hoynes, William (2006) *The Business of Media: Corporate Media and Public Interest*. Thousand Oaks: Pine Forge Press.

Curran, James (2002) *Media and Power*. London and New York: Routledge.

Czepek, Andrea et al. (eds.) (2009) *Press Freedom and Pluralism in Europe: Concepts and Conditions*. Bristol: Intellect.

Dahl, Robert (1979) "Procedural Democracy" pp. 97–133 [in] Laslett, P. and Fishkin, J. (eds.) *Philosophy, Politics and Society: Fifth Series*. Oxford: Basil Blackwell.

Deuze, Mark (2003) "The web and its journalism" [in] *New Media & Society*. 5 (2): 203–230.

Deuze, Mark (2011) „Media Life" [in] *Media, Culture & Society*. 33 (1): 137–148.

Deuze, Mark (2012) *Media Life*. Cambridge and Malden: Polity Press.

De Wilde, Jaap (2011) "The Mirage of Global Democracy" [in] *Academia Europea*. 19 (1): 5–18.

De Witte, Bruno (1995) "The European Content Requirement in the EC Television Directive – Five Years After" pp. 102–127 [in] Barendt, E. et al. (eds.) *Yearbook of Media and Entertainment Law*, Vol I. Oxford: Oxford University Press.

DG Enlargement (2013a) *EU Enlargement: Speaking out: the EU supports freedom of expression in enlargement countries* (available at: http://ec.europa.eu/enlargement/pdf/publication/20130617_speaking_out_the_eu_supports_freedom_of_expresion.pdf; retrieved 22.10.2013).

DG Enlargement (2013b) *EU Enlargement Fact Sheet: Safeguarding freedom of expression and the media* (available at: http://ec.europa.eu/enlargement/

pdf/publication/20130617_safeguarding_freedom_of_expresion_and_the_media.pdf; retrieved 22.10.2013).

DG Enlargement (2013c) *Speak-up!2. Conclusions*. (available at: http://ec.europa.eu/enlargement/pdf/speak_up_2/20130801_speakup-conclusions.pdf; retrieved 22.10.2013).

Digital Europe (2013) *Digital Europe response to Green Paper: Preparing for a Fully Converged Audiovisual World: Growth, Creation and Values*. 11 September 2013. (available at: http://www.digitaleurope.org/Pressroom/Policyinformation.aspx; retrieved 30.10.2013).

Digital TV Europe (2013) *Europe moves closer to digital switchover*. (available at: http://www.digitaltveurope.net/37402/europe-moves-closer-to-digital-switchover/; retrieved 15.07.2013)

Dobek-Ostrowska, Bogusława and Głowacki, Michał (eds.) (2008) *Comparing Media Systems in Central Europe: Between Commercialization and Politicization*. Wrocław: Wydawnictwo Uniwersytetu Wrocławskiego.

Downey, John and Mihelj, Sabina (2012) *Central and Eastern European Media in Comparative Perspective: Politics, Economy and Culture*. London: Ashgate.

Downey, John (2012) "Transnational Capital, Media Differentiation, and Institutional Isomorphism in Central and Eastern European Media Systems" pp. 113–135 [in] Downey, J. and Mihelj, S. (eds.) *Central and Eastern European Media in Comparative Perspective: Politics, Economy and Culture*. London: Ashgate.

Doyle, Gillian (2002), *Media Ownership. The Economics and Politics of Convergence and Concentration in the UK and European Media*. London: Sage Publications.

Drok, Nico (1998) *Local and Regional Journalism in Europe*. EJTA: European Journalism Training Association.

EBU (2013) *EBU reply to the European Commission Green Paper – Preparing for a Fully Converged Audiovisual World: Growth, Creation and Values*. 10.10.2013 (available at: http://www3.ebu.ch/files/live/sites/ebu/files/Knowledge/Initiatives%20-%20Policy/Topical%20Issues/Hybrid/EBU_reply_to_Green_Paper_convergence_final.pdf; retrieved 30.10.2013).

Economisti Associati et al. (2011) *Feasibility Study for the Preparatory Action "Erasmus for journalists". Final Report*. (available at: http://ec.europa.eu/information_society/media_taskforce/doc/mobility/erjo_part1_report.pdf; retrieved 24.11.2013).

Einstein, Mara (2004) *Media Diversity: Economics, Ownership and the FCC*. LEA Publishers.

ENPA (2011) *Preserving Pluralism in a Rapidly Changing Media Environment*, October (available at: http://stakeholders.ofcom.org.uk/binaries/consultations/measuring-plurality/responses/ns-annex-enpa.pdf; retrieved 11.02.2013).

Erstad, Ola et al. (2012) *Meta-analysis of reviews on media literacy and media studies*. A working Paper delivered at the European Science Foundation seminar *Forward Looks* held at the University of Helsinki in June 2012.

European Audiovisual Observatory (EAO) (2006) *Television in 36 European States: The Yearbook*. Strasbourg.
European Audiovisual Observatory (EAO) (2009) *Television in 36 European States: The Yearbook*. Strasbourg.
European Audiovisual Observatory (EAO) (2011) *Television in 37 European States: The Yearbook*. Strasbourg.
EU Media Futures Forum (2012) *Fast-forward Europe: 8 solutions to thrive in the digital world*. A report for European Commission Vice-President Neelie Kroes to reflect on the future of the media industries from a global perspective (available at: http://ec.europa.eu/information_society/media_task-force/doc/pluralism/forum/report.pdf; retrieved 26.12.2013).
European Commission (1993) *Growth, Competitiveness, Employment. The Challenges and Ways forward into the 21 Century*. White Paper. COM (93) 700. 3.12.1993, Brussels.
European Commission (1994) *Europe and the Global Information Society*. Recommendations to the European Council. Bangemann Report. Brussels.
European Commission (1997) *Green Paper on the Convergence of the Telecommunications, Media and Information Technology Sectors, and the Implications for Regulation*. Towards an Information Society Approach. COM (97) 623. 3.12.1997, Brussels.
European Commission (1999) *Principles and Guidelines for the Community's Audiovisual Policy in the Digital Age*. Communication from the Commission to the Council, the European Parliament, the European Economic and Social Committee and the Committee of the Regions. 14.12.1999. COM (1999) 657 final, Brussels.
European Commission (2000) *Enlargement Strategy Paper: Report on Progress Towards Accession by Each of the Candidate Countries* (available at: http://ec.europa.eu/enlargement/archives/pdf/key_documents/2000/strat_en.pdf; retrieved 5.01.2014).
European Commission (2001) *Communication from the Commission on the application of State aid rules to public service broadcasting*. O.J. 15.11.2001 C 320/5–11 (available at: http://eur-lex.europa.eu/LexUriServ/LexUriServ.do?uri=OJ:C:2001:320:0005:0011:en:pdf; retrieved 5.01.2014).
European Commission (2003) *Towards an International Instrument on Cultural Diversity*. Communication from the Commission to the Council, the European Parliament, the European Economic and Social Committee and the Committee of the Regions. COM (2003) 520 final, Brussels.
European Commission (2005a) *On Accelerating the Transition from Analogue to Digital Broadcasting*. The Communication from the Commission to the European Parliament, the European Economic and Social Committee and the Committee of the Regions. 24.05.2005. COM (2005) 204 final, Brussels.
European Commission (2005b) *Proposal for a Directive of the European Parliament and of the Council amending Council Directive 89/552/EEC on the coordination of certain provisions laid down by law, regulation or administra-*

tive action in Member States concerning the pursuit of television broadcasting activities. 13.12.2005. COM(2005) 646 final. Brussels.

European Commission (2005c) *Issues Paper for the Liverpool Audiovisual Conference: Media Pluralism – What should be the European Union's role?* Brussels: DG Information Society and Media.

European Commission (2006) *White Paper on a European Communication Policy*. Brussels, 1.02.2006. COM (2006) 35 final. (available at: http://europa.eu/documents/comm/white_papers/pdf/com2006_35_en.pdf; retrieved 17.07.2013).

European Commission (2007a) Commission Staff Working Document: *Media Pluralism in the Member States of the European Union*. 16.01.2007. SEC (2007) 32, Brussels.

European Commission (2007b) *A European Approach to Media Literacy in the Digital Environment*. Communication from the Commission to the European Parliament, the Council, the European Economic and Social Committee and the Committee of the Regions. 20.12.2007. COM (2007) 833 final, Brussels.

European Commission (2007c) *On a European agenda for culture in a globalizing world*. Communication from the Commission to the European Parliament, the Council, the European Economic and Social Committee and the Committee of the Regions. 10.05.2007. COM (2007) 242 final, Brussels.

European Commission (2008) Commission Staff Working Document – Accompanying document to the Communication from the Commission to the European Parliament, the Council, the European Economic and Social Committee and the Committee of the Regions: *Eight Communication on the application of Articles 4 and 5 of the Directive 89/552/EEC 'Television without Frontiers', as amended by Directive 97/36/EC, for the period 2005–2006*. 22.07.2008. SEC (2008) 2310.

European Commission (2009a) *Communication from the Commission on the application of State aid rules to public service broadcasting*. O.J. 27.10.2009 C 251/1–14 (available at: http://eur-lex.europa.eu/LexUriServ/LexUriServ.do?uri=OJ:C:2009:257:0001:0014:EN:PDF; retrieved 5.01.2014).

European Commission (2009b) Commission Recommendation *on media literacy in the digital environment for a more competitive audiovisual and content industry and an inclusive knowledge society*. 20.08.2009. C(2009) 6464 final, Brussels.

European Commission (2011) *Enlargement Strategy and Main Challenges 2011–2012*. The Communication from the Commission to the European Parliament and the Council. 12.10.2011. COM (2011) 666 final.

European Commission (2012a) *The Digital Agenda for Europe – Driving European Growth Digitally*. The Communication from the Commission to the European Parliament, the European Economic and Social Committee and the Committee of the Regions. 18.12.2012. COM (2012) 784 final, Brussels.

European Commission (2012b) *Promoting cultural and creative sectors for growth and jobs in the EU*. The Communication from the Commission to the European Parliament, the European Economic and Social Committee and the Committee of the Regions. 26.09.2012. COM (2012) 537 final, Brussels.

European Commission (2012c) *Enlargement Strategy and Main Challenges 2012–2013.* The Communication from the Commission to the European Parliament and the Council. 10.10.2012. COM (2012) 600 final.

European Commission (2012d) *Audiovisual Media Services and Connected Devices: Past and Future Perspectives.* First Report from the Commission to the European Parliament, the Council, the European Economic and Social Committee and the Committee of the Regions on the application of Directive 2010/13/EU "Audiovisual Media Service Directive". 4.05.2012. COM (2012) 203 final.

European Commission (2012e) *Promotion of European works in EU scheduled and on-demand audiovisual media services.* Report from the Commission to the European Parliament, the Council, the European Economic and Social Committee and the Committee of the Regions: First Report on the Application of Articles 13, 16 and 17 of Directive 2010/13/EU for the period 2009–2010. 24.09.2012. COM (2012) 522 final.

European Commission (2012f) Commission Staff Working Document: *Promotion of European works in EU scheduled and on-demand Audiovisual Media Services – PART I – on the Application of Article 13 of Directive 2010/13/EU for the period 2009–2010.* 24.09.2012. SWD (2012) 269 final.

European Commission (2012g) Commission Staff Working Document: *Promotion of European works in EU scheduled and on-demand Audiovisual Media Services – PART II – on the application of Articles 16 and 17 of Directive 2010/13/EU for the period 2009–2010.* 24.09.2012. SWD (2012) 269 final.

European Commission (2012h) Commission Staff Working Document: *Promotion of European works in EU scheduled and on-demand Audiovisual Media Services – PART III – Annex to PART II on the application of Articles 16 and 17 of Directive 2010/13/EU for the period 2009–2010.* 24.09.2012. SWD (2012) 269 final.

European Commission (2013a) Green Paper: *Preparing for a Fully Converged Audiovisual World: Growth, Creation and Values.* 24.04.2013. COM (2013) 231 final, Brussels.

European Commission (2013b) *Enlargement Strategy and Main Challenges 2013–2014.* The Communication from the Commission to the European Parliament and the Council. 16.10.2013. COM (2013) 700 final.

European Council (1989) *Directive 89/552/EEC of 3 October 1989 on the coordination of certain provisions laid down by Law, Regulation or Administrative Action in Member States concerning the pursuit of television broadcasting activities.* O.J. 17.10.1989 L 298/ 23–30.

European Initiative for Media Pluralism (2013) *European Citizens' Initiative proposed by the coalition European Initiative for Media Pluralism.* (available at: http://www.mediainitiative.eu/downloads/European_Initiative_for_Media_Pluralism-Annex_I-Background%20Info.pdf; retrieved 13.07.2013).

EU Media Futures Forum (2012) *Fast-forward Europe: 8 solutions to thrive in the digital world*. Final Report, Brussels.

European Parliament, Directorate General Internal Policies of the Union (2007) *The State of Community Media in the European Union*. Report by Kern European Affairs, IP/B/CULT/FWC/2006-169/Lot03/C01.

European Parliament (1992) *Media concentration and diversity of opinions*. Resolution of 16.09.1992. OJ 2.11.1992 C 284/44.

European Parliament (2004) *The risks of violation, in the EU and especially in Italy, of freedom of expression and information (Article 11(2) of the Charter of Fundamental Rights)*. Resolution of 22.04.2004 (2003/2237(INI)). P5_TA(2004) 0373.

European Parliament (EP) (2007) *The State of Community Media in the European Union*. IP/B/CULT/FWC/2006-169/Lot03/C01.

European Parliament (2008a) *Report on Community Media in Europe* (2008/2011(INI)). A6-0263/2008.

European Parliament (2008b) *Community Media in Europe*. Resolution of 25.09.2008. (2008/2011(INI)). P6_TA (2008) 0456.

European Parliament (2008c) *Media Literacy in a Digital World*. Resolution of 16.12.2008. 2008/2129 (INI). P6_TA (2008) 0598.

European Parliament (2011) *Media Law in Hungary*. Resolution of 10.03.2011. 2011/2510 (RSP). P7_TA (2011) 0094.

European Parliament (2013a) *Implementation of the Audiovisual Media Services Directive covering the period 2009–2010*. Resolution of 22.05.2013. 2012/2132 (INI). P7_TA-PROV(2013)0215.

European Parliament (2013b) *Freedom of Press and Media in the World*. Resolution of 13.06.2013. 2011/2081(INI). P7_TA-PROV(2013) 0274.

European Parliament (2013c) *The situation of fundamental rights: standards and practices in Hungary*. Resolution of 3.07.2013. 2012/2130 (INI). P7_TA-PROV(2013) 0315.

European Parliament (2013d) *The EU Charter: standard setting for media freedom across the EU*. Resolution of 21.05.2013. 2011/2246(INI) P7_TA(2013) 0203.

European Parliament and the Council (1997*) Directive of the European Parliament and the Council of 30 October 2007 amending Council Directive 89/552/EEC on the coordination of certain provisions laid down by law, regulation or administrative action in Member States concerning the pursuit of television broadcasting activities (Television Without Frontiers Directive)*, O.J. 30.07.1997 L 202/0060–0070.

European Parliament and the Council (2002a) *Directive 2002/21/EC of the European Parliament and the Council of 7 March 2002 on a common regulatory framework for electronic communications networks and services (Framework Directive)*, O.J. 24.04.2002 L 108/33–50.

European Parliament and the Council (2002b) *Directive 2002/19/EC of the European Parliament and the Council of 7 March 2002 on access to and inter-*

connection of electronic communications networks and associated facilities (Access Directive), O.J. 24.04.2002 L 108/7–20.

European Parliament and the Council (2002c) *Directive 2002/20/EC of the European Parliament and the Council of 7 March 2002 on the authorisation of electronic communication networks and services (Authorisation Directive)*, O.J. 24.04.2002 L 108/21–32.

European Parliament and the Council (2002d) *Directive 2002/22/EC of the European Parliament and the Council of 7 March 2002 on universal service and users' rights relating to electronic communications networks and services (Universal Service Directive)*, O.J. 24.04.2002 L 108/51–77.

European Parliament and the Council (2002e) *Directive 2002/58/EC of the European Parliament and the Council of 12 July 2002 concerning the processing of personal data and the protection of privacy in the electronic communications sector (Directive on Privacy and Electronic Communications)*, O.J. 31.07.2002 L 201/37–47.

European Parliament and the Council (2002f) Decision No. 676/2002/EC *of the European Parliament and the Council of 7 March 2002 on a regulatory framework for radio spectrum policy in the European Community (Radio Spectrum Decision)*, O.J. 24.04.2002 L 108/1–6.

European Parliament and the Council (2007) *Directive 2007/65/EC of the European Parliament and the Council of 11 December 2007 amending Council Directive 89/552/EEC on the coordination of certain provisions laid down by law, regulation or administrative action in Member States concerning the pursuit of television broadcasting activities (Audiovisual Media Services Without Frontiers Directive)*, O.J. 18.12.2007 L 332/27–45.

European Parliament and the Council (2009a) *Directive 2009/140/EC of the European Parliament and the Council of 25 November 2009 amending Directives 2002/21/EC on a common regulatory framework for electronic communications networks and services, 2002/19/EC on access to, and interconnection of, electronic communications networks and associated facilities, and 2002/20/EC on the authorisation of electronic communications networks and services*, O.J. 18.12.2009 L 337/37–69.

European Parliament and the Council (2009b) *Directive 2009/136/EC of the European Parliament and the Council of 25 November 2009 amending Directive 2002/22/EC on universal service and users' rights relating to electronic communications networks and services, Directive 2002/58/EC concerning the processing of personal data and the protection of privacy in the electronic communications sector and Regulation (EC) No. 2006/2004 on cooperation between national authorities responsible for the enforcement of consumer protection laws*, O.J. 18.12.2009 L 337/11–36.

European Parliament and the Council (2009c) *Regulation (EC) No. 1211/2009 of the European Parliament and of the Council of 25 November 2009 establishing the Body of European Regulators for Electronic Communications (BEREC) and the Office*. O.J. 18.12.2009 L 337/1–10.

European Parliament and the Council (2010a) *Directive 2010/13/EU of the European Parliament and the Council of 10 March 2010 on the coordination of certain provisions laid down by law, regulation or administrative action in Member States concerning the provision of audiovisual media services (Audiovisual Media Services Directive) (codified version).* O.J. 15.04.2010 L 95/1–24.

European Parliament and the Council (2010b) *Charter of Fundamental Rights of the European Union (2010/C 83/02).* O.J. 30.03. 2010 C 83/389–403.

European Publishers Council (2005) *Memorandum on Pluralism and Media Concentration addressed to the Members of the European Parliament's Intergroup on the Press, Communication and Freedom*, (available at: http://epceurope.eu/memorandum-on-pluralism-and-media-concentration-addressed-to-the-members-of-the-european-parliaments-intergroup-on-the-presscommunication-and-freedom/; retrieved 1.06.2013).

European Publisher's Forum (2005) *21st Century Publishing in Europe "Promoting Knowledge, Information and Diversity": Calls for Action*, Brussels December 6th, 2005, (available at: http://europa.eu.int/information_society/media_taskforce/doc/publishing/calls_for_action.pdf; retrieved 1.06.2013).

European Union (2010) *Consolidated Version of the Treaty on the Functioning of the European Union.* O.J. 30.03.2010. C 83/47–199.

European Union (2012) *Consolidated versions of the Treaty on European Union and the Treaty on the Functioning of the European Union.* O. J. 26.10.2012. C 326/01–407.

Fabris, Hans H. (1995)"Westification?" pp. 221–232 [in] Paletz, D. L. et al. (eds.) *Glasnost and After: Media and Change in Central and Eastern Europe.* Creskill, New Jersey: Hampton Press.

Fischer, Frank (1982) *Politics, Values, and Public Policy.* Boulder, Colorado: Westview Press.

Fischer, Frank (2003) *Reframing Policy Analysis: Discursive Politics and Deliberative Practices.* Oxford: Oxford University Press.

Fossum, John E. and Schlesinger, Philip (eds.) (2007) *The European Union and the Public Sphere. A Communicative Space in the Making?* London and New York: Routledge.

FRA (EU Agency for Fundamental Rights) (2010) *EU Agency for Fundamental Rights: Annual Report.*

FRA (EU Agency for Fundamental Rights) (2011) *Fundamental Rights: Challenges and Achievements in 2010.* Luxembourg: FRA.

FRA (EU Agency for Fundamental Rights) (2012) *Bringing Rights to Life: The Fundamental Rights Landscape of the European Union.* Luxembourg: FRA.

FRA (EU Agency for Fundamental Rights) (2013) *Fundamental Rights: Challenges and Achievements in 2012.* Luxembourg: FRA.

Freedman, Des (2008) *The Politics of Media Policy.* Cambridge: Polity Press.

Freedom House (2011) *Freedom of the Press 2011: Slovakia.* (available at: http://www.freedomhouse.org/report/freedom-press/2011/slovakia; retrieved 20.09.2013).

Freedom House (2013) Freedom of the Press (Reports on Czech Republic, Hungary, Poland and Slovakia). (available at: http://www.freedomhouse.org/report-types/freedom-press; retrieved 17.09.2013).

Füg, Oliver (2008) „Content Ratings Harmonisation and the Protection of Minors in the European Information Society" pp. 165–186 [in] Ward, D.(ed.) *The European Union and the Culture Industries: Regulation and the Public Interest*. Ashgate: London.

Gálik, Mihály and Vogl, Artemon (2008) *Searching for Yardstick to Measure Concentration in the Marketplace of Ideas*, a paper presented at the ECREA 2 European Communication Conference in Barcelona, 25–30 November 2008.

Gandy, Oscar H. (1998) *Communication and Race: A Structural Perspective*, London: Arnold.

Gardam, Tim And Levy, David A. L. (eds.) (2008) *The Price of Plurality: Choice, Diversity and Broadcasting Institutions in the Digital Age*. Oxford: Reuters Institute for the Study of Journalism.

Gemius (2011) *Do you CEE? The overview of the Central and Eastern Europe internet market in 2011*. 3rd Edition. (available at: http://doyoucee.gemius.com/pl/doyoucee_about; retrieved 28.12.2013).

Gemius (2013) *Chasing Western Europe: CEE online market 2012/2013*. (available at: https://www.gemius.com/reports-and-presentations-arch/chasing-western-europe-cee-online-market-20122013.html; retrieved 27.12. 2013).

Goban-Klas, Tomasz (1999) *Media i komunikowanie masowe. Teorie i analizy prasy, radia, telewizji i Internetu*. Warszawa, Kraków: Wydawnictwo Naukowe PWN.

Goetz, Anne Marie and Gaventa, John (2001) "Bringing Citizen Voice and Client Focus into Service Delivery" [in] *Working Paper 138, Institute of Development Studies (IDS)*. Brighton: Sussex (available at: http://peoplebuildingbettercities.org/wp-content/uploads/2013/04/Goetz-Gaventa-2004.pdf; retrieved 6.01.2014).

Golka, Bartłomiej (2004) *System medialny Stanów Zjednoczonych*. Warszawa: Wydawnictwa Szkolne i Pedagogiczne.

Goodman, Ellen P. (2007) "Proactive Media Policy in the Age of Content Abundance" pp. 363–382 [in] Napoli, P.M. (ed.) (2007) *Media Diversity and Localism: Meaning and Metrics*. Mahwah, New Jersey and London: LEA Publishers.

Graham, Andrew et al. (1999) *Public Purposes in Broadcasting: Funding the BBC*. Luton: University of Luton Press.

Grande, Edgar (2001) *Institutions and Interests: Interest Groups in the European System of Multi-Level Governance*, Working Paper No. 1/2001.

Gruffydd Jones, Elin H. (1998) "Mass media, cultural activities and regional or minority languages" [in] *International Conference on the European Charter for Regional or Minority Languages*. Strasbourg: Council of Europe Publishing.

Gulyás, Agnes (2003) "Print Media in Post-Communist East Central Europe" [in] *European Journal of Communication* 18 (1): 81–106.

Habermas, Jürgen (1996) *Between Facts and Norms: Contributions to a Discourse Theory of Law and Democracy*. Translated by William Rehg. Cambridge, Mass.: The MIT Press.

Habermas, Jürgen (2006) "Political Communication in Media Society: Does Democracy Still Enjoy an Epistemic Dimension? The Impact of Normative Theory on Empirical Research" [in] *Communication Theory*. 16 (4): 411–426.

Hall, Edward T. (1959) *The Silent Language*. New York: Doubleday.

Hallin, Daniel C. and Mancini, Paolo (2004), *Comparing Media Systems: Three Models of Media and Politics*. Cambridge: Cambridge University Press.

Hallin, Daniel C. (2009) "Comment: State Size as a Variable in Comparative Analysis" *International Communication Gazette*. 71 (1–2): 101–103.

Hans Bredow Institute for Media Research et al. (2011) *INDIREG Final Report: Indicators for independence and efficient functioning of audiovisual media services regulatory bodies for the purpose of enforcing the rules in the AVMS Directive* (SMART 2009/0001). (available at: http://ec.europa.eu/avpolicy/docs/library/studies/regulators/final_report.pdf; retrieved 31.12.2013).

Harcourt, Alison (2003) "The regulation of media markets in selected EU accession states in Central and Eastern Europe" [in] *European Law Journal* 9 (3): 316–340.

Harcourt, Alison (2005) *The European Union and the regulation of media markets*. Manchester and New York: Manchester University Press.

Harcourt, Alison (2008a) "Institutionalisng Soft Governance in the European Information Society" pp. 7–31 [in] Ward, D. (ed.) (2008) *The European Union and the Culture Industries: Regulation and the Public Interest*. Aldershot: Ashgate.

Harcourt, Alison (2008b) *Report on Methodology for the Monitoring of Media Concentration, Pluralism and Diversity*. Report for the Group of Specialists on Media Diversity (MC-S-MD), Council of Europe.

Harcourt, Alison (2012) "Transnational Media Regulation in Central and Eastern Europe" pp. 137–155 [in] Downey, J. and Mihelj, S. (eds.) *Central and Eastern European Media in Comparative Perspective: Politics, Economy and Culture*. London: Ashgate.

Harro-Loit, Halliki (2010) „From Media Policy to Integrated Communication Policy: How to Apply the Paradigm Shift on a European and National Level" pp. 45–58 [in] Klimkiewicz, B. (ed.) *Media Freedom and Pluralism: Media Policy Challenges in the Enlarged Europe*. Budapest: CEU Press.

Helberger, Natali (2012) "Exposure Diversity as a Policy Goal" [in] *Journal of Media Law* 4 (1): 65–92.

HLGMFP (High Level Group on Media Freedom and Pluralism) (2013) *A free and pluralistic media to sustain European democracy*. January 2013. (available at: http://ec.europa.eu/digital-agenda/sites/digital-agenda/files/HLG%20Final%20Report.pdf; retrieved 25.12.2013).

Hitchens, Lesley (2006) *Broadcasting Pluralism and Diversity: A Comparative Study of Policy and Regulation*. Oxford: Hart Publishing.

Hochelová, Vlasta (2007) „Podoba regionalizmu v slovenskej tlači a slovenskej televízii" pp. 28–32 [in] Waschková Císařová, L. (ed.) *Regionální média v evropském kontextu*. Brno: Masarykova Univerzita, Institut regionální žurnalistiky.
Hong, Y. (2011) "Reading the Twelfth Five-Year Plan: China's Communication-Driven Mode of Economic Restructuring" [in] *International Journal of Communication*, (5): 1045–1057.
Hoskins, Colin et al. (2004) *Media Economics: Applying Economics to New and Traditional Media*. Thousand Oaks and London: Sage Publications.
Howlett, Michael and Ramesh, M. (1995) *Studying Public Policy: Policy Cycles and Policy Subsystems*. Oxford and New York: Oxford University Press.
Humphreys, Peter J. (1996) *Mass Media and Politics in Western Europe*. Manchaster: Manchaster University Press.
Humphreys, Peter J. (2008) "The Principal Axes of the European Union's Audiovisual Policy" pp. 151–182 [in] *Communication and Cultural Policies in Europe* (eds.) Fernández Alonso, I. and de Moragas i Spà, M. Universitat Autònoma de Barcelona: Barcelona.
Humphreys, Peter J. (2012) "A Political Scientist's Contribution to the Comparative Study of Media Systems in Europe: A Response to Hallin and Mancini" pp. 157–176 [in] Puppis, M. and Just, N. (eds.) *Trends in Communication Policy Research: New Theories, Methods and Subjects*. Bristol: Intellect.
Hutchison, Davis (1999) *Media Policy: An Introduction*. Oxford: Blackwell.
INDICATOR (2012) *Pluralizm w polskich mediach elektronicznych*. Warszawa. (available at: http://www.krrit.gov.pl/Data/Files/_public/Portals/0/publikacje/analizy/1_1-prezentacja_pluralizm-w--polskich-mediach-elektronicznyc.pdf; retrieved 4.01.2014).
Institute of European Media Law (2005) *Media Market Definitions – Comparative Legal Analysis: Final Report*. Saarbrücken (available at: http://ec.europa.eu/competition/sectors/media/documents/disclaimer_introduction.pdf; retrieved 6.01.2014).
Iosifidis, Petros (ed.) (2010) *Reinventing Public Service Communication: European Broadcasters and Beyond*. Basingstoke: Palgrave Macmillan.
Jakubowicz, Karol (2004a) "A Square Peg in a Round Hole: The EU's Policy in Public Service Broadcasting" pp. 277–301 [in] Bondebjerg, I. and Goldberg, P. (eds.) *European Culture and the Media: Changing Media – Changing Europe Series Volume 1*. Bristol: Intellect.
Jakubowicz, Karol (2004b) "Ideas in Our Heads: Introduction of PSB as Part of Media System Change in Central and Eastern Europe" [in] *European Journal of Communication*. 19 (1): 53–74.
Jakubowicz, Karol (2006), *Revision of the European Convention on Transfrontier Television in the Context of International Media Policy Evolution*. Paper presented during the meeting of Working Group 3 of COST Action A30, Budapest, 22–23 September 2006.
Jakubowicz, Karol (2007) *Rude Awakening: Social and Media Change in Central and Eastern Europe*. Creskill, New Jersey: Hampton Press.

Jakubowicz, Karol (2011) "European Melting Pot? European Integration and EU Audiovisual Policy at a Crossroads" pp. 272–320 [in] Sükösd, M. and Jakubowicz, K. (eds.) *Media, Nationalism and European Identities*. Budapest–New York: CEU Press.

Jakubowicz, Karol (2012a) "Battle of the Paradigms: Defining the Object and Objectives of Media/Communications Policy" pp. 237–259 [in] Puppis, M. and Just, N. (eds.) *Trends in Communication Policy Research: New Theories, Methods and Subjects*. Bristol: Intellect.

Jakubowicz, Karol (2012b) "Post-communist Political Systems and Media Freedom and Independence" pp. 15–40 [in] Downey, J. and Mihelj, S. (eds.) *Central and Eastern European Media in Comparative Perspective: Politics, Economy and Culture*. London: Ashgate.

Jakubowicz, Karol and Sükösd, Miklós (eds.) (2008) *Finding the Right Place on the Map: Central and Eastern European Media Change in a Global Perspective*. Bristol: Intellect.

Just, Natascha (2009) "Measuring Media Concentration and Diversity: New Approaches and Instruments in Europe and the US" [in] *Media, Culture and Society* 31(1): 97–117.

Kaitatzi-Whitlock, Sophia (2008) "The Political Economy of the Media at the Root of the EU's Democratic Deficit" pp. 25–48 [in] Bodenbjerg, I. and Madsen, P. (eds.) *Media, Democracy and European Culture*. Bristol: Intellect.

Karppinen, Kari (2013) *Rethinking Media Pluralism*. New York: Fordham University Press.

Karppinen, Kari and Moe, Hallvard (2012) "What We Talk about When We Talk about Document Analysis" pp. 178–193 [in] Puppis, M. and Just, N. (eds.) *Trends in Communication Policy Research: New Theories, Methods and Subjects*. Bristol: Intellect.

Katzenbach, Christian (2012) "Technologies as Institutions: Rethinking the Role of Technology in Media Governance Constellations" pp. 117–137 [in] Puppis, M. and Just, N. (eds.) *Trends in Communication Policy Research: New Theories, Methods and Subjects*. Bristol: Intellect.

Keane, John (1991) *Media and Democracy*. Oxford: Polity Press.

Keane, John (2009) "Monitory Democracy and Media-Saturated Societies" [in] *Griffith Review* 24 (4): 79–102.

Kekes, John (1993) *The Morality of Pluralism*. Princeton: Princeton University Press.

Kilman, Larry (2012) *World Press Trends: Newspaper Audience Rise, Digital Revenues Yet to Follow*. World Association of Newspapers. (available at: http://www.wan-ifra.org/press-releases/2012/09/03/world-press-trends-newspaper-audience-rise-digital-revenues-yet-to-follow, retrieved 13.02.2013).

Kleinsteuber, Hans J. (1993) „Mediensysteme in vergleichender Perspektive zur Anwendung komparativer Ansätze in der Medienwissenschaft: Probleme und Beispiele" [in] *Rundfunk und Fernsehen* 41(3): 317–338.

Klimkiewicz, Beata (2004a) "Poland" pp. 363–403 [in] Petković, B. et al. (ed.) *Media Ownership and its Impact on Media Independence and Pluralism*. Ljubljana: Peace Institute.

Klimkiewicz, Beata (2004b) "Media Pluralism: European Regulatory Policies and the Case of Central Europe" [in] *EUI Working Papers* RSCAS No. 2005/19.

Klimkiewicz, Beata (2008) "Media Pluralism and Enlargement: The Limits and Potential for Media Policy Change" pp. 81–104 [in] Ward, D. (ed.) *The European Union and the Culture Industries: Regulation and the Public Interest*. Aldershot: Ashgate.

Klimkiewicz, Beata (2009a) „Structural Media Pluralism and Ownership Revisited: The Case of Central and Eastern Europe" [in] *Journal of Media Business Studies: A special issue on Ownership Policy, Regulation and Business*. 6 (3): 43–62.

Klimkiewicz, Beata (2009b) "Is the Clash of Rationalities Leading Nowhere? Media Pluralism in European Regulatory Policies" pp. 45–74 [in] Czepek, A. et al. (eds.) *Press Freedom and Pluralism in Europe: Concepts and Conditions*. Bristol: Intellect.

Klimkiewicz, Beata (ed.) (2010a) *Media Freedom and Pluralism: Media Policy Challenges in the Enlarged Europe*. Budapest: CEU Press.

Klimkiewicz, Beata (2010b) "Structural Media Pluralism: Introduction" [in] *International Journal of Communication* (4): 906–913.

Klimkiewicz, Beata (2013) "Independence or balance of dependencies? Critical remarks on studying conditions of media regulators and public service media in Poland" pp. 185–212 [in] Schulz, W. et al (eds.) *The Independence of the Media and its Regulatory Agencies : Shedding New Light on Formal and Actual Independence Against the National Context*. Bristol: Intellect.

Klinger, Ulrike (2012) "Veto Players and the Regulation of Media Pluralism: A New Paradigm for Media Policy Research?" pp. 139–153 [in] Puppis, M. and Just, N. (eds.) *Trends in Communication Policy Research: New Theories, Methods and Subjects*. Bristol: Intellect.

Klukan, Petr (2007) "Jihlavské listy, poslední 'České noviny'" pp. 104–106 [in] Waschková Císařová, L. (ed.) *Regionální média v evropském context*. Brno: Masarykova Univerzita: Institut regionální žurnalistiky.

Koltay, Tibor (2011) "The media and the literacies: media literacy, information literacy, digital literacy" [in] *Media, Culture & Society*. 33 (2): 211–221.

KRRiT (Krajowa Rada Radiofonii i Telewizji) (2003) *Informacja o podstawowych problemach radiofonii i telewizji* (The Information about Basic Issues of Broadcasting), Warszawa, 2003; (available at: http://www.krrit.gov.pl/krrit/sprawozdania/2003/; retrieved 14.12.2013).

KRRiT (Krajowa Rada Radiofonii i Telewizji) (2005) *Strategia Państwa Polskiego w Dziedzinie Mediów Elektronicznych na lata 2005–2020* (available at: http://www.krrit.gov.pl/Data/Files/_public/pliki/publikacje/strategie/strategia_050826.pdf; retrieved 11.12.2013).

KRRiT (Krajowa Rada Radiofonii i Telewizji) (2011) *Strategia Regulacyjna na lata 2011–2013* (available at: http://www.krrit.gov.pl/Data/Files/_public/pliki/publikacje/strategie/strategia_110420.pdf; retrieved 11.12.2013)

K.U. Leuven, et al. (2009) *Independent Study on Indicators for Media Pluralism in the Member States – Towards a Risk-Based Approach. Prepared for the Eu-*

ropean Commission Directorate-General Information Society and Media. K.U. Leuven: Leuven. Available at: (http://ec.europa.eu/information_society/media_taskforce/doc/pluralism/pfr_report.pdf; retrieved 29.11.2009)

Lasswell, Harold D. (1956) *The Decision Process: Seven Categories of Functional Analysis*. College Park: University of Maryland.

Lasswell, Harold D. (1971) *A Pre-View of Policy Sciences*, New York: American Elsevier.

Lengyel, Mark (2010) "Hungary: A Wave of Media Legislation" [in] *IRIS Merlin* 8 (1/34).

Levin, Peter (1997) *Making Social Policy: The Mechanisms of Government and Politics and How to Investigate Them*. Buckingham, Philadelphia: Open University Press.

Livingstone, Sonia (2009) "On Mediation of Everything" [in] *Journal of Communication*. 59 (1): 1–18.

Lowenstein, Ralph L. and Merrill, John C. (1990) *Macromedia: Mission, Message and Morality*. New York: Longman.

Lucht, Jens and Udris, Linards (2010) *Transformation of media structures and media content. A diachronic analysis of five Western European countries*. Working Paper No. 49. National Centre of Competence in Research (NCCR). Institute of Mass Communication & Media Research and Sociological Institute, University of Zurich.

Luhmann, Niklas (2000) *The Reality of the Mass Media*. Translated by Kathleen Cross. Stanford: Stanford University Press.

Masłowska, Katarzyna (2008) "Legality of State Aid for TVP S.A. questioned" [in] *IRIS* 2008 (6) 16/22 (available at: http://merlin.obs.coe.int/iris/2008/6/article22.en.html; retrieved 5.01.2014).

McChesney, Robert W. (1999) *Rich Media, Poor Democracy: Communication Politics in Dubious Times*. Urbana and Chicago: University of Illinois Press.

MM-CM, Council of Europe's Committee of Experts on Media Concentrations and Pluralism (1994) *The Activity Report of the Committee of Experts on Media Concentrations and Pluralism* submitted to the 4th European Ministerial Conference on Mass Media Policy, Prague, 7–8 December 1994.

McGoonagle, Tarlach (2008) "The Quota Quandary: An Assessment of Articles 4–6 of the Television without Frontiers Directive" pp. 187–212 [in] Ward, D. (ed.) (2008) *The European Union and the Culture Industries: Regulation and the Public Interest*. Aldershot: Ashgate.

McLuhan, Marshall (1967) *Understanding Media. The Extension of Man*. London: Routledge and Keagan Paul.

McQuail, Denis (1992) *Media Performance. Mass Communication and the Public Interest*. London: Sage Publications.

McQuail, Denis (1994) "Mass Communication and the Public Interest: Towards Social Theory for Media Structure and Performance" pp. 235–253 [in] Crowley, D. and Mitchell, D. (eds.) *Communication Theory Today*. Stanford: Stanford University Press.

McQuail, Denis (ed.) (2002) *McQuail's Reader in Mass Communication Theory*. London: Sage Publications.

McQuail, Denis and Siune, Karen (eds.) (1998) *Media Policy: Convergence, Concentration and Commerce*. London: Sage Publications.

Meier, Henk E. (2003) "Beyond Convergence: Understanding Programming Strategies of Public Broadcasters in Competitive Environments" [in] *European Journal of Communication*. 18 (3): 337–365.

Meyer, Thomas (2002) *Media Democracy: How the Media Colonize Politics*. Cambridge: Polity.

Monti, Mario (2012) "A defining year for Europe" [in] *The Economist: The World in 2013*. 8 November 2012, p. 54.

Nagy, Krisztina (2013) "Hungary: New Amendments to Media Law" [in] *IRIS Merlin* 4 (1/17) (available at: http://merlin.obs.coe.int/iris/2013/4/article17.en.html; retrieved 15.10.2013).

Napoli, Philip M. (1999) "The Unique Nature of Communications Regulation: Evidence and Implications for Communications Policy Analysis" [in] *Journal of Broadcasting and Electronic Media* 43 (4): 565–581.

Napoli, Philip M. (ed.) (2007) *Media Diversity and Localism: Meaning and Metrics*. Mahwah, New Jersey and London: LEA Publishers.

Napoli, Philip M. and Karaganis, Joe (2010) *On Making Public Policy with Publicly Available Data: The Case of U.S. Communications Policymaking*. Working Paper, The Donald McGannon Communication Research Center. (available at: http://www.fordham.edu/images/undergraduate/communications/on%20making%20public%20policy%20with%20publicly%20available%20data.pdf; retrieved 6.01.2014).

Nicholson, Tom (2012) *Gorila*. Bratislava: Vydavateľstvo Dixit.

Nielsen, Kleis Rasmus (2012) *Ten Years that Shook the Media World. Big Questions and Big Trends in International Media Developments*. Reuters Institute for the Study of Journalism, University of Oxford. (available at: https://reutersinstitute.politics.ox.ac.uk/fileadmin/documents/Publications/Working_Papers/Nielsen_-_Ten_Years_that_Shook_the_Media.pdf, retrieved 12.02.2013).

Nielsen, Kleis Rasmus and Linnebank, Geert (2011) *Public Support for the Media: A Six-Country Overview of Direct and Indirect Subsidies*. Reuters Institute for the Study of Journalism: Oxford.

Nieminen, Hannu (2010) "Towards Democratic Regulation of European Media and Communication" pp. 3–26 [in] Klimkiewicz, B. (ed.) *Media Freedom and Pluralism: Media Policy Challenges in the Enlarged Europe*. Budapest: CEU Press.

Nieminen, Hannu and Sparks, Colin (2012) *Discussion paper for the workshop on Digital divides and their relation to class, gender, generation, ethnicity and region*. European Science Foundation, 7–8 June, 2012, Helsinki.

Nissen, Christian S. (2006), *Public Service Media in the Information Society*, the Report prepared by the Group of Specialists on PSB in the Information Society (MC-S-PSB), Strasbourg: Media Division, Directorate General of Human Rights, Council of Europe.

Noam, Eli (1994) "The impact of competition on television's public interest performance" [in] *Social responsibility of television in the United States*. The European Institute of the Media (available at: http://www.citi.columbia.edu/elinoam/articles/social_responsibility_tv_us.pdf; retrieved 1.09.2013).

Noam, Eli (2009) *Media Ownership and Concentration in America*. New York: Oxford University Press.

Ociepka, B. (2003) *Dla kogo telewizja? Model publiczny w postkomunistycznej Europie Środkowej*. Wrocław: Wydawnictwo Uniwersytetu Wrocławskiego.

OECD (2010) *The Evolution of News and the Internet*. DSTI/ICCP/IE(2009)14/FINAL (available at: http://www.oecd.org/sti/interneteconomy/45559596.pdf; retrieved 13.02.2013).

OSF (Open Society Foundations) (2012a) *Mapping Digital Media in the European Union. A report for the High-Level Group on Media Freedom and Pluralism*. (available at: http://www.opensocietyfoundations.org/sites/default/files/Mapping_Digital_Media_EU_20121217_0.pdf; retrieved 12.02.2013).

OSF (Open Society Foundations) (2012b) *Mapping Digital Media: Hungary*. (available at: http://www.opensocietyfoundations.org/projects/mapping-digital-media; retrieved 11.12.2013).

OSF (Open Society Foundations) (2012c) *Mapping Digital Media: Poland*. (available at: http://www.opensocietyfoundations.org/projects/mapping-digital-media; retrieved 11.12.2013).

OSF (Open Society Foundations), Access Info Europe (2012) *Transparency of Media Ownership in Europe. A report for the High-Level Group on Media Freedom and Pluralism*. (available at: http://www.opensocietyfoundations.org/sites/default/files/Transparency_Media_Ownership_Europe_20121217_0.pdf; retrieved 28.12.2013).

OSF (Open Society Foundations) (2013a) *Mapping Digital Media: Czech Republic*. (available at: http://www.opensocietyfoundations.org/projects/mapping-digital-media; retrieved 11.12.2013).

OSF (Open Society Foundations) (2013b) *Mapping Digital Media: Slovakia*. (available at: http://www.opensocietyfoundations.org/projects/mapping-digital-media; retrieved 11.12.2013).

Open Society Institute (2005) *Television Across Europe: regulation, policy and Independence*. Budapest: OSI/EU Monitoring and Advocacy Program).

OSCE (2010) *Analysis and Assessment of a Package of Hungarian Legislation and Draft Legislation on media and Telecommunications* (available at: http://www.osce.org/fom/71218; retrieved 30.12.2013).

O'Sullivan, Tim et al. (1994) *Key Concepts in Communication and Cultural Studies*. London and New York: Routledge.

PEFMPNM (Pan-European Forum on Media Pluralism and New Media) (2013) *Wider? World? Web? Summary Report: Key Observations and Recommendations* (available at: http://www.mediapluralism.eu/wp-content/uploads/2013/03/NMF27_SUMMARY-REPORT.pdf; retrieved 3.01.2014).

Petković, Brankica et al. (eds.) (2004) *Media Ownership and its Impact on Media Independence and Pluralism*. Ljubljana: Peace Institute.

Pickard, Robert (2011) *Mapping Digital Media: Digitization and Media Business Models*. Open Society Foundations. (available at: http://snap3.uas.mx/RECURSO1/libroselectronicos/BIBAS%20PERIODISMO%20-%20DIGITAL/OSF-Media-Report-Handbook_Digitization_and_Media_Business_Models-final-07-18-2011-WEB.pdf; retrieved 24.11.2013).

Postman, Neil (1985) *Amusing Ourselves to Death: Public Discourse in the Age of Show Business*. New York: Penguin Books.

Potter, James (2011) *Media Literacy*. 5th edition. Sage Publications: Thousand Oaks, London.

Price, Monroe et al. (eds.) (2002) *Media Reform: Democratising the Media, Democratising the State*. London and New York; Routledge.

Princen, Sebastian (2011) "Agenda-Setting Strategies in EU Policy Processes" [in] *Journal of European Public Policy* 18 (7): 927–943.

Psychogiopoulou, Evangelia (ed.) (2012) *Understanding Media Policies: A European Perspective*. Basingstoke: Palgrave Macmillan.

Puppis, Manuel (2008) "National Media Regulation in the Era of Free Trade: The Role of Global Media Governance" [in] *European Journal of Communication* 23 (4): 405–424.

Puppis, Manuel (2009) "Media Regulation in Small States" [in] *International Communication Gazette* 71 (1–2): 7–17.

Puppis, Manuel and Just, Natascha (eds.) (2012) *Trends in Communication Policy Research: New Theories, Methods and Subjects*. Bristol: Intellect.

Puppis Manuel and Maggetti, Martino (2012) "The Accountability and Legitimacy of Regulatory Agencies in the Communication Sector" pp. 75–94 [in] Puppis, M. and Just, N. (eds.) (2012) *Trends in Communication Policy Research: New Theories, Methods and Subjects*. Bristol: Intellect

Rebillard, Franck and Loicq, Marlène (eds.) (2013) *Pluralisme de de l'information et media diversity: Un état des lieux international*. Brussels: De Boeck.

Reuters Institute for the Study of Journalism (2012) *Hungary*. Oxford. (available at: https://reutersinstitute.politics.ox.ac.uk/fileadmin/documents/Media_Landscapes/Hungary.pdf; retrieved 22.12.2013)

Ringen, Stein (2007) *What Democracy Is For: On Freedom and Moral Government*. Princeton and Oxford: Princeton University Press.

Roudakova, Natalia (2008) "Media Political Clientelism: Lessons from Anthropology" [in] *Media, Culture and Society* 30 (1): 41–59.

RWB (Reporters Without Borders) (2013) *2013 World Press Freedom Index: Dashed Hopes After Spring*. (available at: http://en.rsf.org/press-freedom-index-2013,1054.html; retrieved 20.09.2013).

Sabatier, Paul A. (1988) "An Advocacy Coalition Framework of Policy Change and the Role of Policy-Oriented Learning Therein" [in] *Policy Sciences* 21(2/3): 129–168.

Sadurski, Wojciech (2003) "Accession's Democracy Dividend: From Conditionality to Post-Accession" pp. 5–46 [in] *Implications of Enlargement for the Rule of Law, Democracy and Constitutionalism in Post-Communist Legal Orders*. European University Institute, Florence: Workshop Papers.

Sarikakis, Katharine (2004), *Powers in Media Policy: The Challenge of the European Parliament*, Oxford: Peter Lang.

Sarikakis, Katharine (2008) "Communication and Cultural Policy Research in Europe: A Review of Recent Scholarship" pp. 293–315 [in] *Communication and Cultural Policies in Europe* (eds.) Fernández Alonso, I. and de Moragas i Spà, M. Universitat Autònoma de Barcelona: Barcelona.

Sasse, Gwendolyn (2003) "How Deep is the Wider Europe: The Europeanisation of Sub-National Governance in Central and Eastern Europe" pp. 123–160 [in] *Implications of Enlargement for the Rule of Law, Democracy and Constitutionalism in Post-Communist Legal Orders*. European University Institute, Florence: Workshop Papers.

Sasse, Gwendolyn (2004) "EU Conditionality and Minority Right: Translating the Copenhagen Criterion into Policy" [in] *EUI Working Papers*. RSCAS No. 2005/16.

Scharpf, Fritz W. (1999) *Governing in Europe: Effective and Democratic?* Oxford: Oxford University Press.

Schimmelfennig, Frank and Sedelmeier, Ulrich (2004) "Governance by conditionality: EU rule transfer to the candidate countries of Central and Eastern Europe" [in] *Journal of European Public Policy* 11(4): 661–669.

Schlesinger, Philip (1995) "Europeanisation and the Media: National Identity and the public Sphere" [in] *ARENA Working Papers*. No. 7/95.

Schlosberg, Justin (2013) "Modelling Media Ownership Limits: The Impact of Current Policy Proposals on the UK Media Market" [in] *Media Policy Brief 10*. LSE Media Policy Project. (available at: http://www.lse.ac.uk/media@lse/documents/MPP/LSE-MPP-Policy-Brief-10-Modelling-media-ownership-limits.pdf; retrieved 25.12.2013).

Schudson, Michael (1998) *The Good Citizen: A History of American Civic Life*. Cambridge, Mass. and London: Harvard University Press.

Schulz, Wienfried (2004) "Reconstructing Mediatization as an Analytical Concept" [in] *European Journal of Communication* 19 (1): 87–101.

Schulz, Wolfgang et al (eds.) (2013) *The Independence of the Media and its Regulatory Agencies: Shedding New Light on Formal and Actual Independence Against the National Context*. Bristol: Intellect.

Siedentop, Larry (2001) *Democracy in Europe*. New York: Columbia University Press.

Simpson, Seamus (2008) "The Changing Totems of European Telecommunications Governance: Liberalization, Market Forces and the Importance of the EU Regulatory Package" pp. 105–124 [in] Ward, D. (ed.) *The European Union and the Culture Industries: Regulation and the Public Interest*. Aldershot: Ashgate.

Školkay, Andrej and Ondruchová-Hong, Mária (2012) "Slovakia: Reinventing Media Policy Without a Practical Perspective" pp. 182–197 [in] Psychogiopoulou, Evangelia (ed.) (2012) *Understanding Media Policies: A European Perspective*. Basingstoke: Palgrave Macmillan.

Skrzypczak, Jędrzej (2011) *Polityka medialna w okresie konwersji cyfrowej radiofonii i telewizji*. Poznań: Wydawnictwo Naukowe WNPiD UAM.

Šmíd, Milan (2004) "Czech Republic" pp. 141–164 [in] Petković, B. et al. (ed.) *Media Ownership and its Impact on Media Independence and Pluralism*. Ljubljana: Peace Institute.

Sparks, Colin (1998) *Communism, Capitalism and the Mass Media*. London: Sage Publications.

Sparks, Colin (2008) "After Transition: The Media in Poland, Russia and China" pp. 43–72 [in] Jakubowicz, K. and Sükösd, M. (eds.) (2008) *Finding the Right Place on the Map: Central and Eastern European Media Change in a Global Perspective*. Bristol: Intellect.

Splichal, Slavko (2001) "Imitative Revolutions: Changes in the Media and Journalism in East-Central Europe" [in] *Javnost/The Public*. 8 (4): 31–58.

Stasiak-Jazukiewicz, Ewa and Jas-Koziarkiewicz, Marta (2011) *Polityka medialna w Unii Europejskiej*. Warszawa: Wydawnictwo Poltext.

Štetka, Václav (2010) "Struggling with Diversity: Objectives, Outcomes, and Future of the European Quota Policy in the Context of the Television Scene in the Czech Republic" pp. 97–124 [in] Klimkiewicz, B. (ed.) *Media Freedom and Pluralism: Media Policy Challenges in the Enlarged Europe*. Budapest: CEU Press.

Štetka, Václav (2013) "The Rise of the Tycoons: Economic Crisis and Changing Media Ownership in Central Europe" [in] *Eurozine*, 31.05.2013 (available at: http://www.eurozine.com/articles/2013-05-31-stetka-en.html; retrieved 22.12.2013).

Stevenson, Nick (1995) *Understanding Media Cultures: Social Theory and Mass Communication*. London: Sage Publications.

Stolte, Yolande and Craufurd Smith, Rachel (2010) *The European Union and Media Ownership Transparency: The Scope for Regulatory Intervention*. Open Society Media Programme: London (available at: http://mediapolicy.org/wp-content/uploads/the-european-union-media-ownership-transparency.pdf; retrieved 11.12.2013).

Straubhaar, Joseph D. (2008) "Global, Hybrid or Multiple? Cultural identities in the Age of Satellite TV and the Internet" [in] *Nordicom Review* (Special Issue on 18th Nordic Conference on Media and Communication Research), 29 (2): 11–29.

Sükösd, Miklós and Bajomi-Lázár, Péter (eds.) (2003) *Reinventing Media: Media Policy Reform in East-Central Europe* Budapest: CEU Press.

Sükösd, Miklós and Jakubowicz, Karol (eds.) (2011) *Media, Nationalism and European Identities*. Budapest–New York: CEU Press.

Szczerski, Krzysztof (2008) *Dynamika systemu europejskiego: Rozważania o nowym kształcie polityki w Unii Europejskiej*. Kraków: Wydawnictwo UJ.

Tambini, Damian (2011) "Reforming Consumer Representation in UK Communications" [in] *Media Policy Brief 4* (available at: http://www.lse.ac.uk/media@lse/documents/MPP/LSEMPPBrief4.pdf; retrieved 5.01.2014)

Tehranian, Majid (1994) "Communication and Development" pp. 274–306 [in] Crowley, D. and Mitchell, D. (eds.) *Communication Theory Today*. Stanford: Stanford University Press.

Thacher, David (2004) *Value Rationality in Policy Analysis*. University of Michigan: Working Paper.
Tsebelis, George (2002) *Veto Players. How Political Institutions Work*. Princeton: Princeton University Press.
Telewizja Polska (TVP) (2008) *Odpowiedź Telewizji Polskiej S.A. na kwestionariusz Komisji Europejskiej w ramach przeglądu komunikatu Komisji w sprawie udzielenia pomocy państwa dla radiofonii i telewizji publicznej* 18.03.2008. TVP-P-220/2008 (available at: http://ec.europa.eu/competition/state_aid/reform/comments_broadcasting/tvp.pdf; retrieved 5.01.2014).
Tkaczyński, Jan W. (ed.) (2013) *Lizbońska Unia Europejska: Zagadnienia wybrane*. Kraków: Wydawnictwo Uniwersytetu Jagiellońskiego.
Tyner, Kathleen (ed.) (2010) *Media Literacy. New agendas in Communication*. New York: Routledge.
UNESCO (2001) *Universal Declaration on Cultural Diversity*.
UNESCO (2005) *Convention on the Protection and Promotion of the Diversity of Cultural Expressions*.
Van Cuilenburg, Jan and McQuail, Denis (2003) "Media Policy Paradigm Shifts: Towards a New Communications Policy" [in] *European Journal of Communication*. 18 (2): 181–207.
Van Cuilenburg, Jan and van der Wurff, Richard (eds.) (2000) *Media and Open Societies: Cultural, Economic and Policy Foundations for Media Openness and Diversity in East and West*. Amsterdam: Het Spinhuis.
Van den Bulck, Hilde (2012) "Towards a Media Policy Process Analysis Model and its Methodological Implications" pp. 217–231 [in] Puppis, M. and Just, N. (eds.) *Trends in Communication Policy Research: New Theories, Methods and Subjects*. Bristol: Intellect.
Van der Wurff, Richard (2011) "Do audiences receive diverse ideas from news media? Exposure to a variety of news media and personal characteristics as determinants of diversity as received" [in] *European Journal of Communication* 26(4): 328–342.
Van Dijk, Jan (2008) "One Europe, Digitally Divided" pp. 288–304 [in] Chadwick, Andrew and Howard, N. Philip (eds.) *The Handbook of Internet Politics*. London and New York: Routledge.
Varga, Peter J. (2011) "Pan European-Media: Attempts and Limitations" pp. 119–151 [in] Sükösd, M. and Jakubowicz, K. (eds.) *Media, Nationalism and European Identities*. Budapest–New York: CEU Press.
Venturelli, Shalini (1998) *Liberalising the European Media: Politics, Regulation and the Public Sphere*. Oxford: Clarendon Press.
Verhulst, Stefaan and Goldberg, David (1998), "European Media Policy: Complexity and Comprehensiveness" pp. 17–49 [in] d'Haenens, L. and Saeys, F. (eds.), *Media Dynamics and Regulatory Concern in the Digital Age*. Berlin: Quintessenz Verlags GmbH.
Voltmer, Katrin (2000) *Structures of diversity of press and broadcasting systems: The institutional context of public communication in Western democracies*.

Discussion Paper FS III 00-201. Wissenschaftszentrum Berlin für Sozialforschung (WZB).

Voltmer, Katrin (2013) *The Media in Transitional Democracies*. Cambridge: Polity Press.

Voorhoof, Dirk (1998) "Guaranteeing the Freedom and Independence of the Media" pp. 35–57 [in] *Media and democracy*. Strasbourg: Council of Europe Publishing.

Ward, David (2002). *The EU Democratic Deficit and The Public Sphere: An Evaluation of EU Media Policy*. Washington, D.C.: IOS Press.

Ward, David (2006), *Final Report on the study commissioned by the MC-S-MD 'The Assessment of content diversity in newspapers and television in the context of increasing trends towards concentration of media markets'*. MC-S-MD (2006) 001. Strasbourg: Council of Europe.

Ward, David (ed.) (2008) *The European Union and the Culture Industries: Regulation and the Public Interest*. Aldershot: Ashgate.

Waschková Císařová, Lenka (ed.) (2007) „Vybrané aspekty strukturální transformace českých lokálních a regionálních médií" pp. 62–71 [in] Waschková Císařová, L. (ed.) *Regionální média v evropském kontextu*. Brno: Masarykova Univerzita, Institut regionální žurnalistiky.

Westphal, Dietrich (2002) "Media Pluralism and European Regulation" [in] *European Business Law Review*, 13 (5): 459–487.

Wheeler, Mark (2010) "The European Union's Competition Directorate: State Aids and Public Service Broadcasting" pp. 49–62 [in] Iosifidis, P. (ed.) *Reinventing Public Service Communication: European Broadcasters and Beyond*. Basingstoke: Palgrave Macmillan.

Wildman, Steven (2007) "Indexing Diversity" pp. 151–176 [in] Napoli, M. Philip (ed.) *Media Diversity and Localism: Meaning and Metrics.* Mawhaw and London: LEA Publishers.

Woods, Lorna (2008) „Jurisdiction of the Television without Frontiers Directive" pp. 145–163 [in] Ward, D. (ed.) *The European Union and the Culture Industries: Regulation and the Public Interest*. Aldershot: Ashgate.

Working Group 5 (2005) *Final Report on Media Pluralism*. Audiovisual Conference 'Between Culture and Commerce' (Liverpool 22.09.2005).

Zahariadis, Nikolaos (2013) „Building Better Theoretical Frameworks of the European Union's Policy Process" [in] *Journal of European Public Policy* 20 (6): 807–816.

Editor in chief
Anna Poinc-Chrabąszcz

Proofreader
Tytus Ferenc
Monika Skowron

Jagiellonian University Press
Editorial Offices: Michałowskiego St. 9/2, 31-126 Cracow
Phone: +48 12 663 23 81, +48 12 663 23 82, Fax: +48 12 663 23 83